Shaggy Man's Ramblings

Also by Leslie Evans

BOOKS

Outsider's Reverie

China After Mao. Chinese edition: *Mao Zedong yihou de Zhongguo*

AS EDITOR

Peru: Education at a Crossroads: Challenges and Opportunities for the 21st Century. World Bank, Production Editor

Investing in Health Research and Development. World Health Organization, Production Editor

The China Democracy Movement and Tiananmen Incident: Annotated Catalog of the UCLA Archives, 1989–1993

Losses in the Los Angeles Civil Unrest, April 29–May 1, 1992

The Chinese Communist Party in Power by Peng Shu-tse.

Leon Trotsky on China (with Russell Block)

James P. Cannon as We Knew Him

The Struggle for Socialism in the American Century: James P. Cannon Writings and Speeches, 1945-1947

The Socialist Workers Party in World War II: James P. Cannon Writings and Speeches, 1940-1943

Shaggy Man's Ramblings

Essays by

Leslie Evans

Boryanabooks
Los Angeles

Published by   Boryana Books
                    3941 Veselich Avenue, Suite 262
                    Los Angeles, CA 90039
                    www.boryanabooks.com

ISBN: 978-1475137323

Cover: The Shaggy Man, adapted from an illustration by John R. Neill for
L. Frank Baum's 1909 *The Road to Oz.*

To my sister, Heather Jill Evans, with much love

Contents

Preface

The majority of these essays first appeared on my website, The Shaggy Man's Place (www.shaggyman.com). All but one were written between 2006 and early 2012. Just over half are biographical sketches of people who interest me: Sayyid Qutb, the central theorist of jihadi Islam, polemicist Christopher Hitchens, George Bernard Shaw, and a group of figures prominent in Los Angeles history who lived or are buried in my turn-of-the-twentieth century West Adams neighborhood.

The collection traces several disparate themes, which is fitting for a ramble through time and place. I have divided the essays into six parts by topic. Part 1, *The Unfolding Ecological Crisis and Solutions Better Left Untried*, examines the risk of social collapse from pitting the ever increasing demand for food, oil, and other limited natural resources against the insatiable needs of a population speeding past the 7 billion mark and bent on closing in on European and American living standards.

This opens with a review of Jared Diamond's 2005 *Collapse: How Societies Choose to Fail or Succeed.* Diamond shows how seemingly small mismatches between agricultural productivity and population have destroyed bustling civilizations of the past, and shows how precarious are our world's present stocks of arable land and potable water.

"$4 Gas Is Only the Beginning" hones in on the flatlining of world oil production since 2005 while demand, fed by the economic fires of China and India, has continued to grow, only slightly tamped down by the world recession. Escalating fuel prices, symptoms of "peak oil," promise to soon price the energy source on which our modern civilization depends out of reach except for the rich and key government agencies. And oil is only one of the resources hitting a production wall, from phosphorus to uranium and the rare earth metals essential for computer screens. A growing number of specialists now say that the spiking prices of oil and other natural resources, due to declining supplies and the lower quality and increasing costs of extracting what remains, as well as the impact of rising oil prices on transportation and fertilizer that in

1

turn push food prices up, have been an underestimated cause of the world recession that began in 2008.

Every economic crisis gives new hope to dead panaceas, religious and secular. "Anticapitalism, the Hyperstate, and the Current Crisis" examines the flickering revival of Marxist hopes that capitalism can be blamed for this one, and if the downturn deepens, open the door to a new opportunity to plump for total state ownership of the economy. I review the deadly experience of this idea in power, in particular, because of my own long illusions here during a few decades in the Trotskyist movement, looking at the bloody trail of the Lenin dictatorship in the much romanticized early days of the legendary October Revolution, drawing on sources that dug into the archives of the Soviet state after the fall of communism.

The second section, *Militant Islam and the Left*, attempts to weigh the import for Western society of the post-World War II Islamic awakening. In part out of the tradition of Enlightenment rationalism, in part because of the mendacity of the George W. Bush administration and its "war on terror," and in part because a Marxist left found itself with no constituency after the collapse of communism and the rightward shift of the proletariat, there has been a disturbing tendency among Western liberals and leftists to range from neutral to supportive of Islamic militancy.

The first two articles in this section examine the beliefs of the Islamic radicals and the extent of their influence and activity. Sayyid Qutb, the Qur'anic theorist of the Muslim Brotherhood, executed by Nasser in 1966, lives on in a large literary legacy urging the destruction of the decadent and idolatrous West and of communism and their global replacement by Islamic rule. "The World Islamic Revolution" traces Islam's bloody borders, its widespread calls for genocide of the Jews, and its rejection of the secular notion of the separation of church and state.

The last two articles in this part, a commemoration of the late Christopher Hitchens and a review of Pascal Bruckner's *The Tyranny of Guilt: An Essay on Western Masochism,* challenge the mid- and far-left's illusions that Western imperialism is a greater evil than their new-found Islamic rebels.

Part three, *Vernon and Its Discontents*, looks at the history of the small industrial city of Vernon, south and east of downtown Los Angeles, and at the overblown civic corruption scandal that has fascinated the media since 2005. I became interested in this when, in researching the history of the 1910 Craftsman house my wife Jennifer and I bought in 1988, we discovered that it had been owned, between 1921 and 1958, by members of the Furlong family, one of the two founding families that created Vernon in 1905 as an exclusively industrial city and who ruled it as a corporate fiefdom down to recent times.

Part four, *Miscellany*, is what the title promises: an article on computer role playing games, a memorial to a beloved cat, an internet search for the history of an odd little left-wing bookstore in Missoula, Montana, and reviews of two authors, one Romanian, the other Japanese.

Part five, *Remembering the Edwardians*, is biographical and literary sketches of three prominent English and Irish writers: children's author Edith Nesbit and playwright George Bernard Shaw, both Fabian socialists, and fantasist Lord Dunsany, the pro-British Irish aristocrat who invented strange gods and dreamlike cities. I was drawn to Nesbit and Shaw primarily because I like their work, but also because they became socialists in the 1880s and it helps to understand this current in Western thought to see it in its early earnest and somewhat naive formation.

The last part, *West Adams Sketches*, owes its place here to an interest in the history of the neighborhood where my wife and I live. West Adams is centered on a stretch of Adams Blvd., an east-west thoroughfare just under three miles south of City Hall. The dirt tract began to be developed with a few palatial homes in the late 1880s, then took off as the center for the city's wealthy when oil magnate Edward Doheny built his Chester Place compound at Adams and Figueroa in 1901. First came the business class, in a pioneer age when everything was wide open and penniless adventurers more than struck it rich. Doheny had arrived in town dead broke and living in a run-down hotel and ended as the richest man in America; Secundo Guasti, an Italian farm laborer, came to America and worked as a dishwasher in a restaurant, and rose to become the biggest wine maker in California. There were many others. After them came the film stars — Fatty Arbuckle and Theda Bara. The era ended in 1917 when Beverly Hills supplanted West Adams.

An age of decline followed. The old architect-designed mansions became rooming houses. When the racial covenants were ruled unconstitutional in 1948, West Adams became a black neighborhood. In the nineties Latino immigrants in turn became the dominant ethnicity, along with the remaining blacks and a small number of white old house enthusiasts.

When Jennifer and I moved here in 1988 we joined the local historic preservation organization, the West Adams Heritage Association. In 2007 I became their webmaster and wrote a number of sketches of the early residents. This stretched to people buried in the old local West Adams cemetery, Angelus Rosedale.

I have included here six of those sketches, the people who I found most intriguing: Wyatt Earp, the famed Western lawman and hero of the OK Corral, who spent his last years in Los Angeles while prospecting for gold in the Mojave Desert. Dirty Dan Harris, smuggler, Indian fighter, and founder of

Bellingham, Washington, poisoned for his money in a dingy Los Angeles hotel. Katherine Putnam Hooker, writer and close friend of John Muir, astronomer George Ellery Hale, and psychologist William James. William G. Kerckhoff, lumber and electric power millionaire who created the hydroelectric dam system in the Sierra Nevadas that supplies much of Los Angeles's electricity. John Randolph Haynes, the millionaire socialist who practically invented California's system of ballot box initiatives and a hundred other reforms that shape our city and state government to this day. And finally, Doctor Margaret Chung, daughter of a prostitute and a vegetable peddler who became the first Chinese woman doctor in the United States, adopted mother to 1500 American flyers in World War II, and creator of the Navy women's auxiliary, the WAVES, which the government refused to allow her to join because they believed she was gay.

All of these pieces appear largely as first published. I have done some light editing, and where needed added an introduction or a postscript to bring the subject up to date.

Oh, yes. Why the Shaggy Man? When I was about eight my parents bought three of L. Frank Baum's Oz books, which my father read to me and my sister Heather. Besides *The Wizard of Oz*, which everyone knows, we had two further adventures where Dorothy returns to the magic kingdom: *Ozma of Oz* (1907) and *The Road to Oz* (1909). In this last, a lifetime favorite, the Shaggy Man, an old raggedy tramp, approaches Dorothy on Uncle Henry and Aunt Em's Kansas farm, asking directions for the road to Butterfield. Dorothy goes to show him the crossroads and they find themselves instead in the center of a circle with roads branching in every direction. The one they take leads on into fairyland and to Oz. The Shaggy Man becomes a permanent resident of Oz, as Dorothy eventually becomes a princess there.

In my teen years I collected the Oz books. When I married and went away to New York in 1967 to serve on the staff of the Trotskyist Socialist Workers Party I gave my collection to my first wife's little sister in Oakland, California. When I married Jennifer Charnofsky in 1984 I collected them all again, all thirty-two, the original fourteen by Baum and the nineteen more by his successor, Ruth Plumly Thompson. When I started my website in 2006 the symbolism of Oz seemed the most natural, and the Shaggy Man, the ragged wanderer, the closest of the Oz characters to my own life. So he is today my alter ego.

Leslie Evans
West Adams, Los Angeles
March 20, 2012

Part 1:
The Unfolding Ecological Crisis and Solutions Better Left Untried

The Threat of Agrarian Collapse

Collapse: How Societies Choose to Fail or Succeed — Jared Diamond
(New York: Viking, 2005)

If you thought human society risked collapse because of global warming, exhaustion of fossil fuels, and overpopulation, UCLA geographer Jared Diamond has a whole new list of things to worry about. Diamond is the author of the insightful *Guns, Germs, and Steel*, which theorized a nonracial explanation for European supremacy over the New World and Africa based on the availability of domesticable animals and grains and a greater exposure to, and hence immunity to, common diseases. In *Collapse* Diamond traces in exhaustive detail the ecological disasters that destroyed four ancient and medieval societies, and points to parallels in our own time as warning signs. Diamond's examples are comparatively small, isolated units living in fragile, unforgiving landscapes. The advantage of concentrating on such otherwise marginal peoples is that by their isolation it is easier to piece together the factors that led to their destruction. Diamond chooses the Polynesian people of Easter Island off the coast of Chile; the vanished Anasazi of the deserts of northeastern Arizona, northwestern New Mexico, southeastern Utah, and southwestern Colorado; the Maya of the Yucatan Peninsula; and the Norse colonies in western Greenland.

While there are important differences in the factors that led to social failure between these examples, a common thread is deforestation, leading to a loss of building materials and fuel; extermination through over-hunting of local animals and birds used for food; and erosion and salinization of croplands as a consequence of the loss of woodland cover on hillsides.

A cardinal risk factor unearthed in Diamond's study is cultural expansion into territories that appear to be the same as the homeland but in fact have difficult-to-detect but crucial differences. Dust carried ashore by the Southeast Asian monsoons provides a natural fertilizer that renews croplands and encourages rapid growth of coconut palms and other trees on many South Pacific islands.

As Polynesian colonies spread further east across the Pacific toward South America, Diamond says, they eventually outran the monsoon effect. At Easter Island, located 2,200 miles west of continental Chile, the lack of monsoon-carried dust meant the land was poor and trees grew far more slowly than in the western Pacific. Harvesting wood at the same rate as in the monsoon area eventually denuded the island's forests, with disastrous consequences. Colonized around 900 AD, there may have been 15,000 inhabitants at the height in the thirteenth century. By the time European ships arrived in 1722 there were 2,000 left, and these were quickly decimated by slave traders and smallpox.

Searches through garbage middens reveal that for the early inhabitants dolphin was a major food source, with fish far scarcer than in most Polynesian societies. This was apparently because of the rocky coast that left few places to fish. The dolphins were caught at sea from ocean-going canoes. Over time the big trees used to make such canoes were all cut down. When the trees were gone, the diet changed as well.

"Porpoises, and open-ocean fish like tuna, virtually disappeared from the islanders' diet. . . . Land birds disappeared completely from the diet, for the simple reason that every species became extinct from some combination of overhunting, deforestation, and predation by rats."

With the trees, palm nuts also disappeared, removing another important food source. The latest carbon date for a palm nut shell found on the island is 1500. The population crashed in the century that followed. Crops also failed. "Deforestation led locally to soil erosion by rain and wind, as shown by huge increases in the quantities of soil-derived metal ions."

For the Norse colony in Greenland, again the land looked a lot like home, in this case Norway, but in fact the soil was far poorer. The colonists tried to replicate their home ecology, raising cattle and sheep and growing crops. Founded in 984, the colony, based in two fjords on the southwest coast, lasted some 450 years. They prospered until the Little Ice Age set in after 1300. They then faced competition from the invading Inuit, saw crop failures from the deepening cold and the thin topsoil, and made fatal cultural mistakes, the most important of which was relying on sheep and cattle that could no longer be fed when the hay harvests failed, rather than on seal and fish as the Inuit did.

What bearing do these isolated local tragedies have for our globalized world? Diamond makes an analogy with the two Norse colonies in Greenland. In fact, he says, the more southerly one had a chance to survive, or at least its largest farms did, with great barns where they housed their cattle in the winter. The outlying areas evacuated and migrated to the better-off places in hopes of staving off the disaster. They succeeded only in swamping the lifeboat and all drowned together.

Diamond sees the globalized world of today as more subject to ecological shocks than the relatively self-isolated nation states of a century ago. He has been criticized for not having an economist's tools to weigh more accurately the growth of wealth as a balance against ecological costs. Cambridge economist Partha Dasgupta in a review in the May 19, 2005, *London Review of Books* pointed out that deforestation in Britain in the nineteenth century spurred that country to switch to coal and become the leader of the Industrial Revolution while well-forested France fell behind. Dasgupta asks "how should we recognise the trade-offs between a society's present and future needs for goods and services?" and scores Diamond for lacking a clear concept of sustainable development.

This is an approach that has a great many economists blind-sided. Dasgupta's premise, ingrained in his profession, is that markets have a near infinite capacity to supply substitutes if only the price makes them competitive. What has changed since his nineteenth century example is the vast expansion of human population, wedded to an ecologically costly industrially based living standard currently expanding on the planet from a few rich countries to a growing set of developing ones. The better known threats are in human caused climate change and the tapping out of key natural resources, particularly the end in sight for fossil fuels. If the British made a killing by turning to coal, they at least knew that coal existed during the end days of the great forests. We are now in the end days of coal, though there can be debates over how near or far off that is. And there is no replacement on the horizon.

Diamond focuses on the less understood vulnerability of world agriculture and global food supply. There is today a world market in food grains. The principal suppliers of this market for some years have been the United States, Canada, and Australia. One ominous sign has been China's transition from grain self-sufficiency to become a major grain importer.

As the world's most populous country, China's relations to the world grain market can have an enormous impact. Historically, China with its intensive, irrigated garden farming and extremely limited arable land has lived far closer to the edge than the countries of Western Europe and North America with their large tracts of rainfall farming.

Population growth, even with the government's one-child policy, is having powerful impacts on the country's capacity to feed itself. Diamond writes:

"By world standards, China is poor in fresh water, with a quantity per person only one-quarter of the world average value. . . . Of the water required for cities and for irrigation, two-thirds depends on groundwater pumped from wells tapping aquifers. However, these aquifers are becoming depleted, permitting seawater to enter them in most coastal areas, and causing land to sink under some cities as the aquifers are becoming emptied. . . . China's soil problems start with its being one of the world's countries most severely damaged by erosion, now affecting 19% of its land area and resulting in soil loss at 5 billion tons per year. Erosion is especially devastating on the Loess Plateau . . . and increasingly on the Yangtze River, whose sediment discharge from erosion exceeds the combined discharges of the Nile and Amazon. . . .

"Soil quality and fertility as well as soil quantity have declined, partly because of long-term fertilizer use plus pesticide-related drastic declines in soil-renewing earthworms, thereby causing a 50% decrease in the area of cropland considered to be of high quality. Salinization . . . has affected 9% of China's lands, mainly due to poor design and management of irrigation systems in dry areas. . . . Desertification, due to overgrazing and land reclamation for agriculture, has affected more than one-quarter of China, destroying about 15% of North China's area remaining for agriculture and pastoralism within the last decade."

The World Watch Institute in a January 11, 2006, report said that China in 2005 consumed 32 percent of the rice output of the world, and that "If Chinese per-capita grain consumption were to double to roughly European levels, China alone would require the equivalent of nearly 40 percent of today's global grain harvest."

At the same time, Jared Diamond reports, Australia, one of the current pillars of world grain exports, is faced with its own erosion and salinization problems that are likely to move it from an exporter to an importer in the next decade. This spells a global food supply in which a single bad year will mean large scale famine in many countries.

At root the world as a whole is confronting a growing pressure on mostly limited resources, including agrarian ones that are most often overlooked, from both a growth in population and a simultaneous growth in per capita use of resources.

Skeptics can quibble, but their counter arguments have to rest on two risky assumptions: that new technology fixes will turn up in time to solve the growing food and energy problems, as the turn to coal did for the British 200 years ago, and that governments will be brave and energetic enough to confront their populations with unpopular demands to reduce population growth and conserve resources. Not to mention the opposition such measures face now from Muslim forces in the Middle East and Indonesia, and fundamentalist Christian forces that wield enormous power here in the United States, who oppose such measures on the ground that God will take care of it or take his followers up to heaven soon where it won't matter.

Jared Diamond himself is not a pessimist, or at least so he says. He points to the amazingly effective forest management efforts of the Tokugawa Shogunate in Japan after 1600 that protected the country's forests even to the point of inventorying individual trees. And no doubt there is growing awareness of the rising risks and public and private projects to conserve and to find alternatives. We will see.

2006

$4 Gas Is Only the Beginning

Republicans and Democrats are scrambling in a blame game over the sky-rocketing price of gasoline, which is rapidly approaching the historic highs of the 2008 oil shock. As of April 29, 2011, pump prices for regular had topped $4 in thirteen states and crested $3.90 in eleven more. The April 23 *Christian Science Monitor* carried the headline "Obama faces trouble with $4 gasoline." The story led off: "Polls show Americans blame Democrats more than Republicans for $4 gasoline prices, and President Obama's poll numbers show it."

Of course, Americans traditionally hold incumbents responsible for any bad thing that happens. New Jersey governor James F. Fielder was voted out of office in 1916 as punishment for shark attacks off the Jersey shore. And drought-stricken states throughout the twentieth century voted against incumbent presidents who failed to make rain.

Things aren't made easier by a Republican and Tea Party establishment that lives on a different planet, where global warming is a hoax, oil is an inexhaustible gift from God to Americans as a reward for their exceptionalism, and all we need to do to put cheap gas in the tank is to "Drill, Baby, Drill!"

Without belaboring the rebuttal here, U.S. oil companies are already sitting on leases on millions of acres of land that they don't drill because wells are expensive and they have no good reason to think there is oil underneath. After all, more then 1 million wells have been drilled on American soil and in shallow offshore seas. The companies pretty well know what is out there.

And even if we desecrate the Arctic National Wildlife Refuge in Alaska, the U.S. Energy Information Administration, the best informed entity on the subject, in its 2008 report projected that if work began promptly in the nearly year-round ice-bound region it would be ten years before any oil appeared and production could hit 780,000 barrels a day by 2027, declining steadily after that. That is not going to put much of a dent in U.S. daily oil consumption of 21 million barrels a day.

Unhappily, President Obama's counterpunch has been more symbolic than real. He has called for rescinding tax breaks for oil companies, which are reporting record profits from the run-up in crude prices of the last year. The idea that American oil company profits are the root cause of rising gas prices, though loudly trumpeted by the Democrats and much of the liberal media, is simply not true, and while comparatively big profits may be reprehensible, the notion that cutting them by government action can have any noticeable effect on the price of gas is living in a past that has been gone for forty years.

At best you would have to say that all wings of the political establishment are in determined denial. In January 2011 the ever-optimistic U.S. Energy Information Administration, which is supposed to know the most about this stuff, predicted that there was only a 10% chance that gas would hit $4 by the end of the summer driving season in September.

Who Owns the Oil? Not Americans

The past that Obama and apparently many Americans seem to be thinking of was the era of the "Seven Sisters," when privately owned — mostly American — oil companies dominated the global petroleum industry. This lasted from the mid-1940s to the 1970s. The famous seven were the Americans — Standard Oil of New Jersey, Standard Oil of New York (now Exxon-Mobil), Standard Oil of California, Gulf Oil, and Texaco (now Chevron) - joined by two from other countries, Royal Dutch Shell, and the Anglo-Persian Oil Company (now BP). In 1973 the Seven Sisters controlled 85% of the world's petroleum reserves.

Today the six largest privately owned oil companies are BP (United Kingdom), Royal Dutch Shell (Netherlands and UK), Total S.A. (France), and only three American corporations: Chevron, ConocoPhillips, and ExxonMobil. The six together control only 6% of world oil and gas reserves. The balance has shifted overwhelmingly to foreign, state-owned companies. State owned companies control 77% of world reserves, led by Aramco of Saudi Arabia, which was pumping 8.2 million barrels a day (mbd) in 2010 with a claimed capacity of 12.5 mbd, followed by National Iran at 3.5 mbd, Petroleos Mexicanos (2.9), Iraq National Oil (2.5), Petro China (2.3), Abu Dhabi National Oil Co. (2.3), Kuwait Oil Co. (2.3), and Petroleos de Venezuela (2.2). ExxonMobil is the only publicly traded company that even makes the top ten, at 2.5 mbd. Other significant players include Russia and Nigeria. (*Forbes*, July 9, 2010)

Clearly the U.S. oil companies have only extremely marginal ability to affect the price of oil or gas, and no tinkering with their tax status is going to change that. This is another measure of the relative decline of the United States as a world power, also testified to by the long series of lost, stalemated, or indecisive wars of the last generation.

So when we come in for a reality check we find that the United States produces and has reserves of only about 2% of world oil. That tail is not going to wag the dog of world fossil fuel prices. It consumes 25% of world output, about half from imports. It makes up the difference by pumping out its existing supplies at a far greater rate than any other major oil producer, for which future generations will pay the price.

Supply, Demand, and Peak Oil

Gas prices in turn depend on the price of crude oil, and that has been rising rapidly. Crude oil sold for about $3 a barrel for some 65 years, from 1880 through 1945. It rose marginally to about $5 a barrel for the next thirty years, until the OPEC oil embargo of 1973, when it began to spiral upward. It hit $21 a barrel in 1981, then roller-coasted down to $10 in 1990, followed by another spike, to a little over $30 a barrel that year following Saddam Hussain's invasion of Kuwait and the outbreak of the First Gulf War, only to turn downward again a few years later. What is striking, however, is that each trough is higher than the last time and each peak sets a new record.

The present huge upward curve began in 2000. It topped out in 2008 when crude oil briefly hit $147 a barrel, probably contributing as much to the U.S. and world financial collapse as the sub-prime mortgage crisis.

What has happened is that world demand has risen faster than supply. Worse yet, global output plateaued in 2005. Wikipedia summarizes: "Worldwide oil production, including oil from oil sands, reached an all-time high of 73,720,000 barrels per day in 2005. By 2009, production had declined to 72,260,000 barrels per day." This defies the standard economic model that big increases in sale prices will bring more product to market. Can't do it if it ain't there.

The cause is the once-controversial phenomenon called peak oil. It was first proposed by Shell oil geologist M. King Hubbert in a 1956 paper. Hubbert discovered that output from any given oil well followed a bell shaped curve: rising to its highest point when about half of the total oil had been extracted, and declining steadily thereafter, with a substantial portion of the second half unrecoverable. Further, the first half of the output was the easy part, with the second half deeper, more difficult to recover, and more expensive.

Eventually on the downhill side you hit the Energy Return on Energy Invested (EROEI) limit. Simple crude oil out of a fresh well gives you about 100 to 1 return. That is, it took only the equivalent energy of one barrel of oil to harvest 100 barrels. That has dropped in the U.S. today to one barrel invested to harvest only eleven barrels of return, and far less for biofuels such as corn ethanol, which may take as much energy to produce as it gives back.

Small wonder that the cost of oil has gone up. But at some point on each oil well, even when there remains a large amount of oil in the ground, EROEI falls to one for one. That is the point at which efforts to get the last part of the oil stop. It is why most figures on so-called oil reserves are grossly misleading, as they are to some degree guesses to begin with, and at best include the large percentage of unrecoverable oil ruled out by the prohibitive energy costs that would be needed to extract the product.

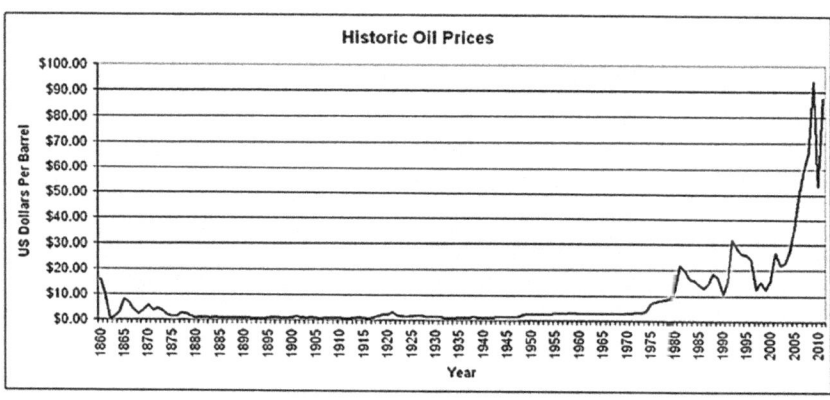

Hubbert in 1956 predicted that U.S. domestic oil production would peak between the late 1960s and early 1970s. That is exactly what happened, with U.S. output going into irreversible decline, leading to the U.S. going from self-sufficiency in oil to dependency on imports, particularly from the Middle East. Production in the continental 48 states peaked in 1970. Alaska's famous Prudhoe Bay wells peaked in 1989. And production in the shallow parts of the Gulf of Mexico peaked in 1998.

But Hubbert's curve works not just for a single well or country but globally. And more and more official sources have concluded that global oil peaked in 2005. Virtually all major oil producing countries have already peaked. Saudi Arabia is essentially the only significant oil producer with a fairly persuasive claim to have any available excess capacity, and that is not much on a global scale, amounting to a claimed 4 mbd. The Saudis promised at the beginning of the Libyan revolution to increase their output, then about 9 mbd, to cover the loss of about 2 mbd from Libya, but their increase never exceeded 10 mbd.

The other side of the coin is the rapid rise in world demand on an engine that is stuck in neutral. There have been slight declines in use in Western Europe and the U.S. through conservation and efficiency improvements. But demand growth has simply shifted to the developing world. China alone increased its daily oil use from 3.5 mbd in 1999 to 9 mbd in 2010, this alone more than eclipses the whole of Saudi Arabia's claimed excess capacity.

Unwillingness to Recognize that Resources Are Finite

While fossil fuels are finite — the decayed remains of prehistoric plant materials that took millions of years to turn into oil — human population has been growing at exponential speed, from 2.5 billion in 1950 to 7 billion in 2010. Add industrial development and a rise in living standards to that, and world demand for fossil fuels has been increasing dramatically while production has stagnated. In most producing countries it has in fact declined, often by very large margins.

For understandable reasons politicians of any stripe do not want to be the bearers of vastly bad news. Denial becomes an obligatory part of the profession. And that is what we have gotten. While officialdom mostly avert their eyes, there has been a small coterie of whistle blowers who have been trying to wake the country up. They tend to refer to themselves as the peak oil community. These include James Howard Kunstler, whose *The Long Emergency* lays out one of the most pessimistic scenarios, where oil decline and astronomical price increases shatter modern civilization altogether and we return to the life of the nineteenth or even eighteenth century, with vast loss of life along the way as modern agriculture collapses due to prohibitive costs of transportation and oil-based fertilizers.

Other figures include the prolific Richard Heinberg, where you might look at his *Peak Everything: Waking Up to the Century of Declines* or his large and comprehensive volume coedited with Daniel Lerch, *The Post Carbon Reader: Managing the 21st Century's Sustainability Crises.* Along similar lines is *The Ecotechnic Future: Envisioning a Post Peak World* by John Michael Greer. Then, among the least apocalyptic of this school, there is Jeff Rubin's *Why Your World Is About to Get a Whole Lot Smaller.* Rubin limits his prediction to the collapse of globalization and most air travel due to high fuel costs, leading on the positive side to a revival of American manufacturing industry. For ongoing current news one of the best sources is the Energy Bulletin website of the Post Carbon Institute.

Remember as you read in this literature that no one is talking about oil running out. It doesn't have to do that to become too hard to get and too expensive for the uses we have built our civilization on, particularly cheap car and truck transport.

To be frank, pioneers are sometimes outsiders who champion several fringe ideas at once. Kunstler warned repeatedly that the Y2K computer clock threat would crash the world economy, and he was a vitriolic critic of suburban sprawl on esthetic grounds long before he had the idea that gas prices would turn the hated suburbs into wastelands.

Richard Heinberg was a personal assistant to the famous crank Immanuel Velikovsky, who wrote numerous books trying to prove that catastrophes described in the Bible such as Noah's flood were real and were caused by drastic changes in the orbits of other planets in the solar system — in living human memory. Heinberg is also a 9-11 Truther.

John Michael Greer, who writes admirably clear and factual books on fossil fuel depletion, leads another life as a self-proclaimed Arch Druid, where he has a long beard, dresses in ankle length white robes, and writes books claiming that magic and magical beings are real.

Happily Jeff Rubin has more plausible credentials, having served for twenty years as Chief Economist for CIBC World Markets, the investment banking subsidiary of the Canadian Imperial Bank of Commerce.

Heinberg's *Post Carbon Reader* presents contributions by 36 authors, many of whom are tenured professors or the heads of established nonprofit agencies, above any suspicion of bizarre agendas.

If some of our path breakers have something a bit kooky about them, in the last year a number of long-reluctant official agencies have begun to confirm the peak oil community's worst fears. One of the first was the U.S. military. The UK *Guardian* reported April 11, 2010:

"The US military has warned that surplus oil production capacity could disappear within two years and there could be serious shortages by 2015 with a significant economic and political impact. The energy crisis outlined in a Joint Operating Environment report from the US Joint Forces Command, comes as the price of petrol in Britain reaches record levels and the cost of crude is predicted to soon top $100 a barrel.

"'By 2012, surplus oil production capacity could entirely disappear, and as early as 2015, the shortfall in output could reach nearly 10 million barrels per day,' says the report, which has a foreword by a senior commander, General James N. Mattis."

Most notable has been the turnabout by the International Energy Agency (IEA), the Paris-based intergovernmental advisory body for the OECD countries. The IEA had long been accused of doctoring its figures under pressure from the United States to present an unreasonably optimistic picture. Then, in November 2010, in its *World Economic Outlook*, it dropped a bomb, predicting that "Crude oil output reaches an undulating plateau of around 68-69 mb/d by 2020, but never regains its all-time peak of 70 mb/d reached in 2006." Whoa! after years of denying there would be any supply problem for crude for decades to come, the IEA now announces that world crude production peaked back in 2006, with a total output that would never be reached again!

The IEA tried to soften the blow with projections that the shortfall would be made up by gas liquids, tar sands, and other unconventional (and very expensive) sources, claims that were widely regarded as improbable. It capped its peering into the future with a prediction that crude oil would reach $113 a barrel — in 2035! On April 27, 2011, Brent crude was selling for $125, twenty-four years ahead of schedule and already $12 over budget.[1]

The unraveling by one-time peak oil skeptics has continued. Ronald Stoeferle of the Erste Group, the leading financial provider in the Eastern European Union with more than 50,000 employees, reported on March 14, 2011, on oilprice.com that "the British Department of Energy and Climate Change is collaborating with the Ministry of Defence and the Bank of England on a study about the consequences of peak oil." He added that "peak oil is not just a chimera of doomsday prophets, scaremongers, and congenital pessimists, but rather imminent reality," citing a report that 64 countries "have already reached their maximum production levels."

Stoeferle then cites a recent study by a German government think tank warning of the risk of a "tipping point" in which "the economic system would tip over." He summarizes the risks the German government study considers possible:

- The Western industrialised powers lose their influence
- Dramatic shifts of political and economic balances of power
- Massive reduction of mobility
- Further erosion of trust in governmental institutions and politics
- Negative impact on democracy, since a systemic crisis would create "space for ideological and extremist alternatives to existing forms of government"
- Possible partial or full failure of the markets, which could result in a regression to barter trade

---

[1] There are two international standards for oil prices. The conventional one for the United States is West Texas Intermediate (WTI), set at oil storage depots in Cushing, Oklahoma. This is the amount usually cited in the American media for current oil prices. The other, European, price, based on the UK's North Sea wells, is called Brent crude (for a well named for the Brent Goose). Normally the spread between the two is about 75 cents, but in the last year it has grown to more than $10. It is widely accepted that the WTI price (on April 27 at $112) is artificially low due to limited storage in Cushing, which is overfilled. Large parts of the U.S. pay the Brent price, not the WTI price, including the Gulf of Mexico states and the West Coast.

- Shortages in the supply of essentially important goods, such as food, and famine as a result
- Price shocks in practically all areas of the industry and in almost all stages of the value chain
- Banks would lose their basis of business, since companies with low creditworthiness would not survive
- Loss of confidence in currencies, as a result hyperinflation, and return to barter trade on local level
- Mass unemployment and state bankruptcies

This vision is hardly less apocalyptic than the most pessimistic scenarios of James Howard Kunstler and Richard Heinberg.

Retired CIA analyst Tom Whipple, who has specialized in the study of peak oil since 1999, looked at the future in his February 17, 2011, column in the *Falls Church News-Press* (Falls Church, Virginia):

"With declining quantities of fossil fuels, and the likelihood that renewable forms of energy cannot be developed and expanded quickly enough, continued worldwide economic growth is unlikely. While countries that are self-sufficient in fossil fuels and those able to get a lock on a share of fossil fuel production (most likely the Chinese) will be able to grow for a while. Eventually, however, they are certain to encounter other constraints. At the minute fresh water and food seem poised to follow fossil fuels into scarcity, but there are many other natural resources that soon will be too expensive for common use.

"Taken together, the decline and eventual near cessation of fossil fuel production and that of many other minerals, disruption in global weather patterns, and the growing food and water scarcity will constitute the third great transition [the first being agriculture, the second the Industrial Revolution]. Unlike the previous transitions in which life arguably got better for some, if not most, of the world's peoples, any upside to this transition seems to pale in the face of what is to come. Obviously the seven billion of us are going to have to shrink to some more sustainable number. Some demographers are already arguing that this might be under 1 billion."

Small wonder that virtually every prominent politician sees leveling with the public on this one as a career ender.

What Can Be Done?

It's when you start to think about what can be done that you really get why the politicians won't touch this one but just keep hoping the worst will hold off until they are out of office, or better yet, have made it to the end of their lives ahead of the storm. It is true that, while the storm looks to be beginning right here and now, there is always some chance that the decline will be put off for a while, and the downward slide will be slow. But the end is pretty clear and even an optimist is not likely to plan for it being more than a century away. World population, heavily dependent on fossil fuels for transportation, heating, electricity, and food production, is climbing toward an estimated 9 billion. Arable land is being eroded, global warming is already disrupting harvests, water tables, many of irreplaceable one-time deposits of "fossil" water, are being over pumped, and the price of oil keeps climbing.

Even uranium, if we were to choose to go the nuclear route after Fukushima, is within decades of exhaustion. And so far only oil — and liquefied natural gas at steep costs — can be pumped into a gas tank. Solar and wind power have extremely low return on energy invested, depend on oil to manufacture and transport the equipment, and are not going to run any airplanes or ocean going cargo ships.

There are things that can be done, so long as there remains a substantial amount of oil available. These are mostly fossil fuel extenders rather than true replacements. But they are steps that should be taken, in fact should have been taken thirty years ago. One step would be to build or re-build a nationwide system of electric railways and street cars. Electricity can be and is generated in large quantities by natural gas and, with its ecological overhead, by coal. Both of these are finite as well, and probably have less than a century to go, but they will be around for a while after the oil has become too expensive for ordinary passenger cars and many other of its customary uses.

America needs to begin replacing, or at least supplementing on a large scale, the agribusiness model of food production. Organic farming, apart from its health claims, has the great virtue that it does not depend on fertilizers made with fossil fuels (mainly natural gas). As oil becomes more expensive and more restricted in its allowable uses America will need to reverse the flight from the land that was one of the major demographic transitions of the twentieth century. Today's economy in which a huge portion of the population do not produce any tangible product is possible only because of the expenditure of the huge equivalents of human energy stored in finite, one-time deposits of fossil fuels. As these tangibly decline, standards of living will decline as well, and a far larger proportion of the population will have to be committed to the production of food and physical commodities.

Living space will also have to be redesigned. The incomprehensibly large investment in automobile-enabled urban sprawl with its concomitant long commutes in private automobiles of the post World War II period will prove to be too expensive to maintain. Higher density city and small town cores will become the new norm, with much of the abandoned suburbs being returned to the farmland they had concreted over. Urban front and back yards will be dedicated to raising food in the pattern of the Victory Gardens of the last world war.

One dead end that unfortunately has been endorsed by the Obama administration is ethanol. Declining arable land, droughts and fires, and the rising cost of fertilizer are causing rising food prices, already putting the very survival of a large part of the world's population at the mercy of a single bad global harvest. Diverting corn and sugar from the food supplies of poor nations to fill the gas tanks of rich ones is an unconscionable act.

Every U.S. president since Nixon has pledged to wean the country from dependency on foreign oil. So far this has been mostly just talk. A formidable obstacle to ending the paralysis in U.S. energy policy is the continually reinforced evidence of the solidity of our civilization. Like the citizens of Eternal Rome, it seems so established, so predictable, so real as to be unshakable. Surely it will go on, if not forever, than at least for our lifetimes, even for those of us who are pretty young. A good antidote to that kind of mesmerizing thought process is Jared Diamond's 2005 book *Collapsem* reviewed elsewhere in this volume. He traces the unanticipated and unexpected collapse of several mostly small ancient societies. The Polynesian inhabitants of Easter Island, having come from the Western Pacific where a more lush growing season saw palm trees growing faster than people harvested them, got in the habit of chopping down the trees in their new home at the same rate, for firewood, for building materials, and to make ocean going canoes. Over time the more barren Easter Island couldn't keep up. There were fewer and fewer palm trees. When the last tree was cut and there was no wood to make ocean going canoes for fishing the population collapsed to a tiny handful of survivors. What do you suppose the Easter islander was thinking when they cut down the last tree, or the next to last one?

April 28, 2011

Anticapitalism, the Hyperstate, and the Current Crisis

The Dragons of Expectation: Reality and Delusion in the Course of History, Robert Conquest. New York: W. W. Norton & Company, 2005, 256 pp.

"The Return of an Illusion," John Gray. *The New Republic*, June 23, 2011.

The global economic crisis that began in 2008 has revived many salvationist dogmas that we should have thought were well past their shelf life. Most notably in the United States this has been Christian theocracy, but also, to some extent at least, the Marxist notion that the problems of inequality and declining living standards can best be solved by scrapping the whole existing system and abolishing private property tout court. Where the former has secured a commanding influence among Tea Party activists, the latter has been seeking, with a good deal less success, to persuade the Occupy movement campers.

The encouraging Occupy movement arose under the brilliant slogan, "We Are the 99%." Scanning a Google search for Occupy Wall Street signs shows the vast majority call for specific reforms: raise taxes on the rich, guarantee jobs and healthcare for all, rein in corporate power and profits, pass serious regulations for the financial sector, start a new WPA to repair America's infrastructure and create jobs. Many are funny and most are home made. At the edges a few proclaim "Capitalism is a crime," "Capitalism is a disease," or simply "Anticapitalist." No doubt these warm the cockles of my elderly Marxist friends' hearts, but we should stop for a moment and ask just what those slogans actually call for.

Slogans of an activist movement are words of power. And like any magic, you should be careful what you wish for.

Before the collapse of the Soviet Union, the disintegration immediately thereafter of the Communist regimes of Eastern Europe, and China's turn to capitalism, there was broad agreement on the meanings of the terms capitalist and anticapitalist. The counterpoint was between an economy that was based primarily on private ownership of the means of production and regimes where the great majority of productive property was owned by the state.

"Anticapitalist" had a clear and well understood meaning: nationalize the means of production, usually with a subtext about this being done under workers' control. With the global implosion of Communism — Cuba and the nightmare slave state in North Korea being the spars left floating after the ship sank, even Vietnam having followed China into the free market in 1986 — the Marxist screen on which was inscribed what comes next after capitalism went dark. Something vaguely better but unspecified is often all the antiglobalists and anticapitalists of today will venture.

By and large the demands of the Occupy movement could be satisfied by a European-style welfare state. These all have universal healthcare and better welfare and job protections than the rugged individualist and religious-sect-ridden United States.

Speaking about these options is complicated by the muddled meanings of the word "socialist." For the right wing, most of Europe is "socialist." Even the middle-of-the-road Obama is a socialist, when he isn't a secret Kenyan Muslim conspirator. On the left "socialist" is the self-identification both of democratic socialists and Marxists, the first being advocates of extensive but limited state intervention to reduce inequality and provide certain minimal protections for all citizens, the second mean by it the first stage of communism, which begins with the destruction of the capitalist state and its institutions. To convolute further, some call themselves Marxists who have drifted away from such fraught imperatives as the dictatorship of the proletariat, while others who remain as hard core as ever nevertheless like to think of themselves as champions of some kind of proletarian democracy superior to what actually exists in what are called the Western democracies.

Sweden, though currently governed by a center-right bloc, is the prime example of European noncommunist socialism. For most of the twentieth century the dominant party was the Social Democrats, a socialist party. It remains the largest party in parliament. The country boasts the greatest equality in Europe, including gender equality, universal taxpayer-funded healthcare, strong trade unions, and mass participation in politics. At the same time Sweden is a constitutional monarchy, its industry is primarily privately owned, and by any reasonable economic definition it is a capitalist country.

By contrast, in no country where the economy was entirely statized — those, that is, that really were anticapitalist — has there been any kind of free press, elections, or any citizen organization, including trade unions, except those controlled by the one-party state. All had large numbers of political prisoners, and the great majority of these states murdered outright or deliberately starved to death hundreds of thousands or millions of their own citizens. All have been marked by extensive poverty, total censorship, and a ubiquitous secret police. Not a single one came to power through an election or ever afterward submitted to validation of its rule by allowing a vote on anything that mattered, leaving us to take their word that they represent the will of their people.

With the sole exception of Cuba — a paternalistic police state with a lackluster economy brightened by some notable social welfare measures, and which has begun, with Fidel's retirement, to also dip its toe into the private enterprise stream — the Communist regimes were matched in savagery toward their own people only by the most zealous of the fascist states. Hitler Germany was worse, but fascist Italy was considerably less repressive than Stalinist Russia, China while Mao was alive, Pol Pot's Cambodia, the Kim dynasty's North Korean serfdom, or even the Soviet Union in its first years under Lenin. Since there have been no examples of a democratic nationalized-property state, opponents of capitalism who call for its outright abolition need to look more critically at the theory, propounded by Karl Marx, on why we should expect such a state to be liberating compared to the existing order.

The evils that face the United States today are real and serious. A vast increase in inequality; growth of corporate power; prolonged joblessness, at 9 percent with much higher rates for youths and ethnic minorities; a bitter political paralysis at both national and local levels; and the ominous turn of the Republican Party toward religious obscurantism, rejection of modern science, and a drive to dismantle the social safety net and the modern welfare state, which would return the United States to the immiseration of Charles Dickens' England.

Clearly there are big battles to be fought here. It is essential to clarify the goals. Robert Conquest's 2005 reflections on the lingering attraction of the Soviet model and John Gray's more fundamental critique of the Marxist enterprise are helpful here. They are both brief, meant as smelling salts to wake up day dreamers with a sudden jolt, not to provide a definitive account.

I picked up Conquest's book on the recommendation of Christopher Hitchens, in his most recent essay collection, *Arguably*. Conquest, a poet as well as historian, is best known for *The Great Terror: Stalin's Purge of the Thirties* (1968), considered by many to be the definitive work on the subject. If we focus on our own domestic evils, violations such as waterboarding suspected al-Qaeda militants, government wiretapping, the extraordinary inflation of CEO salaries, and threats to Social Security and Medicare loom large.

Placing absolute, unrestricted power in the hands of government, as the Russian abolition of capitalist decentralization did, gave the state the power to do evil on a wholly different scale.

Conquest in *The Great Terror* put the number murdered or deliberately starved to death by the Soviet regime at 20 million. In the debates over such numbers, even after the collapse of the Soviet Union and the opening of its secret archives, Conquest's estimate proved to be far from the highest. Political scientist R. J. Rummel, the leading authority on democide, the intentional killing of citizens by their own government, put the number of those deliberately killed by the Soviet government in the Stalin era at 43 million. There were several categories Conquest left out, including most of those who died in the Gulag before 1936 or after 1939, the huge death rates among ethnic minorities such as the Crimean Tatars forcibly deported to Siberia. and the extensive executions in Eastern Europe as the Soviet army established its control at the end of World War II, including anti-Nazi fighters who did not happen to be Communists as well as many who were.

The dragons Conquest wants to slay are ideological, tendencies on the political left to magnify the evils of capitalism while finding rationalizations to discount the awful human cost of the statist experiments as irrelevant to their calls to try that road again. Every age, he suggests, and every people and culture within it, has its fanaticisms, fixed perceptions of reality that a later time can only look back on with horror. The Spanish Inquisition, the French Catholic massacres of the Huguenot Protestants, Spanish and English slavery in the Americas, defended by references to the Bible, all had their devoted followers who believed they were doing God's work — and never changed their minds. Conquest treats the hopes placed in state totalitarianism as only the most recent of these terrifyingly false mass expectations. And as the most recent, this one still has a grip on the minds of living people, many of whom are as immune to evidence or argument as any deeply religious believer. As their predecessors did, the devotees convince themselves their sacrifices for the cause were service to humanity. I should know, as I was one myself for a good part of my life.

"Whatever feuds or attitudes exist in the democracies," Conquest writes, "they count for very little compared with the vast and essential conflict between 'Western' society and the worldwide fanaticisms facing it."

As political battles within the democracies become polarized there is a tendency for the partisans to look favorably on the totalitarian state or movement that appears to share some of their aspirations. We see "a preference for the more appealing totalitarians over opponents within their own culture, with whom they actually have far less real substantive disagreements. If the trouble is largely from a left, it is partly because of a certain reluctance to admit that Communism was not only physically lethal and mentally repressive but also a total failure."

Conquest rejects all versions of socialism that place the whole of economic life in the hands of the state. This, of course, is what is generally meant by the term anticapitalist. Who, Conquests asks, "is to run the economy after you have eliminated the capitalists?"

"The answer," he writes, "was that it would be done by 'society.' But who would represent 'society'? A simple enough point, but one that has proved refractory." Referenda have been tried since the days of Napoleon and had little effect. So it can't be society as a whole directly. It will be representatives of some sort and a professional governmental cadre. In fact, no state that went so far as nationalizing the great majority of productive property has ever relinquished power back to the people it supposedly represents, or submitted to any election to validate its claim to rule — except in the throes of collapse when the nationalized property was being reprivatized as well.

Marx in his *Capital* both predicted and advocated that "Centralization of the means of production and socialization of labour at last reach a point where they become incompatible with their capitalist integument. This integument is burst asunder. The knell of capitalist private property sounds. The expropriators are expropriated." So it was in those countries where militant armed movements or the Soviet army carried this process out. But the resulting maw swallowed not only the capitalist expropriators but the proletariat, the peasantry, and all the intermediate classes as well. The state and the small cliques that came to control it were revealed as the greatest expropriators of all.

Conquest summarizes laconically, "Highly centralized and doctrinaire regimes have time and again proved deeply destructive." He was eighty-eight when he set out to battle old dragons. Hitchens calls the book "marvelous" and credits Conquest, rightly I think, with "invincible common sense and courage in the fight against totalitarian thinking." The book is also a bit the musings of a very old man irritated that what should have been long-settled issues return to plague him. He is beyond the point in his career where he needs to footnote every quotation or even name most of his targets. He does, however, take the occasion to weave in some of the most recent discoveries on his topic.

Anticapitalism in the Soviet Union — The Stalin Years

Stalin famously said to Churchill at Tehran, "When one man dies it is a tragedy, when thousands die it's statistics." Perhaps the camera has to zoom in from the numbingly large numbers to focus on a recognizable scene. Stalin,

Conquest reports, personally signed orders for forty-four thousand executions. Only fairly high ranking party and army functionaries rated such personal attention.

Death warrants for the *nomenclatura* were the least of it. For the Soviet masses there were kill quotas, like burger goals in a MacDonald's franchise or a cop giving parking tickets. "We now have a set of decrees, starting in July 1937, ordering specific execution and imprisonment targets . . . in each province and republic. The largest single category was 'anti-Soviet elements.' This included former kulaks, former officials of the tsarist state and army, former members of non-Bolshevik parties [including the Marxist parties!], religious activists, 'speculators' . . . a significant proportion of the population." The anonymous victims were selected at random by their match to some sociological criteria. Bureaucrats who failed to find enough of this or that category were themselves shot, on suspicion of being soft on enemies of the state. A fictional account that captures the stifling air of this necrotic system better than any mere recital of facts is Victor Serge's *The Case of Comrade Tulayev*. Serge spent three years in a Stalinist prison before being expelled from the Soviet Union in 1936.

As in the rest of the Mordor economy, overfulfilling your quota was met with approval, even when it was a quota of corpses. A recently discovered document from the head of the Novosibirsk NKVD, the secret police, authorizes his agents to double their death quotas at will. Now, for any Republicans listening, that was a real death panel.

In 1935 the death penalty was extended to apply to twelve-year-olds.

Deaths from starvation and other such "indirect" causes were a politicized weapon. Infant mortality in 1943, admittedly a war year, was .47 percent for ordinary Russian mothers; it was 41.7 percent for the children of mothers in the camps.

There is a record that 170 "blind, legless, and otherwise disabled men" in Moscow were arrested and shot for begging. The justification was that they would be useless in a labor camp.

The regime lied about everything — about the standard of living in the West, about its own economic output, about the mass killings, and about individual state assassinations. Avram Slutsky, Stalin's chief of foreign intelligence, was given a hero's funeral when he reportedly died of a heart attack in February 1938. We now know that deputy people's commissar Zakovsky pinioned him while Alekhin, head of the poisoning department (yes, there was such a unit!) ran in and gave Slutsky a fatal injection. Zakovsky was in turn executed that August.

"Torture was massively employed throughout the Stalin period, as with the victims of the secret 1952 Jewish Anti-Fascist Committee trial."

A whole army of interrogators and clerks were employed throughout these years to concoct "page after page of ever more complicated falsehood" about what happened to the millions of victims and why. This reached every aspect of life. The whole of the social sciences were destroyed. Conquest concludes that the German Nazis were more brutal, but Stalin's Russia was by far a more thoroughgoing totalitarianism, where private thought reservations about the government were almost impossible to retain and a slip of the tongue could result in execution, which could come at the whim of any local bureaucrat.

In May 1937 Stalin had Mikhail Tukhachevsky, commander in chief of the Soviet Army, arrested along with seven other generals. They made outlandish confessions of being agents of Trotsky and Hitler, and were executed the following month. A special crime was put on the books, being the wife of an enemy of the people. Many were shot, including Tukhachevsky's widow. Many other such widows were sent to the labor camps, from which few returned. The Soviet command structure was still decimated when Hitler attacked the USSR in June 1941. Stalin had other senior commanders killed during the war.

Afterward as well. In January 1947 two generals, Gordov and Rybalchenko, were caught by a secret police bug saying to each other that the population was "beggared" and there should be "genuine democracy." They were arrested and shot.

"Dead bodies were a common product of the Stalinist system. But minds did not do well either. They had to endure a continuous barrage of untruth. It can be argued that the Soviet Union's main negative characteristic — with plenty to choose from — was falsification. One finds it right from the start. But in the 1930s, after the disastrous failure of collectivization, the disjunction was complete. Henceforth, two different Soviet Unions existed — the official one, a flourishing and happy country (beset, though, by traitors), and the real one, overrun by poverty, squalor, and terror, and with a crushed population."

Conquest cites a moment of black comedy in 1964 as the regime was beginning to "rehabilitate" some of its many victims. A local party committee had to publish a group photo that included Faizulla Khodzhayev, an Uzbek Communist leader who had been shot in 1938. Not certain whether or not he was soon to be posthumously pardoned, they left him in the picture but airbrushed a big black beard over his face.

The details here are new but the general picture of the Soviet regime has been known since the 1920s. Conquest's reason for writing his book was to counter the remnants of sympathy for the idea of drastic state centralism as the cure for capitalist injustice. This has survived the collapse of Communism, though even among the small choir who still call themselves Marxists many, unlike their Leninist progenitors, have become vague about just what "post-capitalist" society is to be.

"Over the past half century," Conquest writes, "Western minds that were diverted by the socialist idea largely abandoned it as a serious program. . . . Socialism has thus largely petered out. . . . But the cluster of social and other ideas that accompanied socialism persists. And the idea of using state power to impose them has, of course, flourished and more than flourished both as a mental habit and as a political reality. Its adherents are now no longer social-ists but . . . remain implacably hostile to 'capitalism' without seriously ad-vancing any real alternative."

The old Marxists had a clear goal: crush the capitalist class and its sup-porters and establish a state monopoly of the means of production under firm communist control. The generally monstrous experience with that experiment, and the evaporation of Communism, depriving such advocates of even a "de-formed" example of what they advocate, leaves that section of the left that still champions anticapitalism with no generally accepted agreement on what the slogan entails. Conquest calls this "negative utopianism," adding, "it is a bit much to go on finding sub-Marxism and such still thumping away."

Such currents are broadly recognizable on the American and European left, though Conquest is less than specific about who his targets may be, spending a few pages on an obscure CNN book on the Cold War, on Simone de Beauvoir's lamentable embrace of the violent and cultish Maoist Cultural Revolution, and the ever floggable pro-Moscow historian Eric Hobsbawm.

Starting Again from the Enlightenment

With John Gray we encounter an intellect of a different order. Where Conquest largely limits his presentation to the past evils of hyperstatism, Gray rises immediately above the anecdotal. He confronts the rejuvenated hopes of the Marxist left that the global economic crisis offers a chance to emerge from their long sojourn in the wilderness:

"An intellectual revival of Marxism is one of the predictable conse-quences of the financial crisis. In the twenty years before the storm broke, the *Marxisant* intelligentsia was more marginal in politics and culture than it had ever been. This was not because Marxism had been falsified — an event that occurred a century or more before, when it became clear that no advanced industrial society was developing as Marx had predicted. Rather Marxist intellectuals had become unfashionable — an experience far more galling than the refutation of their theories."

You might suppose at this point that Gray is going to refute the Marxist catastrophists by promising a rapid economic recovery and a return to market stability, saving capitalist democracy. You would be wrong. John Gray, emeritus professor at the London School of Economics, is, if anything, at least as pessimistic about the future of capitalism as the Marxists, but sees the forces in motion as utterly different from those Marx expected and predicted.

Gray's philosophic roots lie not in the social engineering ambitions of Marxism and a section of liberalism inspired by the Enlightenment, but in the dissenting historical interpretation by that great Jewish-English liberal theorist Isaiah Berlin, whose world view Gray defended in his book *Berlin* (1995).

Berlin called his distinctive viewpoint "value pluralism," by which he signified that no human society could reach agreement on a single standard of right. This was a radical departure from the outlook of the European Enlightenment, which believed that reason would discover truth, that truth, like Newton's laws of motion, had only one solution to each equation, and that as ignorance was swept away by education, people would come to a common view of the social good.

When that did not happen, in the late nineteenth and early twentieth centuries a political current arose that sought to cut through the obvious failure to find agreement on how to achieve human improvement. The solution they hit on was to abolish electoral democracy by force, establish a statist dictatorship, and impose by violence their particular view of the social good.

These movements arose on both the left and the right, sharing a common disdain for the corrupt and sluggish democratic institutions. The left called itself communist, the right fascist. Both outlawed all political parties but their own, dispensed with elections, crushed trade unions, executed real and suspected critics, imposed censorship and thought control, and nationalized industry or placed it under constrictive state tutelage. They silenced or did away with those they could not persuade — or who fit their profile of the inassimilable. One side chose the Jews and Slavs, the other the better off peasants and the well-to-do. Both agreed on destroying the intellectuals — and the Marxists. On the fascist side that meant all Marxists; on the Bolshevik side, all Marxists who were not members of Lenin's party, and quite a few of those who were.

If you think about it for a moment, does anyone really believe that the only obstacle to abolishing capitalism in the United States is the economic and military power of the 1%? If that were really so, the change could be accomplished under the existing electoral system, or at least that system could reveal that the 99% want something radically different. Yet the system to date has been unable to produce a majority vote for even the far more limited demands of the Occupy movement: for a more progressive tax system, for greater government regulation of corporations and banks, for strengthening and extending pensions and healthcare.

Why does Obama not just impose these things now? Obviously because a large percentage of the population, not just the wealthy 1%, vote Republican, and the Republicans in state and national legislatures oppose the reform agenda. And behind the Republicans are the very numerous adherents of authoritarian Christian fundamentalist sects. The United States, after all, was largely founded by dissenting religious fanatics fleeing the power of the more moderate state churches of England and Germany. It was an unusual conjunction that placed at the head of the American Revolution that amazing group of rationalists and deists who wrote the Declaration of Independence and the Constitution. Out in the hinterland were people who looked on with uncomprehending distrust, whose intellectual horizons were firmly girdled by holy writ. Uniquely among the developed countries today, 40% of Americans deny outright that humans are descended from other animals; 20% more say they are not sure.

Notably, the Republican base includes a majority of the industrial workers who are supposed to be the bedrock of the Marxist revolutionary class. Narrow majorities may shift here, allowing significant changes, but overwhelming agreement on total restructuring of the existing society comes up against the impenetrable obstacle of the plural and irreconcilable values Berlin insisted must be accommodated if democracy is to survive.

In the heyday of popular illusions in the magic of ruthless statism the advocates of radical social change were quite clear sighted about the impossibility of ending these differences of view by persuasion or by electoral means. Both left and right, communist and fascist movements, based their politics on the violent crushing not only of capitalism but first of all of electoral democracy, the independent press, and the existing intellectual class. Then they moved to create their centralist states where only a single viewpoint was permitted, solving by brute force the problem of the large swaths of the population that did not agree with them.

The original Marxist project for the abolition of capitalism rested on the expectation of increasing proletarianization and an emergent shared agreement on the need to abolish private property. That is, the Enlightenment perspective on the triumph of human reason wedded to theories of onward and upward progress powered by class struggle.

It is not so much the failure of the economic crises Marx predicted to appear on schedule as the failure to materialize of the anticapitalist social forces required to do anything about it. Isaiah Berlin is perhaps the most important theorist in grasping why that happened.

In a series of essays beginning in 1955, collected in his *Against the Current: Essays in the History of Ideas*, Berlin carried out a then-shocking reevaluation of the Enlightenment, which was still hailed in liberal tradition as the movement in defense of reason against religious dogmatism and superstition, and the wellspring of a host of movements for human betterment, including Marxism itself.

Berlin said that the Enlightenment also had a dark side. That lay precisely in the social engineering dreams that were its hallmark, and its notion of a single universal human society superseding existing nations and cultures. Berlin popularized the term Counter Enlightenment for the thinkers that culminated in the late eighteenth and early nineteenth centuries in German Romanticism. On its face, seeing something positive here seemed unpromising. Figures such a J. A. Haaman championed intuition against rationalism, mysterious vitalism against biological science, and the idea of society as an organic whole, which regarded any organized attempt to impose universal improvement as destructive of irreplaceable human values. Though neither Berlin nor John Gray had much use for Hegel, this was a case where it could really be said that truth lay in a dialectical synthesis of two opposite schools of thought.

The extreme left wing of the Enlightenment imagined an entire world united along rationalist lines, in a universalist super government that was to expose religion as a vapid dream, leave national differences in the past, and erase ethnic and racial distinctions. For Marx, this meant the dissolution of national identities into universal humankind.

The thinkers of the Counter Enlightenment objected that what makes all real human communities function is their sense of place, of lineage, of a shared history, and traditions, customs, and culture, including religion, language, and ethnic or national identity. Strip people of these identifiers and they become atomized cogs in an impersonal machine, a change that most people will fiercely resist. Even a false propaganda hint of this prospect has the Tea Party in a frenzy, and they are tapping roots that run much deeper than their own ersatz movement.

John Gray, following Isaiah Berlin's lead, sees the collapse of Soviet and East European Communism and the hollowing out of its Chinese variant as due, not to economic backwardness or some technical unpreparedness for socialism, but to the artificiality of these presumed universals. In his *New Republic* article he writes:

"Like most nineteenth-century thinkers, Marx expected religion to fade away with the increase of prosperity and the advance of scientific knowledge. Instead religion is at the heart of politics and war, just as it has always been. Marx never doubted that the globalization of capital would occur in tandem with the decline of nationalism. In fact globalization has triggered a nationalist backlash in many parts of the world."

Scientific Socialism

Marx in his theory of communism did take one step beyond the other social engineering movements of the liberal Enlightenment, an extremely negative borrowing from the Enlightenment's critics. He grafted the Romantics' idea of organic unity, their idea of extending the values of real communities to embrace the whole of emergent nation states, onto his plan for the communist future.

"A fantasy of German Romanticism that enchanted not only Marx but also movements of the radical right," Gray writes, "the dream of organic social unity, has always been repressive in practice. And this is not because the ideal has been wrongly interpreted. Hostility to minorities is the very logic of organicist ideology. Marx located his ideal society in the future; but like that of the German nationalists who looked backward to an imaginary folk culture, his communist dream-world could be entered only by shedding particular identities (including that of Jews, who would be emancipated by ceasing to be Jews and becoming specks of universal humanity). In a society of the kind of which Marx — along with Herder and his disciples — dreamed, anyone who resists being absorbed into the social organism will be stigmatized as deluded or diseased."

Outside of his study of capitalism, where Marx was in his element, his and Engels' projections for the future were speculative and deductive. In describing their theories about the future as scientific socialism they sought to claim the authority of modern science. In fact the revolutionary duo were totally wrong about two of most important discoveries of their time: Malthus's theory of population and Darwin's theory of evolution. In both cases their political prejudices and deductive method misled them.

Malthus's basic observation was that population grows geometrically while food supplies expand only arithmetically, a fact observable in animal and even bacterial as well as human populations, for the same reasons. The consequences of this fact today confront the planet with the threat of mass starvation. Marx vehemently denied Malthus's verifiable observation on the grounds that it let capitalist society off the hook. But one didn't have to look very far into the future to see the outcome of human reproductive rates. England had a population of 14,866,000 in 1841 when its first census was taken. By 1861 this had grown to 18,776,000, a 26% increase. On the same principal as compound interest, a few centuries of unchecked growth like this would produce a mass of human bodies that covered every square inch of dry land on the earth.

Marxists frequently cite the few vague words of praise Marx and Engels uttered affirming an unspecified similarity between their historical materialism and Darwin's theory of evolution to show that Marx and Engels were on the cutting edge of the science of their day. Between themselves, however, they rejected natural selection, Darwin's essential discovery, which today is the foundation of biological science. Their reason was that Darwin explicitly said the idea of natural selection had been suggested to him by reading Malthus. Marx and Engels praised Darwin for his *Origin of Species* as a widely understood public symbol for the idea of "evolution," but had their own and very different theory of evolution which was more supportive of their theories of social evolution than Darwin's work.

Marx wrote sniffily to Engels: "It is remarkable how Darwin rediscovers, among the beasts and plants, the society of England with its division of labour, competition, opening up of new markets, 'inventions' and Malthusian 'struggle for existence'." (June 18, 1862). Engels, writing to P. L. Lavrov, astonishingly proclaims: "Of the Darwinian theory I accept the *theory of evolution* but only take Darwin's method of proof (struggle for life, natural selection) as the first, provisional, and incomplete expression of a newly-discovered fact. . . . If, therefore, a so-called natural scientist permits himself to subsume the whole manifold wealth of historical development under the one-sided and meagre phrase, 'struggle for existence,' a phrase which even in the sphere of nature can only be taken with a grain of salt, such a proceeding is its own condemnation." (November 12, 1875).

Marx praised, as far superior to Darwin, a book by the long-forgotten Pierre Tremaux (not important enough to even warrant a Wikipedia entry) which theorized that evolution's motor was the geological, not biological, evolution of the earth's crust, species being inextricably linked to specific soil types that appeared in sequence as the physical earth "evolved." Tremaux's crank theory appealed to Marx because it propounded a steady progression of ever higher stages, analogous to Marx's historical materialism for human society.

Darwin's natural selection in contrast did not contain a theory of progress. It stated only that individual organisms with some biological or behavioral advantage left behind more progeny in the competition for survival, leading to adaptation to their environments and eventually speciation. Darwin's natural selection makes no predictions of future stages. It does not suppose that natural selection is in particular geared to higher complexity — only a tiny segment of life forms, such as the giant reptiles and the later mammals, are exceptionally complex — much less a drive toward intelligence or the appearance of humanity. From the standpoint of natural selection the HIV virus could be regarded as a more successful adaptation to its environment than homo sapiens.

"Evolution" leaving out Darwin's natural selection became a term often commandeered by religious and political progressives in the nineteenth and early twentieth century to depict humans as the apex of the evolutionary tree and to concoct schemas to prove that humanity was continuing to evolve toward still greater perfection in the near future. In that usage it was not science but a bogus justification for the self-congratulatory Victorian belief in progress.

I write this not to pillory Marx. What he did was to choose the view that corresponded to his predilections rather than the one that was scientifically valid. Between the two he made an inspired — and mistaken — guess. Unhappily the guess he made reinforced his confidence that he had discovered the key to predicting future stages of social evolution, as Tremaux had done for the biological past. Had he understood Darwin's natural selection he would also have understood much of the argument against trying to predict society's future. Marx here, and in his expectation of a collectivist utopian future, was operating within the parameters of nineteenth century thought and its mental habits. His inheritors are the ones principally at fault for taking his theoretical constructs for reality.

John Gray, in his 2007 *Black Mass: Apocalyptic Religion and the Death of Utopia,* challenged conventional assumptions about human progress. Gray acknowledges obvious technical, scientific, and even administrative progress in human history. But he denies any concomitant moral improvement. Our biological inheritance, which has not changed in significant ways since Cro Magnon times, includes savagery as well as sociability. For Gray, greater technical and scientific progress has improved human health, but it has also put more destructive weapons in the hands of fanatical and authoritarian movements and regimes.

This sobering and rather pessimistic view does not lead Gray to see no distinction among existing human societies. Echoing Robert Conquest, he writes:

"The notion that the excesses of contemporary capitalism are on par with the crimes of Stalinism and Maoism is crazy. Contemporary Western capitalism has many faults, some of them conceivably fatal; but it cannot be placed in the same category with systems that perpetrated the mass murder of their own citizens, and which were responsible for the worst ecological catastrophes in modern times, possibly in all history."

The Anti-Stalinist Marxists

Gray's *New Republic* piece is a scathing review of *Why Marx Was Right* by British literary critic Terry Eagleton, and Eric Hobsbawm's *How to Change the World: Tales of Marx and Marxism,* both published in 2011 and both professing a certain nostalgia for Stalin's Russia.

Gray rejects the common view that the evils of the Soviet system were mainly attributable to economic backwardness, Russia's authoritarian traditions, and the early civil war.

"The repression that defined Soviet life from the beginning to the end flowed principally from the communist idea itself, which requires that any group that defines itself differently from the rest of society must eventually be destroyed. Interestingly, Eagleton does not deny this. Like many others, he writes as if repression became severe only under Stalin, which is nonsense."

This last is a particularly sore point for the Trotskyists, with whom I had a long association. They have been among the most bitter critics of Stalin, his regime, and the later Communist states influenced at the outset by the Moscow pattern. At the same time they reject the modern capitalist welfare state in even its most humane guise, disparaging "bourgeois democracy" as a sham. Their attitude toward the now defunct Communist regimes was, nevertheless, ambiguous. Trotsky was among the first to reveal and denounce the crimes of Stalin, yet he continued to regard the Soviet Union as more progressive than the United States because of its retention of the purportedly advanced property relations from the days of the October Revolution.

Trotsky and his followers occupied an ultimately untenable ground on the outskirts of the far larger Communist movement. Trotsky was an attractive personality, a polymath who had served the Bolshevik regime as diplomat and founder of the Red Army, leading it to victory in the civil war. A gifted historian and orator, he was finally a martyr to Stalin's assassin. In the early years of the revolution he was in its most authoritarian wing, championing the militarization of labor, defending the crushing of the Kronstadt sailors' rebellion, and raising no objection to the mass killings by the Cheka.

Trotsky won credit in exile in publicizing the crimes of the Stalin government, often when the liberal press didn't want to hear such things. But while he now advocated socialist democracy, this bore little resemblance to democratic institutions as they actually evolved in European and American history. He had helped to create the one-party state, with Lenin used the Soviets to consolidate Bolshevik power and then stripped them of any authority, helped to destroy the trade unions, and endorsed the arrest and imprisonment of the members and leaders of all the other political parties, including the widely popular far leftist ones.

As he envisioned it for the future, socialist democracy was plainly conditional on accepting all the essential positions of the predominant party that was to smash the capitalist state. In Trotsky's program the monopoly of productive property was to remain the centerpiece, and the new government was to be unicameral, rejecting any separation of powers or independent judiciary. The government was to centrally control the press as well as industry and the land. Other parties were to be tolerated only insofar as they accepted these conditions. He did not promise the right of free speech but only of speech that agreed with all the essential features of the communist state. We have been there before. Archimedes said if he had a long enough fulcrum and a place to stand he could move the world. Trotsky's projected revolutionary government left dissenters no fulcrum and no place to stand.

Trotsky never reconsidered or regretted the bloody repression of the years when he and Lenin headed the government. He promoted a cult of Lenin that bore little resemblance to the dictator's real place in history. He condemned the murders of the Old Bolsheviks by Stalin, but not the imprisonment and many executions of the Social Revolutionaries and the Mensheviks, much less the members of the liberal parties, by his own government. And he clung to the view that the brutal Communist states should be defended against the Western democracies as well as against the fascist states.

George Orwell, who remained a socialist and had a limited sympathy for Trotsky, nevertheless wrote, in 1939:

"Trotsky, in exile, denounces the Russian dictatorship, but he is probably as much responsible for it as any man now living, and there is no certainty that as a dictator he would be preferable to Stalin, though undoubtedly he has a much more interesting mind. The essential act is the rejection of democracy — that is, of the underlying values of democracy; once you have decided upon that, Stalin — or at any rate something *like* Stalin — is already on the way."

Though the Trotskyists long supposed that if Stalinism could be somehow eliminated they would then fill the revolutionary vacuum, the unhappy reality was that they were too inextricably tied in history, outlook, and goals to the discredited Soviet Union. When it foundered, interest in the Lenin era and its Trotskyist champions faded as well. For the few who remain, the cult of Lenin and the October Revolution as heroic models stands in fatal opposition to their self-image as champions of socialist democracy.

Lenin and the Early Soviet Union

What truth is there to the view that Lenin was the great emancipator whose work was undone by Stalin the betrayer? Conquest and Gray devote most of their fire to Marxite currents that were sympathetic to the Soviet system in its Stalin and post-Stalin years. But they have little patience for myth making on Lenin's account.

Conquest writes, "The Bolshevik Revolution brought an atavistic ideocracy, with a narrowly sectarian mind-set, and a total, and indeed self-admitted, amorality of action. And its long-term effects have been overwhelmingly negative. Its real nature was understood by many even at the time. But its myth, especially among the ideas-and-ideals thirsty of the West, still vaguely survived."

Conquest first dismisses the legend that the October Revolution, unlike the mass outpouring in February 1917, was sought by any significant force in Russian society. "Lenin had great difficulty in getting a majority even of his own Central Committee to support the seizure of power, and reports from its own agents in the city districts spoke in most cases of a lack of enthusiasm for the coming revolution."

On November 11, 1917, four days after the Bolshevik coup, a meeting of the Central Committee (with Lenin and Trotsky absent), voted unanimously to form a coalition government with the other left parties. On November 18, Kamenev, Rykov, and three other members of the Central Committee resigned, warning that the failure to set up a coalition government would result in "a purely Bolshevik government by means of political terror." The Bolsheviks never thereafter permitted the people to vote on their regime. In the Constituent Assembly elections in late November the Bolsheviks won only 175 seats out of 703. All the other parties were of the left except for the moderate liberals, the Constitutional Democrats (Cadets), who won only 17 seats. The Bolsheviks forcibly dispersed the only elected legislature in Russian history, thirteen hours after it convened its first session.

In reports to the Bolsheviks at the time, long hidden from the public, factory after factory in St. Petersburg, after the Bolshevik seizure of power, voted solidly for the Mensheviks and Social Revolutionaries. There were many strikes in 1918, which the Bolsheviks crushed mercilessly.

Conquest comments:

"One reads, to this day, in books published by reputable university presses, such things as 'the Bolshevik Party was a product of idealistic, egalitarian, and socially progressive strands in the Russian intelligentsia and working class.' Something missing here, you may think — for example fanatical hostility to and finally total suppression of other groups with the same ostensible aims."

The killings without trial and far from the front in wartime began not under Stalin but under Lenin and Trotsky. "There are now many documents available in which Lenin insists on mass shootings and hangings. And Bertrand Russell, who met him when he was in power, reports that 'his guffaw at the thought of those massacred made my blood run cold.'"

Conquest gives only a few examples to make his point. For those who would like to look further into repression in the early Soviet years there are many books. I could suggest as places to begin Dmitri Volkogonov's *Lenin: A New Biography* (1994) and Alexander N. Yakovlev's *A Century of Violence in Soviet Russia* (2002), both based on access to the long-sequestered archives of the Soviet state and its secret police.

The first Soviet secret police organization, the Cheka (All-Russian Extraordinary Commission for Combating Counter-Revolution and Sabotage), was formed in December 1917, hardly a month into the new power. Volkogonov writes, "The Cheka quickly became virtually the chief element of the state, arousing fear not only among the mass of the population, but also among the Bolsheviks themselves." The secret police had unlimited powers of arrest and execution. "Tens of thousands of people were shot without trial in the cellars of the Cheka."

Volkogonov recounts that Revolutionary Tribunals "disposed of thousands of people, often merely for belonging to the 'exploiting' class." There was no appeal and those sentenced were shot within twenty-four hours. The Cheka did the same thing on a vaster scale, including executing Communist Party members suspected of dissenting from its methods. Trials were rare, and when held, Yakovlev reports, the Politburo decided the sentences in advance.

The Cheka was given special authorization to secretly arrest and even execute persons they were certain would be acquitted in any public trial because there was no evidence against them.

In March 1921 a group of Chekists on the Turkestan front dared to write to the Bolshevik Party Central Committee protesting the executions of Chekists by their own organization. "[Chekists] are being shot for various crimes, and none of the Communists working in these proletarian punitive organs has any guarantee that he won't be shot tomorrow under some heading or other."

Only Lenin personally had any influence with this ruthless and secretive agency, and he gave it his unstinting support against protests and critics from within his own party.

The Bolsheviks established a system of concentration camps largely to hold various kinds of hostages and to silence the other left parties. Volkogonov writes:

"As early as 1918 the Bolsheviks began organizing concentration camps, and those who were spared the bullet began filling them. On 20 April 1921 the Politburo under Lenin's chairmanship approved the building of a camp for ten to twenty thousand people in the region of Ukhta in the far north." Another camp was built in Kholmogory, also in Siberia. In a short time there were 84 of the camps. This system did not begin with Stalin.

"The first deportations to the camps took place during the civil war. An especially large number of women and children were 'resettled' from the Don and the Kuban following the savage reprisals against the Cossacks. Thousands of them died, either in camp or on the way there."

The camps were initially for hostages, first of families of army officers, then of peasants to compel their families to deliver up their grain, and then for the members of the other left and Marxist parties. The camp regimes were not as deadly as later under Stalin, and the numbers incarcerated were far fewer, but their use to imprison tens of thousands for even small deviations from the views of the government, for mere suspicious "class origins," or to force obedience from family members where no crime had been committed were marks of an inhumanity not anticipated in the works of Marx or in Lenin's soporifically rosy *State and Revolution*. To have quoted Marx's prediction that after the socialist revolution all officials would be subject both to election and recall and that everyone would participate in carrying out the functions of supervision so there would be no bureaucrats was enough to earn a bullet from the Cheka.

The left parties, which had far larger followings than the Bolsheviks at the time of the October Revolution, were driven out of the Soviets by violence, then falsely accused of aiding the counterrevolution, and finally their members exiled, arrested, or executed. In March 1922 in a speech to the 11th Congress of the Communist Party, Lenin instructed the courts (no independent judiciary here!): "For public evidence of Menshevism our revolutionary courts must order executions, or else they are not our courts."

The Mensheviks and the Social Revolutionaries were incessantly accused in the Bolshevik press and in show trials of being in league with the White Guards and foreign imperialists. Yakovlev reports that the secret archives show these slanders were lies. The same tactic was used to justify the crushing of the Kronstadt sailors' uprising in March 1921, where "the government published an announcement headlined 'A New White Guard Conspiracy!' It declared that everything that had happened in Kronstadt 'was undoubtedly prepared by French counterintelligence' and that the 'spies have been apprehended.'" The sailors in fact raised only the demands that the Bolsheviks themselves had championed in 1917: for all power to the Soviets, for all socialist parties to have the right to participate, for freedom of the press. These were all now denounced as counterrevolutionary.

A formal investigation of the uprising headed by Ya. Agranov in April immediately afterward concluded that it was impossible to show any links between the Kronstadt uprising and White Guards or foreign governments. More than 2,000 of the sailors were executed; Agranov's report was kept secret. Fifteen years later, Stalin staged the first of the infamous Moscow Trials of the Old Bolsheviks. The only supplement to Lenin's playbook was having the victims confess to the false charges.

There is also the myth that the secret police, repressive as they may have been, directed their imprisonments and liquidations against capitalist saboteurs, ultra rightists, military conspirators, and the like. In January 1922 six of the ten subdivisions of the secret police, recently renamed the OGPU, were assigned to infiltrate and repress the socialist and anarchist parties and their suspected sympathizers.

The government made widespread use of hostages, including executing them either in reprisals for acts of resistance or when their family members refused to do what the government demanded of them. In September 1918 the Petrograd secret police shot 500 hostages. The government routinely used children as hostages in large numbers, from the families of army officers, to compel them to serve in the new Red Army, and from peasant families to make them surrender their grain. In 1919 the families, including the children, of an entire army unit, the Eighty-sixth Infantry Regiment, that had gone over to the Whites were shot. Yakovlev adds, "In May 1920 the newspapers told of the execution in Elizavetgrad of the elderly mother and four daughters, ages three to seven, of an officer who had refused to serve the proletarian regime. Arkhangelsk, where the Cheka shot children of twelve to sixteen, was known in 1920 as the 'city of the dead.' . . . The fall of 1918 saw the creation of concentration camps whose prisoners at first were largely hostages, including women with infants, taken as relatives of the [peasant] 'rebels.' The minutes of the meeting of 27 June 1921 of the commission on the maintenance of child hostages in concentration camps in Tambov province notes a sizable influx of minors, including infants . . . and it speaks of the inadequacy of these camps for long-term support of children and the resultant intestinal and respiratory diseases."

Lenin personally issued numerous orders for ever broader categories of shootings. In August 1918 he wrote to the party secretary in Saratov, telling him "shoot conspirators and waverers without asking anyone or any idiotic red tape." In December he ordered Shlyapnikov to "catch and shoot the Astrakhan speculators and bribe-takers" Volkogonov summarizes:

"During the civil war Lenin told his commanders to shoot miscreants for a widening range of offences: for taking part in a conspiracy, resisting arrest, concealing arms, disobedience, backwardness, carelessness and false reports." Conscious of his reputation as a humanitarian liberator Lenin kept these orders out of all public documents and his speeches. They were recorded in telegrams and written notes marked confidential, filed away in the secret archives of the state, not revealed until after 1989.

Volkogonov records that in early 1922 during a Soviet campaign to seize the valuables of the Russian Orthodox churches, "between fourteen and twenty thousand clergy and active laymen were shot." For many there were refinements. Yakovlev recounts that Metropolitan Vladimir of Kiev was castrated before being shot. Metropolitan Veniamin of St. Petersburg was frozen alive into a block of ice. One was tied to the wheels of a paddle boat and mangled, another buried alive. Archbishop Vasily was crucified; others were given Communion with molten lead.

Lenin on December 25, 1919, on the eve of the Nikola, the celebration of the relics of St. Nicolai, issued an order: "[T]o put up with 'Nikola' would be stupid — the entire Cheka must be put on the alert to see to it that those who do not show up for work because of 'Nikola' are shot."

Annoyed that prostitutes were encouraging disorder among Red Army troops, Lenin on August 9, 1918, sent out a telegram ordering, "impose mass terror immediately, shoot and deport hundreds of prostitutes who have been getting soldiers, former officers, and so on drunk. Not a minute's delay."

The Bolsheviks from the outset made enemies of the vast Russian peasantry. Coming to power while promising All Power to the Soviets and Land to the Tiller, the Bolshevik government then nationalized the land. Even in Lenin's public writings and speeches he insisted that the peasantry, the overwhelming majority of the Russian people, should have no voice in Soviet government policy. But within the distrusted peasantry Lenin decided to exterminate the so-called kulaks, the better off peasants. This layer mostly came into existence only in 1906, when the Stolypin reforms broke up the big landed estates. Kulaks were defined as any farm larger than eight acres per male family member. Between 13 and 16 percent of the farmers met this standard, something around 2 million people.

In August 1918 Lenin called for "Merciless war against these kulaks! Death to them!" The idea that these people were rich was mostly a communist mirage. When Stalin seized their valuables during his forced collectivization a few years later at the beginning of the 1930s the average kulak family had goods worth less than $200.

Armed grain requisitions, nominally of "surplus" grain, began to leave the peasants starving, and for kulak families the government began to issue orders to leave them with no food at all. On the 10th of August 1918 Lenin sent out a telegram to one district leader ordering: "1. Hang (by all means hang, so people will see) no fewer than 100 known kulaks, fat cats, blood-suckers. 2. Publish their names. 3. Take all their grain. 4. Select hostages in accordance with yesterday's telegram. Do it so that for hundreds of miles around people will see and tremble."

In a similar vein he ordered the Executive Committee in Livny: "Essential . . . to confiscate all the grain and property of the rebellious kulaks . . . take hostages from among the rich and hold them until every last bit of grain is removed from their districts." That is, the district was condemned to die of starvation. He added that in the nearby fight against White Guard Yudenich, reinforcements should be rounded up for the Red Army: "can we not mobilize some 20,000 more Petersburg workers, plus 10,000 or so bourgeois, place some machine guns behind them, shoot several hundred and bring some real mass pressure against Yudenich."

In Tambov province the peasants were eating nothing but grass, bark and nettles. "Chief Commissar Sergei Kamenev in October 1920 speaks of crowds of hungry peasants in adjacent Voronezh and Saratov provinces pleading with the local authorities to give them at least some of the grain taken at the collection centers. Often, Kamenev writes, 'these crowds were mowed down by machine guns.'"

In the midst of the dire famine caused by the government grain seizures, which had enveloped thirty-six million people, the Politburo on December 7, 1922, voted to export almost a million tons of grain. The Russian philosopher and one-time Marxist Nicolai Berdyaev commented, "There is something other-worldly in the Bolsheviks, something alien. That is what makes them terrifying."

In August 1920 the peasants in Tambov and Voronezh provinces finally rebelled. Red Army records document that in June 1921 General Tukhachevsky, later Soviet commander-in-chief, faced with peasants who had sought refuge in a wooded area, ordered poison gas "be made to spread through the forest killing anyone hiding there." A Politburo decree of June 11, 1921, on the Tambov situation provided that anyone who refused to give their name was "to be shot on the spot without trial," and "Any family which harboured a bandit [!] is subject to arrest and deportation from the province, their property to be confiscated and the eldest worker in the family to be shot without trial."

In the late twenties the Romanian author and Soviet sympathizer Panait Istrati traveled around the Soviet Union with Soviet diplomat Christian Rakovsky and revolutionary novelist Victor Serge. Some functionary sought to justify the visible negatives by citing Lenin's favorite exculpatory proverb about having to break eggs to make omelets. "All right, I can see the broken eggs," Istrati replied. "Where's this omelet of yours?"

It is easy to feel self-righteous and blameless when campaigning against the evils of capitalism far from the countries that have done away with it. The great majority of the European and American followers of the Communist parties, pro-Stalin though they were, saw themselves this way. Ultimate aims are not on the table. The battles are for needed reforms, where the Marxists, using the term loosely, share common aims with broader sections of the population that have no desire for a communist future.

Most of the Trotskyists I have known see themselves in the same light: heroic opponents of America's foreign wars, champions of civil rights, of feminism, and gay liberation, warriors against the power and influence of the very rich, enemies of the "twin capitalist parties." But there always lurks "the program," the "solution" to the whole bag of injustices, toward which every partial struggle is supposed to lead, and for which the model is the Russian October Revolution. By and large these militants have not cared to look the real Lenin in the face and confront what it is they advocate. A few have and decided to quietly withhold their approval. Unhappily, at least a few of my Trotskyist comrades have looked, and seeing, shrug their shoulders and say this is the way of great revolutions. And so they wander off into the totalitarian swamp and political irrelevancy.

This is not the place to pursue this further. You get the idea. Both Volkogonov (1928-1995) and Yakovlev (1923-2005) were lifelong Russian Communists. Volkogonov, a colonel general in the Soviet army, was an orthodox Communist in the Brezhnev years. He became a military historian, and was slowly disillusioned. For some years he held the view that the Soviet degeneration dated from Stalin, but his research in the archives finally convinced him that all the essential elements of the totalitarian state began with Lenin. He was fired by Gorbachev for his critical views, but supported perestroika and became Boris Yeltsin's military advisor.

Yakovlev first became disillusioned while attending Khrushchev's famous de-Stalinization speech in 1956. He was the first to reveal, in 1989, the secret agreements between Nazi Germany and the Soviet Union. He was a key advisor to Gorbachev and a principal architect of perestroika. In his last years he chaired Russia's Presidential Commission for the Rehabilitation of Victims of Political Repression, where he had access for the first time to the secret files of the KGB and other state agencies of repression, on which he based his book.

I have limited this brief excursion to Russians, for their intimacy with the subject. Also worth reading are Jean-François Revel's *Last Exit to Utopia: The Survival of Socialism in a Post-Soviet Era,* and François Furet's *The Passing of an Illusion: The Idea of Communism in the Twentieth Century.* And for the very bold Marxist ready to rethink their world view there is A. James Gregor's *The Faces of Janus: Marxism and Fascism in the Twentieth Century.*

Decentralized property ownership, that is, capitalism, despite its known evils has proven able to give more leverage to people seeking some level of freedom and well being than systems of total state control. The Marxist project rested on the premise that the people would be able to retain control of the state after the state won control over the means of production. Why this would fail should have been evident from the premises of Marxism itself. The capitalists' disproportionate power over society is because they own the means of production, the most elementary truism of the Marxist canon. In capitalist societies, despite relatively free elections and the right to form organizations and raise funds to influence government, the power of the property owners remains predominant. What, then, happens when the government, which is composed of career functionaries, owns not only the means of production but also all means of communication and controls all channels by which funds can be raised and all forms of political organization? The mere "class origins" of these functionaries should, by Marx's own understanding, not long outweigh their actual social situation as masters of "capital." If legal electoral forms do not counteract the advantages capital has in the decentralized West, why should anyone have imagined that mere electoral forms — which were never even permitted anyway — could hold the masters of the state to account when they hold many more of the levers of power than the capitalists ever did?

The Current Crisis Is Not an Ordinary Recession

The whole reason for this exercise is to try to discourage, as people cast around for some way to dig out of the now long-lasting economic slump, the revival of self-defeating proposals that have already produced almost unimaginable human misery. So what is it we are up against in this latest disaster?

John Gray is far more sympathetic to Marx's critique of capitalism than to Marx's theorizing about a communist replacement. "Marx," he writes, "was closer to reality than generations of mainstream economists. His insights are particularly relevant at a time when the economics profession devotes itself to the mathematical modeling of delusional harmonies."

He disparages "fundamentalist believers in the market [who] imagine that a deregulated economy would lead to a kind of universal bourgeoisification — a society in which nearly everyone could aspire to a solidly middle-class life. The reality is that for a majority of people in the United States, Britain, and parts of Europe, middle-class life is rapidly ceasing to be a viable option. With their houses and pensions depleted in value and the job market increasingly fragmented and insecure, many who thought they were middle-class are finding themselves in something like the position of Marx's propertyless proletarians."

What has been emergent from this process has not been mass socialist movements and nations. For Gray, "free market's successors are much more likely to be other versions of capitalism — the state capitalism of China, the social-market capitalism that has made Germany the most successful advanced economy, and other varieties of capitalism that are yet to develop."

I remember when first reading Gray's *Black Mass* when it came out in 2007, thinking that his prediction then that the coming century would be marked principally by resource wars was something I hadn't heard or thought of before. Four years later it seems all too prescient.

Our industrial civilization was made possible by the discovery of finite deposits of fossilized energy. Unlike most mineral resources, which are abundant in the earth's crust and date from the formation of the planet, coal, oil, and natural gas are the compressed remains of plant and animal matter, created in comparatively more recent geological epochs, and preserved only in a limited number of particularly favorable locations where conditions were uniquely right.

No one in the nineteenth century considered the amount of these materials to be of cardinal importance. Most economists today still do not, assuming without evidence that any rising prices due to scarcity will spark more intense exploration for new deposits, as well as technological innovation to conserve energy and seek new energy sources.

Perhaps this blindness to the ecological foundation of our civilization stems from our religious inheritance, which sees us as the God-given masters of the earth. But time appears to have run out. World crude oil output has not increased by any significant amount since 2005 — demand has. Every major oil producer is in rapid decline save Saudi Arabia, which still claims it has a small reserve that could be thrown into the world market to slow price rises.

The current world financial crisis, which erupted in 2008, is not a classic Smithian or Marxian crisis of over production. It is not a consequence of the falling rate of profit. This one is unprecedented, a crisis of insufficient natural resources to meet the growing demand of a geometrically expanding world population at prices that do not induce recession.

The mainstream press and the left have repeated endlessly that the economic meltdown was precipitated by greedy marketing of subprime mortgages and their collateralization into worthless mutual funds. That explanation provides an easily understood and conventional villain. If it were the whole story the crash should be fairly short-lived and readily overcome. as were all the previous crashes of the capitalist business cycle except the Great Depression.

A growing number of recent studies are pointing to a more irremediable cause. James Hamilton in a paper for the Brookings Institute (http://www.econbrowser.com/archives/2009/04/consequences_of.html) presents results from a computer modeling that indicate the sharp run-up in oil price that began in 2000 and topped out in 2008 was a larger cause of the recession than the more famous housing bubble.

Historically, high oil prices have been the trigger for American recessions, and they are headed to exceptionally high levels now. Chris Nelder and Gregor MacDonald in the October 4, 2011, *Harvard Business Review Blog* write:

"The connection between oil shocks and recessions has been understood for decades. We have ample historical evidence that when petroleum expenditures reach 5% of GDP, recession typically follows. Annual energy expenditures rose from 6.2% of U.S. GDP in 2002 to a painful 9.8% in 2008, which was immediately followed by an economic crash. And now oil is sending energy expenditures back above 9% of GDP, just as we see fresh indications that the recession persists. This is not a coincidence."

The explosion of debt after the turn of the millennium was itself not due solely to bankers arbitrary voraciousness, guilty as they were. Oil for the first time in a century reached $10 a barrel in 1980, triggering a recession that year and another in 1981, which drove prices down. It spiked in 1990 to over $30 a barrel, launching an eight month recession that, with conservation efforts, lowered prices for a decade. But a sharp upward spiral hit in 2000 that threatened to wipe out the prosperity of the mid and late 1990s. Banks and consumers responded by prolonging the good times on a wave of debt — maxed-out credit cards, steadily inflating home prices, home equity loans to supplement income, liar loans to buy houses people couldn't afford.

In 2008 international competition, especially from China and India, for a piece of the stagnant global oil supply drove the price through the roof, briefly hitting $147 a barrel, in the process blowing out the foundation of the debt pyramid. Significantly, even with Europe and the United States deep in recession, sharply reducing the use of gas and oil in all their forms, the price never got below about $55 a barrel, a level it had reached for the first time in history only in 2005, the year world crude oil peaked and hit the plateau it has been stuck on ever since.

In mid-November 2011 the U.S. domestic price was briefly back above $100 while European Brent oil, a more realistic measure of world oil cost, was at $112. (The U.S. price, West Texas Intermediate, is set in Cushing, Oklahoma. Inadequate storage facilities there have produced a local glut, holding down the nominal U.S. price. The Brent price is what is paid on the American Gulf Coast and in California, as well as the rest of the world, and is the more accurate figure.)

Oil doesn't need to run out to deal a body blow to the world economy. There is still a great deal of oil, but what remains is lower quality, harder to extract, far more expensive than the crude of an earlier day, and can't be extracted fast enough to increase total supplies. As price goes up the costs of everything dependent on oil, above all transportation, increase, with food prices moving in lock-step.

There is no longer enough crude oil to meet current world demand, the still-flatlined total being maintained by additions of expensive and low grade processed liquids. Nelder and MacDonald write:

"Conventional crude ended its 150-year-long growth trajectory in 2004 and flattened out around 74 million barrels per day. Crude supply did not budge when oil prices tripled from 2004 to 2008, but global demand remained firm, shrugging off a recessionary dip in 2009. All the growth in supply since then was not crude but unconventional liquids, including natural gas liquids, biofuels, refinery gains, synthetic oil from tar sands, and other marginal resources. These liquids are by no means equivalent to crude."

Demand in Europe and the United States is relatively flat, but is growing rapidly in China and India as those countries seek first-world living standards. Global population reached the seven billion mark this year, as arable land continued its decline, from erosion, over cropping, and exhaustion of underground aquifers. Global warming, still in its earliest stages, has magnified floods and droughts.

Global food prices are closely tied to the price of oil, because of the costs of transport and fertilizer, though they have their own independent drivers, all of which are working against us.

The *New York Times* summarizes: "The rapid growth in farm output that defined the late 20th century has slowed to the point that it is failing to keep up with the demand for food, driven by population increases and rising affluence in once-poor countries. Consumption of the four staples that supply most human calories — wheat, rice, corn and soybeans — has outstripped production for much of the past decade, drawing once-large stockpiles down to worrisome levels. The imbalance between supply and demand has resulted in two huge spikes in international grain prices since 2007, with some grains more than doubling in cost. (June 4, 2011)

Both capitalism and Communism were founded on a need for perpetual economic growth. For both societies there is a need to provide food, lodging, and employment for an ever expanding population, not to mention expectations of higher living standards, and in the capitalist case there is the additional need to sell products.

The politics of growth as the engine of employment and prosperity is no longer viable. Increasing costs, rising demand, and impending declines in supplies of key energy sources and industrial raw materials promise not just recessions but a decline in the standard of living of world civilizations as a whole, or worse. While the political establishment largely avoids talking about this unpleasant subject, militaries around the world have been alarmed for some time. Their own reports (http://www.energybulletin.net/stories/2010-09-28/energy-security-annotated-militarysecurity-bibliography-2010-update) consider seriously the possibility not merely of decline but of collapse of society as we know it. Many show thorough familiarity with the facts of peak oil. One that I thought was particularly interesting, and which has since disappeared from the Internet, was an article by Major Cameron Leckie in the July 2010 issue of the *Australian Defense Force Journal* urging a drastic simplification of his country's weapons systems on the premise that a sharp decline in civilization could make parts for their current high tech arsenal unobtainable. He ominously titled his contribution "Lasers or Longbows."

All the variants of our social systems arose and based their collective livelihoods and expectations on cheap energy and abundant food rolling on into the future. None have contingency plans for steady and unstoppable decline, much less for Gotterdammerung. The first whiff of sulphur even in the wealthy nations has had people casting around for who to blame and rummaging through the inventory of discarded belief systems for something that can save them. The first signs of this in the U.S. date from the oil shock of 1973, and the American defeat in Vietnam two years later. Before that Republicans and Democrats alike held a comfortable trust in the federal government. Afterward, trust in government eroded sharply, the left from the years of opposing the war, the right from the sense of inescapable decline when the Arabs turned off the spigot and the U.S. proved unable to win a long war against the guerrillas of a small Asian nation. The right shifted its Norman Rockwell embrace of Washington to a fascination with the impending Rapture that would let them escape this place. Bible literalist Evangelical Christian sects, hitherto confined to the backwoods, went mainstream, and then succeeded in capturing one of the two major political parties.

The deepening sense of national decline, economic threat, and, for many whites, the vision of an America with a black and brown majority underwrites the bitter partisanship that marks American politics. The risk is the revival of extremist schemas that were tried and failed the first time around.

The Tea Party looks to God. While waiting to be Raptured they remain busy trying to shut out the unwanted immigrants; radically weaken government except where they can use it to pass religious-based legislation to control women's reproductive lives and restrict gay rights, while amputating much of the rest, creating still more unemployed; roll back taxes used to help the unemployed, the sick, or the elderly; and free corrupt financial institutions and polluting industries from regulation. Their guts tell them these projects will restore prosperity and American power, and to reject all unpleasant facts that cast doubt, particularly those that come from scientists, academics, and the "lamestream" media. The leadership of the Republican Party professes to find this witches brew convincing.

Liberals and the left are fighting to roll back the extraordinary increases in income and wealth the financial elite pocketed in the last two decades, to protect the frayed social safety net, and to defend jobs, wage levels, and pensions in face of ever more severe federal, state, and local cutbacks. The tax fight can possibly be won, and most serious economists believe that the deficit can ride for a while, that it is more important to provide more stimulus.

What we know about overpopulation, resource depletion, and global warming tell us that sooner or later we will arrive at a second stage of these battles. Ultimately, governments that can't pay their bills end up like Greece, even the United States. If the future is as it appears, that day is not a possibility but an inevitability, only the date being unknown. That means at some point it will be impossible to sustain our present standard of living, not because America is capitalist but because the historically brief window of plentiful cheap energy and a population small enough to feed itself without that subsidy is over and no change of social system is going to bring it back. Then the job becomes saving what can be saved and finding ways to live where not only growth, but perhaps even gasoline and electricity are no longer options, an age where the U.S. Marines will be armed with longbows.

November 28, 2011

Part 2:
Militant Islam and the Left

Sayyid Qutb: The Karl Marx
of the Islamic Revolution

From Secularism to Jihad: Sayyid Qutb and the Foundations of Radical Islamism — **Adnan A. Musallam. Westport, Connecticut: Praeger, 2005. 261 pp.**

"The Philosopher of Islamic Terror" -- Paul Berman. *New York Times Magazine,* **March 23, 2003**

Sayyid Qutb (October 9, 1906-August 29, 1966), the Egyptian literary critic, philosopher, and theorist of the contemporary jihadist movement is only becoming a familiar name in the West in recent years, but his voluminous writings have had, and continue to have, enormous impact in the Muslim world. It is not an overstatement to say that it is hardly possible to understand the reasoning and goals of the Islamic militants without some familiarity with the outlook Qutb (pronounced KUH-tahb) enunciated.

A search of Amazon.com returns no less than seven books in English about Sayyid Qutb as well as collections of his writings and many of his own books in translation. The two works touched on here are only a random sampling of a very large literature, which is again but a minute fraction of what exists in Arabic. These two are quite different in scope and attitude. Adnan Ayyub Musallam, a Palestinian native of Bethlehem, holds a doctorate from the University of Michigan and is currently professor of history, politics, and cultural studies at Bethlehem University in the West Bank. His generally sympathetic but critical biography concentrates on the evolving politics of Qutb's affiliations and thought. The quite brief and more critical piece by Paul Berman for the *New York Times* looks at Qutb's theology and helps to clarify his argument with Christianity and Western secularism.

Brilliant from his earliest youth, Sayyid Qutb was an unlikely figure to serve as the inspiration for a global revolutionary movement. Although for a brief period he was a member of the militant Muslim Brothers, where he served as an editor, not as an organizer, he spent most of his life as a lone intellectual. Where Marx, the theorist of world communism, labored in the British Museum, Sayyid Qutb wrote his most influential works in an Egyptian prison, where he spent most of the last eleven years of his life, until his execution by the Nasser government in 1966. Even his turn to Islam in any serious way did not take place until he was past forty, yet in prison in his fifties he produced a controversial rethinking of the religion that reverberates around the world.

Qutb was born in the village of Musha, between Cairo and Aswan into a family of small landowners. He was sent to the local madrasa, the government school, rather than the still more religious kuttab, the Islamic school, but he won a contest between the two schools for the best memorization of the Qur'an. He recalled his life there in his only biographical work, *A Child from the Village,* recording local customs and superstitions. From that period he acquired a belief in the world of spirits that he carried with him all his life.

At fifteen Sayyid Qutb went to Cairo to live with an uncle. This was in 1921, in the midst of the 1918-22 nationalist revolt against British rule led by the secular Wafd Party of Sa'd Zaghlul. Qutb attended intermediate and high school in Cairo, then college, graduating in 1933 from Dar al-Ulam with a BA in Arabic language and literature and in education. Around that year his father back in Musha died and his brother and two sisters came to Cairo to live with him. At the age of nineteen he began to write and publish poetry. Musallam describes Qutb's poems as fascinated with death, travel in the spirit world, and idealization of a fantasy beloved. He also, however, wrote a poem in support of the Palestinian anti-Jewish uprising of 1936-39.

The Secular Literary Critic

Responsible for supporting his siblings, Qutb became a teacher in government schools, writing literary criticism on the side for various small magazines. In 1940 he got a job with the Ministry of Education. In a pattern common for Egyptian intellectuals, Qutb built his literary reputation while holding down a full-time government job. During the 1930s he came strongly under the influence of Abbas Mahmud al-Aqqad, a prominent journalist, literary critic, and poet. Al-Aqqad was a modernist supporter of the Wafd Party and secular nationalism, and these were Qutb's views as well into the 1940s.

Musallam quotes a reminiscence of Qutb in the 1930s penned many years later by the journalist 'Adel Hammuda, who said "there is no doubt he was audacious. . . . His words were sharp sometimes. His expressions were sticks of fire. . . . His pencil was a whip. The one who sees him does not believe that he is the same person who writes. . . . For with people he was milder than the breeze. . . . With the paper and the pencil, he was a hell which does not cool off." Similar sentiments were often voiced about George Orwell, who was gentle in person but vitriolic in print.

Sayyid Qutb was a prolific writer. He published some twenty books and monographs during his lifetime, or in a few cases posthumously. One of them, *In the Shade of Islam*, by itself runs to fifteen or more volumes depending on the edition and language. Half a dozen of Qutb's works are available in English translation, but except for his youthful autobiography, *A Child from the Village*, the rest are from his Islamic period and do not include the few volumes of his poetry from the 1930s or his literary criticism of the 1940s and two novels, *The Bewitched City* (1946) and *Thorns* (1947).

Sayyid Qutb is credited with being one of the first to write laudatory reviews of the work of Egyptian novelist Naguib Mahfouz, who was awarded the Nobel Prize for literature in 1988 and who died in August 2006.

Qutb's transition into Qur'anic studies began as an extension of his literary criticism, with a study of artistic images in the Qur'an begun in 1939. Musallam recounts how Qutb when he was drawn back to the Qur'an he had memorized as a schoolboy was enthralled by its stories. A favorite was the tale of the Virgin Mary (Maryam in the Qur'an), her hostile reception by her family when she returned home with her baby and claimed to her incredulous relatives that it was not the product of sex with a human being. At risk of retribution for her apparent sin, Maryam is saved when the infant Jesus cries out from his crib, "Lo! I am the slave of Allah. He hath given me the Scripture and hath appointed me a Prophet." Sayyid Qutb himself dated his serious reattraction to the Qur'an to the writing and publication of this work, published as *Artistic Portrayal in the Qur'an* in 1945.

Musallam makes the point that in Qutb's return to religion neither he nor al-Aqqad had ever been Western-style materialists. Al-Aqqad advocated a kind of nationalist rationalism but he remained a believer in Islam and rejected both Marxism and materialism. Qutb even more than al-Aqqad always retained a belief in the supernatural. In the 1930s, Musallam characterizes Qutb as a "Muslim secularist," not irreligious but inclined to see religion as a private matter. He did go so far, Musallam avers, as to have doubts about his faith. This was a view he would put behind him in the 1950s.

Musallam notes that Qutb's new interest in Qur'anic studies was part of a broad current among the liberal Egyptian intelligentsia in the 1940s, "inspired by resentment against Western hegemony in Egypt and the Arab world and a gradual loss of faith in the popular appeal of liberal nationalist parliamentary ideals." This period also saw a decline in interest in the pre-Islamic civilization of the ancient Pharaohs, to which several periodicals had been devoted.

The death of Qutb's mother Fatimah in 1940 and the collapse of what seems to have been his only serious love affair, in 1942 or 1943, appear to have propelled Qutb to devote the rest of his life to religious studies. By 1946 in an article entitled "Schools for Indignation" (Madaris lil-sakht) his writing became openly theological. In this period he wrote admiringly of Jamal al-Din al-Afghani (1838-97), advocate of a pan-Islamist religious and cultural revival to counter European influence, as an example of the need for a spiritual dimension to political reform movements. He also began to look back to an imagined golden age of "the first towering flow" of Islam in the days of the Prophet and the first caliphs.

Moral puritanism emerged in Qutb's thought before his general rejection of the separation of religion and the state. Already by 1940 he repudiated his earlier somewhat bohemian ways, campaigning in his essays against broadcasting popular music on Egyptian radio. Musallam recounts that Qutb "asserts in his writings that such songs destroyed Egyptian social structure and personal character because they corrupted the virtues of men and women." He advocated the formation of a censorship committee "empowered to prevent, if necessary, the broadcasting of songs, the production of records and tapes, and the showing of films." He also called for new laws to prosecute singers of disapproved songs.

World War II further hardened Qutb's anti-Western views. Egypt had been essentially a British colony since 1882, and as such was attacked in the war first by the Italians and then by the Nazi armies under Rommel, who was under orders to break through Egypt to exterminate the Jewish population of Palestine and try to spark an Arab revolt (study of Nazi archival documents by Klaus-Michael Mallmann and Martin Cueppers of Stuttgart University reported by Agence France-Presse on April 13, 2006). Rommel penetrated deep into Egypt and the country endured severe hardships in the war. Qutb, according to Musallam, was particularly outraged by the arrogance of British troops stationed in Cairo.

A Growing Hostility to the West

The end of the 1940s saw Sayyid Qutb's transformation, as Musallam puts it, into "a stern moralist, an anti-Western thinker, and an anti-political, anti-literary establishment intellectual."

Much like the Manchu rulers of China in the last years of the Qing dynasty, Qutb advocated retention of Islamic and Egyptian religion and culture while adopting Western science and technology. Even here, however, he rejected Darwinism and biological materialism.

"By the mid 1940s," Musallam writes, "Qutb became fiercely anti-Western. In 1944, he attacked Western civilization and hailed its demise. In his view the West has failed and it is now the turn of the East to take over the leadership of the world and create by the power of its spirituality a new civilization." He condemned French colonialism from the days of Napoleon's invasion of Egypt to more recent French suppressions of nationalist movements in Syria, Morocco, Tunisia, and Algeria. The British were excoriated as the colonial masters of Egypt, particularly for imposing a Wafd cabinet on the king in February 1942. And the Americans were censured for their support of Jewish immigration to Palestine.

In an article in *al-Risalah* (The Message) of October 21, 1946, Qutb wrote, "How I hate and despise those Westerners! All without exception: the British, the French, the Dutch and now the Americans who were at one time trusted by many. . . . And I do not hate or despise these alone. I hate and despise just as much those Egyptians and Arabs who continue to trust Western conscience."

At about this time Sayyid Qutb became more strongly concerned with reducing inequality, which led to his disillusionment with the existing nationalist parties such as the Wafd. He condemned the Egyptian upper classes for their privileges and their subservience to the British, as well as the press, broadcasting, and well-known literati figures both for defending the status quo and for disseminating material he regarded as immoral. Still, at this time his views have more of pan-Arabism about them than Islamism.

In the late 1940s Qutb appeared ideologically restless. Though not a member of any party or definite group, he was briefly but prominently associated with two different radical journals, *The Arab World* (al-'Alam al-'Arabi, a pan-Arabist monthly) and *The New Thought* (al-Fikr al-Jadid, a weekly published between January and March 1948 by a member of the radical Islamic Muslim Brothers). While exposed at this time to frequent solicitation from the Muslim Brothers, or Muslim Brotherhood or Ikhwan as it is also known, Qutb was not yet convinced that any existing Islamic organization was what he was looking for. He did see Islam as the alternative to communism, which was then on the rise among Egyptian nationalists. Qutb and the other editors and writers of the short-lived *al-Fikr al-Jadid* preached a fiery sermon on the need to feed, house, and clothe the Egyptian poor and to find new ways within traditional Islam to redistribute wealth and power for a more egalitarian society. Qutb called for taking a portion of the land of large landowners and distributing it to the landless peasants, forming cooperative societies, and adopting legislation ameliorating the conflicts between capital and labor.

The monarchy responded to these appeals by ordering Qutb's arrest. He escaped only because the prime minister, Mahmud Fahmi al-Nuqrashi, an old acquaintance from the Wafd days, ordered Sayyid Qutb's superiors in the Ministry of Education to send him abroad to America on a mission to study the U.S. educational system. He left for New York in November 1948, leaving behind the just-completed manuscript of his first fully Islamic political work, *Social Justice in Islam* (al-'Adalah al-Ijtima'iyyah Fi al-Islam). This book was published in an English translation by the American Council of Learned Societies in 1953 and remains the best-known work of Sayyid Qutb in English, though there are various editions involving numerous changes by both the author and translators.

In this work Qutb expounds the thesis that only the earliest days of Islam should serve as the model for successful social life. Musallam writes, "According to Qutb, as long as Muslims adhered to Islam (including its political and economic systems), they manifested no weakness and no tendency to abdicate their control of life. When they deviated from their religion, however, weakness overtook them." In Qutb's view the fatal drift away from true Islam began not with modern Western imperialism but already with the Umayyad dynasty (661-750) only a few years after the death of Muhammad in 632. True Islam lasted for only 29 years. Islam, he contended, was corrupted by the tyrannical monarchy of the Umayyads. Here Qutb develops his idea of the utopian golden age of Islam marked by "charity and benevolence, mutual help and responsibility, tolerance and freedom of conscience and human equality, payment of the poor-tax and the alms." He regards the succeeding history of Islam as one long decline from these noble principles, even in the heyday of its expansion and intellectual vigor, culminating in its "final overthrow" at the hands of European colonization in the nineteenth and twentieth centuries.

Qutb takes a firm stand in the debate that raged throughout the colonial world over how to relate to modernism. Where the Chinese in the 1920s became enamored of the slogan "Science and Democracy," Qutb in the 1940s urged Muslims to reject borrowings from Western ideas with the exception of technology. In economics Qutb advocated an Islamic welfare state that would redistribute income from the rich to the poor and offer universal health care and education. At the same time he rejected Western democracy as based in a human-oriented materialism no different in kind from communism.

Qutb in America, November 1948-August 1950

Sayyid Qutb sailed from Alexandria to New York in November 1948. During his brief stay in the United States he lived in New York; Washington, DC; Greeley and Denver, Colorado; and finally California, where he spent time in San Francisco, Palo Alto, and San Diego. As an outsider and sexual prude he felt revulsion at American society, particularly its overt sexuality (this, almost two decades before the free love movement of the 1960s). Musallam draws on Qutb's correspondence to illuminate this period of his life:

"[H]e found harried crowds resembling an excited herd that knew only lust and money. He describes love in America as merely a body that lusts after another body, or hungry animal that craves another animal, with no time for spiritual longings, high aspirations, or even the flirtation that normally precedes 'the final step.'" Qutb accused Americans he had observed of "absolute licentiousness." He was particularly offended by homosexuality and the failure of the government to enforce laws against it that were then still on the books.

Qutb was no more impressed by American music. Jazz, he wrote, "was created by the negroes to satisfy their primitive inclinations and their desire." He also disapproved of U.S. participation in the Korean War, which broke out in July 1950.

Musallam concludes, "Qutb's stay in the United States reinforced his earlier belief that the Islamic way of life was man's only salvation from the abyss of godless capitalism." When he left Egypt in 1948 Sayyid Qutb was critical of the militant Islamist society of Muslim Brothers founded by Hassan al Banna in 1928. The Brothers were so anti-British that they allegedly established relations with the Nazis in the 1930s. After the war they had turned to assassination in an effort to overturn the Egyptian monarchy. The government responded by banning the Muslim Brothers in December 1948. The Brothers retaliated by assassinating Prime Minister Nuqrashi Pasha the same month. Egyptian government agents then tracked down Hassan al Banna and killed him, in February 1949. Sayyid Qutb, in his strongly alienated state in America, reacted angrily to U.S. and British news reports celebrating the death of the radical Islamist leader, and reconsidered his relations with the Brothers. On his return to Egypt in August 1950 he was met at the airport by a delegation from the Muslim Brothers.

Visions of an Islamic World Government

Qutb's writings in the period before the Nasserite coup in 1952 had a sharp anticapitalist edge, eloquently berating the rich parasites, the corrupt and immoral court, and mistreatment of the poor. He began to develop a pan-Islamist doctrine calling for a global struggle between three forces: capitalism, communism, and Islam. He more and more began to visualize Islam as a political power, not as a personalized religion, transcending national boundaries as a world government. Musallam summarizes:

"Islam must rule; it must not be confined merely to places of worship, to hearts, or to conscience like Christianity. The system of belief is not in itself valuable; it must be translated into a 'Shari'ah,' an all-encompassing law which governs personal, penal, civil, and commercial affairs." Qutb cited the admonition of the Qur'an 5:44: "Whoso judgeth not by that which Allah hath revealed: such are wrong-doers." That included all non-Muslims, and all Muslims content to practice their religion in private while ceding lawmaking to politicians and parties not based on the Qur'an. Qutb added that rejection of God's supremacy must be resisted if international harmony was to be achieved. For that to happen, Muslims must be entrusted with the welfare of humanity. "The most serious injustice," Qutb wrote in that period, "is luring people from the worship of God and forcing them to deify those rulers who empower themselves to legalize what God has prohibited and prohibit what God has allowed."

This was the beginning of his doctrine of world domination by Islam that has come to inspire militant Islamists around the planet.

"When dealing with its enemies Islam takes one of three courses: they may adopt the religion, or pay tribute or fight. . . . If the enemy rejects the religion and also refuses to pay tribute, Muslims must declare war (jihad) on those who obdurately stand between men and Islam's righteous and peaceful principles. If the enemies are defeated they are obliged to pay the tribute in return for which they become wards of the Islamic state." (Sayyid Qutb, *Islam and Universal Peace,* Indianapolis, 1977, pp. 73-74)

He called for a single Islamic state, becoming more and more hostile to nationalist Arab leaders, accusing them of playing into the hands of imperialism "by tearing up the Muslim nation into narrow national entities."

In 1951 Qutb began writing regularly for publications of the Muslim Brothers. He publicly hailed them for engaging in an armed struggle against the British, who still exercised what amounted to a protectorate over Egypt. The Muslim Brothers were organizing guerrilla units for battles with British troops stationed along the Suez Canal.

Several thousand of the Muslim Brothers had been imprisoned after terrorist actions at the end of the 1940s, but by May 1952 when martial law ended the society was again legal. After the July 1952 officers' revolution that ended the monarchy there was a period of uneasy collaboration between the

Muslim Brothers and the new government, originally headed by General Muhammad Naguib but ultimately led by Colonel Gamal Abdel Nasser.

The revolution had been planned, in part, at Sayyid Qutb's home and he knew many of the leaders, including Nasser, well. When the new government was formed Qutb was given an office in the Revolutionary Command Council (RCC) building, where he was in charge of revising the school curricula. He was being considered for the post of Minister of Education. He now moved away from the pluralism within Islam he had advocated in the past and called for a strict dictatorship to defend the revolution. Initially tolerant of the communists, he supported executing two workers who took part in a communist-led strike in August 1952 at the Misr Fine Spinning and Weaving Company in Fafr al-Dawwar.

Naguib and Nasser's Revolutionary Command Council of the Free Officers came to power in alliance with the Muslim Brothers. But it was not willing to make post-revolutionary Egypt an Islamic state. The RCC soon purged from its own ranks officers too close to the Brothers. In January 1953, all political parties were dissolved except the Muslim Brothers, who were exempted as a religious organization. But the military government founded its own rival movement, the Liberation Rally. Qutb objected and resigned from his government post. That ended his chance to become Minister of Education.

About that time Sayyid Qutb accepted an appointment to head the Muslim Brothers' propaganda department, called the Propagation of the Message Section. In a statement written in prison in 1965 looking back he said he joined the Muslim Brothers because of their effectiveness "for confronting Zionist and imperialistic Crusader schemes about which I knew a lot especially in the period of my stay in America." This was language that would become more familiar to the outside world many years later from Qutb's intellectual descendants in al-Qaeda.

The Muslim Brothers became increasingly critical of the Naguib-Nasser military government, claiming it was insufficiently anti-British. After a January 1954 protest meeting by the Brothers the government declared the organization a political party and added it to the previous ban, briefly arresting many of its leaders including Sayyid Qutb. Shortly after, Nasser succeeded in reducing General Naguib to a figurehead president and consolidated power in his own hands. In October 1954 the Muslim Brothers attempted to assassinate Nasser during a rally in Alexandria. He retaliated by placing President Naguib, who he accused of complicity, under house arrest. The government sentenced Hassan Isma'il al-Hudaybi, the head of the Muslim Brothers, to life imprisonment, and hung six leaders of the Brothers' secret paramilitary section. The Brothers were then outlawed. Qutb was arrested in November 1954.

The following year he was sentenced to fifteen years at hard labor. He remained in prison until May 1964 when his poor health secured his release.

A Decade in Prison: The Excommunication of Secular Society

Sayyid Qutb spent much of his prison time in hospitals for lung and heart ailments. During the decade behind bars he became increasingly radical. A key event was the shooting of twenty-one Muslim Brother prisoners in Liman Tura prison on June 1, 1957, when they refused to report to their labor assignment.

Qutb was permitted to write. While he was in prison, Musallam writes, he produced "many works that would eventually make him the leading ideologue of radical and jihadist Islamists. Indeed, Qutb's prison writings in 1954-1965 would become an integral part of Islamic resurgence in the next forty years."

Two central concepts, adapted from the Pakistani radical Islamist Abul A'ala Maududi, became central to Sayyid Qutb's thought and later became the "common denominator among extremist factions in the Islamic awakening movements." These were al-Jahiliyyah (paganism), and al-Hakimiyyah (God's rule on earth). As you might guess, these are mutually exclusive opposites.

Jahiliyyah is an Arabic term with many overtones. It was used by Muhammad to describe Arab societies before Islam. But this was a period in which contention between the Byzantine Eastern Roman Empire at Constantinople and the Persian Empire had led to decimation of the trade routes to the east that had passed through Arabia. The Arab economy and civilization itself declined into a dark age. In Muslim history, Muhammad and Islam rescue Arabia from this darkness, the age of Jahiliyyah. Hence Jahiliyyah has extremely negative connotations. Sayyid Qutb adopted the term to mean secular society in general; all societies, including Muslim ones, that were not governed under Sharia law.

Sayyid Qutb's prison output was phenomenal. His first project, begun before his arrest, and continued in prison under a court order on a lawsuit by his publisher, who claimed they would lose money if it was not finished, was to complete his multivolume masterpiece, *In the Shade of the Qur'an* — see below Paul Berman's comments on this work. Qutb went on to write six more books during his prison years. *In the Shade of the Qur'an* was a vast lyric verse-by-verse commentary on the whole of the Qur'an, today widely published in both print and online editions including partial publication in English.

Of the later six books the most widely read was *Milestones on the Road* (Ma'alim fi al-tariq, sometimes translated as Signs on the Path), first published in Cairo in 1964. This was the clearest statement of his later views rejecting compromise with Jahili states and institutions, and has become a core text of the jihadist movement. Here he proposed that all existing human societies, including those with Muslim majorities, were Jahiliyyah, pagan. The Islamic utopia was yet to be created. He wrote, "We may say that any society is a Jahili society that does not dedicate itself to submission to God alone, in its beliefs and ideas, in its observance of worship, and in its legal regulations. . . . Our foremost objective is to change . . . the Jahili system at its very roots."

This led him to one more concept, excommunication (*takfir*). Qutb called for the excommunication of all existing pagan societies and their replacement by Islamic ones reflecting al-Hakimiyyah. He called for "Jihad through sword" to achieve "the establishment of the sovereignty of God and His Lordship throughout the world, the end of man's arrogance and selfishness, and the implementation of the rule of the Divine Shari'ah in human affairs."

In a kind of mirror image of Leninism, the once-mild-mannered literary critic proposed that the world Islamic revolution be led by an Islamic revolutionary vanguard (tali'ah). Like the Leninist denunciation of capitalism, Qutb poses a Manichean division in the world. In another work of his prison period, *The Religion of Islam* (1962), he makes this clear. There are two parties in the world, "that of God and that of Satan. The party of God stands beneath the banner of God and bears His insignia. The party of the Devil embraces every community, group, people, race, and individual who do not stand under the banner of God." In another of his works, *Islam, the Religion of the Future* (1965), he writes that "the civilization of the white man has already exhausted its restricted usefulness . . . because [it] did not issue from that Divine source and origin [but] was established on bases repugnant to the nature of life and human beings."

Qutb was released from prison at the end of 1964 at the behest of the then Prime Minister of Iraq, Abdul Salam Arif. He immediately joined an underground group of the Muslim Brothers. Musallam says that the group's aim was long-term education of the Egyptian people to prepare for the creation of an Islamic state. However, they made plans to assassinate Egyptian leaders in the event they were discovered. The plans were never carried out, but were discovered by the government. At the end of July 1965 the government began to arrest the Muslim Brothers, picking up Sayyid Qutb on August 9.

The group's leaders were charged with planning the assassination of Nasser and trying to overthrow the government. Qutb and his book *Milestones on the Road* figured prominently in the government's case. Despite protests by Amnesty International, Sayyid Qutb was sentenced to death and hanged on August 29, 1966.

Paul Berman on Qutb's Critique of Christianity

It was Paul Berman in his *New York Times* article who coined the apt comparison of Sayyid Qutb with Karl Marx, or as he put it, "the Karl Marx of Jihad." Berman in his brief essay began to explore Qutb's most substantive work, *In the Shade of the Qur'an*. In print in Arabic for decades, an English edition is underway that is expected to run to fifteen large volumes. Berman at the time of his writing in 2003 had read the part that had already appeared in print, about half of the projected total.

Shades highlights the centrality of the law, or Sharia, to Islam. The Qur'an and its subsidiary literature like the Torah and the Talmud of Jewish holy writings, contains a vast body of legal opinion on every aspect of life by authoritative spokesmen of the religion. This is quite unlike the Christian scriptures, which are not law-centered. For staunch literalists and traditionalists within Islam it is this jurisprudential tradition that makes separation of church and state so unacceptable.

Berman writes of *Shades of the Qur'an*:

"He quotes passages from the chapters, or suras, of the Koran, and he pores over the quoted passages, observing the prosodic qualities of the text, the rhythm, tone and musicality of the words, sometimes the images. The suras lead him to discuss dietary regulations, the proper direction to pray, the rules of divorce, the question of when a man may propose marriage to a widow (four months and 10 days after the death of her husband, unless she is pregnant, in which case after delivery), the rules concerning a Muslim man who wishes to marry a Christian or a Jew (very complicated), the obligations of charity, the punishment for crimes and for breaking your word, the prohibition on liquor and intoxicants, the proper clothing to wear, the rules on usury, money lending and a thousand other themes. . . . As he makes his way through the suras and proposes his other commentaries, he slowly constructs an enormous theological criticism of modern life, and not just in Egypt."

Qutb, he says, "wrote that, all over the world, humans had reached a moment of unbearable crisis. The human race had lost touch with human nature. Man's inspiration, intelligence and morality were degenerating. Sexual relations were deteriorating 'to a level lower than the beasts.' Man was miserable, anxious and skeptical, sinking into idiocy, insanity and crime. People were turning, in their unhappiness, to drugs, alcohol and existentialism."

This is familiar ground, the well-known moral crisis of modern industrial society, grounded in the growth of urbanism, the expansion of scientific knowledge discrediting the earlier certainties of tribal religions, and the extensions of states and empires bringing together believers in many creeds and world views while abjuring the previous practice of imposing state religions, thus reducing these beliefs to mere private affirmations. Though many regret the loss of externally assured certainty, purpose, and protection, we generally get on with our lives. In contrast, every utopian or millenarian movement offers to repair the loss through its particular panacea. Each recites more or less that same litany of social disintegrative evils (although the religiously based utopians have their own list of sexual offenses that secular utopians such as the communists usually do not share), then rides off on its own reformative hobby horse, from communism to the second coming of Christ, or in Qutb's case, Islamic world government.

Qutb did put his finger on a cardinal difference between Islam and Christianity's attitude toward the world. Islam meant to rule in the here and now, while Christianity in agreeing to the separation of church and state conceded the function of rulership to someone else while viewing this world, as Berman puts it, as "something alien to spirituality or as a way station on the road to a Christian afterlife."

As Qutb saw it, Berman writes, "Europeans, under Christianity's influence, began to picture God on one side and science on the other. Religion over here; intellectual inquiry over there. On one side, the natural human yearning for God and for a divinely ordered life; on the other side, the natural human desire for knowledge of the physical universe. . . . Everything that Islam knew to be one, the Christian Church divided into two." Qutb in a dramatic image called this separation of society and religion, of science and belief, of church and state as a "hideous schizophrenia."

As might be guessed, the Jews come in for a particularly negative assessment in Qutb's cosmology. Beginning with the Egyptian captivity in the time of Moses, Berman summarizes, "the Jews acquired a slavish character, he believed. As a result they became craven and unprincipled when powerless, and vicious and arrogant when powerful. And these traits were eternal. The Jews occupy huge portions of Qutb's Koranic commentary — their perfidy, greed, hatefulness, diabolical impulses, never-ending conspiracies and plots against Muhammad and Islam. Qutb was relentless on these themes. He looked on Zionism as part of the eternal campaign by the Jews to destroy Islam."

Qutb rejected the United States not because of its deeds but because of its values and system of organization. He wrote: "But in reality the confrontation is not over control of territory or economic resources, or for military domination. If we believed that, we would play into our enemies' hands and would have no one but ourselves to blame for the consequences." Qutb in *Shades of the Qur'an* repudiated "an effort to confine Islam to the emotional and ritual circles, and to bar it from participating in the activity of life, and to check its complete predominance over every human secular activity, a pre-eminence it earns by virtue of its nature and function."

Berman comments: "The true confrontation, the deepest confrontation of all, was over Islam and nothing but Islam. Religion was the issue. Qutb could hardly be clearer on this topic."

Unluckily for non-Islamists who can look forward to having their every secular activity regulated by Sharia law, Qutb and his followers are strict constructionists, far more so than most of the Jews who adhere to the legal texts of Deuteronomy and the Talmud. Berman writes:

"Qutb cited the Koran on the punishments for killing or wounding: 'a life for a life, an eye for an eye, a nose for a nose, an ear for an ear.' Fornication, too, was a serious crime because, in his words, 'it involves an attack on honor and a contempt for sanctity and an encouragement of profligacy in society.' Shariah specified the punishments here as well. 'The penalty for this must be severe; for married men and women it is stoning to death; for unmarried men and women it is flogging, a hundred lashes, which in cases is fatal.' False accusations were likewise serious. 'A punishment of 80 lashes is fixed for those who falsely accuse chaste women.' As for those who threaten the general security of society, their punishment is to be put to death, to be crucified, to have their hands and feet cut off, or to be banished from the country."

Qutb often insisted that Sharia means freedom of conscience, though Berman qualifies this. "Freedom of conscience, in his interpretation, meant freedom from false doctrines that failed to recognize God, freedom from the modern schizophrenia. Shariah, in a word, was utopia for Sayyid Qutb. It was perfection. It was the natural order in the universal. It was freedom, justice, humanity and divinity in a single system. It was a vision as grand or grander than Communism or any of the other totalitarian doctrines of the 20th century. It was, in his words, 'the total liberation of man from enslavement by others.'"

The Jihadist Movement and Sayyid Qutb's Legacy

Sayyid Qutb's influence has continued to grow since his death. Adnan Musallam quotes prominent Lebanese intellectual Radwan al-Sayyid to the effect that *Milestones on the Road* is "the founding text for the jihadist Islam.

From between the lines of that booklet, all groups in jihadist Islam, in the Arab domain at least, came out."

Adnan Musallam lists some of the groups that publicly trace their ideological lineage to Sayyid Qutb and his Islamist permanent revolution. These include the Taliban, the Moro Islamic Liberation Front in the Philippines, and "Islamists in Europe and the former Soviet Republics" as well as the extremely violent Armed Islamic Group in Algeria and the Muslim Brothers of Syria.

The military officers who assassinated Anwar Sadat in 1981 were members of Egyptian Islamic Jihad, one of two violent Islamic groups that grew out of the Muslim Brothers. The principal leader of Egyptian Islamic Jihad is Ayman al-Zawahiri, the Egyptian physician who is the second in command and principal ideologist of al-Qaeda. In his autobiography published in a London Arabic newspaper in 2001-02 al-Zawahiri talks about the impact of Qutb in his own decision to become a jihadist. In 1998 al-Qaeda formed an alliance with jihadist groups from the Middle East, Europe, Asia, and Africa called the International Islamic Front for Jihad against the Jews and Christians which, Musallam writes, "called on every Muslim to kill Americans and their allies in any country 'in which it is possible to do it.'"

The other Egyptian offshoot of the Muslim Brothers imbued with Qutb's theology is the Islamic Group (Al-Gama'a al-Islamiyya, also transliterated as Jamaat al-Islamiyya) led by the blind Sheikh Omar Abd al-Rahman. By far the most devastating of the Islamic Group's attacks occurred on November 17, 1997, in Luxor, when terrorists opened fire on tourists at an ancient temple, killing 58 and injuring 20 more. The Council on Foreign Relations described the Islamic Group as "Egypt's largest Islamist militant organization" and said it "has a presence both in Egypt and worldwide." The Islamic Group is said to have participated with Egyptian Islamic Jihad in the assassination of President Sadat. Sheikh Omar prior to the assassination issued fatwas excommunicating Sadat and calling for setting up an Islamic state through jihad. He was arrested in 1981 but released in 1984 and expelled from Egypt.

Sheikh Omar spent much of the 1980s in Afghanistan where he reportedly worked closely with Osama bin Laden and al-Qaeda in the armed struggle against the Soviet Union. He moved to New York City in 1990. His New York followers were involved in the World Trade Center bombing in 1993. Shortly after, several were arrested for conspiring to blow up the United Nations, the Lincoln and Holland tunnels, the George Washington Bridge, and a federal building housing the FBI. Government prosecutors showed videotapes of defendants mixing bomb ingredients in a garage before their arrest in 1993. Al-Rahman was arrested in 1993 along with nine of his followers. In October

1995 he was convicted of seditious conspiracy and was sentenced to life in prison. He was also accused of soliciting the murder of Egyptian president Hosni Mubarak.

Musallam quotes the Palestinian Islamic Jihad as describing itself as "the Islamic vanguard Sayyid Qutb talks about," and includes Hamas in the circle of Qutb's disciples. The Islamist organization Hizb al-Tahrir, founded in Jerusalem in 1952 and active in various countries of the Middle East and also in Britain, has also come under the influence of Qutb's framing of the global issues.

Musallam theorizes that had Qutb not spent so many years in prison his writings might not have been so embittered, and not provided so fruitful a basis for the jihadist movement. Nevertheless he summarizes Qutb's final work, *Components of the Islamic Conception*, left unfinished and published only in 1986, as maintaining that Jahiliyyah "has no right to exist" and that "there is no meeting between Islam and al-Jahiliyyah." In regard to Christians and Jews, Qutb grants them the right to maintain their religion but only if they are submitted to Muslim rule and pay the Jizya, "the land tax imposed on infidels out of humiliation and servility."

Musallam cites a criticism of Qutb's radical interpretation of the Qur'an by Sheikh Yusuf al-Qaradawi, "a noted Egyptian Islamist propagator," who accuses Qutb of selective quoting of only the "sword-oriented" verses of the Qur'an while ignoring many Qur'anic verses that call for peace with non-Muslims. Qaradawi is himself a controversial figure, calling for death to homosexuals, endorsing the Iranian fatwa calling for the murder of Salman Rushdie, calling for killing all Americans found in Iraq, and stating the Allah sent Hitler to inflict a just punishment on the Jews.

Fawaz A. Gerges in his book *The Far Enemy: The New Definition of Jihad* (Cambridge University Press, 2005) describes Qutb's position as Islamic Permanent Revolution. Gerges writes:

"More than anyone else, Sayyid Qutb . . . inspired generations of jihadis, including Al Qaeda's senior leaders, Osama bin Laden and his deputies, . . . theoretician Ayman al-Zawahiri, and thousands of others — to wage perpetual jihad to 'abolish injustice from the earth, to bring people to the worship of God alone, and to bring them out of servitude to others into the servants of the Lord.' Far from viewing jihad as a collective duty governed by strict rules and regulations (similar to just war theory in Christianity, international law, and classical Islamic jurisprudence, or fiqh), jihad, for Qutb, was a permanent revolution against internal and external enemies who usurped God's sovereignty. He attacked Muslim scholars and clerics with 'defeatist and apologetic mentalities' for confining jihad to 'defensive war.' There is no such thing as a defensive, limited war in Islam, only an offensive, total war."

* * *

Excerpts from *Milestones on the Road* by Sayyid Qutb

The Right to Judge

It is not the function of Islam to compromise with the concepts of Jahiliyyah which are current in the world or to co-exist in the same land together with a jahili system. This was not the case when it first appeared in the world, nor will it be today or in the future. Jahiliyyah, to whatever period it belongs, is Jahiliyyah; that is, deviation from the worship of One Allah and the way of life prescribed by Allah.

It derives its system and laws and regulations and habits and standards and values from a source other than Allah. On the other hand, Islam is submission to Allah, and its function is to bring people away from Jahiliyyah towards Islam. Jahiliyyah is the worship of some people by others; that is to say, some people become dominant and make laws for others, regardless of whether these laws are against Allah's injunctions and without caring for the use or misuse of their authority.

Islam, on the other hand, is people's worshipping Allah alone, and deriving concepts and beliefs, laws and regulations from the authority of Allah, and freeing themselves from the servitude to Allah's servants. This is the very nature of Islam and the nature of its role on earth.

Islam cannot accept any mixing with Jahiliyyah. Either Islam will remain, or Jahiliyyah; no half-half situation is possible. Command belongs to Allah, or otherwise to Jahiliyyah; Allah's Shari'ah will prevail, or else people's desires: "And if they do not respond to you, then know that they only follow their own lusts. And who is more astray than one who follows his own lusts, without guidance from Allah? Verily! Allah guides not the people who are disobedient."[28:50]; "Do they then seek the judgment of (the Days of) Ignorance? And who is better in judgment than Allah for a people who have firm faith"[5:50].

The foremost duty of Islam is to depose Jahiliyyah from the leadership of man, with the intention of raising human beings to that high position which Allah has chosen for him. This purpose is explained by Raba'i Bin 'Amer, when he replied to the Commander in Chief of the Persian army, Rustum. Rustum asked, "For what purpose have you come?" Raba'i answered," Allah has sent us to bring anyone who wishes from servitude to men into the service of Allah alone, from the narrowness of this world into the vastness of this world and the Hereafter, from the tyranny of religions into the justice of Islam."

December 15, 2009

The World Islamic Revolution

[David Selbourne's book was published in 2005, and I completed this review in September 2006, almost six years ago. He wrote to me shortly after it appeared on my website to say mine was the best review of his book he had seen. How much has changed in the global confrontation with Islam in the six years since? Al-Qaeda has been significantly weakened, particularly with the death of Osama bin Laden. The frail Iraq regime installed by the American invasion has survived, but still faces daily killings and bombings by its Islamist opponents. In Afghanistan the Taliban is arguably stronger than it was in 2006. The Arab Spring has deposed tyrants in Tunisia, Libya, Egypt, and Yemen, but so far failed in Bahrain, and stands on the verge of civil war in Syria. In all these places militant Islamic movements are major players and the ultimate shape of governments and their place in the world order is still unknown.

[In Egypt, despite the Arab Spring overthrow of Mubarak, the Muslim Brotherhood is a strong contender for power, while there have been new attacks on the Coptic Christians. Iran is as belligerent as ever and closer today to having the bomb than it was six years ago. In Nigeria, massacres of Christians by the northern Muslims are in full swing. Hezbollah has become the unchallenged ruler of South Lebanon and much of Beirut. The kinds of triumphalist plans for world conquest and submitting all peoples to Islamic rule cited by Selbourne still are voiced regularly by high religious and political functionaries from Saudi Arabia to Indonesia. Islamic militants are still lobbing rockets into southern Israel while Hamas holds firm to its goal of expelling the Jews from the region. Europe is as concerned today as it was then by the large unassimilated Muslim immigration. Taken as a whole, the Islamic revolution is a bit weaker than in 2005 but remains a formidable challenge to secular society. Selbourne's great merit is in putting together in one place a global summary of this determined if decentralized movement. For a century it was common for the Marxist left to speak of a world communist revolution as though this were a real unfolding event. There is far more evidence today of a religious Islamic world revolution in process, unexpected as

71

that might be from the standpoint of yesterday's Western radicals. — Leslie
Evans, March 19, 2012*]*

*   *   *

**The Losing Battle with Islam by David Selbourne. New York: Prometheus
Books, 2005. 541 pp.**

*"We will control the land of the Vatican, we will control Rome and introduce
Islam in it. Yes, the Christians . . . will yet pay us the Jizya [poll tax paid by
non-Muslims under Muslim rule], in humiliation, or they will convert to Islam."* — Sheikh Muhammad bin Abd al-Rahman al Arifi, imam of the
mosque of the King Fahd Defence Academy, Saudi Arabia, cited by Middle
East Media Research Institute, dispatch 447, December 6, 2002

Question: *"What can the West, especially the US, do to make the world
more peaceful?"*
   Abu Bakar Bashir *[jailed leader of the Indonesian Jemaah Islamiyah]:
"They have to stop fighting Islam. That's impossible because it is sunnatullah
[destiny, a law of nature], as Allah has said in the Koran. If they want to have
peace, they have to accept to be governed by Islam."* — The First Post Online
Daily Magazine (UK), September 16, 2006

   *"Democratic civilization is the first in history to blame itself because
another power is trying to destroy it."* — Jean-François Revel, 1970

More than a decade ago Harvard professor Samuel Huntington in *Foreign
Affairs* published his famous thesis that future world conflict would unfold
along cultural rather than national or ideological lines as it had in most of the
twentieth century, in a clash of civilizations between the secular West and
Islam, as well as potentially with the reemergent civilization of East Asia represented by China. Others such as Mark Juergensmeyer in his 1993 book *The
New Cold War? Religious Nationalism Confronts the Secular State* began to
warn that the roots of secular democracy were extremely thin in large parts of
the world, particularly in the Muslim Middle East and Hindu India, where
much of the population takes its identity from traditional religions rather than
from political affiliation. This, Juergensmeyer said, threatens to pose irresolv-
able conflicts between the truth claims of rival religions, each of which asserts
that it possesses the only valid and moral world view and rejects governments
not based solely on its own religious exclusivism.

For some years these assessments were met with skepticism. If they were exaggerated, it was feared, they could serve to justify U.S. and European aggression against other societies. On the other hand, however, if they were true, the parliamentary democracies of the West and of East Asia, whatever their bad behavior toward the former colonial world, could well face an opponent that, while lacking the technical and material base of Western capitalism, rests on a huge population united in a common world view with a large activist minority possessing a level of determination largely lacking in the highly individualistic and often politically divided societies of Europe and America.

Five years after 9/11 with Muslim insurgencies flaring on three continents and widespread rejection of the U.S. government's idea of what a democracy should look like in Afghanistan and Iraq, the thesis of a clash of civilizations appears far more plausible. British author David Selbourne in his provocative book *The Losing Battle with Islam* attempts to compile the evidence of just how widespread the Islamic awakening has been in the last two decades, amounting, he holds, to a world revolution that the West is ill-prepared to meet.

The West, or as David Selbourne more inclusively prefers, the non-Islamic world, has been unwilling to look too closely at what it is up against in what George Bush misleadingly calls a "war on terrorism." The term, Selbourne argues, drops from sight the issues the fight is about. Selbourne insists that the hot spots of today's clashes with militant Islam — the Iraq war, Afghanistan, the Israel-Palestine conflict, and even Iran — are only episodes in a far wider struggle that began just after World War II and promises to become more intense in the years to come. "It is a long drawn-out struggle for dominion which is in progress, generated by the gradual reawakening of Islam to a sense, God-inspired, of moral entitlement to inherit the world. For its part, America and its allies, with all their fire-power, are squaring up to foes whom they cannot or will not name, and about whose 'sensibilities', or sense of history, they know little."

To enunciate such a thesis generally provokes a firestorm of criticism that this maligns moderate Muslims. Yet the scale and sweep of Islamic violence is hard to deny. Selbourne's book is a catalog of wars, civil wars, secessionist movements, mass demonstrations, and speeches by authoritative Muslim religious leaders or articles in government sponsored newspapers in Muslim countries that constitute or advocate violent action to achieve the advancement of Islam. The rise of militant Islam certainly is paralleled by a decline in its principal rivals in the Arab and Iranian worlds, secular nationalism and Marxism. Persian secularism took a severe blow with the overthrow of the pro-Western shah in 1979 and the crushing of unions and other non-Islamic organizations by the Revolutionary Guards. Arab nationalism peaked with Nasserism in the 1960s and has been in sharp decline since the defeat of secular Ba'athist Saddam Hussein in the First Gulf War, leaving a wide field for religious leadership. The Bush administration and some moderate Muslims clearly exaggerate when they claim that radical Islamists are a small isolated fringe. It is beyond dispute that the Islamists command a substantial active minority in many countries and the passive support of many more.

Certainly many millions of Muslims choose to live in peace with their neighbors and would prefer a modern democratic government. In Los Angeles there are thousands of Iranians who bitterly oppose the theocracy in their home country, while the city's head of counter terrorism is himself a Muslim. But even if it were the case that a majority of Muslims do not advocate, engage in, or favor violence most revolutions are made by determined minorities whose victory often requires only that the majority be modestly in favor of the militants' goals, neutral, or even just not well organized or motivated. Looking back over the great Western revolutionary movements from the U.S. war of independence from Britain to the French revolution of 1789, or the Communist revolution of 1917 in Russia, powerful as these were and with long-echoing international repercussions, none was the act of a majority. Important in the relations of majority and militant minority in Islam is that disagreements are more about methods than about ends, as the militants, even Osama bin Laden, are comparatively orthodox and traditionalist in their theology, advocating the imposition of Sharia law and elimination of non-Islamic political and cultural influences and institutions.

David Selbourne is a British political philosopher and historian of ideas. He taught at Ruskin College, Oxford, 1966-1986. He has written for *New Society,* the *New Statesman,* the *Independent*, and the *Guardian*, traveled widely, published plays as well as nonfiction works. He chronicled the fall of communism from behind the lines in Poland. In June 2001, he was awarded the Order of Merit of the Italian Republic by president Carlo Azeglio Ciampi. His fourteen previous books have covered a wide swath from civic theory to British politics to China and India. *The Losing Battle with Islam*, as he states at the outset, is based not on previously unknown classified documents but mainly on a mountain of newspaper clippings from the early 1980s to its writing in the summer of 2005. This material has the advantage of laying out hundreds of episodes, declarations, sermons by imams well known and obscure, that build up a broad canvas filled with detail. Its disadvantage is the lack of precision of such sources, compounded because Selbourne writes in a popular style without footnotes.

A Global Islamic Insurgency

To summarize Selbourne's argument, the U.S. government and mass media have a short attention span, treating each outbreak of Islamic violence as a distinct story rather than seeing each as a component part of a broad sweep of growing Islamic militancy in a score of countries over several decades. Too much attention, he says, is paid to al-Qaeda because they happened to be the group behind 9/11, while Islamic insurgencies, civil wars, large scale communal violence, and campaigns of intimidation or assassination of critics of Islam have raged around the world.

> It is a war of great complexity which has taken millions of lives in open and bloody conflicts, as in Afghanistan, Algeria, Bangladesh, Biafra, Bosnia, Chechnya, Iran, Iraq, Lebanon, Nigeria, Somalia, Sudan, Tajikistan, Xinjiang, and so on. The Algerian civil war from 1992 has cost between 150,000 and 200,000 dead. The Pakistan-Bangladesh war in 1971 is said by some to have taken the lives of two million; some estimates suggest that as many as a million — Iraqis and non-Iraqis alike — were killed by Saddam Hussein during his twenty-five-year rule. . . . Since 1983, civil wars, famine (as in 1998) and displacement in Sudan, Africa's largest country, have led to more than 2 million deaths.

He goes on to list a million dead in the civil war in northern Nigeria in 1967-70 in which the Chrstian Igbo people of the secessionist Biafran republic charged the Muslim northerners with genocide against them, 150,000 in the Lebanese civil war between 1975 and 1990, tens of thousands in the Tajikistan civil war of 1992-97. Muslim separatist rebellions have claimed tens of thousands more lives in each of several theaters, from the Chechen separatists to the Armenian-Muslim wars of Nagorno-Karabakh, Indonesia and the Philippines, the Palestinian intifadas, Kashmir, and Kosovo. There were Muslim separatist uprisings in Xinjiang, China's far western province, in 1981, 1988, and 1989-90. Muslim parties were banned in Tanzania and Kenya in the 1990s after violent clashes.

Taken together, while these conflicts have arisen from different causes and in a few cases it is the non-Muslims who were the aggressors, there is much exchange of funding, battle-hardened combatants, intelligence, and heroic legend between the Islamic fighters on these many fronts. Selbourne sees the battles and the networks emerging from them as proof of a global Muslim "awakening," no less than the world revolution that the communist left expected in vain for a century to arise from the industrial proletariat. But this growing assertiveness is in the name not of a universalist doctrine of so-

cialist egality but of an exclusivist religion whose militants class all unbelievers in an inferior political and social status, where they are allowed to exist at
all (Saudi Arabia denies citizenship to all non-Muslims, while in nominally
secular Algeria only those who can prove that their fathers and paternal grand-
fathers were Muslims are eligible for citizenship. Jews are prohibited from
living in most Arab states).

While there is no Islamintern counterpart to the international organization of Soviet Communism, there are many links between the different Islamic
struggles.

> Iran helped fund and otherwise supported the Algerian, Egyptian,
> and Iraqi Islamist insurgencies; was a key ally of the Sudanese Islamist
> regime; supplied arms to the Bosnian Muslims; inspired and aided the
> formation of Lebanese Hezbollah; armed Hamas; and worked hard to
> develop its nuclear programme. It was also active in the insurgencies in
> Tajikistan, Turkmenistan and other Central Asian Muslim countries.

Iraq under Saddam Hussein aided anti-government Islamic groups in Egypt;
Libya supported the attempted coup against Gorbachev in the last days of the
Soviet Union; Sudan gave aid to the Islamist insurgencies in Algeria, Egypt,
Tunisia, and Somalia. Pakistan's support to the Taliban and the Kashmiri
Islamists is well known but it also aided the anti-Russian Chechen secession-
ist movement, gave nuclear technology to North Korea, and has been accused
of involvement in Islamist bombings in India. Saudi Arabia funded "violent
Islamist groups in Algeria and Chechnya" and founds thousands of mosques
around the world, including in the United States, committed to the puritanical
Wahhabist version of Islam that is one of the principal ideological founts of
contemporary Islamic militancy.

The scope of Islam's spread is often unappreciated in the United States.
Islam is universally known to be the dominant religion in the Arab and Persian Middle East, North Africa, and Indonesia. Selbourne reminds us that
some 50 percent of the population of Africa is Muslim and not all in the Arab
north: 80-90% in the Black African states of Mali, Niger, and Senegal; 50% in
Nigeria; and 25% in East Africa. There are 3.5 million Muslims in Germany,
and as many as 7 million in France with some estimates putting Muslims at
25% of the whole French population under 25. There are projections that see a
Muslim majority in France by 2050.

To this picture should be added the territorial holdings of the militants or
regions dominated by the militant ideology as distinguished from Arab or
majority Muslim states in general. This consists foremost of Khomeinist Iran

and Wahhabist Saudi Arabia, each with huge oil incomes. Sudan could be considered in this category, with a larger land mass than the United States, followed by states-within-a-state, notably the Hezbollah enclave in southern Lebanon, Hamas in Gaza, the militant enclaves in northwestern Pakistan, the reviving Taliban in Afghanistan, and land held by the Southeast Asian insurgencies in Thailand and the Philippines.

In taking up the touchy subject of Western-Muslim conflict Selbourne feels no need to gloss over oppressive acts and exploitive policies toward Muslims and Muslim states by the United States, Israel, or Europe. Clearly the rise of Islamic militancy has as one of its principal causes the failure of secular nationalism to secure full independence of Muslim countries from non-Muslim control or influence. But Selbourne argues that the very globalized character of the Islamic insurgency shows that it has its own dynamic and is not merely a response to harsh treatment of the Palestinians by Israel, or the U.S. war in Iraq or its support to Arab dictators. This can also be plainly seen from the oft repeated claims by leading Muslim figures that Islam will defeat Europe and America and that the Christian West will be ruled by Islam or will have to convert. Consequently Selbourne holds that reforms of U.S., European, or Israeli policy, while needed, cannot plausibly be expected to establish peaceful relations with the Islamic revolutionaries.

Brutality Not from Fanaticism But for Shock Value

A second characteristic of the global struggle for Islam has been the conscious use of extremely brutal shock tactics. Best known have been suicide bombings aimed almost exclusively at civilians, from Tel Aviv to Baghdad, Istanbul, Bombay, Madrid, and London. Selbourne does not seek to avoid the fact that the United States and Israel use air power in military actions that also kill civilians fairly indiscriminately. His point is that the spectacular attack specifically on civilians has become a hallmark of the Islamist movement. Selbourne cites many examples, of which some of the most extreme took place in Algeria. There the Islamist movement, mainly the Armed Islamic Group, fighting back after the government canceled an election the Islamists had won, involved such events as cutting eleven women teachers' throats in front of their students in September 1997.

> Horror on horror was recorded: as of village women decapitated in Tlemencen province in western Algeria in November 1997; of burnings alive, and . . . even of burials alive, as of a taxi driver, Mahieddine Ahmed, in February 1995 at Tighrine; of "hackings"-to-death of women and children in the village of Omaria in April 1997; of the July 1997

slaughter in the village of Aonaria in Algeria's Medea province where, according to El Watan, even a pregnant woman is said to have been "disembowelled".

Since Selbourne's book was published the remaining active Algerian militant Islamic organization, the Salafist Group for Preaching and Combat (GSPC from its French initials), originally part of the Armed Islamic Group, confirmed earlier rumors by announcing in mid-September 2006 that it was joining al-Qaeda. Al Jazeera reported September 14, 2006, that al-Qaeda's second in command, Ayman al-Zawahiri, responded by urging the GSPC to punish "Crusader nation" France.

Bombings of public places such as movie theaters have also been widely used in many countries. Selbourne gives numerous examples including the killing of 255 people in Mumbai (formerly Bombay) by eleven explosions in a single day in the early 1990s. And of course there was the Beslan school hostage crisis in Russian North Ossetia in September 2004 in which Islamist separatists killed 366 people in explosions, including 186 children.

Selbourne criticizes the Western media presentation of these events for focusing on their gory details and emphasizing "terrorism." This makes the public lose sight of the political point of such events, a blow struck for the cause of Islamic power using tactics consciously chosen despite their risk for negative blowback. "The engendering of fear bloodied the Islamist cause but simultaneously promoted it to disaffected young Muslims, while helping to disable and cow responses to its advance." Islamist movements have frequently themselves circulated videos of their most vicious actions, such as beheadings, both to intimidate their enemies and to impress potential recruits with their boldness.

From the standpoint of the closed jihadist theology the use of extreme violence and the rejection of coexistence with other religions or secular law is neither fanaticism nor irrational. It is a proven winning strategy. One should not expect much result from negotiations here. As Selbourne has it, "Those who think that a culture of 'human rights', for example, can be introduced into Muslim polities, or who believe that Western Enlightenment notions of freedom of thought, conscience, religion and expression are compatible with Islam in its revival and advance are themselves guilty of delusion."

The non-Islamic governments and media, Selbourne maintains, for fear of alienating Muslims, or in hopes of encouraging divisions among them, overstate the distinction between extremist and moderate Muslims and between secular and Islamic states. Selbourne cites a British Muslim leader, the president of the Bradford Council for Mosques, as saying in July 1989, "I cannot accept that there are liberals and fundamentalists within Islam. For me, you are either Islamic and hold to your beliefs; or you do not hold to them and you are not Islamic." Secular Pakistan's parliament unanimously condemned Pope Benedict XVI for his citing of a hostile comment on Islam in his September 2006 address in Germany.

The U.S., Europe, and more recently China prop up unpopular dictatorships in the Arab world to fend off Islamic militancy and retain access to oil on which their economies depend. Selbourne points out that many of these states while nominally acquiescing to their non-Muslim patron at the same time fund or otherwise facilitate Islamic radicals, either out of conviction or to try to buy them off. This goes far beyond the usual mention of Saudi Arabia and includes Jordan, Egypt, Pakistan, Qatar, Yemen, Sudan and other states further afield.

Muslim Immigrant Communities in Non-Muslim Countries

Selbourne is also concerned that domestically in Europe and the U.S. large-scale Muslim immigration has been accompanied by frequent demands that non-Islamic societies concede to standards and sensibilities that derive exclusively from Islam and that are in conflict with long-established Western protections of freedom of religion and speech, or that Muslims be exempted from laws or school curriculum that conflict with their religion. Many Muslims do accept the rules of their new societies, and Muslim immigrants often face discrimination or racist attacks. Still, important minorities within the Muslim immigrant communities of Europe pose explicit reservations about the meaning of citizenship.

"French Muslims . . . have demanded to set their own rules as to which doctors or teachers they will permit to treat or teach them in French hospitals or schools, or which lessons they will or will not attend and which texts they will or will not read." Saudi-funded schools in Britain and Germany in 2002 and 2003 were found to teach mainly Islamic religion with few lessons in the language of the country in which they were located. Fears of the nonassimilation of Muslim immigrants have been fueled by reports such as that "Asian" radio stations in Britain two months after 9/11 announced "that '98 per cent' of London Muslims under the age of forty-five would 'not fight for Britain' against bin Laden's al-Qaeda, and that '48 per cent' would take up arms for him." Selbourne comments that this makes "nonsense" of multicultural assumptions, as Muslim youth, while living in Western countries, "see little or no virtue in the civic orders to which they had chosen to belong."

Selbourne offers numerous examples of efforts by Muslims in non-Muslim countries or in secular Muslim states to impose their religious views on others by force, including retribution for criticism of Islam of sorts that would not even be controversial in most non-Muslim societies if directed at Christianity or Buddhism. These range from trashing a French butcher shop by Muslim youth because of pork on a pizza to an attack with iron bars on non-fasting youth in Marmara, Turkey, during Ramadan, to the murder of Salman Rushdie's Japanese translator and the wounding of his Norwegian publisher and Italian translator, the offer by an Iranian charity of $2.5 million in 1997 to Salman Rushdie's bodyguards in Britain if they would kill him, or the murder of Dutch filmmaker Theo Van Gogh for his film criticizing the status of women in Muslim countries. In 2001 a Pakistani professor, Mohammed Younnus Shaikh, was sentenced to death for blasphemy for suggesting in a college lecture that the Prophet Muhammad's parents could not have been Muslims because the religion had not been created yet. While his sentence was reduced to imprisonment, a fellow prisoner was supplied with a gun and Shaikh was shot to death in prison. The president of Iran in March 1989 is said to have called for the death of "any writer who criticizes Islam."

In October 1995 in London the Hizb ut-Tahir, an Islamist group, demanded the exclusion of Jewish students from British schools.

A serious warning sign was the response of Muslims in non-Muslim states to the February 1989 fatwa issued by Iran's Ayatollah Khomeini calling for the murder of British-Indian author Salman Rushdie on the grounds that his novel *The Satanic Verses* insulted Islam. As Selbourne recounts, some 20,000 Muslim demonstrators in Westminster in May 1989 carried banners demanding "Kill the Bastard" and "Rushdie Must Be Chopped Up" (with a drawing of a bloody knife). Bookstores throughout Europe were threatened by local Muslims and ordered not to display the book. Many obeyed. Rushdie's Japanese translator Hitoshi Igarashi was stabbed to death. In Milan his Italian translator was stabbed; his Norwegian publisher was shot and badly wounded. Copies of the book were burned in London's Parliament Square. Abdullah Ahdel, a leader of the Belgian Muslim community, was shot and killed when he refused to endorse a call to ban the *Satanic Verses* in Belgium.

A London bookstore was burned, and Iranian groups threatened to target Britons "all over the world" if the arsonist was not freed. "His release followed." A British radio station was threatened with violence by the Muslim Youth Movement if they broadcast an interview with Rushdie. The since-famous head of Hezbollah, Sheikh Hassan Nasrallah, in a speech to a crowd of 5,000 in Beirut in February 1989, threatened that if Rushdie came out of hiding he "will be killed." Years later he was credited with saying that if

Rushdie had been killed in acordance with the fatwa the Danish cartoons of the prophet would never have been published in 2005. The Palestinian Popular Front for the Liberation of Palestine declared that Rushdie would be "hunted down and killed, in order to defend Islam and its prophet." A BBC poll in 1990 found that 42 percent of British Muslims supported the demand to kill Rushdie.

Writer Anthony Burgess defended Rushdie, declaring "They cannot have the privileges of a theocratic state in a society which, as they knew when they entered it, grants total tolerance to all faiths, so long as those faiths do not conflict with that very principle of tolerance." But other Brits caved in to the Muslim pressure. Keith Vaz, Labour MP from Leicester East, where there is a large Muslim population, on May 27, 1989, spoke at an anti-Rushdie demonstration of tens of thousands of Muslims in Parliament Square who were shouting "Rushdie die, Rushdie scum!" and "We want Rushdie, dead dog Rushdie!" Vaz, Selbourne recounts, "described the occasion as a 'great celebration of freedom.'" Roy Hattersley, deputy-leader of the Labour Party, elected from a constituency that had 43 percent Muslim voters, denounced as "racist" opposition to the rallies organized to urge Rushdie's murder, declaring, "The proposition that Muslims are welcome in Britain if, and only if, they stop behaving like Muslims is a doctrine which is incompatible with the principles which govern and guide a free society."

Public toleration of death threats by British Muslims against their critics and opponents became so common in the following decade as to lead the *Times* of London in February 2002 to opine that a "certificate of immunity" appeared to have been "unofficially issued to Muslims, and to Muslims alone, who publicly call for people to be murdered."

We have seen similar Muslim campaigns to conduct literary criticism by death threats and bombings, notably in the furor over the cartoons of Muhammad published in the Danish newspaper *Jyllands-Posten* in September 2005. At least 139 people were killed in protests according to the website www.cartoonbodycount.com, mainly in Nigeria, Libya, Pakistan, and Afghanistan. In February 2006 after David Selbourne's book went to press the Indian provincial Uttar Pradesh government, not some fringe group, offered a 51 crore (US$110 million) reward for "anyone who beheads the Danish cartoonist who caricatured Prophet Mohammad," as the *Indian Express* reported in its February 17, 2006, edition. Note that most of the protests were for printing any kind of picture of Muhammad, which is regarded as idolatry and punishable by death. Insulting Islam, even in a very mild way, is also punishable by death, as in one of the cartoons whose author is slated by the Indian state government for beheading, showing Muhammad on a cloud welcoming a smoking suicide bomber to paradise with the warning "Stop! There are no more virgins!"

There have also been growing numbers of bombings, attacks on Jews, and other exemplary actions across Europe and Southeast Asia, as well as a general rise in threats. "From April to August 2004, for example, there were threats by Ahmet Azzuz of the Arab European League against the city of Antwerp — attacks were 'nearly unavoidable', he declared — if the Antwerp Jewish community did not 'distance itself from the state of Israel.'" There has been a rise in actions by converts as well, as in the case of a Filipino convert to Islam who planted a bomb on a ferry in Manila Bay in February 2004 killing more than 100 people.

A year after the cartoon rampage a new crisis appeared over the pope quoting a fourteenth century Byzantine emperor who said Muhammad's command to spread Islam by the sword had produced "evil and inhuman" results. Certainly the pope meant this as a criticism of Muslim violence. The Muslim retort used still stronger words. In Turkey, Salih Kapusuz, deputy head of the ruling party, told the press that the pope "is going down in history in the same category as leaders such as Hitler and Mussolini" (Canada.com, September 16, 2006). Also in Turkey the Welfare Party demanded the pope be arrested and put on trial for inciting religious hatred. In Iraq the Mujahedeen Shura Council, an umbrella organization of Sunni Arab insurgent groups, reiterated the now familiar promise of global conquest: "We will break up the cross, spill the liquor and impose head tax, then the only thing acceptable is a conversion (to Islam) or (be killed by) the sword." (CBS News online, Sept. 18, 2006) The Muslim response was not limited to words. It included the fire bombing of seven Christian churches by Palestinians in Gaza and the West Bank, and shooting a nun to death in Somalia.

Israel and the Jews

"'Anti-Americanism' has increasingly become a leitmotif as the Islamic 'reawakening' has advanced," Selbourne writes, "and as muddled Western responses to Islam and Islamism have intensified. . . . Overheated obsessions with the Jews and the making of Israel into the root-of-all-evil have also clouded judgment, as have equally aberrant forms of hero-worship of the malefactor."

Rather than viewing Israel, or U.S. support to Israel, as the core issue in dispute between Islam and non-Islam, Selbourne is more inclined to view the Israeli-Palestinian conflict as an exemplar and microcosm of the global conflict. He writes:

Illegal Israeli settlement on Palestinian lands is a rank injustice. So, too, has been the deliberate Israeli strangulation of the Palestinian economy, the latter made more threadbare by corruption and inertia. They are injustices matched by the injustice of desires to end the existence of Israel entirely.

To begin with, he maintains that the centrality of Israel as well as its strength have been vastly inflated because of the religious issues involved in the conflict with Islam. Israel, Selbourne reminds his readers, is about the size of San Bernardino County, ten miles wide at its narrowest point, with a population half the size of Mexico City, 20% of whom are Arabs. Its four contiguous neighbors have sixty times its land area, and if Iran, Sudan, and Saudi Arabia are added they have more than three hundred times the land area of Israel. There are 14.5 million Jews in the world and 1.3 billion Muslims. The Jew, he suggests, plays an exaggerated role in both Christian and Muslim concepts of the world. "Israel becomes the anti-Christ among nations," to use the Christian image. It is seen and treated in ways different from other nations and viewed stereotypically as a Zionist monolith which does not reflect its actually very diverse internal politics and ethnic composition. In Israel's actuality "there are Arab members of Parliament, Arab political parties, and an Arab supreme court justice."

The Israel-West Bank fence was singled out by the International Court of Justice in 2004 to be a violation of human rights law "despite the existence of similar security barriers between India and Pakistan, between Saudi Arabia and Yemen, between Turkey and Syria, between the Turkish and Greek sectors of Cyprus, and between Morocco and the Western Saharan region."

Although Israel has been a member of the United Nations since 1949, its destruction "remains the avowed aim of some of its fellow UN members, contrary to the UN charter." Holocaust denial, publication of extreme anti-Semitic literature, and calls to kill Jews in general are widespread in the Arab and Muslim world.

While the Palestinian grievance against Israel has as a focal point the some 700,000 Palestinians who fled or were driven out during the Arab states' military invasion of the Jewish areas that became Israel in 1948, Selbourne also mentions the usually forgotten flight or expulsion of the "hundreds of thousands of Jews" who lost their homes and property in Egypt, Iraq, Lebanon, the Maghreb, Syria, and other Arab states. Most historians put their number at 866,000. There have certainly been injustices on both sides in this long and bitter conflict, but the rights of the matter, including on the claims for land within the eastern Mediterranean, are not all on the Arab side.

Above all Selbourne condemns as a moral evasion "the desire to separate the conflict between Israel and the Palestinians from the broader collision between the Islamic and non-Islamic worlds, as if it were a lethal but 'private' quarrel which could be settled by negotiation between the parties, rather than a fierce confrontation upon one of the many front-lines of a larger war." He particularly excoriates Western leftists — and neo-Nazi rightists — who are prone to argue that U.S. support to Israel is the root of Muslim hostility to America. This looking to the Jews as the cause of evil in the world has all too many historical precedents, Selbourne suggests. In its most extreme form, he cites an April 2004 article by the deputy editor of the Egyptian government daily *al-Gumbouriya* asserting that Jews have carried out "all terrorism worldwide."

For those who imagine that the anti-Jewish sentiment is just a response of Arabs sympathetic to the Palestinian cause Selbourne notes a January 2004 poll in Italy in which more than a third "agreed 'totally' or 'substantially' that the Jews 'secretly control economic and financial power and the media.'" He concludes: "From the 'far right' to the 'left', and from the world of Islamism to the world which seeks to oppose it, such concord of opinion has more of neurosis about it than considered judgment, for all the wrongness of Israel's acts. At its prompting it becomes possible to argue, from 'neo-Nazi right' to . . . 'left', that 'anti-US hatred' derives principally from the failure to meet Palestinian grievances against Israel."

Even if the Palestinian-Israeli conflict were resolved "it would have minimal 'transformatory' effect, or no effect at all, upon the warring parties in other conflicts generated by the Islamic 'reawakening' from Algeria to Sudan, Iraq to Indonesia, and the Philippines to Nigeria. During the last decades most Islamist attacks on the non-Islamic world, attacks on Israel apart, have not made the Palestinian issue their first cause, or made it their cause at all."

Yet Israel is often castigated for responding to armed attacks on itself in ways that any other nation would be expected to do and which are certainly the routine response of Muslim states when confronted by assaults by Islamists. "Even international organisations, such as the European Union, con-tributed to the free fall," Selbourne comments, "with their open financial and covert political support for Palestinian paramilitary organizations." This moral free for all has not been a boon to the Palestinians any more than to the Is-raelis. The demonization of Israel facilitates the growth of Western anti-Jewish feelings as well as inflaming Muslim sentiment and making any kind of settlement less likely. Selbourne gives many examples, ranging from Syr-ian President Bashar al-Assad's assertion in March 2001 to a group of Arab leaders that Israeli society is "even more racist than the Nazis," to the claim in the Egyptian government-controlled newspaper *al-Akhbar* that same year that Israel is "worse than the Nazis," while the German *Der Spiegel* in December 2001 "likened the policies of Ariel Sharon to those of Adolf Hitler." Cartoons using swastikas imposed on Israeli flags or politicians have become a commonplace. Selbourne cites here only the example of the Spanish liberal daily *Cambrio 16* in May and June 2001 which "depicted Sharon as a swastika-wearing Nazi," but a Google image search for "Israel Nazi" turns up hundreds of others.

Holocaust denial is a staple of the Muslim press, but there are exceptions. Selbourne notes, "In the Egyptian government-sponsored *al-Akhbar* . . . the fact of the Holocaust was not denied but lauded in April 2001. 'Thanks be to Hitler of blessed memory', wrote one of its columnists. 'on behalf of the Palestinians he took revenge in advance . . . on the most vile criminals on the face of the earth. Still, we do have a complaint. His revenge on them was not enough.'"

While comparisons to the Nazis are almost always overblown, if one were to make such a comparison it would seem that the Muslim side is by far the more extreme in promoting racial hatred. Among many examples Selbourne points to a public statement in November 2003 by the Turkish Abu Hafs al-Masri Brigades after bombing synagogues in Istanbul to the effect that "Jews around the world" would "regret that their ancestors even thought about occupying the land of Muslims," while the British Muslim group al-Muhajiroun in October 2000 conducted a poster and leaflet campaign using posters with the slogan "Kill the Jews." The Indonesian Muslim militant Amrozi after being convicted in August 2003 of participating in the Bali bombing shouted "Burn the Jews!" and "The Jews should be annihilated!" Fawaz Mohammed Damra, imam of the Islamic Center of Cleveland, Ohio, after using the common Qur'anic description of the Jews as "monkeys and pigs" in a sermon "called in the next breath for 'rifles' to be 'directed at' Jews."

Noting a Palestinian television broadcast in August 2001 that invoked "blessings upon him who shot a bullet into the head of a Jew," Selbourne dissented that "here there could arguably be heard the accents not of political resistance to a 'colonial occupier' or 'settler state', but those of hatred of the members of an entire race, wherever they might happen to be. Those who decapitated the American Jewish journalist, Daniel Pearl, in Karachi and made him declare 'I am a Jew' to a video-camera before his throat was cut, appeared to be acting in the same spirit."

This kind of talk has not been limited to Muslims. Selbourne quotes Labour MP George Galloway at a London University meeting in May 2002 saying "We must support the Palestinians and assist them in wiping out the Zionist entity." Selbourne concludes, "The language of 'replacement', 'destruction', 'erasure', 'obliteration' and 'extermination', whatever else it is, has not been the language of peace."

Elsewhere he writes, "With those who feel such hatred, Israel, being perceived as 'the Jew' writ large, has attracted odium less for what it does than for what it is." Ominously the growing Muslim immigration to Europe, given the dependence of European society on Muslim oil and existing anti-Semitic feelings on the continent, risks an opportunistic abandonment of Israel to its Islamic enemies. A UPI dispatch of May 2002 commented that "from Paris and London to Berlin and Brussels, European leaders are likely to fear outbursts of violence from their huge, recent, Muslim immigrant populations far more than angering tiny Israel."

George Bush and the Export of Democracy by Force

In the Muslim east itself, Selbourne dismisses as "naive" the Bush administration's efforts to create parliamentary democratic states. He sums up the actual Muslim position on this by quoting an Iraqi Shi'ite cleric on the eve of the U.S. invasion: "Preaching to tens of thousands of worshippers at the Qadhimaya mosque in northern Baghdad, Sheikh Mohammed al-Tabatabi said: 'The west calls for freedom and liberty. Islam is not calling for this. Islam rejects such liberty. True liberty is obedience to God and to be liberated from desires.'" (This quote, which I have tracked down, is from the May 3, 2003, London *Guardian*).

Selbourne quotes another Iraqi Shi'ite leader, Ayatollah Mohammed Baqer al-Hakim, who is said to have "declared that even were 'democracy' to come to Iraq, it would not be a 'western-style democracy' but a 'democracy' which prohibited 'behaviour acceptable in the West but forbidden in Islam.'" A sharper rendition of this thought came from al-Qaeda in Iraq leader Abu Musab al-Zarqawi in January 2005 who charged that replacing the rule of God with the rule of the people was "infidelity itself."

In contrast, Selbourne writes, "the West, and especially the United States, persists in transposing to the Islamic world its own preferences for 'free thought', for the separation of God's realm from Caesar's, for the 'free market' and so on." The notion that these are forms of social organization desired by Muslims Selbourne dismisses as a self-defeating illusion. He cites Salman Rushdie saying "actually existing Islam has failed to create a free society anywhere." He adds: "It is not universal suffrage but universal knowledge of Islam, and not the sovereignty of the people but the sovereignty of God, to which pious Muslims aspire. There might be differences among the faithful about the means to attain such ends, but not about the ends themselves."

In this broader framework Selbourne rejects the idea popular on the left that George Bush's war in Iraq is, perhaps with the Israeli-Palestinian conflict, the principal source of Islamic hostility to America or that the U.S. losing the war would have much effect on the global Islamic insurgency.

However much the U.S. invasion of Iraq has provoked Islamic hostility, "non-intervention would . . . have had no impact upon the wars in Kashmir, Sudan or Chechnya, upon the insurrection in Thailand, upon the strife between Muslims and Christians from the Philippines to Nigeria, upon Islamism's assaults in India, north-western China and Central Asia, or upon the struggles of the rulers of the Gulf kingdoms and sheikhdoms to keep their thrones."

Is the Insurgency a Response to Imperialism's Wrong-Doing or to Religious Conviction?

A common view espoused by critics of the American government, particularly of the Bush administration, is to see the world as composed of two counterposed segments, rich and poor countries, north and south, imperialist and Third World. In this frame, hostile acts against the United States or Israel are most often regarded as part of a liberation struggle, as responses to prior crimes by the imperialists, and so on. Selbourne mentions a London *Guardian* commentator who in November 2003 posed the question "Who is tackling the global causes of suicide bombing?" Selbourne comments that "The view implicit in many such . . . questions was that the non-Islamic world was to blame for whatever blows were struck against it; they could be variously attributed to 'disadvantage' and 'exclusion' of Muslim citizens in the diaspora, US partiality in the Palestinian issue, 'abusive American detention methods', 'unemployment and poverty' in the Muslim world and so on."

Selbourne counters, "However, to attribute 'blame' for Islamism to the United States was again to understate the degree to which the Muslim advance is governed by its own internal dynamic and by dictates of belief which the non-Muslim world cannot alter." To see Islamic violence always as a response rather than an initiative "can therefore provide Islamism with grounds for a permanent evasion of responsibility, or a moral carte blanche."

For many this approach is based on the conviction that the United States is the worst evil in the world. This view is very popular in Europe, in Latin America, in the Third World, and among American leftists and even liberals. Certainly there is a long history of colonialism by European powers, which drew to a formal close in the 1960s and even its successor neocolonialism has faded much more since. There was a far shorter colonial period by the United States, which overturned many governments or seized territory, from its wars with Mexico, the Spanish-American war, interventions in Latin America, the Philippines, Iran, Chile, and Vietnam.

Anti-Americanism frequently conflates America's wealth with its actual power, which has been in retreat since the defeat in the Vietnam War thirty years ago and possibly since the stalemate in the Korean War in the 1950s. The Bush administration's ill-considered invasion of Iraq and the resulting incapacity of the U.S. forces there to impose their will on the situation confirm this. As the U.S. in reality becomes less involved in controlling the affairs of other countries its critics escalate the image of the evil enemy of humanity. Selbourne notes the May 2004 assertion of the late Susan Sontag that the high-handed and brutal detention of some hundreds of accused "terrorists" at Guantanamo and in secret CIA prisons in Eastern Europe initiated by the Bush administration goes "beyond Soviet Russia's Gulag system" in which perhaps 50 million people died. Similarly, the head of Turkey's parliamentary human rights group in November 2004 claimed that the U.S. "genocide" in Iraq was on a scale "never seen in the time of the Pharaohs nor of Hitler." Osama bin Laden accused the U.S. of inventing AIDS.

It could be argued that as new countries emerge as serious forces on the world scene, such as China and India, or Islam itself, that the world is becoming more decentralized than in the old two-pole Leninist vision rooted in a colonialist past. The most active of the Islamists, however, do not focus their demands on the types of things one would expect if this was a movement that aimed mainly at the independence of Muslim states. Selbourne notes the Israeli Arab leader Ra'ed Salah who four days after 9/11 declared "If Bush wants peace and security the only solution is for him to convert to Islam."

This is consistent with Islamic theology, which rejects concessions to infidelity. As long as communications were limited between Muslim lands and other nations, Islam's struggle to punish and suppress infidelity was local, or at most on its borderlands. One effect of globalization has been to make this a world conflict, as the unacceptable moral, cultural, and religious standards of the U.S., Europe, or China, become better known to Muslims and pose a direct challenge to Islamic morality and belief.

For the most pious — and the most militant — the natural and ordained fate of the infidel is to be subordinate to Muslim rule, combined with the death penalty for Muslims who leave the faith or those of other faiths who attempt to convert Muslims. Christian missionaries, for example, were killed by Muslims in Lebanon and Yemen as well as Christian nurses in Pakistan, in 2002. Attacks on Buddhist monks and temples in Thailand in 2004 and 2005 "included decapitations." These are taken from among many more examples Selbourne provides from throughout the Muslim world in the last few years.

The Left and Islam

The European and American left since the end of the Vietnam War, the collapse of the Soviet Union, China's turn to market capitalism, and the failure of the workers' radicalization hoped for in the 1960s and 1970s, has been in serious need of a mass constituency. It has been tempted by the Islamic revolution into seeing this as a national liberation movement against imperialism. Selbourne writes that this creates an insoluble problem because Islamism is "hostile to most 'left' or 'progressive presuppositions.'" While he does not use the term "Islamo-fascist," he does point out many similarities between the characteristics of European fascism and the Islamic movement:

> The principle of submission to authority; the reduction of all "out-groups" to inferior status; disbelief in the virtues of free thought; contempt for democracy; the corporatist dissolution of distinctions between the public and the private realms; the perception of all cultures save that of Islam as morally decadent; the subordination of women to men and to the home; and the readiness to use extremes of personal cruelty and violence, together with the odium expressed for Jews and homosexuals, were among the main constituents of the fascist creed.

He adds that the secular Ba'athist parties of Syria and Iraq were consciously modeled on European fascist parties, that Chechen Muslim irregulars fought on the Nazi side in World War II, while a number of Arab leaders of the 1930s and 1940s were pro-Nazi, including the Grand Mufti of Jerusalem, the Iraq government, and many prominent Egyptians such as Anwar Sadat, who later became president. Nevertheless, "for much of what remained of the Western 'left' — with its own 'socialist project' in ruins — the appeal of a politics of anti-colonialism, anti-racism and (especially) anti-Americanism weighed more heavily in the ethical scales than did the defects of Muslim and Arab societies." Here both the Marxist left and a number of European neofascists such as the Austrian Jorg Haider and the Russian Vladimir Zhirinovsky found themselves on the same side.

Selbourne calls the Western anti-imperialists' embrace of Islamism against America a "suicidal impulse." At best it provides the Islamists "further political space . . . to pursue their ends against a divided non-Muslim world." Islam in fact competes with the left to become the leader of the oppressed, but with very different ends in mind, ends in which the leftists, as no less unbelievers than the Bush administration, will never be permitted to share without converting to Islam.

In truth a large section of American liberalism shares the left's analysis. Sam Harris, the antireligious author of *The End of Faith: Religion, Terror and the Future of Reason*, in a September 18, 2006, op ed piece in the *Los Angeles Times* condemns the "debilitating dogma that lurks at the heart of liberalism" that "Western power is utterly malevolent, while the powerless people of the Earth can be counted on to embrace reason and tolerance, if only given sufficient economic opportunities." He laments, "I don't know how many more engineers and architects need to blow themselves up, fly planes into buildings or saw the heads off of journalists before this fantasy will dissipate. . . . Unless liberals realize that there are tens of millions of people in the Muslim world who are far scarier than Dick Cheney, they will be unable to protect civilization form its genuine enemies."

What Next?

The battle with Islam is a losing one in Selbourne's view not because Islamic values are acceptable to the non-Islamic peoples but because the West, and here he seems to have in mind principally Britain and the United States, have carried the individualism that was the hallmark of their creative age from the Renaissance to the early twentieth century, to a current hypertrophy of social incoherence. These are

> societies increasingly governed by the atrophied ethics of "the market" and by a belief in the self-realisation of the individual as the highest of values. They were also societies over-dependent on a "culture" of consumption, and upon the resources of Muslim lands — among others — which sustained it. Their citizens' aspirations for, and sense of, the future had in many cases similarly shrunk to dimensions compared with which Islam's moral and religious goals were grandiose, however unacceptable they might be to most non-Muslims.

Finally, while Selbourne clearly does not favor conversion of the non-Muslim world to Islamic theocracies, he views the closed and internally logical Islamic theology as highly motivating, the inheritor of almost fourteen hundred years of struggle to impose its view of the world on others in several waves of expansion, beaten back only in the nineteenth century when the Ottoman Turks were finally driven out of Greece and the Balkans.

Islam, Selbourne concludes, has an internal coherence and inspiration of its followers that the West lacks. Europe and America despite their wealth and military power are comparatively fragile societies, deeply internally divided, and "susceptible to large-scale economic, social and moral crises."

Selbourne really offers no proposal to protect and preserve Western secularist democracy except to begin by acknowledging what the world Islamic revolution is about and not dodge the truth by presenting it as a handful of terrorist fanatics or criminals, or the converse, as merely a national liberation struggle on past models. These presentations, he insists, miss the whole point.

September 23, 2006

Christopher Hitchens and
the Two Lefts

I cannot help but feel deeply the loss of Christopher Hitchens, who died on December 15, 2011. I never met him. I read a number of his books, many of his articles in *Vanity Fair* and in the online *Slate* magazine, and saw a few of his speeches on video. Contrarian though he was, he had become for me, with a few other similar thinkers, a political anchor in a time when the world was sorting itself into new and unexpected categories and many old convictions had become sterile and untenable.

In 1965 at sixteen Hitchens joined the British Labour Party, where he became part of its left-wing youth. He was soon expelled for campaigning against the war in Vietnam. He joined the International Socialists, Trotskyist followers of Tony Cliff, in time to be thrilled by the global revolutionary outbreaks of 1968, above all the May-June worker-student uprising in France. Hitchens began to write for their press in 1970. I was then just completing several years as managing editor of the *Intercontinental Press*, the New York weekly news magazine of the Trotskyist Fourth International. In May of that year I became editor of the *International Socialist Review*, the monthly magazine of the U.S. Socialist Workers Party. In 1977 the British International Socialists changed their name to Socialist Workers Party. Despite the confusion of their identical names the two groups were not on friendly terms, though they shared a common ideological heritage in variations on Trotsky's Bolshevism.

Hitchens worked for most of the 1970s for the London left-wing *New Statesman*. He moved to New York in 1981, two years after I left there to go into the iron mines in northern Minnesota. In America he wrote for *The Nation*, excoriating, as we Marxists did, the evils of capitalism in general and American imperialism in particular.

He had an exceptional talent. Like Churchill, who he despised, he read rapidly and widely and had virtually eidetic memory, giving his carefully wrought journalism unusual sweep and depth. He was as much a literary critic as political scourge; erudite and pugnacious, with only a few fixed guiding stars, the most important a hatred of tyranny and of religious obscurantism.

The most shocking scene in his memoir, *Hitch 22*, was not about politics. In April 1973, his mother Yvonne abandoned his father, an austere British naval officer, and ran away to Athens with her lover, a defrocked pastor. There the pair committed suicide. Hitchens was summoned to the grisly scene, guiltily wondering if, had he spoken to her one more time, he could have forestalled the tragedy. While there a major military protest erupted against the right-wing junta. Hitchens filed a story with the *New Statesman* and launched his career as a foreign correspondent.

For the next twenty-nine years he was on the move for various leftist publications, covering events in sixty countries, including Pakistan, India, Chad, Zimbabwe, Uganda, the Darfur region of Sudan, and Iraq under Saddam Hussein.

For the politicized, Hitchens is best remembered for his militant atheism, admired on the left, and his break with the far left after 9/11 and support for the U.S. war in Iraq, from which leftists and most liberals shrank in horror. I never found his atheism particularly interesting. By the time I acquired Hitchens' *God Is Not Great* I had already read Sam Harris' and Richard Dawkins' anti-God books and did not take the time to read Hitchens' addition to the genre. I certainly agreed that militant religion had come to pose a mortal threat to liberal democracy, but felt that a political battle to set secular limits was more likely to have results than trying to change deeply held belief systems.

His support to the Iraq war was grounded in his hatred of totalitarianism and his conviction, already forming a decade before 9/11, that the Arab and Persian Middle East had become a cauldron of right-wing dictatorships and religious fanaticism that threatened democratic societies everywhere. I did not for a very long time pay much attention to that thread in his thinking either.

What drew me to Hitchens was his critique of the Marxist and anti-imperialist left in the age that dawned with the collapse of Communism. I felt by the turn of the millennium that the world lineups that had shaped my politics in the sixties and seventies had morphed into new forms that I was struggling to understand. With Tolkien's Galadriel I could sense that "The world is changed, I feel it in the water, I feel it in the earth, I smell it in the air." Hitchens was articulating what was different and I read him with rapt attention.

A major factor that had attracted both of us to the far left was revulsion at our respective governments' promotion of right-wing dictatorships in what we then called the colonial and later the third world. The litany included the CIA-backed Iranian coup against the liberal Mosaddegh government in 1953; toppling Arbenz in Guatemala in 1954; the failed Bay of Pigs invasion of Cuba and the murder of Patrice Lumumba in the Congo in 1961; the U.S.-backed Pinochet coup against Salvador Allende in Chile in 1973; and above all the decades-long war in Vietnam.

The world that dawned with the collapse of the Soviet Union in 1991 proved to be quite different from the Cold War realm, where a ruthless United States swatted down real and imagined pro-Communist governments wherever it found them. In fact, all of the imperialist sins in the standard list were blows struck against what Washington perceived, somewhat paranoically, as emergent Communist threats. The Manichean Soviet-Western split was gone and with it much of the motivation for the capitalist West's bad behavior toward emergent states.

The disappearance of the Soviet adversary was followed by several years of a drugged up high where the American establishment strutted as the hegemonic power on the planet. Those were the days of Francis Fukuyama's 1992 *The End of History and the Last Man* fantasy, where the American variety of mostly free market capitalism was now to be the unchallenged model for every country. The Republican right puffed itself up with self-congratulatory praise about the power of the United States. Perhaps because they took this stuff too seriously, much of the left succumbed to the illusion that the United States was now more dangerous than ever, king of the world — and hence bringing it low was the cardinal task of the age.

A more sober assessment was Samuel P. Huntington's lecture the same year on "The Clash of Civilizations," framed as a reply to Fukuyama, which proposed that there are multiple civilizations, divided by firmly entrenched cultures, religions, and economic patterns that are not about to go away. He named the Anglo, European, Russian, Chinese, Japanese, Indian, Latin American, and Islamic as the world's major civilizations. This was largely rejected at the time and caricatured as proposing inevitable war between the rivals. That is not at all what Huntington said, only that the other civilizations were not going to adopt the American pattern — the neocons were notoriously over optimistic here — and that the lines where they met were hot spots (famously: Islam has bloody borders).

Instead of American hegemony, multiple rival powers emerged, many of them, the optimism of 1991 notwithstanding, hostile to democratic institutions. There is the authoritarian and Mafia-ridden Russia of Medvedev-Putin; the numerous dictatorial failed states of Sub-Saharan Africa; the Communist dictatorships of China and Vietnam, which have turned capitalist and become

America's economic rivals, along with rapidly advancing India; nuclear armed North Korea; and an increasingly prosperous Latin America distanced by history and inclination from the United States. The Arab and Persian Middle East has mostly been a spoiler in the world system: cripplingly undeveloped suppliers of oil, mired in a stifling religious miasma that ensures their continued backwardness, marked by dictatorships and fanatical Islamic movements locked in many variations of mutual combat, with the jihadis, in and out of power, aspiring to a world revolution that would exterminate modern civilization and replace it with a medieval totalitarianism The Arab Spring offers hope here, though we need to await its further evolution.

Anti-imperialism was a cardinal element of Hitchens' as well as my politics. Beginning with the Islamic Revolution in Iran in 1979, and deepening after the collapse of Communism at the end of the 1980s, the political tectonic plates shifted. The most active opponents of U.S. and British influence became Islamic theocrats, narco terrorists like the FARC in Colombia, the North Korean nightmare state, and various unsavory dictatorships such as Robert Mugabe's kleptocracy in Zimbabwe, or repressive demagogues like Chavez in Venezuela.

Guided by the unreconsidered premise that American imperialism was the most evil force on the planet, much of the far left embraced any regime or movement that claimed the United States as its enemy. In the process many became champions of dictatorships, often of the far right, and of the ultraright religious totalitarians of the Islamic jihad. A common subtext here was endorsement of Hamas' and Hezbollah's drive to destroy Israel, leapfrogging from morally admirable opposition to the Israeli occupation of the West Bank and Gaza to the patently anti-Semitic promotion of jihadi movements that call for the expulsion of the Jews from the region — including the Israeli majority whose families are refugees already expelled from a half dozen Arab states — and commonly for extermination of the Jews altogether.

For both Hitchens and myself the alarm began to sound with leftist support to the Islamist theocracy in Iran.

I began to break with the Socialist Workers Party in 1981, in part over a historical dispute on Lenin's politics, but contemporaneously over their coverage of the Khomeini theocracy in Iran. At a certain point after the 1979 Islamic Revolution the American SWP, in imitation of the Cuban government in Havana, which they hoped to influence, eliminated from their press any reports on the mullahs' crushing of the Iranian liberals, leftists, and unionists, portraying Khomeini solely as an anti-imperialist. At the time I called that kind of politics Third Worldist and rejected it, but did not yet see what it signified about changes in the world alignment of forces.

Hitchens hit the same roadblock a few years later. In a 2003 interview in *Frontpage* he recalled:

"The realization that we were in a cultural and political war with Islamic theocracy came to me with force and certainty not on 11 September 2001 but on 14 February 1989, when the Ayatollah Khomeini offered money in his own name to suborn the murder of my friend Salman Rushdie."

Hitchens, while having hopes for the beleaguered democratic forces in the Arab world, was one of the first on the left to recognize that the new multicentered world contained more newly risen enemies of democracy than victims of imperialist oppression. He derived his insight not from Huntington, but from his hero, George Orwell, who lived in the age of Hitler and Stalin, when it was obvious the world had irreconcilable regimes and that there were far worse things lurking than British or American imperialism.

At root for both Hitchens and Orwell, democracy was worth defending. For the Marxist left, "bourgeois" democracy is a fake, to be swept aside by a totalizing state power. For the narrow anti-imperialist, their own country is the irredeemable villain, while its democratic institutions do not weigh much in the balance. Orwell excoriated the British intellectuals of his own day who imagined that Soviet communism was a utopian alternative to Britain's evils, or saw little to defend in their homeland. In his "The Lion and the Unicorn" essay in 1940 Orwell wrote:

> [T]he really important fact about so many of the English intelligentsia — [is] their severance from the common culture of the country. In intention, at any rate, the English intelligentsia are Europeanized. They take their cookery from Paris and their opinions from Moscow. In the general patriotism of the country they form a sort of island of dissident thought. England is perhaps the only great country whose intellectuals are ashamed of their own nationality. In left-wing circles it is always felt that there is something slightly disgraceful in being an Englishman and that it is a duty to snigger at every English institution, from horse racing to suet puddings. It is a strange fact, but it is unquestionably true that almost any English intellectual would feel more ashamed of standing to attention during 'God save the King' than of stealing from a poor box. All through the critical years many left-wingers were chipping away at English morale, trying to spread an outlook that was sometimes squashily pacifist, sometimes violently pro-Russian, but always anti-British.

This not from a man of the right but from a still-convinced socialist. The people he disparages are of a type quite widespread in the wake of the sixties radicalization. They hardened their political views in the days of the struggle against the Vietnam War. I was one myself for many years. Of course, there was a parallel alienation on the right, in reaction to the upheavals of the sixties and the defeat in Vietnam, visible today in the Tea Party movement.

It was time, Hitchens felt, to accept responsibility to defend a society that is among the better ones in the world rather than campaign to scrap it in hopes that a superior one could take its place. The United States remains the strongest single player, but one clearly facing many unfriendly powers and in rapid relative and absolute decline. One measure of this is that, despite its vaunted technological and economic superiority, the U.S. has not unequivocally won any of the many wars it has waged since World War II (except for the invasion of tiny Grenada, which proves my point).

Of the various enemies of democratic society the most active and threatening in the last decade have been the Islamic jihadists. They do not hold state power outside of Iran, Gaza, and, arguably, southern Lebanon, but have a large following within the Muslim world — we will have to see as the Arab Spring evolves just how large. At the least, 9/11 and the al-Qaeda offshoots in Iraq, Algeria, and in Europe showed they can inflict traumatic damage.

Christopher Hitchens took this struggle to heart. In the introduction to his last book, *Arguably,* written just six months before he died, he says,

> The organizations that find and train men like [9/11 hijacker Mohammed] Atta have since been responsible for unutterable crimes in many countries and societies, from England to Iraq, in their attempt to create a system where the cold and loveless zombie would be the norm, and culture would be dead. They claim that they will win because they love death more than life, and because life-lovers are feeble and corrupt degenerates. Practically every word I have written, since 2001, has been explicitly or implicitly directed at refuting and defeating those hateful, nihilistic propositions, as well as those among us who try to explain them away.

He pursued this theme in many venues. In a July 2005 article in *The Mirror* he summarized the grievances put forward by Osama bin Laden in his various messages to the world, most of which can be found much earlier in the extremely influential writings of that father of modern jihad, Egyptian theorist Sayyid Qutb (see my essay on Qutb's views earlier in this book):

The grievance of seeing unveiled women. The grievance of the existence, not of the State of Israel, but of the Jewish people. The grievance of the heresy of democracy, which impedes the imposition of Sharia law. The grievance of a work of fiction written by an Indian living in London. The grievance of the existence of black African Muslim farmers, who won't abandon lands in Darfur. The grievance of the existence of homosexuals. The grievance of music, and of most representational art. The grievance of the existence of Hinduism. The grievance of East Timor's liberation from Indonesian rule.

In *Arguably* he describes a meeting where he spoke at the American University of Beirut in February 2009. He tried, he says, to highlight positive democratic currents in the Middle East: Egyptian dissident Saad-Eddin Ibrahim, who shortly afterward became an inspirer of the anti-Mubarak revolt; the Cedar Revolution against Syrian domination in Lebanon; the Kurdish struggle against Saddam Hussein and, since his fall, against the revanchist Ba'ath and al-Qaeda "insurgents"; and Salem Fayyad's work to reform the Palestinian Authority. His audience, he said, including most of the Americans, were hostile, responding that revolutionary authenticity belonged to groups like Hamas or Hezbollah. Here Hitchens states his central life credo:

> For me this was yet another round in a long historic dispute. Briefly stated, this ongoing polemic takes place between the anti-imperialist Left, and the anti-totalitarian Left. In one shape or another, I have been involved — on both sides of it — all my life. And, in the case of any conflict, I have increasingly resolved it on the anti-totalitarian side.

Like his mentor, George Orwell, Hitchens remained on the left after his break with those leftists who placed anti-Americanism above anti-totalitarianism, and despite his opponents' fatwas of excommunication. His former comrades of the British Socialist Workers Party in 2004 formed a Marxist-Islamist alliance, launching the Respect Party, which includes supporters of Hamas and of the Muslim Brotherhood. It called not only for an end to the war in Iraq but for the destruction of Israel. The party elected one member to parliament in 2005 and won quite a number of local elections, until it underwent a devastating split in 2007.

The more venerable *New Left Review* in its May-June 2003 issue called for support to the "resistance" in Iraq and for solidarity with North Korea's Kim Jong-Il in his stand against imperialism. The American SWP more recently sent a goodwill mission to the comrades in North Korea.

Hitchens' turn quickly earned the vituperation of the scabrous doyens of anti-Americanism: Noam Chomsky, Alexander Cockurn, Norman Finkelstein, and Edward Herman and their coterie. George Galloway, one-time British Labour politician, inveterate enemy of Israel, and supporter of Saddam Hussein, quipped that Hitchens was "the first-ever metamorphosis from a butterfly back into a slug."

Hitchens, never one to duck a fight, responded in kind. In the afterword to *Christopher Hitchens and His Critics* he replied to the lot:

[T]he years after the implosion of the Soviet Union in 1989 are marked by the recrudescence of danger from different forms of absolutism in Serbia, Iraq, Afghanistan, Iran, Darfur, and North Korea, and, once again, a huge number of "intellectuals" will not agree that the totalitarian principle, whether secular or religious, is the main enemy. There is, apparently, always some reason why this is either not true or is a distraction from some more pressing business or is perhaps a mere excuse for "empire."

The anti-imperialist left underwent a certain devaluation in the last two decades, making a more moderate progressive politics increasingly attractive. Hitchens took this rather farther than I would, claiming a temporary alliance with the neocons and becoming a bit of a friend to neocon-in-chief Paul Wolfowitz. I would say in his defense that the American right is composed of many different currents, and the neocons are far removed from the Christian evangelicals (most of the neocons were Jewish), or even their cynical compatriots in the Bush-Cheney-Rove group. They are best summed up in John Gray's *Black Mass: Apocalyptic Religion and the Death of Utopia* as "armed missionaries" on a quest to export simulacra of the American political structure. They have been described as advocates of a right-centrist version of Trotsky's theory of permanent revolution. This is likely what Hitchens saw in them. Their welcome in the halls of Republican power was short lived.

Though he viewed the American military in Iraq as a means to free the Iraqi people from their fascistlike dictator it did not endear him to George W. Bush, of whom he said, "He is unusually incurious, abnormally unintelligent, amazingly inarticulate, fantastically uncultured, extraordinarily uneducated and apparently quite proud of all these things."

As usual Hitchens was not a sideline commentator. Terry Glavin in his obituary in the *Ottawa Citizen* recounts:

"Reporting from Pakistan's borderlands while American bombers rained guided missiles down on Taliban strongholds, Hitchens learned that at least two American F-16 pilots were women, and he could barely contain the urge to rush to the Taliban embassy with the news: 'It's your worst nightmare, you bastards. She's pissed, she's packing, and she's headed for you.'"

Glavin adds:

"But he wasn't about to flatter American conservatives, either. Invited by a cable news talk show to offer his views on the death of the American celebrity evangelist Jerry Falwell, Hitchens refused to play along, saying that if Falwell were given an enema he could be buried in a matchbox."

No doubt Hitchens after 2001 moved to the right of where he had been, but to the end he regarded himself as primarily a leftist. "He was brilliant and often exasperating," wrote Timothy Noah, a long-time collaborator on *Slate*, in his death notice in *The New Republic*, "even before 9/11 made him an un-repentant Iraq hawk; I won't say 'conservative' because even in his lefty days Hitchens had a conservative streak, especially in his literary taste, and even after he started writing for the *Weekly Standard* he remained in many ways a man of the left."

In his late writings I thought Hitchens was too soft on Trotsky, too hard on Churchill and Clinton. He wrote with great bitterness against the death penalty, submitted himself to water-boarding to prove that it really is torture, and mocked the sainted Mother Teresa and Christian fundamentalism. He went to Chile to testify against the Pinochet government and Henry Kissinger in the murder investigation of the killing of Charles Horman (the case por-trayed in the film *Missing*).

Hitchens and the Iraq War

It is necessary to say something about Hitchens and the Iraq War. There were many good reasons why any democrat or humanitarian should have op-posed Saddam Hussein's dictatorship. The main debate over the war has been whether they affected direct American interests enough to justify military in-tervention, and whether such intervention could succeed in stabilizing a less repressive regime. The well of American public opinion was poisoned at the outset by the Bush administration's decision to try to motivate an invasion by claiming Iraq posed an immediate threat to the United States and had some connection to the 9/11 atrocity. The charge that Saddam had weapons of mass destruction was based on the highly dubious testimony of the defecting Iraqi scientist code named Curveball and some limitations Saddam placed on UN inspections. The idea he was in league with al-Qaeda had an even thinner foundation. When neither proved to be true, Democrats en masse, not just the hard core anti-imperialist left, regarded the already unpopular Bush as a liar and opposed the whole operation. Support for the war never recovered from that false start.

There was a plausible case for the invasion, but it was more indirect and less likely to persuade a largely isolationist public. The Bushies included it in their motivation, but it was drowned out by the furor over the missing WMDs. The problem, as the neocons saw it during their brief ascendency in Washington, was to break up the status quo of economic stagnation, dictatorship, and religious fanaticism that made the whole region a petri dish for toxins that were repeatedly morphing into other parts of the world. This was really a long-term issue in which 9/11 was only the spark that provoked the concern. The aim was not to punish particular authors of the World Trade Center attack but to try to insert a foothold for a more moderate politics into the region. Where to do that? The states most tied to 9/11 were Saudi Arabia and Pakistan, both allies, if dubious ones. Corrupt Saudi princes lavishly funded Wahabi extremists, out of whose ranks came 15 of the 19 hijackers. At the same time they were officially friendly and the single largest source of oil on which the American economy depended. Pakistan's intelligence service had mentored the Taliban, with which it still maintained strong ties, viewing Afghanistan as a pawn in its conflict with India. Here we had another formal ally, and a nuclear armed one at that.

Iran, the largest open enemy, was Shiite, while all the hijackers were Sunnis, making the connection too remote. Its fifty million inhabitants were a daunting opponent, as it appeared that the Islamic government, while less popular than in 1979, still commanded the loyalty of some important portion of the people.

That left Iraq. Saddam was by far the most repressive of the Arab and Persian Muslim dictators. The *New York Times* said in his obituary that he had murdered as many as 1 million of his own people, many with poison gas, apart from the hundreds of thousands who died in his wars. He was also the most expansionist. He had waged a nine-year war against Iran (1980-1988) that left 1 million Iranians and 500,000 Iraqis dead or wounded. Then, only two years later, there came his invasion of Kuwait.

While Bush and Cheney chose to use far fetched and inflammatory claims to justify their pending invasion, the widespread notion that the choice of Iraq was arbitrary and that America had no special interest there since the end of the Gulf War years before is not the case. The U.S. after 1990 remained deeply and militarily involved in Iraq up to the moment of the 2003 invasion. Under three administrations, Republican and Democratic, it maintained, with the UK and France, the risky and costly no fly zones that covered more than half the country — in the north to protect the Kurds, and in the south to guard the Shiite Muslims. The U.S. alone by 1999 had flown over 200,000 sorties over Iraq, facing anti-aircraft fire from Saddam's batteries.

The UN Security Council sanctions, imposed in 1990, by the time of the U.S. invasion in 2003 had resulted in as many as 500,000 deaths from malnutrition, mostly of children (some contested estimates are much higher). The sanctions, pursued by Clinton as well as the two Bushes, were having an unacceptable human cost. They could be withdrawn, or Saddam could be toppled. In the post 9/11 climate, making a major concession to the Iraqi dictatorship was not a likely possibility.

Whether the American people could have been convinced on humanitarian grounds and to help reform Arab dysfunction in America's long-term interests will never be known. Probably not under Republican auspices. Bush's stupidity meant that the war's initial supporters were predominately on the political right, with the liberals and left firmly in opposition. There were, however, a few leftists with a history of defending Saddam's victims who endorsed the invasion. Christopher Hitchens was prominent among them.

As a British citizen and internationalist there was no reason for Hitchens to make paramount America's costs, the focus of the dispute in the United States (except for the hard anti-imperialists who had more fundamental disagreements). He and his closest cothinker, British journalist Nick Cohen, began from the interests of the Iraqis, particularly the threatened Kurdish minority. There are as many as seven million Kurds in Iraq, perhaps 20% of the population. A non-Arab people, religiously Sunni Muslims, there are altogether something between 28 and 35 million Kurds, the largest ethnicity in the world that does not have its own country, split between Turkey, Iraq, Iran, and Syria. Hitchens spent several months in the Kurdish lands in 1991, just after the Gulf War, crossing over the Iraqi border into Free Kurdistan. He describes his experience in his book *Love, Poverty, and War*:

> I enlisted the help of an armed escort hardened by months of guerrilla fighting. Hoshyar Samsam, who knew this country well and had been the personal bodyguard of Jalal Talabani [a central political and military leader of the Kurds, today president of Iraq], was taking care of me. He calmly conducted me through bomb-shattered villages and deserted towns. He foraged for me in an area blighted by famine and helped me dodge Iraqi patrols.

The Kurds in Iraq's north, like the Marsh Arabs in the south, staged massive uprisings after the Americans in the Gulf War forced the Iraqi army out of Kuwait. Bush the Elder promised them support. It never came, and both peoples were massacred. For those who knew and cared about the Kurds this was an unpaid blood debt on America's ledger.

Both Hitchens and Cohen were friends with Kanan Makiya, a Kurdish emigre and Trotskyist who championed opposition to Saddam Hussein. Cohen in his *What's Left? How Liberals Lost Their Way*, says that Makiya was a hero of the left until the U.S. Gulf War, when criticism of Saddam was suddenly dropped and Makiya's liberal and leftist friends shunned him. On the whole, once the United States was involved in 2003 the American and British left refused to have anything to do with democratic, liberal, or leftist Iraqis for fear of seeming to endorse the U.S. invasion.

Orwell grappled throughout the thirties with the implicit disconnect between his socialist beliefs and the attitude he should take toward his country's battles. He finally concluded, as the war with Germany began, that England's democratic tradition justified public patriotism, that patriotism was not a monopoly of the political right, and that patriotism had to be toward the country as it existed, not the usual leftist subterfuge of claiming to be patriotic to the state that was to come into being after the present one is destroyed by the hoped-for revolution.

In Orwell's shadow, Hitchens made the same journey at the turn of the millennium, while much of the international left went the other way. He was a strong advocate for the Clinton administration's military intervention in the Balkans after the breakup of Yugoslavia, in defense of the victimized Bosniak Muslims.

Bush compounded his initial propaganda disaster by the post-invasion decisions to dissolve the existing Iraqi army and de-Ba'athify the government, the newly jobless soldiers and bureaucrats streaming into the ranks of the terrorist insurgency. The small progressive current in America and Britain that supported the war on humanitarian grounds included at the outset Christopher Hitchens, Paul Berman, Nick Cohen, Fareed Zakaria, Thomas Friedman, and a score of other prominent names. Most of the liberals fell by the wayside by 2005 or 2006 as the war dragged and the civil war erupted within it. Hitchens, Cohen, and Berman stuck it out.

I worked out my own views on the war in a long email correspondence with an unrepentant Trotskyist friend. She regarded the American government as malevolent and necessarily ill intentioned, viewing any military action by its forces as totally reactionary. At UCLA, where I worked at the time, I had gotten to know a young couple, Alicia Stevenson and Jonathan Dotan, UCLA seniors who had spent considerable time in Bosnia-Herzegovina as interns in the NATO occupation government set up to protect the Muslim population. Among their duties was to identify bodies excavated from mass graves in Srebrenica, from the 1995 massacre by the Serbs of 8,000 Bosniak Muslims. As editor of the UCLA International Institute's website I published their account,

in October 2003, many of the dead still anonymous eight years after the killings. There was no way that I could view the U.S. intervention as predatory.
Christopher Hitchens had a still more intimate involvement in that conflict.

I would not have advocated the invasion of Iraq, but I rejoiced to see
Saddam overthrown. The die had then been cast and the choice to hurriedly
back out was not really there. Like Spain in the 1930s, it became a contest
between the international jihadi right and their local Ba'athist thugs, opposed
by the weaker if more numerous native forces defending a more democratic
and pluralist future, if still one in which Islam would be a prominent feature. I
felt from that moment, as Hitchens and his cothinkers did, that it was wrong to
weigh the stakes too narrowly, only from the standpoint of U.S. public opinion. An Islamicist victory would give them a major territorial base in the Arab
world, a large source of oil to fund their efforts, and embolden those forces on
a global scale.

Many of my friends on the far left tried to shoehorn the Iraq invasion
into the Vietnam pattern. Saddam was a despot even to his Sunni base, and a
mass murderer toward the 80 percent of his people who were Shiites or Kurds.
I started from that remnant of my Trotskyist training that made me an internationalist. We had gotten the Iraqis into this — again! — and our moral obligation was not to abandon them for a second time to the killers, unless they
clearly wanted us to get out.

Iraq, like Yugoslavia, was a creation of the post-World War I redrawing
of the map of Europe and the Middle East. Both countries, Yugoslavia, which
dates to 1918, and Iraq, from 1920, were cobbled together from pieces of historic enemy peoples. They held together only so long as firm authoritarian
leaders kept the lid on.

When these were gone, a free-for-all bloodbath ensued. In Iraq this was
deliberately exacerbated by the swarm of foreign jihadi militants who flowed
in. Notable of this type was Musab al-Zarqawi's al-Qaeda in Iraq. Al Zarqawi
was a Jordanian who had run an al-Qaeda training camp in Afghanistan. His
initial cadre infiltrated northern Iraq from Iran. Others came through Syria.
They adopted a deliberate strategy of mass murder of Shiites to provoke a
civil war that would, they hoped, make stabilizing the situation impossible.

I do not believe that the crime here is in deposing the dictatorships that
glued these places together. Rather, the ethnic warfare had to be worked
through, stopped if possible. This is a cost that it seems to me unfair to debit
to the American account. The accepted number of deaths of Iraqi civilians
since 2003 is 104,000. The most authoritative source for such numbers, the
Iraq Body Count website, reports that the U.S.-led coalition committed only
12 percent of these killings; the vast majority were by the Ba'athist and al-

Qaeda death squads, the counter anti-Sunni killings by Muqtada al-Sadr's Shiite militia, the roadside and suicide bombings. It can be said that the large majority of the deaths of the last eight years are the final installment of Saddam's exactions from his people, more than some kind of wanton slaughter by the Americans.

From the beginning the Kurdish leadership welcomed the Americans, refrained from the mutual Arab Sunni-Shiite slaughter taking place in the south, and worked to build a peaceful and productive enclave in their northern quadrant.

Among the Shiite majority, the Americans were accepted by the Grand Ayatollah Ali al-Sistani, considered by some the most influential figure in present-day Iraq. Al-Sistani strongly supported the elections that were held under American protection, including urging participation by women, and promoted nonretaliation to the Sunni attacks on Shiites, attributing them to foreign Wahabis.

Prime Minister Nouri al-Maliki may be ineffectual and corrupt, but he is not a monster. Elections are reasonably honest by the standards of the region, Sunnis and Kurds are elected to office and take part in the government, the regime tries to protect the safety of its people. It doesn't have a clean record on torture by European or American standards, but it is far less repressive than either Saddam's dictatorship or even Shiite Iran, with which it has friendly ties. Grand Ayatollah Ali al-Sistani promotes many of the more reactionary tenets of the Quran, but he believes in women's suffrage, endorses abortion when the health of the mother is in danger, and does not accept the Iranian doctrine of rule by the mullahs.

American deaths in Iraq were 4,477, the price of bringing down the worst and most dangerous of the Arab dictators. In Korea, 36,000 Americans died to save only half the country, and that is widely and reasonably chalked up as worth it. I would ask those who think the Iraq War was a wholly negative effort to consider whether the world and the United States would be better or worse off if the North Korean regime, which bears a striking similarity to that of Saddam Hussein, controlled the whole peninsula today and there was no South Korea.

My stepson Eric for a while had a tag line on his emails that read "Not every problem has an American solution." There are many dictatorships and failed states. The U.S. can't do much about most of them. But the frequently heard argument that no military intervention can be fruitful in trying to depose a tyrant in someone else's country is falsified not only by both world wars, but in the Arab east by both Iraq and by the fate of Gaddafi in Libya. Sometimes even a very costly and risky deed should be undertaken.

Christopher Hitchens supported the American effort in Iraq, for his own reasons, which were humanitarian to the core. The war ended within days of his death, with an outcome closer to what he had hoped for than to the pessimistic expectations of most of the war's critics.

Iraq was his most controversial commitment, but his canvas was almost incalculably broad. In his hospital bed as he lay dying he continued to write, to read, to be read to, and to engage, as he loved to do, in interminable conversations. His friend, novelist Ian McEwan, visited him regularly in his last weeks. The day after Hitch died McEwan in the London *Guardian* recounted one of his last visits:

> And this was a man in constant pain. Denied drinking or eating, he sucked on tiny ice chips. Where others might have beguiled themselves with thoughts of divine purpose (why me?) and dreams of an afterlife, Christopher had all of literature. Over the three days of my final visit I took a note of his subjects. Not long after he stole my Ackroyd [a copy of Peter Acroyd's *London Under*], he was talking to me of a Slovakian novelist; whether Dreiser in his novels about finance was a guide to the current crisis; Chesterton's Catholicism; Browning's *Sonnets from the Portuguese*, which I had brought for him on a previous visit; Mann's *The Magic Mountain* – he'd reread it for reflections on German imperial ambitions towards Turkey; and because we had started to talk about old times in Manhattan, he wanted to quote and celebrate James Fenton's *A German Requiem*: "How comforting it is, once or twice a year,/To get together and forget the old times."

McEwan concluded with the best tribute I have seen:

"His unworldly fluency never deserted him, his commitment was passionate, and he never deserted his trade. He was the consummate writer, the brilliant friend. In Walter Pater's famous phrase, he burned 'with this hard gem-like flame'. Right to the end."

January 1, 2012

A French Philosopher Challenges Europe's Sympathy for Third World Despotisms

The Tyranny of Guilt: An Essay on Western Masochism — **Pascal Bruckner. Translated from the French by Steven Rendall. Princeton: Princeton University Press, 2010 (original French version, 2006).**

Pascal Bruckner is one of that inimitable French breed of public intellectuals: philosopher, academic, novelist, and polemicist. Born at the end of 1948, he is a veteran of the sixties, when he had a certain sympathy for Maoism. Today he is a firm liberal, in American terms perhaps a very moderate leftist. He is a leading figure among the New Philosophers who broke with Marxism in the early 1970s, others including Alain Finkielkraut, André Glucksmann, Alain Badiou, and Bernard-Henri Lévy, though even those grouped under this sobriquet share no common platform.

Bruckner presents an unapologetic defense of liberal democracy in its confrontations with religious and third world authoritarians. He endorsed the NATO intervention in Bosnia and Kosovo in defense of Muslims under attack by Serbian forces in the former Yugoslavia. He supported the overthrow of the Saddam Hussein dictatorship in Iraq, though he was later critical of the U.S. conduct of the war. And, like Paul Berman in his *Flight of the Intellectuals*, Bruckner came to the defense of Somali exile Ayaan Hirsi Ali when she was contemptuously labeled an "Enlightenment fundamentalist" by leftist authors Ian Baruma and Timothy Garton Ash for her campaign against Islamic female genital mutilation, the two authors contrasting her unfavorably to the supposed Islamic moderate Tariq Ramadan. Bruckner dismissed Ash and Baruma as epitomizing the "racism of the anti-racists."

He has penned the most cogent argument I have seen to be skeptical of the often hurled charge of "Islamophobia":

At the end of the 1970s, Iranian fundamentalists invented the term 'Islamophobia' formed in analogy to 'xenophobia'. The aim of this word was to *declare Islam inviolate*. Whoever crosses this border is deemed a racist. This term, which is worthy of totalitarian propaganda, is deliberately unspecific about whether it refers to a religion, a belief system or its faithful adherents around the world.

But confession has no more in common with race than it has with secular ideology. Muslims, like Christians, come from the Arab world, Africa, Asia and Europe, just as Marxists, liberals and anarchists come or came from all over. In a democracy, no one is obliged to like religion, and until proved otherwise, they have the right to regard it as *retrograde and deceptive*. Whether you find it legitimate or absurd that some people regard Islam with suspicion – as they once did Catholicism – and reject its aggressive proselytism and claim to total truth – this has nothing to do with racism. Do we talk about *"liberalophobia"* or "socialistophobia" if someone speaks out against the distribution of wealth or market domination. Or should we reintroduce blasphemy, abolished by the revolution in 1791, as a statutory offence, in line with the annual demands of the "Organisation of the Islamic Conference." (SightandSound.com, 3/1/2011)

In *The Tyranny of Guilt* Bruckner returns to a theme he advanced in *The Tears of the White Man* (1983 in French, 1986 in English), that European guilt over the continent's history of fascism, communism, imperialism, and other barbarisms has ended in passive isolationism, a loss of belief in the worth of people's own culture and history, and an unwarranted tolerance of foreign repressive and dictatorial movements and governments, mainly in the third world, often expressed in the name of multiculturalism. This goes hand in hand with a reflex anti-Americanism, and a hatred for Israel completely disproportionate to the actual relations between Jews and Arabs in the Middle East.

Though Bruckner's attribution to excessive remorse of the very real appeasement of despotism is largely his own idea, his general world view is shared by a current that ranges from moderate leftists to staunch liberals. Its exemplars include Christopher Hitchens, Paul Berman, Jonathan Chait, Oliver Kamm, Bernard-Henri Lévy, Nick Cohen, Michael Ignatieff, Bernard Lewis, and the late Jean-François Revel and François Furet, as well as, historically, figures such as George Orwell.

Christopher Hitchens called them the anti-totalitarian left, and counterposed them to the anti-imperialist left. There is little point in arguing that this anti-totalitarian left, or liberal interventionist school, does not share some ground with neoconservatives. It does, though before any kind of conservatives claimed this ground there was a long and honorable leftist tradition of anti-fascism and, for many, anti-Stalinism, that did not shrink from foreign battles against totalitarians outside of the home country.

Today's split largely occurred when a considerable section of the left and of liberalism, particularly in Europe, rejected that tradition when the ultraright religious or secular movements or governments were ensconced in nominally underdeveloped countries — though their victims are no less numerous for that. Unquestionably the issue that more than any other provoked this split has been the attitude to take toward Islamic jihad, one side seeing it as a dangerous right-wing millenarian religious fanaticism that acts as part of a would-be world revolution aiming to destroy non-Islamic societies; the other seeing Islamism as a legitimate insurgency of the oppressed against American and European imperialism, or, for some, as a fairly harmless regional liberation movement, the threat in its verbiage about world conquest and occasional terrorist attacks greatly exaggerated by Western governments.

Bruckner's search for the origins of the self-disparaging guilt that he believes explains the moral paralysis in face of Islamicism and its similars looks beyond the contemporary argument about Islam or even the older politics of left and right, going still further back to the Christian doctrine of original sin. As this was secularized in the late nineteenth and early twentieth centuries, he says, the doctrine of innate guilt remained intact, consolidating in new philosophical schools after the shattering experiences of Hitler and Stalin and the two world wars:

> From existentialism to deconstructionism, all of modern thought can be reduced to a mechanical denunciation of the West. emphasizing the latter's hypocrisy, violence, and abomination. In this enterprise the best minds have lost much of their substance. . . . one applauds a religious revolution, another goes into ecstasies over the beauty of terrorist acts or supports a guerrilla movement because it challenges our imperialist project. Indulgence toward foreign dictatorships, intransigence toward our democracies. . . . critical thought, at first subversive, turns against itself and becomes a new conformism, but one that is sanctified by the memory of its former rebellion.

He sums this up as "The whole world hates us, and we deserve it: that is what most Europeans think, at least in Western Europe." As a consequence,

> the communist idea is becoming seductive again as the memory of the Soviet Union becomes fainter, Third Worldism is flourishing again as Maoism, the Khmer Rouge, and the South American guerrillas are forgotten. It is precisely the failure of these concrete utopias that explains

the resurgence of the doctrine, which has suddenly been freed from the need to correspond to reality.

The guilt-stricken ventriloquize rational explanations for their attackers' behavior. 9/11 and such are reasonable responses to injustice, poverty, imperialist meddling. "It is true," Bruckner responds, that

> when existing pathologies find no outlet, terrorism grafts itself onto them. . . . However, its ultimate motivation is fanatics' hostility to the principle of an open society in which formal equality is recognized for everyone. It is our existence as such that is intolerable for them. But this observation is intolerable for us: in order to remain within the bounds of reason and nourish the idea that "even the enemies of reason . . . must be, in some fashion, reasonable" . . . we must at all cost provide arguments for the killers, even if in doing so we seem to justify their acts.

An extreme case is the British Trotskyists of the Socialist Workers Party, who have formed an alliance with Islamic jihadists. As Bruckner puts it, "A certain revolutionary fringe's hope that Islam might become the spearhead of a new insurrection in the name of the oppressed." Each side tries to deceive the other: "one side supports the Islamic veil or polygamy in the name of the struggle against racism and neocolonialism. The other side pretends to be attacking globalization in order to impose its version of religious faith. . . . it is not hard to predict which one will crush the other once its objectives have been achieved."

Europe, he concedes, "had given birth to monsters, but at the same time it has given birth to theories that make it possible to understand and destroy these monsters." He adds that the fixation on the history of European colonialism more often than not ignores comparable behavior by other peoples:

"All great civilizations — Persians, Mongols, Chinese, Aztecs, Incas — were colonizers. Muslims invaded Persia, India, Southeast Asia, Sudan, and Egypt, destroying the local religions and massacring those who resisted them. But in official history writing this fact is often neglected."

He could have said more about the Muslim conquests. Islamists remain bitter about the Christian Crusades, 1095-1291, which held a few cities of the Levant for a century and generally failed after that. The Muslims on their side conquered Spain in 718 and were not fully expelled until 1492. They held most of Greece as a colony from 1453 to 1821, Bulgaria from 1393 to 1878, as well as the rest of the Balkan states. Muslim armies waged two long bloody sieges of Vienna, in 1529 and 1683, in an effort to conquer Western Europe. The ledger hardly shows the Europeans to have been the greater villains, the

Muslim colonization of Western countries having been infinitely more extensive, far more recent, and of vastly longer duration, even if we add the brief French and British mandates following World War I.

By extension Bruckner regards the aspiration of Saudi Wahabism and the Muslim Brotherhood "to take over European society" as a form of colonialism.

In contrast, Europeans, he insists, see only their own evil. In what is perhaps the central thesis of his book he writes:

> Barbarity is Europe's great pride, which it acknowledges only in itself; it denies that others are barbarous, finding attenuating circumstances for them (which is a way of denying them all responsibility). . . . Decolonization has deprived us of our power, our economic influence is constantly decreasing, but in a colossal overestimation we continue to see ourselves as the evil center of gravity on which the universe depends. We need our cliches about the wretchedness of Africa, Asia, and Latin America to confirm the cliche about the predatory, murderous West.

This syndrome is not at all limited to Europe. I encounter it endlessly from my Marxist friends, with the United States substituted for Europe as the global font of evil. This way of thinking is a form of ethnocentrism. I recall forty years ago in the American Socialist Workers Party trying to discuss Mao's Cultural Revolution with some of the older party leaders, who saw everything the Chinese Communists did as a response to some act of the United States. I knew enough about China to understand that the struggle between Mao and his technocratic opponents had practically nothing to do with America.

Tyrannical forces outside of Europe and America are not mere responses to imperialist crimes but active fighters for their own goals. Bruckner is particularly impatient with Islam's claims:

> It considers itself not the heir of earlier faiths but rather a successor that invalidates them forever. The day when its highest authorities recognize the conquering, aggressive nature of their faith, when they ask to be pardoned for the holy wars waged in the name of the Qur'an and for the infamies committed against infidels, apostates, unbelievers, and women, when they apologize for the terrorist attacks that profane the name of God — that will be a day of progress and will help dissipate the suspicion that many people legitimately harbor regarding this sacrificial monotheism. Criticizing Islam, far from being reactionary, constitutes on the contrary the only progressive attitude at a time when millions of

Muslims, reformers or liberals, aspire to practice their religion in peace without being subjected to the dictates of bearded doctrinaires.

Bruckner is not championing Jesus against Muhammad:

> Let us add that Jewish and Christian fundamentalism are no less grotesque, and that seeing the Republicans in the United States court the most obscurantist and well-organized religious Right is a matter of concern. But apart from the fact that they are not setting off bombs all over the planet, these fundamentalists remain in the minority within their own denominations, where they are restrained by liberals and traditionalists.

What Islam demands of the West to salve Muslim "humiliation" is not negotiable. "We are not going to confine women to the home, cover their heads, lengthen their skirts, or beat up gay people, prohibit alcohol, censure film, theater, and literature, and codify tolerance in order to respect the overly sensitive whims of a few sanctimonious persons."

Where Europe has largely caved in to Muslim ire has been in its fear of offending, hesitancy to defend the right of the Danish cartoonists to portray Muhammad, and general apologetics for Islamic terror. Popular attitudes are quite different when it comes to the United States or to Israel and the Jews:

"For condemned Europeans, there remains one exit that will allow them to avoid decline: shifting the blame to two nations unworthy of European civilization, Israel and the United States, repudiating them in order to redeem ourselves." And if Israel is to be consigned to the outer darkness, "there still remains, to quench their thirst for the absolute, a final noble savage: the Palestinian. He is the great Christ-like icon, the oppressed of the oppressed, whose beatification has been proceeding for the past thirty years. And the fact that his situation has hardly improved makes it possible to keep alive the revolt he incarnates."

Bruckner explains the centrality of the Palestinians to European leftists as due to their poverty, that some of the Jews they are fighting came from Europe, and that the Palestinians are Muslims, "that is, members of a religion that part of the Left thinks is the spearhead of the disinherited." Of course, the final push is the dissipation of the more traditional vectors of leftist hopes: the collapse of communism, the growing conservatism of the proletariat. "What is surprising about this," he adds, "is that the preference of a minority has become a majority choice." And finally:

"People who support the Palestinians are not hoping to aid flesh-and-blood human beings but pure ideas: on the east coast of the Mediterranean, intellectuals, writers, and politicians are not so much engaged in inquiring into a specific antagonism — a real estate dispute involving two equally legitimate owners, as Amos Oz put it — as in settling accounts with Western culture."

There are, of course, legitimate grievances on the Palestinian side (as there are on the Israeli), but these are obsessively promoted by Europeans — and by American leftists — prodigiously disproportionately to the far more distressed peoples of Chechnya, Tibet, Darfur, and the Congo, listed by Bruckner. I could add Zimbabwe, North Korea, Burma, Somalia, and Syria, and probably a dozen other places where there is greater repression or blood-letting than in the occupied territories, even miserable Gaza, for whose suffering certainly Hamas with its actual and threatened violence must bear important though not sole responsibility.

Bruckner explains this, for Europe, as an opportunity to "clear itself of its past offenses against Judaism." Israel's Western critics have shown no second thoughts about the side they are supporting when high levels of the Arab and Iranian governments and commercial media accuse the Jews of fabricating the Holocaust, of secretly carrying out the 9/11 attacks, of creating HIV/AIDS to wipe out the Gentiles, of secretly hiring the Danish cartoonists, and even, Bruckner notes, of having caused the December 2004 tsunami, using a secret underground nuclear blast. There is also the flood in Arabic and Farsi of the *Protocols of the Elders of Zion* and a large swath of old Nazi anti-Jewish propaganda materials. Anyone who follows the Middle East Media Research Institute (MEMRI) translation service would also find that government newspapers and television and very senior religious leaders regularly call for the physical extermination of the whole of the Jewish people, in and out of Israel, who are referred to as descendants of apes and pigs.

"Zionism," which by its Arab and leftist critics has been reduced to any defense of the right of Israel to exist, is little more than a swear-word, while "anti-Zionism" most often means not some dispute over the right of return or Israel's proclaimed status as an international homeland of the world's Jews, what the term has meant historically to Jews, but the much narrower call to disenfranchise the existing Jewish population of Israel, either by way of expulsion from the region or their submersion as a minority in an Islamic state.

In Europe, Bruckner writes, "the Palestinian question has quietly relegitimated hatred of the Jews. Here we can certainly agree with Bernard Lewis when he says that for many of their supporters, 'the Arabs are in truth nothing more than a stick for beating the Jews.'"

Bruckner quotes from a 1986 work by Vladimir Jankelevitch:

> Anti-Zionism is in this respect a rare Godsend, because it gives us the permission and even the right and even the duty to be anti-Semitic in

the name of democracy! Anti-Zionism is anti-Semitism justified, finally made available to everyone. It is the permission to be democratically anti-Semitic. What if the Jews themselves were Nazis? That would be great. We would no longer have to feel sorry for them; they would have deserved what they got.

The leftist Israel haters — and in Europe this current spreads much wider than the left — repeatedly deny that they are anti-Semitic, or that calling for the destruction of Israel has any anti-Semitic coloration, or even that any significant degree of anti-Semitism still exists in the world outside of a few right-wing fringe organizations. For anyone who believes this I would suggest a look at Robert S. Wistrich's *A Lethal Obsession: Anti-Semitism from Antiquity to the Global Jihad*, which in its sections on Europe alone provides shocking evidence that a very large minority of the population of all the major countries (Italy and Spain are the worst but France is a runner-up, where thousands of Jews have fled the country to escape physical attacks and synagogue burnings by Muslim immigrants) harbor extreme hostility toward domestic Jews as well as toward the Jewish state. And in the United States a deep anti-Americanism on much of the far left has included a long campaign against all the currents of Israeli society except a handful of Jewish Marxists and the Arab sector. This has spread to a hostility to American Jews who support Israel, even critically, hardening into a widespread left-wing anti-Semitism.

Observing and opposing this current does not require prettifying the Israeli system as the American Right does. The settler movement is a blot on Israel's honor, the Netanyahu government has stalled the nominal peace process into deep freeze. At the same time, Hamas remains unremittingly opposed to even the presence of Jews in the region much less with a state in any borders, and there is no guarantee that Fatah will remain dominant in the Palestinian lands and not lose ground to Hamas as it did in Gaza. Still, the occupation has gone on too long and its persistence is untenable.

But opposition to the Israeli occupation by Western leftists and liberals has become pathological. There are many repressive regimes in the world, Israel's mainly in the occupied territories, not so much within the 1967 borders. The Israelis are repeatedly accused of being "Nazis." To Nazify the Israelis, Bruckner writes, "is to delegitimize the state of Israel, and it is also to Judaize the Arabs, shifting the ancient battle against ignominy to the banks of the Jordan. Ultimately, it is to justify in advance the possible disappearance of Israel, that 'usurping entity.'"

And:

The counterpart of the extreme Right's ancient accusation that the Jews are cosmopolitans is the Left's claim that the state of Israel is illegitimate. So now the hatred of the West finds its vehicle in hatred of the Jews, who have become its emblematic community after having been, for centuries, its scapegoat. . . . And thus we also find an incredible tolerance among our intellectual, political, and media elites for Palestinian terrorism: attacks and suicide bombers are condemned, but only faintly, and even justified as acts of desperation. . . . In their view, no horror committed by candidates for suicide, with their grotesque mythology of the seventy virgins awaiting them in Paradise, will ever make up for the ignominy of the Israelis. The victims of these explosions matter little, and still less the culture of death spread among the youth of the West Bank and Gaza. Our indulgence is deeply imbued with condescendence; we don't ask whether the encouragements sent out by militants hiding in their European or American bastions isn't suicidal for the Palestinians themselves or burdens their desire for peace and decency.

In some cases this anti-Jewish tilt is not even justified as ideological belief but is crass politicking, as when Pascal Boniface, director of a major French think tank, advised the Socialist Party in 2001 to abandon support to Israel in order to court the French Muslim vote.

Leftist anti-Semitism in Europe is closely linked to anti-Americanism, the penance Europeans do to exculpate their own colonial past:

"The phobia of America, our last civic religion in Western Europe, allows us to escape our guilty conscience by affiliating ourselves with formerly colonized continents. France, Germany, Spain, and Italy, having become political dwarfs, seem to proclaim in the public eye: we are divorcing ourselves from the West in order to come closer to the South." He notes that this is also a concession to Ahmadinejad and al-Qaeda, who have promised to go lightly on Europe if it will break with the United States and Israel.

Judging America's place in the world order depends on how one views its adversaries. For those who see only the, now former, colonial world it looks one way. For Bruckner, the United States "As the victor, along with its allies, over Nazism and then communism, and as the leader of the fight against Islamism, it can be proud of its recent history, despite its flaws." Of course, essential here is how one regards jihadi Islamism, perhaps the single greatest touchstone of contemporary international politics.

Bruckner's instinct is for an interventionist part in global life. It is what he most admires about the United States, its postwar absence much of what he despairs of in contemporary Europe:

"[T]he true crime of old Europe is not only what it did in the past, but what it is not doing today — its inaction in the course of the 1990s in the Balkans, its scandalous wait-and-see attitude in Rwanda, its silence on Chechnya, its indifference to Darfur and western Sudan, and in general its indulgence, its kowtowing, its servility." It leaves "to the Yankee big brother to do the dirty work, while criticizing him harshly later on. Whatever America does, whether it intervenes or stands aside, it is always wrong."

This could be said as well of much of the American left.

The Tyranny of Guilt was written in 2006, so perhaps could be modified a bit by the show of backbone in French and British aid to the Libyan opposition in 2011 and the EU's decision in 2012 to refuse to purchase Iranian oil.

George Orwell during World War II complained of the Europeanized British Left, unable even in a mortal national crisis to bring themselves to feel anything like patriotism to their country. This same mood of detachment from history and place numbs much of Europe today.

> [W]e refuse to defend our societies: we would rather abolish ourselves than show even a tiny bit of attachment to them. This is a double error: by erecting lack of love for oneself into a leading principle, we lie to ourselves about ourselves and close ourselves to others. It is a mistake to think that self-devaluation is going to open us up, as if by a miracle, to distant peoples. . . . In Western self-hatred, the Other has no place. It is a narcissistic relationship in which the African, the Indian, and the Arab are brought in as extras in an endless drama about settling scores.

And finally, "Let us beware of anyone who values the foreigner only out of disdain for himself."

Bruckner's plea for valuing the Western heritage rejects uncritical jingoism. "We are not talking here of falling into extreme nationalistic pride . . . of the kind defended by the extreme Right, which seeks . . . to provide a glorifying vision of history: this school asserts the grandeur of a country despite its crimes, but we have to be proud of ourselves *against* our crimes because we have recognized them and rejected them."

In the later part of his essay Bruckner critiques professional victimhood and the excesses of multiculturalism.

Each victimized people of course supposes that its sufferings have been the greatest the world has ever seen. And because the Holocaust is the gold standard of victimhood, it has been common, even for Holocaust deniers, to say that their people are undergoing a Holocaust, and at the very least a genocide. "It is as if other peoples, competing with Jews for the privilege of annihilation, were to shout: 'Auschwitz is us!'" In England, Sir Iqbal Sacranie, secretary-general of the Muslim Council of Britain, has declared that "Muslims feel hurt and excluded that their lives are not equally valuable to those lives lost in the Holocaust time." He asked that the Palestinians and the Iraqis killed in the U.S. war be included in a general "Day of Genocide."

Bruckner also cites numerous authors who project Nazism far into the past to describe many kinds of governmental atrocity of the eighteenth or early nineteenth centuries as prefiguring Hitler, the gold standard of evil. These excursions into hyperbole are generally claims to pride of place among victims, often staking out an ironclad claim to exemption from any responsibility for crimes or racist acts perpetrated by proclaimed victim people.

Our author similarly has little patience for present-day warriors against neocolonialism. Perpetually rehashing the crimes of the past is very different from having fought them at the time. "They make one think of those Japanese soldiers scattered around the Pacific islands who at the end of the twentieth century still didn't know that the Second World War was over. It is a vocation to be a hero once the fighting is over; it gives you the luster of being a sniper without exposing you to the slightest danger."

In today's globalized world, he says, the real danger for former colonial peoples

> is not expansion but abandonment. . . . According to the economist Paul Bairoch's brusque formulation, "The West doesn't need the Third World, which is bad news for the Third World." In short, to the misfortune of being exploited corresponds the still greater misfortune of no longer being exploitable, of being abandoned. What threatens many deprived countries in the South is not the invasion of the capitalist octopus, but the inverse: no longer interesting either investors or large economic groups, being excluded from global circuits.

Bruckner turns to multiculturalism. If its originating idea is the worthy promotion of ethnic, religious, female, or gay pride, its unintended consequence has been to whittle away at what unites a people:

> Unless there is a federating national or supranational narrative that brings all the diverse components of a country together and gives them a common impulse, the country becomes an agglomeration of black, North African, Gypsy, Antillese, Corsican, gay, etc. tribes unified by their mutual dissensions and relying on the state only as a simple mediating authority. Then identity ceases to coincide with citizenship; it is in fact what makes citizenship impossible.

He explores this theme in its various dimensions. For immigrants — and this is a particular problem for Europe in its general failure to integrate the very large numbers of Muslim immigrants into the majority cultures — if nations are to survive they must have enough self-confidence to inspire allegiance to their general values, not simply provide some sort of housing and living for hostile enclaves within themselves, not a process of homogenization in which minority cultures are submerged but in which they also share core values with the other components of the national body.

On another axis, Bruckner sees a great obstacle for individuals to be seen for themselves if society has segmented itself into many distinct camps, most of them claiming recompense for some form of victimhood. "Individuals exist as such only when their singularity is more important than their nationality, the color of their skin, or their membership in a group." And further:

> All the ambiguity of multiculturalism proceeds from the fact that with the best intentions, it imprisons men, women, and children in a way of life and in traditions from which they often aspire to free themselves. The politics of identity in fact reaffirm difference at the very moment when we are trying to establish equality, and lead, in the name of anti-racism, back to the old commitments connected with race or ethnicity.

The end result is usually the creation of "a micro-nationalism that is just as jingoistic" as the majority state from which it distinguishes itself, "a legal apartheid in which we find the wealthy once again explaining tenderly to the poor that money won't make them happy . . . you have the joys of custom, forced marriages, the veil, polygamy, and clitoridectomy. The members of these little congregations then become museum pieces, the inhabitants of a reservation whom we want to preserve from the 'calamities' of progress and civilization."

Bruckner calls for "a double battle," to protect minorities from discrimination, to preserve their languages where this applies, their cultures, but to at the same time protect individuals from within minorities who wish to break free of constraints from within or without the group that deny them an individual identity.

What, then, are we to make of Pascal Bruckner's message? He challenges many of the beloved shibboleths of much of the American far left: the American evil empire, Israel's uniquely ineradicable guilt, the beatitude of the Palestinian cause, the justification of jihad, the justness of the sectoral protest movements summed up in multiculturalism, the call for open borders and limitless immigration, and the celebration of Third World victims of imperialism. Is all of that overdone, one-sided, or outright wrong? I think so. The views Bruckner critiques, with the exception of left-wing anti-Semitism, which has deeper and darker causes, are left-overs from the sixties, the era when colonialism was just in process of collapsing, when white racism and male patriarchalism remained dominant paradigms in Europe and the United States, and the problem for members of minority groups of establishing identities as individuals not heavily defined by their race, religion, or sexual orientation not yet in the forefront.

It is natural that Bruckner would devote more attention to these flaws in a leftist world view than the claustrophobic truisms of the far Right. In France the Left has been dominant since 1945, the mirror image of the United States. In America the dominant, though declining, paradigm is that of the white religious Right. The whole of the Obama administration has been a defensive struggle against the very effective stonewalling by the ever more conservative Republican machine, while the current bizarre and extended Republican primary has been a contest over which candidate can present himself as the most religiously intolerant, the most ready to divert more money to the super rich, the most hateful toward gays and women, and the most hard-hearted toward the poor or even just the suddenly unemployed.

Curiously, in both countries the liberalism that Bruckner defends is repudiated by the predominant tendency. Speaking of France, Bruckner could just as well be talking about America when he writes: "One word synthesizes this feeling of dread, a word that has become indecent, like fascism or pedophilia: liberalism."

In France it is the far Left that plays the obstructive role occupied by the Religious Right in the United States. "It is to the far Left that we have to justify ourselves, and it is the far Left that is preventing the development of a true social democracy on the English Labour Party model or the Scandinavian model: those who act or legislate must measure themselves against this ideological standard that has replaced the Church and moral authorities. All intellectuals bow down before it and embroider nice variations around its fundamental themes: no speech is accepted if it does not begin with a firm condemnation of the market."

Bruckner concludes that both far Left and Right are obstacles to the necessary reforms: a regulated market economy funding a strong welfare state, as well as recognition that in today's world, democratic countries face genuine threats: "Democracies have to be powerfully armed in order not to be defeated by the forces of tyranny." In such a world a far Left that "supports any dictatorship provided that it is anticapitalist and anti-American" is a wholly negative element.

He sees the split between Europe and the United States as disastrous for the future of democracy. Europe must be taught "that battles are not won by compromise and incantation alone," the U.S. "that it is not the only country on Earth, invested with a providential mission that makes it unnecessary for it to seek the approval of others, to listen and to debate, that trying to do what is good for people no matter what they want is a recipe for disaster."

And finally, "If America were to collapse tomorrow, Europe would fall like a house of cards," but if Europe were to be dismembered by internal and external predators, "America's prospects would not be bright, either."

Ideas that had some validity at some point in time become engrained in people's minds and remain as new eras arise where they are falsified by events but still powerful. Marxists were among the first to grasp this fact with their theory of base and superstructure. Unfortunately the Marxists are as subject to such processes as every other current of thought. The truisms of progressivism of the sixties have in large part become problematic a half century later.

February 26, 2012

Part 3:
Vernon and Its Discontents

The Furlongs of Vernon and Van Buren Place

[This piece, slightly abridged here, was co-authored by my wife, Jennifer Charnofsky, who did much of the research. It was submitted in support of the nomination of our 1910 Craftsman home at 2657 Van Buren Place in the West Adams section of Los Angeles as a city Historic Cultural Monument, on the basis of its architectural merit but principally on the grounds that it was for almost forty years the home of an important part of the Furlong family, founders and long-time leaders of the industrial city of Vernon. The application was approved by the Los Angeles Cultural Heritage Commission in April 2000, which named it The Furlong House, Historic Cultural Monument #678. This article was written in 1999, six years before the Vernon scandal, covered elsewhere in this book, had broken. I have not attempted to update those parts. Because of its formal purpose it is more heavily annotated than the other essays in the book, and constitutes a piece of local history.]

* * *

The house at 2657 S. Van Buren Place was built in 1910 by Hugh M. and Margaret Cowper, apparently with the intention of selling it. The first residents were Shelley W. and Bella Keiser. Shelley Keiser was a real estate broker and later vice president of the Equitable Loan and Investments Co. The Keisers lived in the house from 1910 to 1921, when it was sold to Thomas J. Furlong, the City Clerk and Treasurer of the City of Vernon.

The history of Vernon is intimately tied to the Furlong family. While it was for many decades the principal industrial center for Los Angeles, Vernon was from its inception the creation and virtual property of three men: John Baptiste Leonis (1872–1953), for whom Leonis Blvd. is named, and brothers Thomas J. Furlong (1872–1950) and James Furlong (1876–1941). These three men founded Vernon in 1905 from farmland they owned south and east of the

Los Angeles Civic Center. They envisioned their new city as an exclusively industrial enclave freed from responsibilities to other kinds of residents. While as many as 70,000 people work there during the day, its registered population has dropped from 1,700 in 1905 to fewer than 300 today, almost all of whom are city employees living in rented city housing. Thomas J. Furlong served continuously as City Clerk and Treasurer of Vernon from 1907 until his death in 1950. His brother James Furlong served as Mayor of Vernon from 1907 until his death in 1941. He was succeeded as Mayor by John B. Leonis, who was in turn succeeded by Robert Furlong (1908–1974), the son of Thomas J. Furlong. Robert served as Mayor continuously from 1948 until his death in 1974. Robert lived in the house at Van Buren Place from the time he was thirteen in 1921 until he sold the house in 1958 at the age of fifty. Even today Vernon is governed by Mayor Leonis C. Malburg, grandson of John B. Leonis.

Industrial pioneers James and Thomas J. Furlong were part of a large clan influential in Southern California history in many ways. They were grandchildren of Thomas Furlong (1788-?) and Ann Sinnott of Wexford, Ireland, seat of the Furlong name, which has considerable antiquity in that region.[1] Thomas Furlong and Ann Sinnott had five children. Of these, four emigrated to California—Robert, Luke, James, and Mary.

The Parents' Generation: Emigration from Ireland

The brothers that concern us were grandsons of Thomas Furlong of Wexford through his son Robert (1836-1881). Robert fought in the Crimean

---

[1] The name is dated to the 1390s in County Wexford, and "the name is rarely found outside County Wexford" (*Bardsley* 1875: 255). The Furlong geneology is somewhat difficult to follow because the family was large and favored use of the male names Thomas, James, Luke, and Robert, while for women there are many Marys, Marthas, and Catherines. In brief, the family is traced from Thomas and Ann Sinnott Furlong of Wexford, Ireland. In the next generation, beginning in our account in the 1850s, Robert, James, and Luke come to California, where Robert and James settle in Vernon. Robert's children are the principal subject of our interest. These are Thomas J. Furlong, who owned the house on Van Buren Place, and his three siblings, James, Annie, and Judith. Thomas has four children with Catherine "Kate" Conneally: Robert, Catherine, Mary, and Martha. These are the main characters of this narrative. Others who appear briefly are the older James's son Luke, first cousin to Thomas J., and, as sources of family history, the children of Thomas J.'s daughter Martha Furlong from her marriage to Anthony Tavernelli: Kath-leen Tavernelli Behné, Thomas Tavernelli, and Denis Tavernelli, and Kate Conneally Furlong's nephew, Father Philip Conneally.

War, then took ship for Canada with his older brother Luke, landing in Quebec in September 1857. In Montreal they heard of the gold rush in California and decided to try their hands at mining. Robert and Luke sailed to Panama, trekked across the isthmus on foot, and found a ship bound for San Francisco. From there they headed for the gold fields in Tuolumne County. Later they were joined by their brother James who had deserted from the British army after a fight with a superior officer and spent some years under an assumed name as a gold miner in Australia (Cecilia Anne Furlong 1980: 27-32).

In 1868 Robert and Luke moved south and bought 41 acres of land at Rancho Los Nietos, between the Santa Ana and the Old San Gabriel rivers, where they took up hog raising. After a few years Robert sent for his childhood sweetheart, Martha Kehoe, from Ireland. While Martha, accompanied by her sister Ann, was on shipboard, the president of the Hibernia Bank in San Francisco, where Robert had his life savings, embezzled the whole of the bank's money and fled to France. Robert offered to send his fiancee back to Ireland but she opted to stay with him and they were married in May 1871 at the Mission San Gabriel.

In 1872, after a disastrous flood of the Old San Gabriel River, Robert, Martha, and Luke moved their ranch to land west of Compton, then called Willowbrook. Here Robert and Martha's first three children were born: Thomas (1872), Annie (1873) and James (1876). Martha's sister, Ann Kehoe, who had not intended to remain in America, married Robert's brother James, and they established a ranch at Vernondale, as Vernon was then called.

In 1877 Robert's brother Luke died, leaving a young widow and an infant son, who lived for some time with Robert's family, then moved on to San Francisco. In 1881 Robert and Martha also bought a ranch at Vernon and moved their family there. The property was at what is now 2048 E. 52nd Street and remained a home of the Furlongs until 1972. Robert Furlong moved the original house he and Luke had built on the banks of the Old San Gabriel River in 1868 to this property (it had already been moved once, from Los Nietos to Willowbrook in 1874).[2] Robert and Martha had one more child at the ranch in Vernondale: Judith Mary (1881). Judith lived at the ranch the whole of her long life. Judith's daughter Roberta later recalled a story of her mother's:

> On a day when Grandmother, "Mama Martha," was out in the fields supervising the Mexican and Chinese laborers who worked on the ranch, she left Judith in bed with influenza and a bad cold. By her bed was a bottle of wine and a glass. Mama Martha told her to take a

---

[2] McGroarty 1933: 583; Cecilia Anne Furlong 1980: 37, 45.

small glass every three hours. Judith, never one to waste time, thought it would be better if she finished it off quickly so she could be well again and up and out to play. When her Mother came in she found Judith completely out. From then on she was such a complete teetotaler that if we wanted her to take a toddy for a cold we held her in one arm and the glass in the other hand so she would not go to sleep before we got it down. (Roberta Poxon, undated notes.)

Robert Furlong died of scarlet fever in 1881, when Thomas, his oldest child, was 9. The four children and their mother Martha remained on the ranch, which was managed by Robert's surviving brother James, whose property adjoined theirs. James worked both farms with the help of his two sons and the two orphaned sons of his brother Robert. Thomas's younger brother James was able to attend a Catholic high school, St. Vincent's College,[3] but Thomas had to drop out of school when his father died and had no further formal education, although he was a voracious reader (Cecilia Anne Furlong 1980: 45).

In 1904 Thomas's Uncle James sold his holdings and moved several miles away, leaving the sons of his brother Robert, now in their early thirties and late twenties, to run their mother's farm. That same year Thomas J. Furlong married Kate (Catherine) Conneally and built a home for her on the Furlong ranch. There their four children were born—Robert, Mary, and the twins Martha and Catherine.[4] In 1915 they moved to 322 N. Oxford Street, at Kate's insistence as she feared the effect of industrial pollution on her children and she wanted a neighborhood with a good Catholic school. Thus Thomas was the only one of the four brothers and sisters to move away from Vernon and from the Furlong ranch. This was a cause of serious friction with his brother and sisters, and caused him some trouble later in life as he was challenged by officials in Los Angeles, who often had a hostile attitude toward Vernon, for holding a civic office in Vernon without living in the city. He response was a lifelong habit of putting in extremely long hours on his job.[5] In 1921 Thomas and Kate and their four children moved to the house on Van Buren Place. Here they had a house of three stories with twelve rooms. But in the old-fashioned manner, they rarely used the living room—it was saved "for when

---

[3] This later became Loyola High School.

[4] Cecilia Anne Furlong 1980: 68. Thomas's first cousin, Luke Furlong (the son of his Uncle James, not the brother of Robert and James who had come from Ireland) also married a Conneally bride. The families remain closely linked to the present time.

[5] Interview by Jennifer Charnofsky with Father Philip Conneally, July 10, 1994.

the parson came."[6] Instead they gathered in the little room off the kitchen. Thomas Tavernelli, Thomas's grandson, remembers the Van Buren house from his childhood in the late 1940s. The street still had a rural feel to it. "The people across the street had chickens, and we bought vegetables off a horse-drawn cart. There were some people living on Vermont nearby who got their water from a spring at Beverly and Rampart."[7]

Vernon—The Early Years

Vernon before it was incorporated was mostly pig farms and Chinese-owned truck gardens. It was a terminus for the Butterfield Stage Coach line which ran to Long Beach and San Pedro. Among its prominent residents in addition to the Furlong brothers was the French-Basque immigrant John Baptiste Leonis. Leonis operated a general store in Vernon, and later established a feed barn and winery at 26th Street and Downey Road (Kilty 1963: 18-19). Leonis offered free land to factories willing to locate in Vernon, expecting that the jobs created would mean money spent in town that would repay the cost of the land. By 1905 there were two factories and two lumber yards in Vernon, and some of the pig farms were in transition to becoming meat packers.

About the time of his marriage, Thomas with his brother James began discussions with Leonis, in which Leonis proposed the idea of the first industrial park in Southern California. Between them they owned a large part of the suburb. They sounded out other landowners, such as P. J. Durbin and William M. Stevens, and brought them into the plan. In 1905 this group moved to formally incorporate Vernon as a city, giving it the motto it still proclaims, "Exclusively Industrial." Their experiment was later imitated in the creation of the City of Commerce and the City of Industry, but Vernon was and remains the preeminent industrial-commercial enclave. From that time, Leonis, Thomas and James Furlong, and rancher William M. Stevens entrenched themselves as the dominant force on the new city's Board of Trustees. The eventual boundaries of the City of Vernon were 25th Street and Washington Blvd. on the north, the Los Angeles River on the east, Slauson on the south, and Alameda Street on the west. Cecilia Anne Furlong writes:

---

[6] Telephone interview by Jennifer Charnofsky with Leo Poxon (son of Judith Furlong Poxon, Thomas J.'s sister), 1994

[7] Telephone interview by Jennifer Charnofsky with Thomas Tavernelli (son of Martha Furlong, grandson of Thomas J. Furlong), 1994. Interviews by Jennifer Charnofsky with Kath-leen Tavernelli Behné and with Father Philip Conneally.

After the City was incorporated Tom and James bought and sold pieces of property to new factories, or rented it out to them with life-time leases. Tom traveled from his home in West Los Angeles to his office in Vernon. However, he frequently met with James at the ranch, and as a result, Annie and Judith shared the thoughts of their brothers and were cognizant of the business of running a city.

Vernon established its own school district, and built an elementary school for the benefit of the children of the families of the workers who lived within its five mile radius. Judith Furlong was one of the first teachers. This was only one of her many contributions to the growth and development of this small city, in whose government she later participated as a councilwoman. (Cecilia Anne Furlong 1980: 65-66.)

James Furlong is remembered in Los Angeles history not only as the first Mayor of the new industrial city, but also as one of the first landowners in Los Angeles to sell land for homes to black families. In a retrospective arti-cle in 1995 the *Los Angeles Times* wrote:

> At the turn of the century, the African American community had grown to more than 2,200 people.... Downtown, many blacks settled along Jefferson Boulevard, between Normandie and Western Ave-nue.... Others bought parcels of land about five miles south of Down-town from an Irish farmer named James Furlong.
>
> In 1905, Furlong subdivided his land bounded by Long Beach Avenue and Alameda, 50th and 55th streets. He sold his lots to black families for the going price of $750. From the start, the Furlong Tract was a working-class area, settled by people ... who were barred from other areas by restrictive racial covenants or high prices....
>
> Some families lived in tents while they built their modest homes. Eventually, the tract had more than 200 houses, grocery stores, a pharmacy, doctors' offices, a florist, dry cleaners, an ice cream parlor, a real estate office, an icehouse, a community hall, three churches and a school. (*Los Angeles Times,* February 13, 1995, Metro section p. B3.)

Vernon in the early days was something of a frontier town out of a western movie. Next to the pig farms and new factories a string of bars and brothels opened, where Angelenos clustered on Sundays for the hot night life. Shortly after the town was incorporated there were three saloons, the most popular of which was Jack Doyle's Central Saloon at the corner of Santa Fe Avenue and the well-named Joy Street. Soon Leonis himself founded an even bigger place at Santa Fe and 38th Street, and leased it to Jack Doyle, a former Southern

Pacific engineer, who built Jack Doyle's Saloon into one of the most famous bars in the region. Vernon's prominent citizens quickly split into two factions. On one side was the Board of Trustees majority, led by Leonis, the Furlongs, and Stevens.

On the other was the sole dissenter on the Board, W. S. Holland, supported by wealthy farmer J. G. De Turk and City Marshal J. H. Neiman. The Board of Trustees majority postponed the election scheduled for April 1906, arousing loud protests and a legal challenge from the opposition. Then in 1908 the two factions fought it out in a bitter election. The Leonis-Furlong-Stevens camp called themselves the Independents, while Holland and De Turk created a new Business Men's Party, which accused the Independents of making the town undesirable for business by encouraging drinking and prostitution. One Los Angeles newspaper wrote: "Sunday the town is wide open and drunken men stagger on the streets, toughs shout ribald remarks at passing women and crap games are played" (cited by Kilty 1963: 24).

The Independents, however, had something larger in mind than a rowdy red-light district, and were soon to develop Vernon as not only an industrial city but also a center for Los Angeles night life and major sports promotions. The Independents won, although the election was followed by long court fights as each side accused the other of stuffing the ballot boxes (a total of 174 votes were cast!). When the dust settled, James Furlong was confirmed as Mayor of Vernon, and was not unseated in his lifetime.

The Business Men's faction retaliated by refusing to honor a city contract signed by the incumbents to allow the Union Oil Company to trench an oil pipeline across J. G. De Turk's farm, one piece of the right of way sold to Union Oil by the city government. De Turk repudiated his signature on the permits and his young wife drove the Union Oil crew off her land with a shotgun. The pipeline had to be abandoned. (Kilty 1963: 31.)

Almost simultaneous with the 1908 elections was a second battle between the same two factions which helped to clarify their different perspectives for the city. It seemed that most of the supporters of the Business Men's Party were hog farmers rather than industrialists. The Board of Trustees majority came into conflict with the hog farmers over the importing from Los Angeles of tons of garbage used to feed the pigs. This created odor and vermin that discouraged other kinds of industry from buying land in Vernon. The Board of Trustees passed a law against dumping garbage within the city limits and interpreted it to cover garbage meant for pig feed. William Stevens announced he would arrest all of the prominent hog farmers if they defied the law. This issue threatened to split the Board of Trustees itself, as the Furlongs were hog farmers and James, the Mayor, was one of the "Solid Three" on the Board with Leonis and Stevens.

For several weeks the Los Angeles press speculated as to which way James would vote. In the end the Furlongs were convinced that the practices of the pig farmers would have to change to make room for modern industry. The united Board of Trustees ordered the arrest of seven of the leading hog farmers from the Business Men's Party and the city entered onto its modern path.

As the end of the fight with the hog farmers came into view, the Board of Trustees majority took steps to promote Vernon in the public mind by making it a center for professional boxing. James Kilty, a local sports writer who worked for Jack Doyle and John B. Leonis for thirty years, describes this effort:

> The enterprising little group, under the leadership of John B. Leonis, with James Furlong and his brother, Thomas Furlong, long established residents of the district, started a campaign to advertise the city through sports. That their venture was successful is attested by the fact that the city of Vernon was considered the boxing capital of the world from 1908 until the 1920s. (Kilty 1963: 38.)

Then-heavyweight champion of the world James J. Jeffries, in partnership with New York promoter Baron Long, were authorized to construct the Vernon Arena. This was a 15,000 capacity wooden stadium at the corner of 25th Street and Santa Fe Avenue. For two decades the Vernon Arena was the center in Los Angeles and even in the country for world championship bouts. Fighters such as Bert Colima, Packay McFarland, Danny Webster, Tommy Burns, Aurilla Herrera, Battling Nelson, and many others appeared there. Jack Doyle constructed a boxing training center next to his saloon and expanded the saloon to house the boxing crowds. Jack Doyle's became famous as "the longest bar in the world." The bar boasted 37 bartenders, all imported from Ireland, and each with his own cash register. It was packed on the weekends by the sports aficionados (Kilty 1963).

Vernon also founded its own baseball team, the Vernon Tigers, who were three-time winners of the Pacific Coast Baseball League pennant. They defeated the Saint Paul team to win the American Association pennant in 1919. These big time sporting events kept Vernon in the public eye and led to the construction of restaurants such as Jack Doyle's Stag Hotel and Baron Long's Vernon Country Club. Enough money was flowing into the city that in 1919 Leonis founded his own bank, the First National Bank of Vernon, and appointed James Furlong and Jack Doyle directors (Kilty 1963: 47; McGroarty 1933: 584).

In 1913 the Furlong family, by now far from the difficult times after Robert's death in 1881, built the only church in Vernon, St. Martha's Church, named for their mother and her patron saint. Judith was married in St. Martha's the year it opened, to English chemist George Poxon from Stoke-on-Trent. Poxon was a graduate of the British Royal Academy of Science who "wanted to lease some property and start a pottery where he could test his ideas and glazes."[8] Together they founded the well-known Poxon Pottery and the Vernon Kilns, which made dishes of all kinds under the name Vernon Ware. They are perhaps best known for their collectible commemorative plates, still a staple of antique stores throughout the country.[9] The kilns were located on the Furlong ranch in Vernon, where the Poxon's built their home.

During World War I industry began to move into Vernon in substantial numbers. The Crescent Refining and Oil Company was founded there in 1917, followed by the Gilmore Oil Company, for a time the top independent oil company in the area. The Fernholtz Machinery Company also was started during the first world war. By 1927 there were 300 factories or other industrial enterprises in Vernon employing more than 20,000 workers (Kilty 1963: 49).

The passage of Prohibition in 1919 damaged and eventually destroyed Vernon's night life. James Kilty reminisces:

> At night, Vernon's silent streets that were once alive with thousands of boxing followers and before that with the night life crowd who patronized Baron Long's Vernon Country Club; the sporting fraternity that followed the silent movie stars, the dance girls, harlots and gamblers; this strange little community can only look back with fond remembrance and see it as it once was. (Kilty 1963: 66.)

But the passing of this scene did little to slow the growth of the industrial city. "Presidents of oil companies," Kilty writes, "railroad tycoons, heads of the packing industries, builders and contractors and nearly all of the big businessmen of Vernon's early period met at [Jack Doyle's] restaurant's round

---

[8] Roberta Poxon (daughter of George Poxon and Judith Furlong Poxon), undated copy of handwritten notes recounting stories of her mother. Courtesy of Father Philip Conneally.

[9] Poxon Pottery was sold to Metlox of Manhattan Beach, California, in 1946, and the name was changed officially to Vernonware. See the books by Maxine Nelson in the reference list for further information on Vernon Kilns.

table to discuss business ventures that were later established in Vernon. It was the spawning grounds for hundreds of enterprises that totaled millions of dollars for this great industrial center (p. 139).

Robert Furlong and the Vernon Power Plant

In the 1940s the founding generation of the city began to pass from the scene. But the 1930s was already a time of transition where the next generation began to enter Vernon politics. The principal figure that concerns us is Robert Furlong, Thomas and Kate Furlong's son and the city's future Mayor. Robert graduated from Loyola University in 1929 with a degree in engineering. Better educated than his parents' generation, he went to work for the Edison Company in Vernon as a diesel engineer. The city government predicated its appeal to industrial development on being able to provide good rail transport, cheap land, low taxes, and low rates for electrical power. This last put the city in a long-term argument with the major utilities in Los Angeles from which it bought its power. Counting on Robert's expertise, the City Council—led by his uncle the Mayor, his father the Treasurer, and John B. Leonis—at the beginning of the 1930s decided to outflank the Edison Company by building their own power plant. Never ones to do anything on a small scale, they proceeded to construct the largest diesel power generating plant in the world with the exception of one in Shanghai. The plant, which went into operation in 1933, was important enough to rate a 16-page article in the trade journal *Diesel Power*. Robert Furlong became chief operating engineer of the new 35,000 horsepower diesel plant.

The Vernon plant was cutting edge when it was built, using a newly developed cooling process of continuous filtration of the cooling oil (*Diesel Power* 1933: 616). By filtering the fuel the operators were free to buy whatever fuel was cheapest at the moment and were not restricted to high grade pre-filtered varieties. This same source stated:

> Probably no plant, regardless of its capacity, has a more complete electrical control board than has Vernon. Coordination of the plant and the distribution system is made possible, leading to the highest possible economy. (Ibid.)

The plant was so well built that more than 65 years later it is still in service and provides the majority of the electric power used by Vernon today, despite the enormous increase in demand over these six and a half decades. The plant is itself a Los Angeles Historic-Cultural Monument. The present authors toured the plant in 1994 and interviewed its present superintendent, James L.

Siegert. The building boasts a beautiful Streamline Moderne façade. Its interior is spotless, with the rows of tall dark green turbines looking as though they were just built, but came from the sets for the Emerald City for the "Wizard of Oz."[10]

Robert ran the Vernon power plant until the outbreak of World War II. He was elected to the City Council in June 1941. Shortly after the bombing of Pearl Harbor that December, he enlisted as an army engineer. He saw active service in North Africa and Italy under General Patton.[11]

On his return home, Robert was reelected to the Vernon City Council in 1946. His uncle James had died in 1941, and John B. Leonis, although in failing health, was serving as Mayor. Finally Leonis was compelled by his health to retire in 1948 and Robert was elected to replace him.

In February 1950 Robert's father, Thomas J. Furlong, died. In his obituary *The Tidings* of Vernon wrote:

> During the first decade of the century when the civic leaders of Los Angeles were promoting their city as a pleasure resort for tourists, the Furlongs were working for the establishment of heavy industries. Today the central manufacturing district of Vernon is a tribute to their judicious planning. With their favorite project in mind they refused to subdivide their ranch—holding it for the day when industry would clamor for space. At the time of his death, the late Thomas J. Furlong was still clerk and treasurer of the City of Vernon, a position which he held for nearly 50 years. (February 24, 1950.)

Thomas had devoted his life to the city he and his brother had founded. Father Philip Conneally remembers that Thomas generally ate his dinner in Vernon after work and did not come home until late. At his funeral there was a parade of 100 motorcycle policemen.[12]

---

[10] Actually, the plant was out of operation for many years after the Edison Company abandoned diesel power generation. In the early 1980s the engines were completely rebuilt to meet modern smog emission standards but remaining close to the original design. The current superintendent, James L. Siegert, told the authors that his plant provides power at the lowest price in California and often sells excess power to the City of Los Angeles (interview by the authors with James L. Siegert, power plant superintendent, City of Vernon Light and Power Department, November 23, 1994).

[11] Cecilia Anne Furlong 1980: 74, and interview by the authors with Kath-leen Tavernelli Behné, Ventura, California, 1994.

[12] Interview by Jennifer Charnofsky with Father Philip Conneally, July 10, 1994. Father Conneally is a nephew of Kate Conneally, Thomas Furlong's wife.

Robert Furlong was reelected as Mayor of Vernon regularly until his death in 1974. Nominally Robert's residence was at the Furlong ranch in the City of Vernon, but he continued to live on at Van Buren Place with his sister Catherine until 1958, when they moved together to Ladera Heights. His sister Mary married Joseph Chumbrek, while Catherine's twin, Martha, married Anthony Tavernelli, a truck driver and dispatcher for Union Oil. Catherine remained at home. She devoted her life to caring for her parents, and when they died she kept house for her brother Robert.

During his early years as Mayor, Robert worked closely in politics with his aunt Judith Furlong Poxon, who was one of the main leaders of the Vernon City Council. Judith was a formidable character who would give in to no one when she felt she was right. She and John Leonis had a tremendous fight when Leonis wanted to use land that had been occupied by a slaughter-house he owned to build a gambling casino. Judith opposed this, and she carried the City Council against Leonis![13]

Cecilia Anne Furlong writes of this period:

> The City of Los Angeles wanted to absorb all the small suburbs, but Robert Furlong maintained the independence of Vernon City against insurmountable odds and political chicanery. (P. 74.)

Robert Furlong during his tenure as Mayor was also employed as an engineer by the Edison Company[14] and continued to manage the Vernon power plant both as a civic need and as an avocation. He was a member of the Board of Directors of the Central Basin Municipal Water District from 1964. He was

---

[13] Ibid.

[14] This fact flowed from the complicated history of the management of the Vernon power plant. Robert was an Edison Company employee when the plant was built in 1933. When constructed, the plant was operated by the City of Vernon for five years, but in 1937 the Edison Company conceded to the rates the Vernon City Council demanded and agreed to take over the management of the plant, with Robert Furlong as an Edison Company employee. The plant was little used between 1950 and the early 1980s when the equipment was rebuilt. Robert Furlong was employed by the Edison Company to keep the plant in running order on standby. The job of Mayor was part-time and Robert continued to oversee the power plant during his administration. When the plant was renovated in the early 1980s it reverted to management by the City of Vernon and became a major source of Vernon's power needs once more (interviews by the authors with Emilia McCarthy, assistant manager, Vernon Chamber of Commerce, and James L. Siegert, power plant superintendent, City of Vernon Light and Power Department, November 23, 1994).

also a member of the Southern California Live Steamers. This reflected his principal hobby, operating large rideable model steam trains. The authors interviewed a former resident of the block on Van Buren Place who recalled as a child being taken by Robert Furlong to ride on the miniature steam trains. Thomas Tavernelli, Robert's nephew, remembered that Robert used to run steam trains with Walt Disney, who was also a devotee of this hobby. Some of these sessions took place at Disney's home.[15] Robert did not keep his trains at Van Buren Place, but stored them elsewhere. He had a special truck built that could carry his two trains when he took them out to run.[16] He also had a large collection of conventional and black powder guns.[17]

In an article on Vernon during Robert Furlong's administration, the *Los Angeles Times* wrote:

> Vernon boasts one of the greatest concentrations of industry in the world. Within its five square mile limits are 950 factories and warehouses. More than 500 top names in industrial America have plants in Vernon. Although only 229 call Vernon home, more than 75,000 — 10% of the employed population of Metropolitan Angeles — work there each day....
>
> The meat packing plants, mills, factories and commercial houses in Vernon are contributing $9 million annually in taxes to the Los Angeles City School District....
>
> Because of its small population many of the officials double in duties. Frank A. Ziemer is city clerk, accounting officer. head of purchasing, supervisor of City Hall maintenance, license and utility bill collector. Robert J. Furlong, diesel engineer with the Edison Co., serves as mayor. His father, Thomas J. Furlong, was a founder of the city. Furlong's aunt, Mrs. Judith M. Poxon, 80, the city's senior citizen in age and length of residence (her entire life) is a member of the city council. Her son, Vincent, is city attorney; her son-in-law, administrator. (*Los Angeles Times,* October 16, 1961.)

---

[15] Telephone interview by Jennifer Charnofsky with Thomas Tavernelli, 1994.

[16] Interview by Jennifer Charnofsky with Father Philip Conneally, July 10, 1994. The authors have a photocopy, courtesy of Kath-leen Tavernelli Behné, of a photograph taken in October 1956 showing Robert Furlong driving one of his trains with his sister Martha Tavernelli's two sons and several other children as passengers. The cars stand about two and a half feet high from the track and the train consists of a steam locomotive and three cars.

[17] Interview by the authors with Kath-leen Tavernelli Behné, Ventura, California, 1994.

Robert remembered his long years in West Adams even though he had moved away from the area; in his instructions at his death (at the age of 67 in 1974), in place of flowers, donations were to be made to the St. John of God Nursing Home at the corner of Western Avenue and Adams Blvd. in the heart of West Adams, a few blocks away from his long-time home on Van Buren Place.

Postscript—Van Buren Place after the Furlongs

In May of 1958 Robert and his sister Catherine sold the house at 2657 S. Van Buren Place. City records list the next owner as the Cercle Catholique Français, from 1958 to March 1964, when it was sold to Ernest Johnson, a clerk on the Southern Pacific Railroad, from whom the present authors bought the house in March 1988.

The authors were able to interview several former members of the Cercle Catholique Français at a picnic of the French Women's Charity Club held at Mapleleaf Park in La Puente in June 1994. Louis Audet told us that among the founders of the Cercle Catholique Français was the millionaire pharmaceutical company owner Lucien Brunswig. Brunswig, who died in 1943, emigrated to Los Angeles in 1888 and founded the Brunswig Drug Company, which today is the Bergen Brunswig Pharmaceutical Company. Brunswig owned an imposing house on Adams Blvd. in West Adams, and his company was moved to Vernon immediately after his death. Audet told us that Brunswig's family was of Jewish stock but had converted to Catholicism. His mother was French and his father French-Canadian.

The Cercle Catholique Français used the house on Van Buren Place house as a clubhouse. The Cercle's main function was to provide aid to recent French immigrants. One member of the club lived in the house as a caretaker, but the others came only for meetings. "Only the front rooms were used, for dinners, and picnics in the yard," Audet said. "We never went upstairs." He also told us that visiting priests said mass there. They were part of a group of French missionary priests headquartered on Alvarado near 6th Street. There were perhaps thirty members in the Cercle, and some of them were dual members with the French Club of the International Institute on Boyle Avenue in Boyle Heights. When the house was eventually sold the money was given to French charities.[18]

Simone Steinbroner, who was born in France and was 97 years old at the time we spoke to her, remembered Christmas parties of the Cercle at the Van Buren Place house. Noeline Regla told us that the Cercle had monthly meet-

---

[18] Interview by the authors with Louis Audet, June 12, 1994, at Mapleleaf Park, La Puente, California.

ings and did charity work to support indigent French Catholics, holding bazaars and lunches at the house, and selling hand-made articles such as baby sweaters to raise money for their work.

During the twenty-four years that Ernest Johnson lived in the house it also had a religious function, although it was now once again a private home. Mr. Johnson was an active member of the Mount Zion Missionary Baptist Church on east 50th Street in South Central Los Angeles. The church held regular meetings at the Van Buren Place house for many years, until Mr. Johnson's health failed and he sold the house and moved to Florida in 1988. During his long stewardship Mr. Johnson, although he was a poor man and unable to afford much upkeep, preserved many of the original features and fixtures of the house, so that today it remains much as it was in the days when Thomas and Robert Furlong lived there. Many of the original light fixtures from the time of the house's construction in 1910 are still in service, and he had preserved the fountain in the back yard with its statue of a little Dutch girl pouring water from her jug, although the works had long since rusted away. This fountain was remembered by several of the Furlong family members we interviewed for its water plants and goldfish. In 1999 it was fully restored by the current owners.

June 1999

References

Bardsley, Charles Wareing Endell. 1875. *English Surnames and Their Significance.* London: Chatto and Windus.

Diesel Power. 1933. The City of Vernon, California: A 35,000 Hp. Diesel Municipal Plant Serves This Industrial Community, America's Largest Diesel Station. *Diesel Power,* October: 613-44.

Furlong, Cecilia Anne (Sister Bridget of Mary). 1980. *The Furlongs of California.* Privately published for the Furlong family, 78 pages plus foldout family tree.

Interview by the authors with Emilia McCarthy, assistant manager, Vernon Chamber of Commerce, November 23, 1994.

Interview by the authors with Kath-leen Tavernelli Behné (grandaughter of Thomas J. Furlong), Ventura, California, 1994.

Interview by Jennifer Charnofsky with Father Philip Conneally (Father Conneally is a nephew of Catherine Conneally and first cousin to the children of Catherine Conneally and Thomas J. Furlong), July 10, 1994.

Interview by Jennifer Charnofsky with Leonis C. Malburg, Mayor of Vernon and grandson of John B. Leonis, November 1994.

Interview by Jennifer Charnofsky with Yvonne Chumbrek (granddaughter of Thomas J. Furlong), June 26, 1994.

Interview by the authors with James L. Siegert, Power Plant Superintendent, City of Vernon Light and Power Department, November 23, 1994.

Interviews by the authors with former members of the Cercle Catholique Français—Louis Audet, Simone Steinbroner, Noeline Regla, and Andrea Regla Kostyzak—June 12, 1994, at Mapleleaf Park, La Puente, California.

Kilty, James. 1963. *Leonis of Vernon.* New York: Carlton Press.

Los Angeles Times. 1932. Silver Jubilee of Fr. N. Conneally's Ordination Sunday [Kate Furlong's brother]. Los Angeles: *Los Angeles Times.*

———. 1941. James J. Furlong, Vernon Mayor, Dies: Rosary to Be Recited Tonight for Official, 75. Los Angeles: *Los Angeles Times,* June 10.

———. 1961. Only 229 Residents in Fast Shrinking Vernon: City with Lots of Factories Has More People Working for It Than Living There. Los Angeles: *Los Angeles Times,* October 16.

———. 1974. Mass Slated for R. Furlong, Vernon Mayor. Los Angeles: *Los Angeles Times,* January 24.

McGroarty. 1933. *California of the South: A History,* vol. 4. Los Angeles: S. J. Clarke Publishing Co.: 583-84.

Moruzzi, Pete. 1997. Vernon: SoCal's First "Exclusively Industrial City." *L. A. Conservancy News,* September-October: 4.

Nelson, Maxine. *Collectible Vernon Kilns: An Identification and Value Guide.*

———. *Versatile Vernon Kilns Book II.*

Poxon, Roberta. Nd. Copy of handwritten notes recounting stories of her mother, Judith Furlong Poxon. Courtesy of Father Philip Conneally.

Rasmussen, Cecilia. 1995. Honoring L.A.'s Black Founders [includes description of the Furlong Tract]. *Los Angeles Times,* February 13, Metro Section: B3.

Telephone interview by Jennifer Charnofsky with Leo Poxon (son of Judith Furlong Poxon), 1994.

Telephone interview by Jennifer Charnofsky with Thomas Tavernelli (son of Martha Furlong Tavernelli, grandson of Thomas J. Furlong), 1994.

The Tidings (Catholic weekly of the diocese published in Vernon). 1946. Requiem Celebrated for Mrs. Catherine Furlong. Vernon, CA: *The Tidings,* nd.

———. 1950. Thomas Furlong, Noted Vernon Pioneer Dies. Vernon, CA: *The Tidings,* February 24: 30.

Vernon Chamber of Commerce. 1994. *Vernon Industrial Directory, 1994–1995.* Vernon, CA.

How the LA Times After a Hundred-Year Love Affair with the City of Vernon Decided It Really Hated the Place All Along

A more balanced look at the industrial town's history and at some of the (often ill considered) proposals for solving the Vernon problem.

Vernon, California, is an odd little town. Five square miles of meat packing plants, warehouses, and industrial enterprises where 50,000 people work during the day while only 91, belonging to just 23 families, live at night. There are only 26 homes within the city's borders, virtually all occupied by city employees or relatives of the long-serving members of the city council or other city officials.

Vernon lies on the southeast side of Downtown Los Angeles, bounded roughly by Washington Blvd. on the north and Slauson on the south. Its main arteries are Santa Fe Avenue, Soto Street, and Bandini Blvd., the last best known for the fertilizer company of the same name.

If you first read about Vernon in 2005, the last five years would be one unrelieved story of municipal scandal. In April of that year the Los Angeles district attorney issued search warrants at the Vernon city hall in an investigation of alleged misuse of public funds. Boxes of files were seized. A year and a half later, in November 2006, indictments were handed down against longtime mayor Leonis Malburg, city administrator Bruce Malkenhorst, Sr., and several other city officials. The charges mostly amounted to payment of very high salaries and bonuses to the elderly coterie who run Vernon, as well as charges that several, including the mayor and Malkenhorst, live outside of the city, making their votes in the small industrial town illegal.

The scandal soon became conflated in the press and the public mind with another story of municipal corruption in the nearby town of Bell, which shares a border with Vernon. In Bell the mayor and other functionaries also gave themselves supersized salaries. Yet there were differences that were soon lost in the general sense that unrestrained criminality was afoot. Bell, a town of 36,000, mostly very poor Latinos, was virtually bankrupted by secret salary raises, illegal taxes, and secret deals between city officials and businesses that they owned, leaving the city with huge debts. The citizenry rose up in fury and were ready to show up with the traditional pitchforks and torches to administer vigilante justice. In Vernon by contrast it was only the outsiders who got excited. The town is one of the most prosperous in the region.

The handful of well paid city employees, enjoying practically giveaway rents, are the last ones to raise a protest. Even the 1800 businesses in the industrial burg generally love the place, and while they wanted the big salaries reduced and some new leaders, they have consistently resisted the more extreme proposals of Los Angeles city and county politicians to dissolve the city altogether, or the ill-thought-out proposal of the County Board of Supervisors to strip the city of control of 90 percent of the tiny housing stock, which would be likely to open the rich little town to a takeover by genuinely criminal elements far worse than the current leaders.

The *Los Angeles Times* has in large part played a negative role in the Vernon scandal. It was of course a very good thing for the *Times* to expose the excessive salaries of the Vernon officialdom. And no one can deny that the problem is significantly inherent in the founding structure of the city, as a peculiar hybrid between a city and a private corporation. Yet because the roots of the problem lay far in the past the *Times* gave in to the temptation to raise a lynch mob atmosphere against the town by retrospectively painting its whole history as one of criminal malfeasance. This view, asserted extremely forcefully in the years since 2005, is simply not supported by its own archival coverage, both on a factual level and in the overwhelmingly positive opinions the *Times* regularly expressed toward Vernon during its first 100 years. The Vernon leadership may have always been the self-perpetuating dynasty of its two founding families, and that may not be how any normal city is run, but for a century the *Times*, with a few rare exceptions regarded the founding families as good stewards of an industrial park essential to the economic well-being of Los Angeles city and county and responsible for providing tens of thousands of badly needed jobs.

The Unfolding Vernon Scandal

The investigation of the Vernon officialdom began in 2005 Five years later much of the investigation is still in process with very little of it finding enough of a smoking gun to end in a courtroom. The charges were not in themselves particularly egregious, though they could potentially carry long jail terms. The salaries were without question extremely high for town government officials. Bruce Malkenhorst, Sr., was making almost $600,000 a year in salary and bonuses, plus perks such as city-funded limousine service and first class foreign travel. The accusation has been raised that some of this money was illegitimately for personal use but no indictments have been issued years into the investigation. Deputy city attorney Eric Fresch was paid nearly $1.65 million in salary and hourly billings in 2008. Extreme but not in itself illegal, and far less than corporate CEOs and staffs, which as we will see is in some sense what the Vernon officialdom actually are. City administrator Donal O'Callaghan has been charged with conflict of interest for getting his wife a city job.

A number of the Vernon officials were charged with voter fraud, including Mayor Leonis Malburg and his wife, Bruce Malkenhorst, Sr., and a few others. This is for giving a false address to vote in a district where you do not live. It can be prosecuted as either a felony or a misdemeanor at the discretion of the district attorney. This has been a century-long issue for Vernon. As the town is an industrial park with virtually no residential section, its leaders always mostly lived elsewhere, commuting to work and voting in the town. Los Angeles has become fussier about this violation in recent years and initiated several cases against LA politicians, but they have never led to the kind of severe punishments the statute nominally permits. Los Angeles County Supervisor Yvonne Braithwaite Burke, when found in 2007 to be living in a Brentwood mansion instead of the low-income area she represented, escaped charges by retiring. In 2010 Los Angeles City Councilman Richard Alarcon and his wife, as well as California State Senator Rod Wright, were all indicted for giving false addresses on their voter registrations. It is doubtful any of these public servants will do any jail time.

The Bizarre 2006 Election

The Vernon investigation of 2005 was inflamed by a surreal election fiasco that began in January 2006. Eight strangers — the town is small enough so everyone knows who is a stranger — moved into a five-room industrial building and within a few days three of them filed applications to run for the five-member city council. If elected they would have commanded majority control over a city with a $300 million annual budget. The town's microscopic voter base meant that any challenge had some potential to unseat the incumbents and take control of a city on which some 1800 industrial companies and commercial operations depend. The unorthodox living arrangements had been secured by Chris Summers, described by the *LA Times* as "a disbarred attorney who has been convicted of embezzlement and forgery." The *Times* added that Summers had a long-time lucrative relationship with Albert Robles, "a convicted felon who as treasurer of South Gate nearly bankrupted that city." Terrified that this unsavory crew could recruit and register fifty or sixty people to come in and vote to take over the town, the geriatric Vernon leadership grossly overreacted.

Charging that the building had been occupied without the owner's permission, the city council had city police break the locks and evict the eight squatters. The would-be candidates were met by Albert Robles, who was seen giving one of them $100. They then took up residence in an Alhambra hotel, and showed up to vote on April 11. City Clerk Bruce Malkenhorst, Jr., canceled the eight new voter registrations and locked up the ballot box while the case went to court. Meanwhile the town hired clumsy private detectives to ostentatiously shadow their new opposition.

The case took an ominous turn when the county registrar ruled that canceling the voter registrations was illegal and that even homeless people had a right to register to vote. With that ruling the future of Vernon was placed in doubt, as any well-funded speculator could probably find seventy homeless people they could pay to bus into Vernon to outvote the 60 registered residents.

A word here about Albert Robles, the reputed mastermind of the effort to capture a majority on the Vernon city council. The *Times* devoted a single sentence to this character while aiming many columns of vitriol at the current Vernon leadership. Without glossing over the evident greediness of the Vernon elders, they have never been accused of doing a bad job of running the little city, which has manageable debt, a model police force, its own health department, and is even by the *Times'* accounts, remarkably efficient, with the lowest electric rates in the state, clean streets, and graffiti free. The *Times* in the four years of its hostile coverage following the 2006 election has been remarkably unconcerned at what the city would likely have become if the takeover effort had succeeded. Robles is a former mayor, councilman, treasurer, and deputy city manager for the city of South Gate. According to the Wikipedia, "Robles was indicted on federal corruption charges in 2004. This stemmed from his award of contracts worth millions to friends and business associates as well as funneling money through the awarded contracts to himself and family members. He was found guilty of 30 counts of bribery, money laundering, and depriving the electorate. He was sentenced to 10 years in federal prison and ordered to pay the city of South Gate $639,000 in restitution." Nothing remotely on that scale has been charged against the Vernon political coterie and it doesn't take much imagination to see that the aim of the electoral challenge had little to do with democracy but was a gambit to loot the lucrative town treasury.

In October 2006 Judge Aurelio Muñoz ruled that the ballots must be counted. Vernon complied, no laws were broken, and the incumbents were reelected. But the heavy handed methods they had used, exacerbated by the very high salaries they were revealed to be paid and the several who lived out of district but voted in the city, opened up a firestorm.

"Almost since Vernon was established . . . the town has moved from controversy to controversy"

The *LA Times*, which for the previous hundred years had been an enthusiastic promoter of the little city, now saw nothing but evil there and developed an astonishing case of amnesia about its own past coverage, now seeing a century of corruption. An editorial in the April 14, 2006, issue headed "Infernal Vernon" fumed: "HISTORY HAS SHOWN THAT there is no election the city of Vernon will not cancel, disrupt or simply ignore if there is even the possibility it will not benefit the handful of families that have mismanaged the city for a century."

Hector Becerra, who has emerged as the *Times'* point man on the trash Vernon campaign, with backup from two other *Times* reporters, filled in this indictment in a lengthy June 18, 2006, article.

"Almost since Vernon was established a century ago," Becerra et al. wrote, "the town has moved from controversy to controversy." The article then launches into a supposed history of Vernon that is wrong or tendentious on numerous counts. First, it singles out John B. Leonis as THE founder, presumably because he was a colorful character and makes a simple and easily grasped link to the current scandal-plagued mayor, Leonis Malburg, who is John Leonis's grandson.

John Baptiste Leonis

John Baptiste Leonis was a French Basque immigrant and an important figure in Vernon's first half century, but he was never the town boss. A word here about Vernon's founding, as it contained within its initial charter all the issues that made the city praiseworthy for its first century but which are now the basis for condemning it. The idea came from Leonis, who ran a general store amidst numerous pig farms. Leonis persuaded two brothers who owned one of these farms, James and Thomas Furlong, to go in with him in turning their land into what would today be called an industrial park. They in turn persuaded a majority of the other nearby farmers to pool their land and incorporate in 1905 as the city of Vernon.

From the outset Vernon was chartered under the motto "Exclu-sively Industrial." That meant exactly what it said: It was going to be a city with essentially no residential district, exclusively devoted to serving industrial properties. From the

John B. Leonis

outset Vernon was an unusual hybrid, part city but in large part a corporation that leased or sold land to factories and warehouses to which it provided many services. And like any corporation, its owners, who initially also personally owned the land on which the city was built, would remain in office indefinitely. It is not true, as the *Times* has it, that Vernon was born in controversy over this organizational form, which is self-evidently at the heart of the essential charges against it today: that the leadership is self-perpetuating and pays itself corporate-style salaries, that the few residents are essentially employees rather than citizens, and that a number of the city officials live in actual residential parts of town rather than among the slaughterhouses and factories that make up almost all of Vernon. It was only in the twenty-first century that the forms required of a city came to be seen as incompatible with what was in essence the private ownership of the town.

Becerra sets out to prove his charge that Vernon was beset by controversy "almost since [it] was established" with this first salvo:

"A powerful voice on the town's Board of Trustees," [the mayor, who held the strongest single power in the city, was James Furlong from 1905 to 1941], "Leonis initially promoted activities that other jurisdictions spurned: gambling, prizefighting and drinking. He leased land to a saloon owner who opened the 'longest bar in the world.' On one side was a boxing stadium; on the other, a baseball stadium."

Becerra suggests a scene of small scale squalid depravity run by lowlife hustlers. Let's look a bit at this sin city. Note that Leonis became rich by creating a bank and he later owned a stockyard and feed mill. He was not an owner of any of the night life establishments for which Vernon was, in fact, famous during its early days, though he had the vision to bring in promoters who made the little town a center of Los Angeles night life.

There were some brothels in the early days, as there were in other cities, including Los Angeles, but Vernon closed them down in 1913. The gambling, such as it was, took place at Baron Long's Vernon Country Club. This was the one Vernon institution the *LA Times* campaigned against during those years, mainly because the paper didn't like strong drink in the period leading up to Prohibition and Vernon was, along with Venice, California, one of the two "wet" towns in the county.

The gambling issue came to a head in February 1916, a decade after the town's founding, when Harry Ellis Dean, a former county deputy chief district attorney, persuaded a justice of the peace, acting in the mistaken belief that the DA's office had authorized it, to issue an arrest warrant for Baron Long on charges of illegal gambling. The actual county district attorney, Thomas Lee Woolwine, refused to prosecute, saying the gambling in question "was in the form of ongoing contests of a sort long conducted by various businesses. Though technically games of chance, they 'had been allowed to run on the theory that they were within the law'" (2007 Metropolitan News Company story, the internal quote is from an *LA Times* article of the period). The Vernon Country Club was destroyed in a fire in 1929, when the *Times* described it as "one of the most popular dining and dancing resorts of Los Angeles county" (March 1, 1929). Baron Long went on to become the owner of the Biltmore Hotel.

From Hector Becerra's disparaging dismissal of the anonymous "saloon owner" and passing references to prize fighting and baseball the reader would never suspect the central role little Vernon played in Los Angeles sports and night life in its first two decades. The unlikely rise of a mainly industrial park into a major center for Hollywood celebrities and the high-life crowd was due to three men: first of all, the "saloon owner," Jack Doyle, and Vernon meatpackers Peter and Edward Maier.

**Jack Doyle, famed
Vernon fight promoter**

In a case of the left hand not knowing what the right hand is doing, *Times* sportswriter Steve Springer in 2006 gave a more honest account of Vernon and area sports:

"Before football came and went, before the Dodgers and Lakers, boxing was the center of the Los Angeles sporting world. . . . The city of Vernon was the first focal point for the sport in the Los Angeles area, thanks to a bartender and former railroad worker named Jack Doyle, who opened a training camp in Arcadia in 1908 . . . . Two years later, when he opened a bar in Vernon, Doyle decided boxing would be a great vehicle for getting customers into his establishment. So he began to stage four-round fights, the participants lined up by matchmaker Wad Wadhams." (March 30, 2006).

Boxing began in Vernon shortly after the town was founded in an outdoor arena run by Tom McCarey, but it took off in a big way after Jack Doyle opened Jack Doyle's Central Saloon in 1910 at the corner of Santa Fe and Joy Street. It did have a 100 foot bar, with 37 bartenders. He built a small arena next door, which he replaced in 1923 with a 7,000 seat stadium that the *Times* described as "the finest U.S. indoor arena" (January 1, 1924). While it was being built the paper enthused:

Boxing at Jack Doyle's Vernon Arena, 1927

"The manly art of self-defense has a prestige at present in Los Angeles that is hardly second to that of any other city in the Union. True, we are not allowed to swing but four-round bouts, but these short session affairs have become a fad and in many cases are more replete with torrid action than are the longer tilts in the East. So popular has the game become in the last year or so that the home of the four round sport in Southern California — Vernon arena, if you please, is absolutely too small to accommodate the fans when an enticing program is offered." (July 13, 1923)

Doyle in his day was a nationally famous fight promoter and many world championship bouts were held at his Venice Arena. Jack Dempsey fought there in 1924.

The second major sports development was the creation in 1909 by Peter and Edward Maier of the Vernon Tigers, a Pacific Coast League baseball team. The team was bought in 1919 by Hollywood star Roscoe "Fatty" Arbuckle, and won the PCL pennant in 1920 over the Seattle Indians. After being moved to San Francisco for a while the team came back to Los Angeles under the name the Hollywood Stars, where it lasted until 1958.

To try to sort out truth from fiction, in research for this article I did a search of the *Los Angeles Times* archive for the word "Vernon" in article headlines from 1905 to the present. This turned up 4,006 articles. The vast majority were about the city of Vernon. I went through year by year looking at each headline, reading the free abstract wherever it bore on the issues we are looking at, and paying to see the full text of scores of articles on the *Times* pay-per-view archive. What this revealed is that far from Vernon being a center of controversy "almost since [it] was established," the *Times* poured out ink over two decades covering Vernon sporting events and little else about the town. Typically the paper ran 180 to 200 articles a year about Vernon, most about boxing matches, or under titles such as "Vernon Tigers Gnaw the Sacramento Solons."

There is an occasional denunciation of Baron Long or a note that some industrial plant has been built, but sports is not just the main but virtually the only subject worth covering. The sports ended when the Tigers were moved to San Francisco in 1925 and Jack Doyle became the fight promoter for the Olympic Auditorium in downtown Los Angeles in 1927. With sports gone the *Times* lost interest. In 1930 the *Times* ran only 5 articles on Vernon, mostly on industrial construction.

What today's Times reporters don't seem to want to recall is what the Times actually thought of Vernon the city. It was not scandals of supposed mismanagement. A good sample comes from the January 1, 1915, *Times*, under the headline "Vernon —The Coming Industrial and Manufacturing Center of Los Angeles County." This gets us to something else that is objectionable in the *Times'* coverage of the recent five years. Vernon consistently comes across as a little no-account burg whose only interest is as a negative example of a historically bad leadership. It is always mentioned that Vernon is an industrial enclave, but the tone invariably suggests that it is not an important place except for concern about its bad government. In the genuine history of our area Vernon was the keystone of Los Angeles industrial growth and remained indisputably so until the incorporation of the City of Industry in 1957. The *Times*, singing a song that it would reprise many times over the next ninety years, added in its 1915 article:

"One of the greatest factors for real progress and prosperity in Southern California for a decade or more has been the industrial development in the ... manufacturing suburb of Vernon."

An Exposé that Wasn't

Hector Becerra doesn't find his first supposed nugget of scandal until twenty years after the city was founded. No scandal in twenty years wouldn't be bad for most cities. Here is how he tells it:

"In 1925, *The Times* did its first front-page expose of Vernon. The paper quoted one foe as saying of Leonis: 'In that town, you do not file papers at the City Hall. You simply hand them to John and he puts them in his pocket. If he is in favor of the proposition, it goes through; if he is opposed, that's the last you hear of it.'"

By definition an exposé is a revelation of wrongdoing, crime, or corruption based on FACTS. When we look at the actual piece Becerra and his team refer to, dated June 19, 1925, it doesn't claim to be any of those things. It merely quotes an unsupported opinion by one of John Leonis's enemies on which the *Times* ventures no opinion of its own as to its truthfulness. Becerra retails this stuff as fact eighty-one years later, with all the principals long dead, maybe thinking no one will bother to go back and read his source. Sorry, fella. The article is headlined "Vernon Run by One Man Is Protest." The "foe" Becerra doesn't name was John T. Gaffey and the occasion was a long-simmering court battle over a piece of land that Vernon had wanted to annex. Gaffey was not a resident of Vernon but was a wealthy real estate developer in San Pedro. He was married to the richest woman in California, Arcadia Bandini, heiress of a Spanish land grant and worth some $8 million. Vernon ultimately did not get the land.

Gaffey was prominent in area politics, having served briefly on the Los Angeles City Council and the Board of Equalization. But he was also convicted in 1915 of overcharging the residents of Palos Verdes for their water, which he controlled, and compelled to make restitution, so he was no saint. No reputable reporter would present Gaffey's unsubstantiated outburst during a land fight as fact, but Becerra does just that. The *Times* back in 1925 also asked John Leonis to respond:

"When Leonis was told of Gaffey's statements, he laughed and declined comment. 'Just let him have his say; I don't care to answer him.'"

Note that Gaffey in the quote from the *Times* does not claim to have given Leonis such a paper, or even to have witnessed anyone else do so, nor does he say from whom he heard this story. This makes Becerra's effort to slip the quote in as allegedly part of a factual "exposé" a con job.

The 1943 Legal Case

The first time the issues that presented themselves in the last few years came up was in 1943, thirty-eight years into Vernon's existence. Not exactly a story of perpetual and unrelieved mismanagement and scandal. Becerra reports that a county grand jury indicted six Vernon leaders, including John Leonis, on charges of voter fraud and that four were convicted while Leonis and one other were acquitted. It would have been more useful to the present debate over Vernon's future to have examined more closely the legal debate in the 1943-44 case. The Vernon functionaries were defended by John W. Preston, a former justice of the California Supreme Court. The charges for each of the accused hinged entirely on the pretty much undisputed fact that the six regularly voted in Vernon while living elsewhere, much the same situation recently charged against Vernon mayor Leonis Malburg and city administrator Bruce Malkenhorst, Sr. The court verdict, delivered in January 1944, was strangely split in seemingly identical situations. The police and fire chiefs, a city councilman, and the deputy city clerk were all convicted. They were given token fines of $500 each and permitted to keep their city jobs. They did not move into the city. Leonis, who had become mayor in 1941 on the death of James Furlong, and Thomas J. Furlong, the city clerk, both had the charges dropped outright, with the approval of the prosecutor as well as the judge (there was no jury).

There was no dispute over the fact that Leonis lived at 647 S. Hudson Avenue in Hancock Park, while Furlong, along with his son, Robert Furlong, who would succeed Leonis as mayor in 1948, lived on Van Buren Place in the West Adams section of Los Angeles.

So why were the charges dropped? In a January 19, 1944. editorial, the *Times* said that the judge had agreed with the defendants that Vernon was basically not a residential city and that "technical residence" through working there on a daily basis was sufficient to establish voting rights. Thus the issues that seem so clear to the *Times* and local politicians in 2010 were not at all clear to the legal system when they first came into a courtroom, in 1943. The *Times* in its 1944 editorial objected, not that the setup in Vernon was illegal or should be abolished, but merely that a nonresident officialdom risked getting out of touch with the town it administered:

"Since Vernon is a 'city in which nobody lives,' except technically, it has in effect been run by carpetbaggers. This is not a healthy situation. The decisions in regard to the Mayor and the City Clerk are presumably good law. But it would seem to be good practice to require the principal officials of any city to reside in it actually and not merely technically. Nobody can know what is going on in a town unless he spends most of his time there; staying there just in business hours is not enough."

From left: James Furlong with his son, Robert Furlong, and Thomas J. Furlong

John Leonis was far from the feudal lord of Vernon that the *Times* painted him during the 1943 legal case or Becerra does today. He became mayor only reluctantly despite serious illness in 1941. He tried, before he retired in 1948, to persuade the Vernon city council to let him build a gambling casino, like the ones then in Gardena, on a piece of land he owned that had been a slaughterhouse. He was opposed by council member Judith Furlong Poxon, James and Thomas Furlongs' sister, who had been a founder of the famous Vernon-based Poxon Pottery company. Judith won and Leonis didn't get his casino. (July 10, 1994, interview by Jennifer Charnofsky with Father

Philip Conneally, a nephew of Thomas J. Furlong's wife, Kate Conneally Furlong.)

Leonis died in 1953. He had been succeeded as mayor in 1948 by Robert Furlong, the son of Thomas J. Furlong, who was reelected repeatedly until his death in 1974 and never the subject of any scandal.

Later Legal Challenges to the Vernon Officials

The courts occasionally returned to the Vernon conundrum in the years that followed. Not persistently and uninterruptedly as the *Times* writers try to imply but more like once in a generation. And until 2009 their efforts were even less conclusive than the 1943-44 trial.

Thirty-four years passed after the 1944 case before the issue of nonresident officials voting in Vernon was raised again. By this time the mayor was Leonis C. Malburg, John Leonis's grandson, who was to become the focus of the 2005 scandal, still in office then and only the town's fourth mayor. A Los Angeles County Grand Jury in December 1978 indicted Malburg along with City Administrator Bruce Malkenhorst, Sr., and City Attorney David Brearley. The case was intimately tied to a dispute with the 101-member Vernon Fire Department, who were on strike. One of the firemen, Carlton Claunch, filed to run for the Vernon city council and began a lawsuit against Malburg, charging him with holding the office of mayor illegally because he didn't live in the city. The indictment against Malburg was for voting in Vernon while living in his grandfather's former home in Hancock Park; against Malkenhorst and Brearley for having allegedly held up renewing a contract with the Vernon fire fighters until they agreed to withhold support from Claunch and to repudiate his lawsuit. The charges were not criminal and if they had resulted in conviction would have removed the defendants from office but did not include any threat of jail time.

In the end the court decided that the whole thing was part of the dispute over the fire fighters' contract and dismissed the cases against all three, which never went to trial. A contract was signed in November and the dispute with the fire fighters was said to have been amicably resolved. Not much there to stir the scandal pot.

I would add that the judge could not have seriously believed that Malburg, who had inherited $8 million from his grandfather, really lived in an apartment over an office building in Vernon rather than in his 7,371 square foot Italianate mansion on Hudson Avenue in Hancock Park. Back in 1944 the court had actually confronted the issue and ruled that "technical" residence by working there was legal for voting. The court in 1978 dodged it entirely, presumably not thinking it a good idea to shatter the government of an otherwise well-run town that was important to the economic health of the region over what was essentially a misdemeanor, especially as there was pretty much no residential section of Vernon.

What Can Be Put on the Plus Side?

In its "Infernal Vernon" editorial the *Times* had opined that the city had been "mismanaged . . . for a century." That judgment would have come as a surprise to its own editors who covered the Vernon beat over that hundred years.

In truth, apart from the sports coverage of the early years and the once-a-generation voting scandals that petered out without much issue, the *Times'* rare coverage was almost all about new enterprises, investments, and the occasional fire or industrial accident. In October 1961 a piece on Vernon's shrinking population treated the city with great friendliness, noting that it accounted for 10% of the employed population of metropolitan Los Angeles and contributed $9 million in annual taxes to the LA school system. It quoted a resident as saying "Living here is like living in a small country town. You know everyone. You feel you really have a voice in government. And you know your vote really counts." This doesn't fit well with the image of the recent past of a serflike handful of city employees afraid to open their mouths.

In July 1962 there was a still more adulatory article, headed "Industrial Park Idea Typified by Vernon" that lauded the idea of dedicated industrial parks devoted to industry and separated from residential areas, declaring Vernon "the pioneer, the granddaddy, and still the biggest of them all." It praised the small city for "putting up modern public buildings, and ... expanding its water and other public utilities systems." The writer noted that the entirety of Vernon is zoned for industry and "There is not one hotel or motel in Vernon," not to mention movie theaters or stores. But the *Times* saw that as a good thing then:

"Perhaps it is because of rather than in spite of these oddities in a municipality that Vernon is so ably fulfilling its chosen role of handmaiden to industry. It is a role which seems destined to become even more important as its facilities and the region develop."

It was a decade later before the *Times* got back to the little town, this time with an article on how industry was being replaced by less profitable warehouses as factories aged and new ones wanted more space in outlying suburbs (July 20, 1975). It said "there are more of Fortune Magazine's top 500 businesses in the city than in any other comparable area in the nation." The writer reminisced a bit on the old sporting days, even having a good word for Baron Long's Vernon Country Club, demonized by the *Times* back in the day and part of the stuff the present-day *Times* dismisses as scorned by neighboring towns:

"Baron Long's sprawling Vernon Country Club became a gathering place for silent screen stars like Charlie Chaplin, Rudolph Valentino and Blossom Seeley."

The 1975 piece had nothing but good to say about the place, how it had the only municipal health department in the county "designed to help industry solve problems of food handling, noise, dust, fumes and internal environmental quality control." And a police department that "claimed the average response time is under two minutes."

Another twenty-five years on, the *Times* ran another general article about Vernon, in its April 4, 2000, issue. The subhead read: "Amid the factories and industrial odors of Vernon live 85 people who seem perfectly happy with their lifestyle." Yes, elections are routinely canceled, but that's "because incumbents rarely are challenged."

This one is worth quoting at length to get a picture of the bucolic paradise the *Times* found there:

"Residents say that living in the 5-square-mile industrial city takes some getting used to. They have to put up with heavy freight trains that rumble through the city at all hours and the pungent fumes from factories, like the Farmer John pork processing plant and Kal Kan's dog food factory. Still, Vernonites say they are a content group who share a sense of community rarely found in Southern California's urban sprawl. What other city can hold an annual picnic that is attended by nearly every resident? How many cities have a mayor who can name almost every citizen?

"'It's like a big family here,' said Isabel Saenz, who has lived in Vernon for 30 years with her husband, Edward, a water department employee. Their teenage granddaughter, Lorena Saldana, lives with them. . . .

"The utility fees are the lowest in the state and the subsidized rents are cheap, allowing some residents to save up to buy a house elsewhere. A three-bedroom house with wood floors, a backyard and a two-car garage is only $225 a month (if you don't mind living a block from a railroad line). The commute for workers who live in the city is practically nil, and city employees work only Monday through Thursday.

"Maria Kirkland and her husband, Curtis, an electrical technician, recently moved from Fontana, where they paid $1,300 a month for a four-bedroom apartment. In Vernon, they pay $145 for a well-maintained one-bedroom apartment."

Well, mismanagement, especially of the infernal variety, must be a bit in the eye of the beholder.

What Should We Do with Vernon?

An important part of the Vernon old guard were swept away following the 2005-06 scandals. Leonis Malburg was forced from office, sued by Vernon for legal fees, and convicted on the voter fraud count, for which he received probation and the hefty fine of $500,000, though for a multimillionaire it is not going to break him. There is a new mayor in town for the first time since 1974. His name is Hilario "Larry" Gonzales.

City Administrator Bruce Malkenhorst, Sr., resigned, as did his son, Vernon city attorney Bruce Malkenhorst, Jr. These and others who bit the dust — Eric T. Fresch, former city administrator and deputy city attorney; Donal O'Callaghan, former city administrator and utilities director; Roirdan S. Burnett, city treasurer/finance director; Jeffrey A. Harrison, former city attorney — were named in an October 21, 2010, subpoena by California's attorney general and new governor Jerry Brown. This was aimed in large part at investigating and seeking to reduce the huge pensions these recently deposed Vernon officials are now collecting, in Malkenhorst, Sr.'s case, $500,000 a year.

Brown, sensibly, declared, "It's clear to me that we need a state authority to set some standards and curb these excesses." Setting statewide standards for municipal pay is an excellent idea, particularly for a town like Vernon where, while the town remains prosperous, the electorate is essentially hand picked by the town officials, or Bell, where the officials operated in secret to loot the treasury.

Meanwhile a plethora of more extreme solutions are being debated to solve the Vernon problem. Probably the most widespread is a call to disband the city entirely. This has been backed by Los Angeles City Councilmember Janice Hahn, who has introduced a motion to that effect in the LA City Council. This solution has been endorsed by LA County District Attorney Steve Cooley, State Assembly Speaker John A. Pérez, and state Senator Hector De La Torre of South Gate. No city in California has ever been disincorporated against the will of its residents, and in the nation as a whole there are only a handful of such cases, the best known where a landowner in Ohio incorporated a "city" to create a speed trap for motorists, hardly comparable to the Vernon situation. In any case such a move would require an act of the state legislature that would also require majority support in a general statewide election, as one city cannot unilaterally decide it wants to gobble up another. Los Angeles is not the only candidate for such a merger. The other contiguous towns are Huntington Park, Bell, Maywood, and the City of Commerce.

None of these are a very good match. Bell should be out of the question as its own government is in shambles. Huntington Park and Commerce at first seem plausible, the former with 61,000 residents, the latter with 13,000, so they wouldn't have elections that could be captured by seventy outside plants. But here the positives end. Both have high poverty rates, with median income in Huntington Park at $29,844 and in Commerce at $34,000, posing a strong temptation to divert large amounts of funds from the Vernon part of the merger to use for pressing needs in the other partner. Nor does either town have the health, fire, or police resources that make Vernon safe for the dangerous industrial processes that are housed there.

Huntington Park has its own police department but depends on the county health department for fire and health coverage, the last mostly through a health service center in yet another city, Whittier. Commerce has no health, police or fire departments, depending on the county for all of this.

In Commerce the largest employers are a casino, LA County itself, Smart and Final, and the 99 Cent stores, hardly in a league to run Vernon's demanding 1800-firm industrial base, many of which are Fortune 500 companies.

The Vernon business owners have been outspoken as angry at the huge salaries but quite understandably opposed to dissolution or merger of their city, given the virtually certain negative effects that would have on the level of police, fire, and health protections they could count on, not to mention a stiff boost in electric utility rates.

Still, it would seem very risky to leave Vernon with its present microscopic residential sector and large city income, especially if the probably illegal restrictions on residence and voting the old guard insulated themselves with are removed, leaving the town a sitting duck for fast buck takeover attempts.

Steve Freed, president of the Vernon Property Association, told the *Times* that "Many business owners feel that the only way the city of Vernon can truly have a representative government would be for the property owners to be allowed to vote in city elections." That is not currently permitted in any California city. But it is not so out of reach as a solution as it might seem. The National Conference of State Legislatures in the October 2008 issue of its newsletter carried a lead article entitled "Nonresident Property Owners and Voting in Local Elections: A Paradigm Shift?" It reported that ten states — Arizona, Colorado, Connecticut, Delaware, Indiana, Montana, New Mexico, North Dakota, Tennessee, and Wyoming — have authorized cities at their discretion to grant voting rights to non-resident property owners in local elections, though in some cases these are restricted to voting on taxation issues. It adds that there are taxpayer associations agitating for such nonresident voting rights in Florida, Massachusetts, New York, Vermont, and Wisconsin. The article concludes:

"'Taxation without representation' was the cry that started a revolution. More than 200 years later, it is still fueling a debate that could affect a shift in election law."

The city of Vernon was long aware of the problem of its structure with little or no residential housing and hence no independent voter base. The town at its incorporation in 1905 became what is called a sixth class city, which means it has no authority to write its own statutes. In 1953 Robert Furlong, during his tenure as mayor, attempted to resolve the issue that later lay at the heart of scandals in the next century. He formed a committee of Vernon businessmen that proposed to the California State Assembly a constitutional amendment that would convert Vernon to a chartered city, which does have such authority, and that it explicitly include in the charter a provision that nonresident property owners be permitted to vote in city elections. Furlong argued that Vernon at that time, despite its small population, was the state's eighth largest city in assessable wealth. The proposal was approved by the Assembly Committee on Constitutional Amendments. The bill was defeated in the Assembly in May 1955.

It would seem to me that if the political system decides to go further than Jerry Brown's proposal for statewide regulation of municipal salary limits to curb the financial abuses in towns such as Vernon, that another effort to give cities the choice of establishing enfranchisement of nonresident property owners would be the least disruptive solution to the Vernon problem and the least potentially damaging to the regional economy. If legislators are uneasy about offering this option to all of California's charter cities they could choose to narrow a piece of legislation to apply to Vernon alone, as the Assembly's Constitutional Amendments Committee agreed to do in 1953, as Vernon is an almost unique case in California, most nearly matched only by the Los Angeles area City of Industry and Emeryville in Alameda County in the San Francisco Bay Area.

The stupidest and most risky solution is the resolution shepherded through the Los Angeles County Board of Supervisors by Gloria Molina, which calls on the State Legislature to restrict city owned housing in Vernon to 10 percent of the total housing stock. As there is only one apartment building and a total of 26 homes the most likely outcome of this measure would be to open the wealthy little town to takeover attempts by grifters and con artists. There has already been one such attempt. This could guarantee that the next one succeeds. Believe me, they wouldn't limit themselves to exorbitant salaries. The voting and high salary scandals have to be balanced against the huge infrastructural investment the people of Los Angeles County have in the Vernon industrial park and not to take a sledge hammer to the town to deal with a problem that has less drastic solutions. After years of investigation the only conviction that has emerged so far is of former mayor Leonis Malburg, for voting in Vernon while living elsewhere. The city's replacement administrators have drastically reduced salaries, the treasurer topping out at $339,000 with the next highest at $233,000 for the city attorney. City council members make $68,000. These figures are comparable to LA senior officials. Granted LA is an infinitely larger and more important city, but Vernon's per capita income is much higher than Los Angeles.

To put the furor in perspective, for all the *Times'* fuming about a supposed hundred years of mismanagement, their proofs amounted to four $500 fines back in 1944, until we get to 2005. That says there was much that was always positive about the little industrial city, self-perpetuating leadership or not. It is not an accident that several years into the *LA Times* high hysterics about demon Vernon the Los Angeles County Economic Development Corporation voted Vernon its 2008 award as the most business friendly city in LA County with a population under 50,000. There are still 50,000 jobs that depend on how well that town functions. There are other ways to put a cap on the financial excesses of its officialdom, and even to submit them to a real electorate. But the supervisors' notion is patently not the way.

November 27, 2910

By way of disclosure:

In 1988 my wife, Jennifer Charnofsky, and I purchased a home where we have lived since on Van Buren Place in the West Adams section of Los Angeles. Researching the history of the house we discovered that it had been owned from 1922 until 1958 by the Furlong family of Vernon, first by Thomas J. Furlong, one of the three founders of Vernon, who served as Vernon city clerk from 1905 to his death in 1950, when the house passed to his son Robert Furlong, who was Vernon's mayor from 1948 to his death in 1974. Robert Furlong lived in the Van Buren Place house from 1922 until 1958. The Los Angeles Cultural Heritage Commission in 2000 created the Van Buren Place house Los Angeles Historic Cultural Monument #678, under the name the Furlong House in honor of Thomas J. and Robert Furlong. In November 1994 Jennifer Charnofsky spoke to Leonis Malburg on the telephone as part of our research on the history of the house. Other than that neither of us has ever met or spoken to any present or former official of the city of Vernon. We have never had any financial interests, direct or indirect, that concerned Vernon.

Postscript, March 17, 2012:

In May 2011, Bruce Malkenhorst, Sr., pled guilty to improperly billing the city for $60,000 over a six-year period for meals, personal expenses, and installation of a home security system. Restitution plus fines came to $105,000. There was no jail time. Also in May 2011 a bill by State Senator Tony Strickland (R-Moorpark) that would divest the pensions of any public official convicted of abusing public funds was killed in a state Senate committee over concerns that it would overly penalize the families of offenders. On Monday, August 29, 2011, State Assembly Speaker John Pérez's bill, AB 46, to disincorporate Vernon went down to defeat on a 13-17 vote, with 10 senators abstaining. In November 2011, former Vernon city attorney Eric Fresch, who was still billing the city more than $1 million a year for legal services, announced his resignation from work for Vernon effective May 1, 2012. After the departure of Leonis Malburg and the Malkenhorsts, Fresch was seen by many as the last remaining figure of the old guard and the real power in the city.

Vernon has hired former California Attorney General John K. Van de Kamp as its ethics advisor in working on a reform agenda.

Part 4: Miscellany

Wandering in Virtual Landscapes

Some Thoughts about the Early Days of Computer Role Playing Games

Computer games for those over fifty who were not tech adopters are mostly an alien terrain, viewed as the morally questionable province cf teenage boys. There is some truth to that, but it is also true that the whole of this interactive computer entertainment field, which includes computer games proper, video games played on a console attached to a television set, and coin operated arcade machines hit $9.9 billion in 2004 in the United States alone, taking in more money than movie theaters, excepting the sale of popcorn.

That number is tossed out to try to command respect from nonplayers, although it conflates together a wide variety of technologies, entertainment experiences, and subgenres. What they share in common is interactivity, an element missing from films. While it can't be denied that films are better written, where computer games have any writing in them at all, and provide a deeper moral experience, the computer experience offers the player the ability to become an actor or mostly THE actor in the situation or story.

I came to this stuff early in its development but late in life. My interest has pursued one strand of the many in this field: medieval fantasy role playing games, RPGs in the shorthand of the genre. Since the early days of the computer game field at the end of the 1970s and early 1980s, as graphic technology was first added and then rapidly developed, the various genres solidified: flight, ship, submarine, and giant robot simulators; first-person shooters; hex-based war games; point-and-click adventures; sports simulations; life simulations, notably the Sims; adaptations of traditional board and card games; a wide range of turn-based and real-time strategy games such as Sid Meier's *Civilization* and the lengthy *Warcraft* series, and more recently the online persistent worlds of massively multiplayer games such as *World of Warcraft, Everquest,* and *Ultima Online.* World of Warcraft had 6 million subscribers 2006, each paying a monthly fee [$15 per month in 2012 when subscribers were around 11-12 million]. There are even people who make their living brokering game objects such as magical armor and swords for real money, where buyers pay with credit cards to meet purveyors in the game world to collect their merchandise, which can only be used in the game world. There is even a more or less official exchange rate between American dollars and the currencies used in the game worlds, and game mills in China where young players mine gold in virtual worlds all day long, then exchange it for real money.

I am picking out one type among these many variants and ignoring the rest: single player fantasy role playing games.

Infocom and the Commodore 64

My first computer was a Commodore 64, which I bought in the late summer of 1983, a year after they were first released. This proved to be the largest-selling computer of all time, down to the present day. The Apple II had been around longer and already had its own backlog of software game titles.

To pay for my Commodore I sold a 9mm Walther PPK pistol I had purchased from a hard-bitten iron miner on the Mesabi Iron Range in northern Minnesota. I have sometimes regretted that I parted with the Walther and did not find some other way to finance my entrance into the personal computer world.

My Commodore came with a single external disk drive that could write 170K on a single-sided 5-1/4 inch floppy disk. It had a monochrome orangey monitor. The advertised 64K — 64,000 bytes of RAM compared to the 2 gigabytes or 2 billion bytes of memory in my current computer — had to first load the operating system, written in an amazingly small 25K of code, leaving 39K of usable memory. No hard drive. The main application was a pretty nifty word processor called PaperClip which could do all the basic things a word processor should, except it could only save 11 pages of text in a single file. There was some cumbersome way to chain files together for printing to keep the page numbers flowing on longer documents, but when you read an 80 page printout and needed to correct something you had to try to remember if the error was in file 5, 6, or 7 and usually had to open all three before finding the mistake. Oh, and the screen displayed a line only 40 characters wide.

The Commodore was also a game machine. It had the fastest graphics of its time and a music synthesizer to boot. Fascinated with the various things the computer could do, and somehow suspecting in that pre-Internet age that some level of real intelligence lurked behind all of its clever programs, I began to buy or copy games.

The outstanding game was *Zork: The Great Underground Empire*. This was, for those who missed them, a text adventure. No graphics. Just words on the screen. It was written by Marc Blank and David Lebling, and a few others, on a mainframe at MIT in 1977-79. It had to be broken up into three separate games to run on the Commodore 64, the Apple II, and the Atari.

Zork I begins with the now-classic lines:

"West of House: You are standing in an open field west of a white house, with a boarded front door."

The game accepted typed-in commands such as north, south, down (when there was a staircase), pick up (the lantern, the sword, etc.). There was a way into the house through a back window. One of the rooms contained a rug on the floor and if you thought of typing "move rug" you would be rewarded with the message: "There is a trap-door in the floor." Open the trap door, go down, and you were off into the underground empire. Be sure to carry a lighted lantern or the grues would get you. Somewhere lurking in the vast caverns there was also a thief who would steal the treasures you collected. There were puzzles: turning multiple wheels in one room of an installation opened floodgates and drained a passage a few rooms away that would let you into a new area of the underground kingdom. There were inscriptions here and there honoring the long-gone monarch, Lord Dimwit Flathead.

The game, taking up little space since everything was just words, contained 110 rooms and 60 distinct objects, most of which could be picked up and added to the player's inventory. There was a sense of mystery and exhilarating exploration as you wandered from one room to another, encountered trolls, all described to you by the flowing text. The game's parser presented a special challenge: what did it expect you to write to get something to happen? This could be extremely frustrating when nothing seemed to work, but gratifying when you hit on the right phrase to get to the next cave or throne room.

Blank and Lebling in 1979 had founded their own game company, Infocom, which marketed the three installments of the Zork trilogy and then wrote many more, such as *Deadline*, a mystery; *Planetfall*, science fiction featuring a robot companion named Floyd; *Enchanter*; and *Witness*. All of these were intriguing but the one that made the greatest impression on me was *A Mind Forever Voyaging* written by Steve Meretzky and released in 1985.

The premise was that you thought you were a human but were told that you were really a computer. You had, you thought, lived in a small town which proved to be a computer simulation. You were now asked to return to the "town" to record the projected effects of a piece of congressional legislation that would be a major reorganization of the American political system. The first simulation was a projection ten years into the future to look for effects of the social reorganization. Everything was fine, you made your report, and the legislation was approved by Congress. Next you were sent twenty years ahead, but this time things were starting to go wrong. At thirty years everything was terrible, which you experienced by typing in directional commands that took you from intersection to intersection in the imaginary town, or into a few accessible buildings. Here is a sample of the thirty-year mark. The sentences in all caps are your commands:

>LEAVE THE CAFETERIA
   Broadway & Devon
>NORTH
   Entrance to Base Devon Street, which continues to the south, ends here at the gate to the National Guard base for this sector of the city. On the west side of the street is a large, imposing building.

To the east is Devon Park. The front page of a newspaper is pinned against the fence of the base by the wind.

>READ THE NEWSPAPER

(taking the newspaper first) The headline story is about President Mazzotta's defense of the Martial Law Board's decision to lower the mandatory euthanasia age to 55. "Without this ruling," the President is quoted as saying, "we'd have a full-fledged famine by the end of next year." The President agreed that it was a difficult and unpopular step, but blamed it on decades of neglect by previous administrators. The article ends with a reminder that everyone over the age of 55 has two weeks to report to a Euthanasia Center.

I remember vividly entering the town zoo and finding a poster that read "Monkey torturing, 2 pm in the primate cage."

Adventure Games: Sierra's King's Quest Series

In the early days of computer gaming the companies were small and personal. Roberta Williams, unusual in the industry as a woman game designer, founded Sierra software with her husband and business manager Ken, and launched the *King's Quest* series in 1984. These were graphic adventure stories with color pictures on the screen. Your character could walk across the pictured landscape and exit at fixed points where there were roads or doorways. Certain few objects could be picked up or activated by finding the hot spot on the screen and clicking on it — hence the term point-and-click adventures.

King's Quest 1 came out in 1984, but I only dipped into the series in 1986 when the third installment was released. As a general rule in game software, unlike movies when sequels are repetitive and usually worse than the original, because of rapid technological innovation most series improved with each new episode. The graphics got better, the stories more complex, more objects could be activated, and the level of realism rose year after year.

In 1986 the computer of the day was the IBM 286, a whiz-bang system with 640K of memory and a 20 meg hard drive. The monitors were the EGA standard — grainy color in 16 shades only — introduced in 1984, which would be replaced with more or less the current VGA standard in 1987. I started with episode 3 and bought the next two as they came out in 1988 and 1990. By *King's Quest V* in 1990 the screens had a kind of Walt Disney style of fairy tale animation with ambitious background music and a fairly coherent plot. My response to them was mixed. I appreciated the more elaborate situations, artwork, dialogue, and music, but found them frustrating because of the limited number of choices, the lack of freedom of movement, and the frequent stalemates when you couldn't figure out what to click on to get the story to move forward. In the end I abandoned the adventure genre, although with some regret as the stories, which became fewer in the 1990s and 2000s, clearly became much more complex over the years (as per the reviews of the very tempting *Syberia* series of recent years).

SSI's Gold Box Series

Moving in another direction was SSI's series of dungeon and dragons games in its famous Gold Box series. Again, I only touched this series briefly, with its *Champions of Krynn*, released in June 1990. These were adaptations of pen and paper role playing games incorporating the elaborate D&D rules for character advancement. Using an already antiquated EGA crude graphic format, to permit the game to run on the Commodore 64 as well as the IBM and Radio Shack's TRS 80 (known affectionately as the Trash 80), the Gold Box series let you maneuver a party of four over a sketchy landscape to accomplish various missions.

Generally by convention your party included a knight, a mage, a cleric good for healing, and usually a character good with a bow. Your mages had an affiliation as good, evil, or neutral, and their orientation increased or decreased their power with the phases of the moon. Also by convention, the party moved in a square formation with your fighters in the front row and the weaker mage and bowman in the back. Clerics could fight with blunt weapons such as maces or cast healing spells. Setpiece battles would occur as you crossed the terrain and suddenly encountered an enemy party. Winning a turn-based battle was a matter of careful strategy.

Exploring Brittania: Lord British and the Ultima Series

The two games that I spent the most time with in the nineties were *Ultima VI* by the Origin company of Austin, Texas, the sixth episode of a long series whose earlier installments I had missed; and *Daggerfall*, second in the Elder Scrolls series by Bethesda Softworks of Rockville, Maryland. Except for the theme of adventuring in a large territory and using swords and magic these two projects explored opposite ends of how to construct a computer role playing game.

Origin, and its founder Richard Garriott, created their own mythos in a way absolutely unique among computer gaming companies. They were the Arthur and his round table of the industry where everyone else were only gamers and programmers. Garriott was born in Cambridge, England, to an American astronaut father who was also a professor of electrical engineering at Stanford, and a mother who was a professional artist and silver smith

In high school in Texas Garriott was nicknamed Lord British because of his English accent. He studied computer programming on his own, writing one of the first computer role playing games, *Akalabeth*, when he was nineteen for the Apple II. Sales of this were in plastic baggies, but it made so much money that Garriott dropped out of college to found his own game company, Origin Systems, in Austin, Texas. Origin under Garriott's leadership produced the long-running Ultima series.

At the height of the series popularity in the 1990s Garriott built a 4,500-square-foot hilltop house outside Austin, complete with dungeons, secret passageways, a moat, an indoor swimming pool with artificial rain effects, an observatory, and, in the backyard, a 1,150-foot-long suspension bridge. An amateur scientist, Garriott tracked gorillas in Rwanda, canoed down the Amazon, hunted for meteorites in Antarctica, flew a MiG jet in Russia, and dived to view the Titanic in a submersible with his girlfriend. He would appear at trade shows dressed as Lord British, and cut a striking figure in his doublet and crown.

He was an active member of the Society for Creative Anachronisms, a sort of Renaissance Fair organization. He freely incorporated friends into the story line of his games, which made them a kind of role playing *roman a clef*. The fantasy land in which the Ultima series is set was originally named Sosaria. Over time it comes to be ruled by Lord British, Richard Garriott's alter ego, and is renamed Britannia. In *Ultima V* Lord British is imprisoned and the country falls into the hands of the

Richard Garriott

tyrant Blackthorne. The goal of the episode is to unseat Blackthorne, which gamer legend had it was a real associate of Garriottt's with whom he had a falling out.

I arrived in Britannia with *Ultima VI*. The convention of the series was that you play the Avatar, who is called to Britannia from the United States by Lord British when there is a national crisis. The party your Avatar leads can have various members but usually includes the old knight Dupre, said to be modeled on a man Garriott knew in the Society of Creative Anachronisms. Then there was the young blond fighter Shamino, a name transposed from Garriott's Japanese Shimano bicycle. The third was Iolo, a bowman.

In *Ultima VI* your party also included a mouse, that is literally a small rodent, named Sherry. Sherry, the legend had it, was actually the girl friend of one of the programmers. As part of the standard machinery of an RPG, you and each of your party members began very weak, that is, with few hit points and thus easily defeated in combat with enemies. The mouse, naturally, was by far the weakest of all, beginning with perhaps 10 hit points. You needed Sherry because in one of the towns on the south coast you had to have a party member small enough to get through a narrow crack in a wall.

While all my other party members were strong enough to wear armor and carry swords and additional weapons, I found that Sherry was only strong enough to carry a dagger. I thought I would try to match her against some very weak opponent to build up her strength. In some of the dungeons the party was attacked by groups of rats. You could move each party member independently of the others, so I would range a few strong members forward on the sides, then send Sherry the mouse in alone with her dagger to fight the rats. If she got into trouble I would have her retreat and a more powerful fighter take over the combat. Over time each party member was rewarded for their victories in fights by increasing their various stats. Sherry soon was strong enough to carry a sword. Then I had her take on creatures like goblins. Eventually she was able to wear armor, although this was before games showed what your characters were wearing or carrying, as the mouse really had no place to put the armor. By the end of the game many weeks later Sherry the mouse was my strongest fighter.

Garriott, more than any other major game developer, tried to use the limited technology to pose moral issues. He invented his own religion in which shrines of various virtues played a major role. He used semi-religious symbols. The Avatar always wears an Egyptian Ankh, and a symbol of the realm is the Silver Serpent, based on a piece of silver sculpture made years before by his mother. Ultima also used the runic alphabet popularized by Tolkien to label place names on the map included with the game and on all in-game signposts, forcing players to learn the runic script to be able to tell where they were.

In *Ultima VI* Britannia is invaded by the Gargoyles, drawn to look like traditional demons with red skin and horns. In the early stages of the Avatar's arrival he visits hospitals where injured soldiers curse the enemy. Later he meets a bard who expresses some ambivalence about the purposes of the

The Silver Serpent

Gargoyles, and by the end the Avatar discovers that the Gargoyles are responding to the rapid destruction of their world caused by a previous action of the Avatar himself, and he must go to the Gargoyle country where everyone looks like a demon to undo the damage.

Ultima VI despite its top-down graphics and limited resolution had six or seven towns, travel by ship, underground caverns, and nonplayer characters with their own brief stories to tell. In one dungeon, unexpectedly, you are attacked by a group of children. In an interview I read that this was a moral test. If you thought fast enough you could cast a sleep spell on them and not kill them. Other companies have shied away from this dilemma. In the Elder Scrolls series by Bethesda, even though the worlds are larger than the old Ultimas, with hundreds of characters, for several installments there were no children, for fear that some players would kill them deliberately and this would incense the right-wing censors who are always looking for grounds to restrict or ban computer games. In the later installments children are made invulnerable and will run away if you try to hurt them.

In the next installment, *Ultima VII*, there is one place wandering through a forest where you encounter a large troll. By reflex toward all such nonhuman creatures I killed him. Then walked my character into his cave, and there found his wife and children seated around the dinner table. I still regret that action, definitely bad karma, a measure of the power of the interactive medium.

An annoying innovation in *Ultima VII* was that the characters in your party got hungry but expected you to feed them. You would have your group, a straggly line, marching through the countryside to get to some town and first one then another would post a text balloon saying "I'm hungry!" Each character had a backpack which you could click on to have a small window on the screen open showing its contents. If you had thought to pack lots of bread and cheese when in the last town you could click on a loaf of bread and drag it over to the complaining party member, and they would be quiet. Then the next one would start in. You spent an inordinate amount of time dragging food items from backpacks to satisfy the digital hunger pangs of your group of followers. There were many complaints about this and the idea was abandoned in *Ultima VIII*.

In the end Origin Systems ran short of money and Richard Garriott sold the company to Electronic Arts. In short order they sped up the development cycle, released the next few installments unfinished with almost unplayable bugs, and finally killed the franchise except for *Ultima Online*. The failed games had a few memorable advances, notably the seamless connection between building interiors and exteriors where you could enter a structure and look out the windows, something still not duplicated in such state-of-the-art productions as the Elder Scrolls *Oblivion* of 2006. Richard Garriott has gone on to other projects, mostly in online gaming, but has never recovered the old magic.

New World Computing's Might and Magic

A word should be said about the Might and Magic series of Jon Van Caneghem. Van Caneghem founded New World Computing in 1983 and created the Might and Magic role playing games. These were distinguished by a landscape of bright primary colors, a first-person viewpoint, and a party usually of six members represented by faces in a row across the bottom of the screen. The series went through nine iterations between 1987 and 2002. I came into the series with episode three in 1991.

I spent the most time with *Might and Magic VII* published in 1998. Here the party was reduced to four, and the interest was mostly tactical, in that you were often confronted with large crowds of computer controlled opponents. To win against them you needed to strike fast and run, or find a narrow hall-way or defile where only a few could approach your party at one time. As with Origin, New World Computing fell foul of an acquisition. It was sold to 3DO in 1996. 3DO went bankrupt in 2003, taking New World Computing down with it.

Jon Van Caneghem should also be remembered for the turn-based strat-egy spin-off of the Might and Magic series, *Heroes of Might and Magic*. This was a game with almost infinite replayability, especially as it included its own map editor, which spawned an online community of fans who spent endless hours creating their own detailed maps. Many sought to adapt their maps to tell stories, a seriously difficult project in an open ended strategy game based on capturing castles and resource mines. But many tried, creating maps with hero characters and situations based on the Arthurian legend, on Sherlock Holmes, and on other computer games such as the Ultima series. After the collapse of 3DO the *Heroes of Might and Magic* franchise was sold to the French company Ubisoft, which brought out *Heroes V* in 2006, adding a 3D game engine, to mixed reviews.

The World of Tamriel

One of the most successful role playing series is the Elder Scrolls, set in the fantasy world of Tamriel, produced by Bethesda Softworks of Rockville, Maryland. The episodes have been widely spaced in time, with only four ma-jor releases and two minor ones counting from the first in the series, *Arena*, published in 1994. Where the Ultima and Might and Magic series were tightly scripted and every character had fixed lines, the Elder Scrolls world was vast and sometimes disturbingly empty. The programmers concentrated on a first-person realistic landscape of huge dimensions, in the early iterations generated from stock materials on the fly. It was a single player game from the start, no party to manage here, and presented from a first-person perspective through the player's eyes.

Arena gave the first rude idea of what the programmers were trying to do. It was a rebellion against the linear play of graphic adventures or even of the Ultima series. It aimed at the creation of an immersive world in which the player could roam with no definite goal. Endless roads wandered through pixilated landscapes, occasionally dotted with tiny towns or isolated huts, inns, or stone keeps. It was not that there were no people. Plenty of people appeared to walk around the towns, while in the countryside monsters or bandits would attack you. It was that there were too many people and towns for any of them to have any specificity or individuality. The whole place was generated from computer algorithms — the nonplayer characters were walking signboards. If you clicked on one of them they would stop and a text screen would let you ask a few simple questions, like where is the nearest inn. The vastness was impressive but the emptiness dispiriting.

Daggerfall

Two years later with the release of *Daggerfall* the Bethesda vision began to come into focus. The fantasy land was Tamriel, divided into nine provinces (offering significant potential longevity to the series). Daggerfall was a city on the northwest coast in the province of High Rock. *Daggerfall*, the game, contained a plot, something about a scheme by the King of Worms to kill off the existing monarchy, plus subplots of struggles within the royal family and aristocracy. I did a small part of that, with an interesting episode where a woman aristocrat asked me to deliver a cloak to a friend at his rural estate, only to have it turn out that the cloak was poisoned. The local lord died on the spot as he put on the gift, and I was nearly killed by his retainers. But the game was so open ended that you could, and I did, play for months while only touching base with key plot characters on a few rare occasions.

Here I should explain for any readers who don't know what the motor is of role playing games what keeps the player at their keyboard. The core elements, independent of where there is a plot line or not, are straight forward. You begin each of these games as a very weak character. You have a series of attributes such as strength, intelligence, endurance, dexterity, etc., which in turn control your power in a physical fight, what level of magic you have ac-

cess to, how much armor or treasure you can carry around, and whether you
are any good with a bow and arrow, and so on with numerous other attributes
and skills. Most games in the last ten years have more attributes than these
and complex rules for how they can be increased.

As you go out into the open-ended game world you encounter people
who give you quests, and characters or monsters who attack you. In the simplest quests you are asked to deliver a letter to someone far away. In more
complex ones you may have to meet a group, break into a castle, recover
some object, get information from someone, assassinate a well-guarded or
powerful enemy, undergo special training. Along the way you accumulate
gold, better weapons, magical objects, plants that can be sold at an alchemy
shop. Your armor and weapons wear out in combat and must be repaired or
replaced, you become ill with diseases that need to be cured with elixirs or by
a temple priest. The towns are full of stores, the stores are full of merchandise.
Often the proprietor also asks you to do him or her a favor. And of course out
in the hinterlands there are caves, bandit camps, outlaw fortresses, wandering
spirits and magic workers, and wild animals.

Then there are guilds to join, and there is the race issue to consider. The
stock races of these games — usually elves, dwarves, orcs, and humans of two
or three sorts, a generally Tolkienesque cast, plus a catlike or reptilian race —
involve prejudices in which whatever you are in the game will produce favorable or unfavorable reactions from shopkeepers and other nonplayer characters. All of this is comparatively independent of any story line. It's just a place
where a lot of things are going on that you have to react to.

Typically the game will go in cycles. You receive a quest that you know
will involve a difficult fight. You spend time then buying supplies in different
stores, such as better arrows. You get your armor repaired. If you are short of
gold, you find some chore or small quest that can get you enough gold to buy
the new boots you need, or to have your magic sword recharged in a magic
guild. This part is very task oriented and involves careful planning.

Then you set out, walk miles through mountain pathways and forests,
during which you are usually attacked several times by robbers or wild animals. You finally arrive at the required cave, tower, castle, or inn, meet your
enemy, exchange a few words and then get into a major fight. When you win,
if you win, you scour the place for salable items, decide how much of this you
can carry without becoming dangerously overburdened, then walk back to
whoever gave you the quest to claim a reward. When you arrive in town — it
is usually a town but it can be an isolated country inn — you make the rounds
to sell off the objects you have collected, have your equipment repaired at the

right shops, see what better equipment you can now buy with your savings, and then off to find another quest.

Your aim, if you have no other, is to explore the countryside, and to increase those stats; more strength, intelligence, endurance, and dexterity; to acquire better armor, more and stronger magic spells, and better weapons. Early in the game almost anything can beat you and you often have to run away. Later, usually much later, you are a match for most of what you may encounter, although even then often only if you carefully plan out your attack and don't take foolish chances. Of course, you also want to explore. Have you ever been to the village of so and so? What is up on that mountain range to the east? If you had a ship you could get to that island you see off the coast. And there is that dark inland forest. In the early 1990s these landscapes, while very large, were pixilated and often had little you could move around or affect. As the years have gone by the landscapes have gotten better with the higher power of current PCs. The wind now blows in the trees, there are rainstorms, snow, you can swim across rivers, watch the sun rise or the moons (usually plural), read books, eat food (tasteless), and these days the nonplayer characters speak real words instead of printing out their comments.

Now for a few old war stories from. . .

Daggerfall

There were now a few scripted situations, somewhat lost in a sea of cardboard automatons. But the complexity of the world began to be intriguing. Daggerfall was a good sized town containing numerous guilds, many stores, temples, and ordinary houses. Outside the town walls the territory was absurdly huge. It was said that the virtual world of Daggerfall, limited to the province of High Rock, was the size of England. You could walk your character for an hour in real time and not get to the next town, much less to edge of the land mass, except for the coastal sea, where you could wade out a ways but were stopped by the conventions of the program.

The graphics were still fairly grainy, but the game had a true 3D engine and you could explore at will, beginning with the town itself. There were days, when there was a quiet rain or snow falling, when it was a genuinely peaceful experience to meander through the by-now familiar streets and alleyways. I recall once on a journey into the countryside in a winter snowfall seeing a dramatic stone fort on an island in a small river, and feeling a certain thrill in jumping into the river and climbing out onto the island in the shadow of the old walls.

Advancement in life meant joining one or more guilds and taking on quests either for the guild or for individuals. You wanted to work your way up in your guild to gain access to benefits of various kinds. In the mage guild reaching a certain level opened up permissions to enchant objects and to create spells with particular effects and strength. Promotions required that you had achieved certain levels in your attributes or skills. And unlike earlier games where advancement was governed by how many monsters you had killed, in Daggerfall a wide range of skills and magic specialties progressed only through use.

There were various schools of magic. Some had healing powers, others specialized in illusion spells such as invisibility, or spells that influenced people, such as charm spells. And then there was simple destruction, shooting off firebolts and such, a staple of the kind of combat that turned up frequently. Advancing in Destruction magic could only be achieved by using it, not by random battles. It was common for Daggerfall players to hole up their character in an inn or a room in the Mages Guild, and fire off low-level firebolt spells by the hour as a means to raise their levels. I did it, and so did many others.

Then there was exploring the stores. Some paid better prices for booty; some sold their goods at cheaper prices. Some had a better selection of higher level arms or armor. So you spent time figuring out the geography of the town and where to go for what. It reminded me a bit of the first weeks after moving to New York from California in the 1960s.

Quests commonly sent you out to retrieve something from a dungeon. And here the programmers had used the algorithm method to generate what came to be called spaghetti dungeons, places with so many winding tunnels that once lost in them you could spend two or three real hours trying to find your way out again.

When you got in a fight, especially in a dungeon, your character usually was wounded even if you won. If you could sleep, your wounds would heal. But there was always the chance that some creature in the dungeon would find you while you were sleeping, worst of all was if they found you soon, when very little healing had taken place. Then you were forced into another combat under unfavorable circumstances.

Once you had risen high enough in the Mages Guild to have use of the enchanting services, one thing I tried was to enchant a complete outfit — shoes, pants, shirt, and hat, each imbued with a boost (cumulative) to my mercantile skill. On coming back to town loaded with Orc armor and such in my wagon (the game included horses, wagons, and ships), I would take off my armor (here to avoid a lot of extra verbiage let me just refer to my character as me) and put on the suit of mercantile-enhanced clothes. Now I could double the sale price of my goods. I could even, unethical as it was, buy a merchant's goods and sell them back to him for more than I had paid him in the first place. After a while I had enough gold to buy my own house and a ship.

The above raises the issue of how to talk about your activities in virtual worlds. It is unreasonable to prefix every remark with "in the game," "my character," etc. But blending the two worlds also has its pitfalls. Once in 1990 when I was managing a computer service at UCLA, I and a fellow who worked for me were at our respective homes in the evenings both playing a game called *Circuit's Edge*, a cyberpunk adventure set in the Middle East. We were stuck trying to follow clues to an in-game mystery. One night I figured out the next step and was eager to share it with Kevin. In the office the next day I said to him, "I figured out how to get into Mustafa's Pawn Shop last night. I went into that alley behind his store, and there's a way to break in through the warehouse next door. I found proof that Abu Salah was involved in the murder of Kenji Carter!" We were intent on our discussion and didn't notice the three people standing around with their mouths open. Luckily this was before Homeland Security or we would have really been in trouble.

A lot of what you did in *Daggerfall*, as in the real world, had to do with making money. A young fellow who was living with us at the time named Jared also got deep into *Daggerfall*. And while the game did not script moral issues as the Ultima series did, they could arise naturally from how you chose to play.

There was a law in the city of Daggerfall that you could not sleep on the town streets except in an inn or guild, or within a certain distance of the town walls. Jared would camp just outside of town. A pair of guards would show up and try to arrest him — there were jails you could be put in until you paid a fine or did some time. Jared would kill the guards. This would produce a very large number of guards who would show up to subdue this criminal. Jared would systematically kill them all. Pretty soon he would have a huge pile of armor, swords, pikes, boots, and odds and ends, which he would load into his wagon and take back to town to sell, reminiscent of a scene in Clint Eastwood's spaghetti western *A Few Dollars More*.

Now, I was horrified at this behavior. If you are going to suspend disbelief in the reality of the place and its inhabitants, then you are going to want to treat them as you would in the real world. Even in the game world this behavior gave Jared a hideous reputation and most citizens would run from him on sight.

Then I encountered an insurmountable necessity to do some evil myself. Somewhere in one of the dungeons I was bitten by a werewolf. A few nights later my character began to have strange dreams. And by the end of the week I had myself become a werewolf.

I investigated the lore about werewolves in Tamriel and discovered that there were special rules that don't appear in films or Anne Rice novels. Once a month at the full moon (Tamriel did have cycles of its two moons), you would turn into a wolf, complete with muzzle and hairy paws. As a werewolf you could not use any ordinary weapon, armor, or clothing. Worse yet, your hit points would fall to about 15, making you helpless before almost any serious foe. To avoid dying you had to kill a human. Then you would be extra strong for the few days of the full moon.

I considered this killing innocent humans thing for a while. But as there was no alternative I decided to do it with as little repercussion as possible. If I killed anyone in Daggerfall town I would have the guards all over me and an evil reputation that might drive me out of the city. Further, once I had turned furry, everyone I met would flee. I settled on traveling each month to a different tiny village well out in the country, run onto the main street, and kill the first person I got my claws into. Everyone would run from me at sight, but I could always catch some unlucky person. That would galvanize the locals and they would chase me far out into the fields. This led to some close calls, and some moral unease, but it was a way to survive.

Then one day the game revealed just how complex its unscripted interactions could be. Early in the game I had received an invitation to join the Dark Brotherhood, essentially a guild of assassins. I refused. Every now and then in retribution for my refusal I would be attacked suddenly by a would-be assassin. This usually came as a surprise, but had not been too much of a problem, as I was stronger than they were. Then one day I woke up in a bedroom on the second floor of an inn where I had booked a room to recover from wounds, to discover that it was change day and I was in wolf form with no weapons and extremely weak. I headed for the stairs, planning my usual excursion to a remote village to fix my problem, when at the front door I ran into a Dark Brotherhood assassin coming in to get me. He seemed to have no problem recognizing me in my wolf guise and gave chase. By the time I was up on the third floor it was clear that I was not going to get out of this one. I quickly employed my magic weapon: I exited the game and restored from my latest saved position. But I found myself back in my room, just waking up as a wolf. I went to the head of the stairs, and there was the assassin again coming in the downstairs front door.

I thought for a moment and came up with a piece of in-game magic that could give me a way out. There was a teleportation spell that worked by first placing an anchor somewhere, then later teleporting back to it. I went down the stairs, walked right up to the assassin. I cast the anchor spell, then ran up the stairs with the killer on my electronic heels. Up we went to the third floor.

Just as he was about to finish me off with his dagger I cast the return spell, landed instantly on the front doorsill, and ran off down the street. Even for a purely virtual adventure I thought that one was pretty good.

May 15, 2006

Postscript, March 17, 2012

Sales of all computer and video game software and dedicated hardware, though hit by the recession after 2008, reached $25.1 billion in 2010. The demographics have also changed over the years. The Entertainment Software Association in a 2011 report found that 72% of households play video games, the average age of players is 37, and 29% of players are over 50.

The quality and complexity of these kinds of games has moved along with giant strides since *Daggerfall* came out in the summer of 1996. Bethesda Softworks, the creator of *Daggerfall*, has remained in the forefront of the field. The Elder Scrolls world of Tamriel has had three major iterations along with other less memorable releases: *Morrowind* in 2002, *Oblivion* in 2006, and *Skyrim* in 2011, as well as two in the *Fallout* series of a dystopian future in a devastated Washington, DC, and Las Vegas.

In each successive release the graphic quality has improved strikingly. In *Morrowind* weather appeared, rain and dust storms. In *Oblivion*, all the characters were now voice acted from a huge branching script, the talent including Patrick Stewart. Now you could swim under water, hunt deer, enter complex subplots, and in the forests the leaves shook in the breeze. A musical score was written just as for a major film.

By the time of *Skyrim* at the end of 2011 the strategy guide book that can be purchased as an aide runs to 657 8-1/2 X 11 densely packed pages, with scores of local maps, instructions on the use of many plants to compound potions, and a numbing volume of background and detail. In the game itself NPCs carry on extensive lives independent of the player character, working at their trades, discussing with each other, arguing, and fighting over valuables. More than seventy actors were employed to voice the nonplayer characters, including Christopher Plummer and Max von Sydow. The musical soundtrack by Jeremy Soule has been released on four CDs.

Skyrim in its first two months sold more than 10 million units, for more than $620 million. This is vastly more than any film grossed in 2011, and almost twice the income of the year's top grossing film, *Harry Potter and the Deathly Hallows, Part 2*, at $381,011,219.

Under the current Digital Rights Management anti-piracy controls, home users have to log in to the online Steam website to play their own copy. At one point in early January 2012, 5 million players were logged in at the same time, each playing *Skyrim* by themselves. While I have a copy and have spent an hour or two with it and been impressed, the sheer scale and complexity of the game world have told me that it would take an inordinate amount of time to master. Maybe on a long vacation. Below is a screenshot from *Skyrim*. It loses quite a bit from not being in color.

Skyrim

Goodbye Zacky

My wife Jennifer drove us to the vet while I held him in my arms. He hated the vet. I always took him, when it was unavoidable, in a cat carrier, and he screamed all the way. Today I held him in my arms instead. He nestled there quietly, holding his head up to look out at a world he last saw almost twenty years ago. Jennifer told them what we wanted. I sat with him quietly, then they called us into one of the exam rooms, took his weight, just a little over seven pounds, to see how much of the drugs they would need. He screamed for the first time when they picked him up and took him into a back room, to insert a catheter into his right front leg. He was silent when they brought him back, thin, with his once beautiful fur an unkempt disordered tangle.

The name we had given him was Zachary, though we always just called him Zacky. He came to the door one day in September 1990, lost and hungry, a young handsome classic tabby, black and gray with the distinctive circular pattern on his sides like a target. We took him in, meaning to find him a home elsewhere. The vet when we had him examined said that he was about nine months old, so he was probably born in January 1990. We convinced a neighbor across the street to take him. Happily for us, though not for her, Zacky scratched her and she developed cat scratch fever, a large swelling like a goiter on her neck, and she insisted that we take him back.

Zacky proved to be brave and adventurous. He had stopped in for a meal, not agreeing to become a prisoner for life, but that is what happened to him. For years he tried valiantly to escape, to go back to whatever journey had brought him to us in the first place. When a door would open he would make a rush for it, now and then slipping past an unwary giant. I caught him several times as he reached the end of our long porch and was heading off into the bushes. Once he escaped and we went to bed unawares. In our dry arid Los Angeles climate his bad luck was to escape into a rain storm. In the morning we found him clinging spread eagled to the screen on the outside of a back porch window and let him back in.

It wasn't that he didn't like us. He did. And he became more affectionate as he grew older. He was the most lively member of our family. Margaret, a school friend of Jennifer's daughter, lived with us for a while that first year. She and Zacky would play a game. Our big 1910 Craftsman house, in the Craftsman manner, flows one room into another, making circles beloved of children and animals: from the living room into the dining room then into the breakfast room, through the kitchen back to the entry way and then the living room again, round and round. Zacky would chase Margaret round-robin through the course, then she would turn on him and he would take the lead with her in hot pursuit, round and round they went. Margaret was the first human Zacky bonded to, with a fierce loyalty that they both remembered many years later when she would occasionally visit.

He was the most acrobatic of our cats. In the dining room he would leap to the top of an old pine breakfront four feet off the ground, then wind up and from there to the narrow lintel over the big pocket doors, run along that, jump down to the top of a five-foot cabinet, then take a mighty leap to the top of an eight foot high built-in china cabinet. There he would strut as king of the mountain. He could somehow reach almost all the plate rails of our old house, where he would balance precariously while racing along near the ceiling, occasionally knocking a picture off the wall with a crash or breaking one of Jennifer's prize teacups. Once he got past the fire screen and climbed halfway up the chimney of the living room fireplace, tumbling down looking like a furry ball of soot.

For a long time I think he was to me just one more of our several cats, and he had the parallel feeling toward me. Jennifer decided that he should be my cat. She began to carry him in to our bedroom at bedtime and set him down next to my pillow. I was honored when he decided he liked the idea and came every night to jump into bed, most of the time telling me when he had decided it was bedtime. Before Zacky I used to read in bed for a few minutes before dozing off. He wouldn't put up with that. If I wanted his company there couldn't be any split screen or multi-tasking. Open a book and he would stalk off and go sleep somewhere else. I quickly gave up bedtime reading.

Over time we became hooked on each other. Zacky had big green eyes, calm and phlegmatic. For years he was top cat in our household, just, apparently, by some feline charisma, as he was kind hearted, never fought, welcomed new younger cats into the house or ignored them, but seemed to have the respect of all the others, who plainly deferred to him. I put a cat bed for him on my desk, surrendering a good part of it to his domain. Whenever I would walk into the room he would lift a paw to me in welcome.

Somewhere the years slipped away. Jennifer had cats long before she and I got together in 1982, and there were always three or four in our household, one generation succeeding another, as their short cat lives usually ended by the time they were thirteen or fifteen. Zacky outlived many of them. By the time he was sixteen in 2006 signs of old age began to appear. In human years he was already 80. I got sets of cat stairs so he could get to his bed on my desk, to climb into two of his favorite windows, and next to my bed. He understood immediately what they were for, and now at night he would wait for me to get into bed first, then climb up his stairs, stick his head over the edge to confirm that I was there, then climb in. He slept curled up in my arms. He was small for a cat, nine or ten pounds in his best years.

Near the end of the nineties he tested positive for feline leukemia and we thought he would die, but he miraculously threw it off. In 2005 he was diagnosed with hyperthyroidism and an enlarged heart, when again we thought it was the end. From that time he was on two medications I had to push down his throat daily. I stopped traveling then, as his care had become too complicated, I thought, for a cat sitter, leaving Jennifer to visit her oldest son in Cleveland by herself. I knew a fellow at UCLA before I retired who, with his wife, did the same thing for his aging sick cat.

As he became frail in his later years Zacky became still more affectionate. At night when Jennifer and I would watch a movie on television Zacky would come and sleep cradled in the crook of my arm during the program. About three years ago we got a small dog, and had to put our cats' food on top of the dryer to keep it away from the dog. Zacky was too old to get up there, even on a ramp that I built for the others. So began the necessity that I stay with him for every meal to guard him from other hungry household animals. During the night he would get up three or four times to eat, and I would get up with him; if I wasn't there he would have nothing to eat. I became quite used to it, at midnight, two, and four every morning. Now he would sit in my lap if I read a book, or ask to be picked up while I was working at my computer. Luckily I had retired in 2005 and was home most of the time, where I spent much of it with him. I rarely said no, becoming adept at typing Google queries with one hand while cradling him with the other.

I could see he had become stiff and walked with some difficulty. Sometimes he would lose his balance jumping off a footstool or a chair and land on his back. He was generally his phlegmatic self about these mishaps. He turned twenty this January, counted as ninety-six in human years. Yesterday I was reading in an easy chair in the living room. Zacky staggered down the stairs from the second floor and came toward me. I could see his back legs were almost paralyzed. I picked him up and put him on my lap. He sat quietly, but his hind legs twitched, and he lost control of his bladder. When I lifted him up he cried out in pain. That night I brought him to bed, laying out waterproof puppy training pads to protect the sheets, and we slept enfolded with each other one last time. He got up in the night as usual, even ate in my study, but twice cried out. It was time.

At the vet's the young woman doctor carried two syringes in her apron. Zacky sat very still on the examination table and made no protest as she fitted the first into the catheter opening in his front leg. As the fluid cylinder emptied he lay his head down on his paws. With the second syringe he stopped breathing. I stood there crying.

May 16, 2010

Freddy's Feed and Read

This is about a place I never saw, and which has been gone for twelve years. Even longer ago, back in my Marxist days, in New York in the early seventies I was editor of a monthly magazine called the *International Socialist Review*. In 1973 we claimed a circulation of 6,851, a bit less than half from subscriptions and the rest listed as dealers and counter sales. The truth about this last is that almost all of the bundles went to branches of the Socialist Workers Party around the country and very few to bookstores. Now and then I would go downstairs in the party's Manhattan headquarters, where Flax Hermes, the blond athletic business manager, would show me the order lists. Among the handful of nonparty orders one stood out. It was called Freddy's Feed and Read. The name was odd enough but it was located in the unlikely town of Missoula, Montana.

They had a standing order for 10 or 15 copies of our militantly Marxist journal. I often tried to imagine what Freddy's could be like. I think the image that came to mind was Ron Crumb's Mr. Natural standing in front of a shelf of Marxist classics. This lingering romantic picture of a fusion of rural isolation and radical politics was somewhere in the back of my mind when in 1979 I volunteered to move from New York to Virginia, Minnesota, on the Mesabi Iron Range to take a job in the iron mines and help to run a tiny socialist bookstore.

Recently with the magic of the internet I thought I would try to find out more about Freddy's Feed and Read. How did it get there and did it still exist? Obviously it stocked radical stuff. One internet post said they hung a North Vietnamese flag in the store during the Vietnam War. Fairly brave in a small town in a red state. Montana voted Republican in every presidential election from 1952 to 2008, except for backing Lyndon Johnson in 1964 and Bill Clinton, for his first term only, in 1992.

Worse yet, Missoula, in the far west of Montana, is near the border with northern Idaho, the national capital of ultraright-wing survivalist militia nuts, where Rev. Richard Grint Butler built his still-extant anti-Semitic armed Aryan Nations compound at Hayden Lake in the early 1970s. Some years later and even closer there was John Trochmann's Militia of Montana, founded in 1994 at Noxon, Montana, just a bit northwest of Missoula near the Idaho border.

Missoula in 1970 had a population of 29,497, about twice the size of Virginia, Minnesota. The town is isolated in a mountainous valley of the same name. The name comes from a Flathead Indian word for "place of freezing water," referring to the Blackfoot River, which runs through the valley and bisects Missoula. Lewis and Clark passed through the valley in 1805, but the first white settlement didn't appear until 1860. It grew into a small logging town, followed inexplicably by the founding of the University of Montana there in 1895, which helps to explain how Freddy's could survive. Until the end of the 1970s when the timber petered out, the town was mostly divided between the university and the loggers.

Freddy's Feed and Read opened in 1972 in a storefront at 1221 Helen Avenue just a block west of the university, which itself is nestled up against the mountains at the east end of town. I never found out who Freddy was. The store was created by a group of local radicals, some university figures, and a few investors who called themselves collectively Our Gang, Inc. At first it only sold books, then it added a small organic market, and in later years a mostly vegetarian restaurant. It lasted twenty-six years, much longer than the *International Socialist Review* or our ill-fated Iron Range bookstore, closing finally in 1998.

My internet search turned up 205 hits for "Freddy's Feed and Read." A *New York Times* piece from May 12, 1996, titled "The All Too Wild West," set the stage:

"We stopped in Missoula for lunch at a place called the Mustard Seed. Missoula is a college town — the University of Montana is there. . . . At Freddy's Feed and Read, a combination bookstore and deli, I picked up a copy of 'The Journals of Lewis and Clark.' But the shelves were pretty sparse — and so was the entire town, for that matter, which seemed to consist mostly of above-ground municipal parking lots. The streets were a four-lane grid, unnervingly empty in the middle of the day."

Reports from Dark Acres

Not too helpful. I hit pay dirt with a 2006 reminiscence by Bill Vaughn headed "Reports from Dark Acres."

"By the mid-1970s," Vaughn wrote, "Missoula had become one of those towns like Eugene, Madison and Chapel Hill where hordes of baby boomers finished college but refused to leave. And why should we? You simply couldn't find the people and the things you'd come to love in places that didn't have student ghettoes. You bought your bongs and incense and roach clips at the Joint Effort, your organic veggies and tofu at the Good Food Store, and your ramen and your beer and your pinko tracts at Freddy's Feed and Read."

Vaughn had been one of the hard core in his day. "I'd spent my twenties in this dusty warren of offices, obsessed with class struggle, hallucinogenic drugs, and the imminent collapse of monopoly capital. But our lonely campaign of agitprop and radical publishing had been rudely ignored in the crush of our greedy, reactionary countrymen as they boogied down the Disco Highway toward that golden city where the bourgeoisie claimed there would be plenty of cash for everyone."

He describes his effort to organize an antiwar demonstration in front of Missoula's Federal Building in May 1972 to protest Nixon's mining of Haiphong Harbor. Only three people showed up; himself, his girlfriend, and his best friend. Then five tough looking characters appeared, four men and a woman.

"The toughest-looking one made his way through the traffic. I got ready to fight. But when he came closer and I saw that his jaw was the size of a gorilla's I got ready to run. 'What the fuck is this?' he said. 'Who the fuck are you?' I said. He flicked away his cigarette and went to his pocket. I flinched. What he produced wasn't knuckles or a knife, however, but a leaflet I'd printed on an ancient flatbed press in the basement of Freddy's Feed and Read, a leftist book store that also sold groceries to stay in business. '*You're cordially invited to World War III*,' the banner said. 'You guys the demonstration?' I unclenched my fist. 'Yeah. So far.' He called across the street. 'This is it!'"

The four men were Vietnam vets. They and the woman constituted a commune they called the Krik twenty miles out of town. Vaughn and his friends united with the Krik to found Missoula's own underground newspaper, *Borrowed Times*, which lasted until 1980. It drew around it, he writes, " a circus of malcontents — anarcho-feminists, crypto-Wobblies, wildcat unionists, Euro-trash homosexuals, Stalinist poets, Maoist fly fishermen, people who would become lawyers."

This was fascinating but more or less in line with what I had expected to find. As I searched further, however, Freddy's persona began to enlarge.

A post on The Stranger Forums from October 2009 reminisced about a score of places around the United States and elsewhere the author had visited, including:

"Montana has those puppy hill climb mountains so looking down at Missoula as in a basin was always a pleasure. I lived with my dear sweet across from the President's mansion in a nice basement apartment with our black and white cat Chaplin. Managed a half-finished painting that was grand. *Freddy's Feed and Read* was a place I could volunteer and do something while Kathy went to school and held a job. That is where I found and read Martha Gellhorn. She was still alive then and she responded to my letter. It was postmarked *Belize City*."

This was in a standing feature called Eggnog's Corner. A bit more searching disclosed that Eggnog is Mac Crary, son of Ryland Wesley Crary. Ryland had been a World War II Navy veteran and author of several books on education and human rights. Eggnog says that when he was a child a gang of his father's enemies beat him so severely he was left brain damaged and deaf. He sometimes signs himself the Deaf Poet. His posts are mostly deep in conspiracy theories, ranging from Homeland Security being responsible for 911 (wasn't that before Homeland Security was created?) and AIDs as a U.S. plot.

On March 13, 2009, Chicago author Keir Graff in his Likely Stories blog on the national Booklist Online website lamented the passing of independent bookstores. In the comments below, Joel Reese wrote, "R.I.P., Freddy's Feed and Read." Unexpectedly, Graff not only knew what Reese was talking about but he had lived in Missoula as a teenager, where he attended Hellgate High School (yes, that was its real name). Graff responded, "Ah, Freddy's, where I read Jonah Hex on stools made out of tree stumps...."

I next turned up a poem by Mary Scriver, who signs herself Prairie Mary, posted in November 2007. It was a bit long but in part it read:

"Sharon is much braver than I am — she lives in Missoula. For three years I visited Missoula twice a month, staying in a basement full of spiders. . . .

"Sharon is in Missoula — where hippies have shacked up with old broke lumberjacks and mill workers who live in the little rental houses along the river that the lumber company provided and is about to sell out from under them. They met in 'blue collar' bars, which are very trendy among students and attract poets, though out-of-work displaced lumberjacks can get mean.

"Sharon is in Missoula — where the Freddy's Feed 'n Read, a co-op for fine books and organic foods, is no longer and I'm still pouting about it. Commerce is dangerous even in Missoula."

Next came something that was really off in a different direction. A May 2008 piece in *The Missoulian*, the local town paper, was headed "Sweet success — Pastry chef Margaret Ambrose-Barton has made a career out of baking for Missoula's finest eateries."

"If you've dined out in Missoula over the past 17 years or so, chances are you've eaten one of Margaret Ambrose-Barton's fabulous desserts," it began. "A professional baker since 1991, when she graduated from Missoula's Vo-Tech Institute (now the College of Technology), Margaret bakes all the special occasion cakes, including wedding cakes, at Pearl Cafe and Bakery. She also provides desserts for Biga Pizza and The Shack."

After the breakup of her first marriage, as a single mother with two children Margaret took her pastry chef training, remarried to a mostly absentee husband who was a congressional aide in Washington, DC, and got her first job — as pastry chef at Freddy's Feed and Read. A Marxist bookstore with a pastry chef?! She was there for seven years.

"'I worked from 3 a.m. until about 11 a.m., and I baked all the morning pastries and the desserts for the day,' she said, shaking her head in wonder at the schedule. 'I also baked my first wedding cakes then, which set the foundation for what I'd be doing over the coming years.'"

Christianbook.com supplied yet another axis. They carried a post about the book *Sidewalks in the Kingdom: New Urbanism and the Christian Faith* by theologian Eric Jacobsen. Booklinks' review comments, "Jacobsen sees the city as a hopeful place, where community, tradition, and beauty come together on a human scale — a vision that an eclectic mix of architects, city planners, and sociologists has recently promoted as the New Urbanism." What does this have to do with Freddy's? The Christianbook site ran an interview with Jacobsen, who is evidently a native of Missoula:

"**Christianbook.com**: Briefly tell us what inspired you to write *Sidewalks in the Kingdom*.

"**Eric Jacobsen**: About two blocks from my house was a little bookstore/coffee shop called Freddy's Feed and Read which had become an informal gathering spot for the neighborhood. After the owner died, Freddy's couldn't make it financially, so the owner of the building went looking for a new tenant who could continue the role that Freddy's had played in our neighborhood. I won't get into the details here, but this process brought to light the fact that our neighborhood was zoned for residences only which meant that places like Freddy's were illegal according to our current zoning codes. It turns out 60% of our neighborhood was non-compliant with current zoning codes. And yet, ours was the most desirable neighborhood in Missoula. This got me thinking why so many zoning codes make it illegal to build the kinds of traditional neighborhoods that a lot of people want to live in. I'm not the only person to ask this kind of question – there is a whole slew of books reviving the notion of a traditional neighborhood – but at the time of writing *Sidewalks in the Kingdom*, the Christian community seemed to be completely left out of this conversation. I wrote *Sidewalks* to remedy that situation."

Environmental scholar J. W. Smith in his 1994 book *The World's Wasted Wealth 2* thanks Fred Rice, manager of Freddy's Feed and Read, for encouraging him to write the book.

I found an online post by poet Greg Rappleye, winner of the prestigious Brittingham Prize in Poetry for 2000 for his book *A Path Between Houses* (University of Wisconsin Press). The dustcover describes the work:

"These are tough-minded poems about loss, and what comes afterwards — the difficult work of rebuilding a life. Greg Rappleye gathers his material across a vast American landscape, from the Florida Keys through the Nevada Desert to the California Coast, rocketing around the country with some strange friends — Odysseus, William Faulkner, Frank Sinatra, and private eye Jim Rockford. Rappleye is not afraid to implicate the self, building a heroic persona in the classic sense — a person in whom the flaws are as celebrated as the occasional triumph."

In his own post Rappleye celebrates the work of the late short story writer and poet Raymond Carver (1938-1988). Rappleye writes:

"I love all of Carver's work, but the poems in *Ultramarine* (Vintage Books, 1987) are particular favorites of mine. I bought the collection in 1989 in Missoula, Montana, at a great little bookstore called Freddy's Feed and Read, on my way to The Yellow Bay Writers' Workshop. This may be the book that persuaded me my future was in poetry, not fiction."

It seems that many lives were touched, and in unexpected ways, by the little remote bookstore cum deli.

End of the Line

"Final Feed, Last Read" was the headline in the November 15, 1998, *Missoulian*:

"Landmark Missoula bookstore Freddy's Feed and Read is closing after 26 years. A small letter placed in the window of Freddy's Feed and Read on Friday the 13th has been a shocking weekend read for fans of the alternative bookstore. Its message: The university area's one-stop shop for books by local authors and tofu shepherd's pie announced it is closing the doors after 26 years. 'Freddy's has always been a business swimming upstream,' said owner Mark Watkins. 'We've been struggling all year, but the culmination has come very quickly.' Too quickly for some, who learned of the news Saturday as they came to the neighborhood hub for their morning cup of coffee and to thumb through new stock.

"'I'm devastated — it's like a death in the family,' said Judith Holloway. She and her husband, Steven, have been customers since Freddy's opened in the early 1970s. 'It's a part of our daily lives.'"

The final straw had been the opening of a Barnes & Noble chain store in Missoula. Freddy's responded with a last ditch effort to keep alive by enrolling with twenty-six other independent bookstores in a 1997 collective lawsuit against Barnes & Noble/Borders claiming the marketing giant gave secret discounts to its own stores that were denied to the independents. The independents called themselves the American Booksellers Association, which included the Ventura Book Store and the Midnight Special bookstore in Santa Monica, but such famous independents as Moe's in Berkeley, the Strand in Manhattan, and Powell's in Portland, Oregon, did not join. The case wasn't settled until 2001, when Barnes & Noble paid $2.3 million to reimburse the ABA's legal fees but included no damages.

The *Missoulian's* 1998 epitaph eulogy added, "It was a place that tried to keep up with its unique clientele, beginning as a bookstore, expanding into a bookstore with an organic grocery store and bulk food, to its current identity as a haven for local authors and customers who prefer meals prepared deli-style, with sinfully decadent desserts, Watkins said.

"'It is a really supportive environment for first-time authors and local writers,' said Deirdre McNamer, a Missoula author whose first book, *Rima In the Weeds,* found a place at Freddy's. 'It was a warm feeling to go to a book signing there — a small moment of triumph in a place I hung out for years and poked through other people's first novels,' she said.

"It's the down-home quality of Freddy's that will be missed by retirees John and Margie Rasmussen. They bike to Freddy's from their South Side home almost every weekend to enjoy the intimate atmosphere."

When the store was gone a fight began over a pizza parlor request to finally change the zoning to allow it to take over the premises. The *Missoula Independent* described the hearing:

"It was an evening pregnant with childhood reminiscences of the beloved bookstore and grocery, replete with nostalgic accounts of nickel-priced cookies sold out of a glass jar on Freddy's counter, children thumbing through comic books, and university radicals lounging around smoking cigarettes while planning the next socialist utopia."

The once-revolutionary enterprise had mellowed to become a sentimental icon revered for its homey memories. It bore more than a passing resemblance to Jimmy Stewart's bank in *It's a Wonderful Life*, providing inspiration to authors, poets, and pastry chefs.

The city council rejected the pizza parlor. The next tenant at 1221 Helen Avenue was Quarter Moon Books. They were succeeded by the Bear's Brew Coffee House, and finally the property is today shared by the Java U coffee house and the Secret Seconds thrift store.

October 8, 2010

A Romanian Novelist

Eugen Uricaru (left) with Leslie Evans

We sit quietly under the arbor in my backyard. "You are familiar with the Cathars, of course," he says. "Yes," I reply, "French offshoots of the Bulgarian Bogomils, who renounced the material world and its god." This esoteric discussion had been prompted by my giving him a copy of my memoir, *Outsider's Reverie*, in which he had reached the chapter recounting my youthful fascination with the ancient Gnostics, otherworldly progenitors of the medieval sects of which we were speaking. He seems interested and intrigued, to have found an unexpected commonality.

My guest was Eugen Uricaru, a distinguished Romanian novelist. He and his wife Lucia, a university professor, were staying with us for three weeks to attend their daughter Ioana's PhD graduation at USC. Ioana Uricaru, a rising Romanian filmmaker, has lived with my wife Jennifer and me for the last three years, enlivening our lives with her sharp tongue, encyclopedic knowledge of films, and her finely tuned political sensibilities.

When she discovered that Jennifer and I had both spent much of our lives as Marxist activists Ioana was incredulous. Having grown up in one of the more bizarre and repressive Communist dictatorships she asked, "You did this voluntarily?" Happily her bitter experiences with the Marxist left didn't make a right-winger out of her. Ioana actively supported Obama in 2008 and has little use for the Republicans.

Ioana has her own listing in the Internet Movie Database. Photos of her are also fairly widely circulated on the Internet through her film work. She directed one of the stories in Christian Mungiu's 2009 comedy, *Tales from the Golden Age*, which was entered the Cannes Film Festival, and her short film *Stopover* was shown in this year's Sundance film festival. Ioana often watches films with us, but laments our indiscriminate tastes, refusing to join us for the many Lifetime and Hallmark films we settle in with, and as for CSI Miami, she dismisses aging red haired lead investigator David Caruso as "Boiled Carrot."

Eugen was born in 1946, making him four years younger than me. White haired and, like me, a bit plump, he apologizes for his poor English, but makes himself understood perfectly well on a wide range of subjects. In his youth he was an ardent Communist. He supported Nicolae Ceausescu when he first became head of the Romanian Communist Party in 1965, as those were years of unusual liberalization. Controls over literature were loosened, overtures were made to the West, Romania was the only country in the world to recognize both Israel and the Palestine Liberation Organization. Ceausescu condemned the Soviet invasion of Czechoslovakia in 1968, and Romania was the first Communist country to join the International Monetary Fund.

Then in 1971 everything went bad. Ceausescu made a state visit to China, still in the throes of the Cultural Revolution, and Kim Il Sung's North Korea. On his return he lurched into totalitarian madness. Eugen Uricaru became an oppositionist, founding the journal *Echinox*. The years from then until the popular revolution overthrew Ceausescu in 1989 were difficult ones for Eugen and Lucia and their two children. Then came the turnaround. Eugen became the Romanian Cultural Attache in Athens, then Deputy Director of the Academy of Romania in Rome, and finally Secretary of State in the Ministry of Foreign Affairs, 2003-2005. Author of 15 novels, he was elected president of the national Union of Writers, 2001-2005. Today he heads the national copyright organization that protects writers' revenues. On the side he wrote a popular screenplay, translated an opera from the Italian, and has translated works of Aleksandr Solzhenitsyn from the Russian.

I ask him what he thinks now of politics, in particular of Marxism and the left. "The right wing is sterile," he begins. "They look only to the past, create nothing new, and lack humanity. The left looks to the future, explores new trends and has founts of creativity and compassion. But there is a catch, here. The left in power always becomes right wing. Its strength is as a cultural movement or current. Becoming the government ruins it."

I think about that. At first it seems simplistic. If the left is to abjure governing, then the government will always be in the hands of the right, or at best some kind of centrists. But then I consider further. There is clearly a bifurcation between the left as a movement that champions opposition to racism, greater equality, freedom of speech, full rights for women and gays, and, in contrast, the many governments that proclaim themselves leftist, and that in fact emerged from indisputable Marxist movements, that have more in common with fascism, at least of the Italian variety, than with the platforms leftists support while in opposition. Some kind of terrible rupture has taken place and Eugen Uricaru's formulation captures it fairly well.

I also suddenly understand why this man has an interest in the Cathars, dualists who believed there was a complete incompatibility between love and power; the material world and those who hold power in it are incapable of love, those who love would be irretrievably corrupted if they assumed material power. It's another way of stating what he has said to me about leftism.

"Have any of your novels been translated into English?" I ask. "I would love to read them." "No," he replies, "only into German, Polish, Greek, Hungarian, and Russian. But one was just published in 2009 in French, *Ils arrivent, les barbares*! 'They are here, the barbarians.' It's about collaborators with the German occupation in Romania during World War I."

I venture that I know a bit of French, and later that day he presents me with a copy.

During their visit they go to Las Vegas ("More vulgar than I could have imagined."), Catalina ("Very charming"), Hollywood ("Not as much there as we would have expected.") and various other sights. Widely traveled in Europe, Asia, and the Middle East, this was the first time that either Eugen or Lucia had visited the United States.

The Book

I settle down with my gift, *Ils arrivent, les barbares!* and my ancient battered Cassell's French dictionary. The book is published by Les Editions Noir sur Blanc, which is working on a translation of another of Eugen Uricaru's novels. *Ils arrivent, les barbares!* can also be bought from Amazon UK. I found myself looking up words on every page, deciphering as much as reading. Ioana joked with me that this was my Rosetta stone, the dimly understood French as the bridge between my monolingual English and the Romanian of the original.

I found myself in a time and place that were previously unknown to me. Romania, a small country easily tossed about by the Great Powers, sat out the first two years of World War I as a neutral, then, on August 27, 1916, entered the war on the Allied side, hoping to recapture Transylvania, the majority Romanian land to its northwest controlled by the Austro-Hungarian Empire. A German army led by General August von Mackensen invaded Romania from Bulgaria in the south five days later. Russian support promised to Romania quickly evaporated and the German-Austrian-Turkish invasion rapidly crushed the Romanian army. On December 6 Bucharest, the capital, fell to the Germans. The Romanian army and the royal family were not destroyed but retreated into Moldavia, the Romanian province that made up the country's northeast quadrant. They held out there until the war ended in 1918.

Eugen Uricaru's novel follows the fates of five central characters from November 1916 through the early days after the capture of Bucharest at the year's end. The tale opens in the disordered Bucharest bohemian mansion of Leonidas Soroceanu, an elderly comic actor who was once famous on the Romanian stage. He has brought his young nephew Ermil from his home in the quiet provincial town of Ramnic (today Ramnicu Valcea) to find him a job as a journalist and get him started on a career. Ermil watches out the window as exhausted Romanian soldiers and cartloads of the wounded stream by day after day. Ermil is more than half in love with his cousin Sophie Vasiliu, a few years his elder, who remains behind in Ramnic in her parents' home. She is also, by a different sister, a niece of Uncle Leonidas.

We learn that Leonidas is something of a mystic, interested in Theosophy and the writings of Madame Blavatsky and Rudolf Steiner. In his youth he ran away with a gypsy circus run by a mysterious man who called himself Merlin. There Leonidas fell in love with the beautiful Grazia. He followed the circus throughout Europe doing odd jobs just to be near her. Grazia, however, finally refused to allow him to go with her when the circus took ship for America, and his life has been absorbed with her memory for more than thirty years. We learn late in the book that he thinks he sees Grazia in his niece Sophie and secretly imagines himself as her lover despite the more than forty years difference in their ages.

The story next turns to Romanian light cavalry officer Lieutenant Luca Demian. Sent alone on horseback to field headquarters for orders, on his return he finds his entire unit, a thousand men and horses, machine-gunned to death by German gunners hidden in foliage on a ridge. This shocking scene is the first inkling that the Germans have penetrated this far into Romanian territory. Riding on alone he encounters a mounted German officer. The two fight with sabers and, while Lieutenant Demian kills his foe, he suffers a grave head wound.

Next onstage is Tanase Berzea, a somber former military man in his sixties who has worked for thirty-five years in the cloisters of the central state ministry in Bucharest. Excluded from the inner circles of power, he longs to be named a minister but has been frozen in the subordinate technical administrative position of director of the ministry staff. We meet him as the city is preparing to fall to the Germans. He is called into the prime minister's office, who tells him that secret war contingency plans had from the outbreak of hostilities called for abandoning Bucharest and making a stand on the north bank of the Siret River at the Moldavian border. The royal family and the top government officials are leaving for Moldavia. Berzea is ordered to remain behind, to pack and ship the nation's archives and to destroy what can't be sent. Then, the prime minister tells him, he is to take the responsibility to be the government's representative in Bucharest to the German authorities, but with the exile government retaining complete deniability for any of his actions.

Strangely, Berzea accepts this doomed proposition, and, at least briefly, feels an ecstatic sense of freedom. He thinks himself finally in charge, a real minister at last. He will rally the remaining government functionaries to act as a buffer between the citizens and the German army. He drafts a manifesto proclaiming that Romania is occupied but not destroyed and all state employees should remain at their posts.

Berzea spends two weeks overseeing packing the dusty archives, working on his manifesto, and, after a while, day dreaming about his vacation two years earlier in Constanza, a seaside resort city on the Black Sea. There, while out walking, he met a beautiful young woman, none other than our Sophie Vasiliu, and stranger still, Berzea, like Leonidas Soroceanu, was also in the distant past a lover of Grazia, just before she joined Merlin's circus. And, like Leonidas, he sees Sophie as a virtual reincarnation of Grazia, his attraction half to the living woman and half to the ghost of the past. He and Sophie meet innocently for walks a half dozen times, during which he tries to remember everything he can of his life with Grazia, which he retails to Sophie at great length. In the end, however, he confesses to her that he has been shifting his affections from the long-lost Grazia to the very present Sophie. She acknowledges his interest but that is all.

We now turn to the lovely Sophie Vasiliu back at her parents home in Ramnic. The house is on the outskirts of town, on the edge of a square facing what had been a Romanian army barracks and is now a stores depot for the

Germans, including corrals and a slaughterhouse for cattle, sheep, and pigs. One day in crossing the square she is caught in the midst of a herd of horned cattle and risks being gored. She is saved by a German officer on horseback. He is Rolf Timmerman, in civilian life a veterinarian, who imagines himself a great humanist and above such petty things as nationalist hatreds. Timmerman trades on Sophie's obligation to him to pay frequent unwanted visits to her home. He defends his conduct with the argument that he is only collecting food to be sent to the hungry people of Germany. Sophie replies that he is an unwelcome conqueror who is stealing food from hungry Romanians to send out of the country.

Then one afternoon Sophie hears a noise in a shed on her property and finds inside our injured Romanian Lieutenant Luca Demian. She brings him into the house. Then, both fearing his discovery by Timmerman and desperately looking for a doctor to tend his wounds, she hits on the scheme of passing him off as her civilian cousin and persuades Timmerman to use his veterinary skills to treat the patient.

This works well enough while Demian is comatose, but eventually he revives — and flees. Now the rather dense German figures out that he has been had. He has Sophie and her parents arrested. We see them being taken away by soldiers, who burn their house behind them.

Now there comes a strange interlude in which we follow the adventures of Lieutenant Luca Demian. He determines to return to the fight against the Germans, not by rejoining the Romanian army on the Siret but right in the area around Ramnic. He finds and impresses a half dozen lost Romanian soldiers, shooting one of them dead when his orders are questioned. They take up living in a den of bushes in a swamp, venturing out to steal food and to kill an occasional cart driver moving provisions for the Germans. When they encounter a real German patrol one of his men is killed and two wounded, with devastating impact on the little band's morale.

This leads Demian to undertake an entirely mad mission: he and his squad will capture the village of Gherani and ambush the Germans who come to take it back. Ragged and dirty, but well armed, they march in and take over the town hall. The incredulous mayor, Niculae Branea, just wants them to go away before the Germans find out about it. He regards Demian as a lunatic, while Demian denounces Branea as a traitor. It seems the place is too small for the Germans to bother with. They have never entered the village, instead delegating a Romanian merchant to make regular visits there to requisition supplies, an arrangement that both sides find entirely satisfactory.

Lieutenant Demian dragoons local farmers to dig trenches on the Gherani side of a small river, planning to hide his men and jump up shooting as the

Germans cross the bridge to the town. When the collaborator merchant shows up, Demian locks him up in the town hall. Somehow word gets to the Germans and they send a detachment. But instead of walking into the ambush on the bridge they halt on the far side of the river and bombard the town with artillery, leveling the entire place. The luckless Romanian soldiers don't get in so much as a shot. The scene closes as Lieutenant Demian and the now outlawed Mayor Branea make a run for the swamp. At least thus far collaborating has looked the better part of valor.

The last part of the novel focuses on Leonidas Soroceanu, his nephew Ermil, and the minister-collaborator Tanase Berzea. Leonidas takes Ermil to Berzea's office in the capital building. We see Berzea falling further and further under the thumb of the German authorities, who issue daily orders over his signature, requisitioning supplies, making more and more restrictive prohibitions, and finally ordering taking of hostages and reprisals against resistance. The sinister Colonel Hentsch explains to him that it is much easier to maintain order if they have a native front man to screen their rule.

Berzea becomes more and more remote, while his old friend Leonidas seems to be wrapped in a fantasy cloud in which Tanase Berzea is an important figure who can protect them and find a promising position for Ermil on one of the German-censored newspapers. He insists that nothing much has really changed by the occupation and everything will work out well despite the war. As they leave, Leonidas and Ermil enter a nightmarish scene of deserted streets, vandalized houses, and wild dog packs. A madman leads them in circles for hours. They are alone on an empty boulevard when no less than General Mackensen himself passes through in an automobile with a large contingent of horse mounted troops. Called General Death by the Romanians, one of his officers rides to curbside and kicks old Leonidas in the jaw with his steel spur, inflicting a suppurating wound.

Undaunted, Leonidas meets that evening with Berzea, who presses on him a secret personal mission. It seems that neither man knows of the other's past with the captivating Grazia, much less that each imagines they see Grazia returned in Sophie Vasiliu. Leonidas is stunned when Berzea urges him to return to Ramnic and persuade Sophie to move to Bucharest so that Berzea can pursue his courtship. Leonidas, agrees, not revealing that he is her uncle. He secretly plans to press his own suit on the young woman.

Leonidas sets out, but through various mishaps ends up on foot. As he nears Ramnic he is arrested by the Germans, who are looking for hostages to execute in reprisal for the depredations of Luca Demian. The old actor has documents from Berzea stating he is on an official government mission, but these mean little to the occupiers. He is thrown in a dank cellar with a dozen prisoners, including Niculae Branea, the former mayor of Gherani village, a huge powerful man who by now is outspoken in his anger against the German occupation. Called out for an interrogation, Leonidas tries to save his skin by denouncing Branea as a terrorist. The officer in charge finally relents and signs a safe passage for Leonidas, ordering Branea to be shot.

Then, in a tragicomic denouement, as the firing squad takes the Gherani mayor and four others to the execution ground Branea makes a successful run for the forest. The moronic sergeant in charge, feeling his orders require him to produce five bodies, waylays the happy Leonidas and shoots him with the others.

The final chapter takes us back to Leonidas's mansion in Bucharest, where Ermil waits in vain for his uncle's return. Two young women who we have not previously met, Raissa and Myriam, rent a room on the top floor. Ermil out of curiosity and boredom decides to rifle through their things. He is discovered, and after a tense exchange becomes Raissa's lover. Her roommate, and sometime gay lover, Myriam, is a nurse at the nearby German military hospital. Ermil finally decides to ask Raissa to go with him and try to return to Ramnic. As he is waiting to tell her his plan a German ambulance arrives. Myriam has died of typhus and Raissa has the disease. The narrative breaks off at this point.

If with the capture of Gherani we saw the futility of ill-considered resistance, by now the soul-chilling price of collaboration has also been revealed, and the pitfalls of willful ignorance in the mode of Uncle Leonidas.

The novel leaves numerous threads to the reader's imagination. Were Sophie and her parents shot by the Germans after they were led away? What became of Lieutenant Luca Demian and Mayor Niculae Branea? Does Tanase Berzea ever find out what happened to his emissary? To Sophie? To Grazia? Does Ermil find his way to Ramnic, or end with a job on a German-controlled newspaper in the capital? Does Raissa recover, and if so, does she remain with Ermil? The characters strut and fret their hour upon the stage then disappear into the fog of war. Though I have to say that, like Leonidas and Tanase, I would have wished to see Sophie again.

So where does that leave us? First, *Ils arrivent, les barbares!* was written in 1981, during the depths of Ceausescu's Kim Il Sung period. It has been said of the historical novels of Howard Fast that you can hear in them the tramp of modern armies. This is surely no less true of this work by Eugen Uricaru. In working his way through the possible responses to a foreign occupation, the German one of 1916-18 must certainly bring to mind the Soviet occupation after World War II, and even the Ceausescu dictatorship in its various incarnations, which was the child of the Soviet military investment of the country.

The novel brings to mind also the many Chinese dissidents of the 1950s and 1960s who impugned the mad excesses of Mao by writing stories about honest officials who risked their lives to criticize evil emperors of the Tang and Song dynasties.

So how did Eugen Uricaru's characters respond? The Germans of that period, while evil are not the overwhelming evil of the Nazis, as, by and large were not the occupations Romania suffered under Soviet tutelage, bad as they were. Luca Demian met the occupiers head on with a pitiful military force that simply got many innocent people killed. The author I think does not see this as a reasonable course. Sophie rebels in a far smaller way, seeking to save a single victim of the occupation, and becomes in turn a victim of military retaliation.

Tanase Berzea becomes ensnared by good intentions. Seeking to mediate between the victors and the vanquished he is inexorably reduced to a cat's-paw of the cynical Colonel Hentsch, held responsible in the public eye for every privation and execution carried out by the occupation forces over his signature.

Leonidas Soroceanu insulates himself from unpleasantness by wishful thinking, escaping into an airbrushed parallel universe where nothing really bad is going on. When the threat of death finally confronts him he has no moral armor or compass to guide him and in an act of base cowardice tries to direct the executioner's bullets to an innocent man in his place. In an irony of fate the bullet he sought to deflect finds him anyway.

Finally we have Ermil, who essentially has stood aside entirely. He suffers a terrible loss but is not personally harmed. His future is left unknown.

Reviewing the courses chosen by his protagonists it would seem that there are not good choices for the victims, though some at least escape being hopelessly morally compromised.

If there are any good Romanian translators out there they should consider contacting Eugen Uricaru with the aim of introducing his work to the English-speaking audience.

June 30, 2011

Tengo Kawana and Aomame's Adventures in the World with Two Moons

1Q84. **By Haruki Murakami. Translated from the Japanese by Jay Rubin and Philip Gabriel. Audible audiobook edition: 10-25-2011. Narrated by Allison Hiroto, Marc Vietor, and Mark Boyett. 46 hours and 50 minutes. Paper edition: 944 pages. New York: Alfred A. Knopf, October 2011.**

I first encountered Haruki Murakami's work only last year when I "read," as an audiobook, as I do most fiction, his 1985 novel *Hard-Boiled Wonderland and the End of the World.* Literature began as oral storytelling and in our technological age it is to an important degree returning to those roots. It is common in works of fantasy for the conventions of the fantastic world, once established, to be presented with a strict faux realism to promote the suspension of disbelief. Murakami employs realism generously, but to a different end, long sequences of mundane detail are embedded in a world rich in surreal elements, whose rules and reasons are often never explained.

A common device for Murakami is to alternate chapters between two characters who are either intimately connected in some unknown way, or are the same person in different aspects. *Hard-Boiled Wonderland* concerns a nameless Calcutec, an encryption savant, who works for the System, a mysterious governmental agency tasked with keeping data secure. The Calcutec accepts an illicit job for a scientist who is perfecting technology to prevent sound from propagating (his daughter, when rayed by his device, can speak but no sound travels outward). The scientist's laboratory is hidden deep in the sewers under Tokyo. This is the Hard-Boiled Wonderland. If it is bizarre the End of the World place is more so. The second character, in alternating chapters, also nameless, is a recent arrival in a strange walled town. No one who enters ever leaves. The town raises unicorns, who are left to die in the snow each winter. Every town dweller has had their shadow cut away from their bodies, the shadows soon dying, leaving the citizens with no shadow and, they say, no mind, but this seems to mean no affect, a condition that interests Murakami. This character, who has no memory of his previous life, is assigned to be a Dreamreader in the town library, where he spends his days placing his hands on the skulls of dead unicorns, which brings him visions that must be recorded. He makes secret visits to his dying shadow, which pleads with him for the two to try to escape.

We eventually find that the End of the World town is a construct inside the mind of the Calcutec, who in turn is informed that he has only days to live. Does the time his alter ego spends in the unicorn town come after his consciousness is extinguished in Hard-Boiled Wonderland so that is where he will go afterward, or do both of his variants expire when his time is up? It is never clear.

While the life of the Calcutec is frenetic, the chapters in the unicorn town are infinitely slow and meditative. The producers chose different readers for the two halves, the Dreamreader perfectly conveying the curious combination of a patient, memoryless man quietly exploring his new environment, and looking without haste for a way to escape it.

Murakami, who turns sixty-three in January 2012, is regarded as a postmodernist. He lived in the United States for nine years, between 1986 and 1995, where he taught writing at Yale and Tufts. He is criticized by the Japanese literary establishment for his many Western and American references. He has been prolific both as a novelist and as a translator, where he has done Japanese editions of F. Scott Fitzgerald, John Irving, Truman Capote, and numerous other authors. He has received many literary awards and prizes, but mostly from Western countries. Yet his most recent novel, *1Q84*, sold a million copies in Japan the first month. It was published there in three hard-cover volumes in 2009-10. The English translation, by Jay Rubin and Philip Gabriel, runs to 944 pages. It was released in the United States on October 25, 2011.

1Q84 is a love story, an account of a ruthless religious cult, and a tale of parallel worlds, in which none of these terms match conventional expectations. As in *Hard-Boiled Wonderland* the chapters alternate between different characters; in the first two volumes, between the young woman Aomame, a martial arts and sports trainer, and Tengo Kawana, a math instructor in a Tokyo cram school who is an aspiring novelist on the side. In the third volume another voice enters, the morally and physically ugly Ushikawa, tasked by the cult with hunting down Aomame and Tengo.

The story takes place between April and December 1984. It begins with Aomame, thirty, in immaculate business attire, in a taxi caught in a traffic jam on a Tokyo elevated highway. Aomame means "green peas" (think of edo-mame, the green soybeans you get as an appetizer in Japanese restaurants), said to be a very unusual name in Japan. The cab radio is playing Leos Jana-cek's 1926 "Sinfonietta" (now experiencing a surge in popularity due to *1Q84*), which she inexplicably recognizes. We learn later that Tengo played timpani in a high school orchestra performance of this piece that Aomame knew nothing about. Ushikawa also listens to it, with a feeling that it has some significant meaning that he can't quite grasp. The novel is full of these kinds of surreal illuminations.

Aomame, late for an appointment, steps out of the cab and descends an emergency staircase to take a subway to her destination. This marks her entrance into the parallel world she comes to call 1Q84, the Q standing for Question Mark. The title is also a pun in Japanese, as the pronunciation of Q (kyu) is the same as the number 9, so that spoken aloud 1Q84 and 1984 are the same.

Arriving at a high-end hotel, we learn that Aomame is a part-time assassin, there to kill a viciously abusive husband. Posing as a hotel staff member there to inspect the air conditioner, she stabs him in the back of the neck with a special ultrathin ice pick that leaves no mark.

Meanwhile Tengo has been serving as a volunteer reader for submissions to a literary award contest. He is strongly impressed with a novelette written by a seventeen-year-old girl, Eriko Fukada, who signs herself Fuka-Eri, also not a recognizable Japanese name. He proposes it to his editor, Komatsu, as a possible winner. Komatsu agrees but thinks the writing too unpolished. He persuades Tengo to secretly rewrite Fuka-Eri's work in more literary style. This risky subterfuge works, the novelette wins first prize, then is published and becomes a best seller.

We are told that Fuka-Eri's book is a surreal fantasy. It is about the life of a ten-year-old girl who lives in a rural commune in a world with two moons. She tends goats, and is blamed when one goat that is very important to the commune dies. She is locked up with the dead goat, where, during the night, Little People come out of the dead goat's mouth and begin to weave an "air chrysalis," a cocoonlike structure in which a replicant human grows, this image lifted from *Invasion of the Body Snatchers*, but somehow not as sinister when among the seven Little People, who leave the goat's mouth at two inches high and grow to two feet, one is a "keeper of the beat" who says nothing but an occasional "Ho ho!" Charles Baxter in the *New York Review of Books* writes that "It is as if the Seven Dwarfs had gradually made their presence known and their powers understood in a novel by James T. Farrell." Or Jack Finney!

This appears to be fiction until Aomame looks at the sky one night and sees two moons, the ordinary one, and a second, smaller, unevenly shaped, green moon. She is now in the world of 1Q84. The two worlds are almost identical, only a few small differences separate them: Tokyo police uniforms, a violent shootout between a cultish organization a few years back, and, mainly the Little People and the religious commune they dominate, a group called Sakigake (Forerunner), led, we eventually learn, by Fuka-Eri's father.

The menace of Sakigake shadows the whole of the book. It is never clear if the Little People are good, evil, or neither. They come from yet another world. But through them Tamotsu Fukada, the group's founder, is able to hear the Voice, which has become the most important thing in his followers' lives. Publication of his daughter's novel, which reveals the existence of the Little People to the world, even if no one takes it seriously, has stilled the Voice. It has created something like a disturbance in the Force in a Star Wars movie. This turns Sakigake's attention toward Fuka-Eri, and, when they discover his role in the book, toward Tengo.

Aomame crosses paths with the cult through her work as an assassin for an elderly dowager, in which she sends the most brutal husbands of the refugees in the dowager's home for abused women "to the other world." It appears that Tamotsu Fukada, known to Sakigake only as Leader, is raping ten-year-old girls. The dowager puts him on Aomame's transit list.

As children both Tengo and Aomame were denied love by their parents. Tengo's mother disappeared when he was a toddler. His father, a remote and hostile man who made his living as a door-to-door fee collector for the NHK, the national television network, showed the child no affection, but dragged him along on his rounds to gain sympathy from deadbeat clients. Aomame's parents belonged to a strict and self-isolating religious group, something like the Jehovah's Witnesses, and they also forced her as a child to go with them on their door-to-door proselytizing.

The two children were in the same class in elementary school. Tengo was an athletic and math prodigy; Aomame, because of her unpopular religious clothing and manner was an outcast. They never spoke, but once only in the fifth grade she grasped his hand for perhaps a minute. Somehow the two fell in love at that moment. She transferred to another school, and *1Q84* takes up twenty years later, when they both come to realize that they have been carrying this deeply buried love around for two decades. They then begin to search for each other.

There are several murders in the course of the year. The one with the greatest consequences is Aomame's murder of Leader. But nothing in *1Q84* is quite what it seems. A cardinal section of the novel is a long philosophical discussion Leader has with Aomame when she is alone with him in the hotel room where she had gone to kill him. He can read minds. He knows why she is there, and probably arranged it. He knows what Tengo feels for Aomame as well as what she feels for Tengo, even though the fated pair have hardly thought this through themselves. It is not clear that the ten-year-olds he has sex with are real people or the replicants created by the Little People, nor whether his actions have anything voluntary about them.

Throughout the book characters know things they had no means of knowing, or make deductions so improbably accurate that one has to suspect outside mental guidance. At other times they are, more realistically, frustratingly wrong in their surmises. There are occasionally scenes of explicit sex, but more often it will be descriptions of how Tengo's older mistress holds his penis while they abstractedly talk about something else.

Through much of the book Aomame, after killing Leader, is in hiding from the cult, long stretches where the story is filled with the minutia of daily life in the confines of a single small room with the curtains drawn against the outside world. Similarly for Tengo, who spends a lot of time in his tiny apartment. We learn what he had for breakfast, how he cooked his dinner. When he is told his father is in a coma and dying in another town he goes there and long passages have him reading by his father's bedside.

These scenes are reminiscent of the 1950s films by Yasujiro Ozu, such as *Tokyo Story*, depicting the extremely slow unfolding of daily life in tiny increments. In the case of Aomame and Tengo this is a rumination on loneliness and social isolation. The audio reading of this huge novel runs to just short of forty-seven hours. A substantial portion of that were these scenes in Tengo's apartment and at his comatose father's bedside, or at Aomame's hideout. In the right frame of mind I found these prolonged interludes among the most pleasing parts, getting into another person's skin at a time when nothing was happening and living it with them for a while. A little like an Anne Tyler novel.

For a while Fuka-Eri lives with Tengo, giving Murakami the opportunity to have a long digression in which Tengo reads her Chekhov's book on Sakhalin, his 1890 nonfiction investigation of prison conditions on the Russian island just north of Japan. Most of Chekhov's book deals with Russian prisoners, but Murakami has Tengo focus on Chekhov's account of the indigenous Oroks. Even when the Russians built roads, the Oroks wouldn't use them. They made their way across country, seeing no reason to become dependent on the alien construct. Fuka-Eri is fascinated by this point.

The air chrysalis fills with a replicant called a dohta. The dohta is linked mentally to its human model, the maza. The dohta is emotionally stunted. It is never clear if Fuka-Eri herself is the maza or a dohta. She lacks affect, is dyslexic, speaks little and then in an odd stilted way.

While her father, Leader, is genteel, his followers in Sakigake are coldblooded and ready to go to any lengths to reestablish a connection with the Voice of the Little People. They are the dark presence that defines the world of *1Q84*, religious rather than Orwell's political tyranny of that year. Murakami returned to Japan from America shortly after the Aum Shinrikyo cult's sarin gas attack in the Tokyo subway in 1995 that killed thirteen people and injured a thousand more. He interviewed 60 survivors of the attack, and then 8 members of the cult. He published the interviews in a nonfiction book, *Underground*. The Aum Shinrikyo interviews appeared separately in Japan but were included in the U.S. translation that was published in 2000. The transmutation of Aum Shinrikyo into Sakigake also makes them less violent. Insofar as they are a threatening specter it is because they have frozen their lives into acolytes of the Voice, on which they have become desperately dependent for meaning.

The two lovers are only marginally aware of Sakigake. Tengo did not even know of the cult's existence when he worked on Fuka-Eri's manuscript. Aomame killed the cult's founder while knowing almost nothing about its beliefs, having been told only that he is a sexual predator on young children, which was probably not true in the magical circle dominated by the Little People with its incomprehensible rules. Still, *1Q84* was a world to escape from no matter how much it resembled the ordinary 1984.

I have revealed more than I should of the story. I will leave unsaid what happens to Aomame and Tengo in what is coming to be regarded as Haruki Murakami's masterpiece.

January 1, 2012

Part 5:
Remembering
the Edwardians

The Memorable Life of Edith Nesbit

A Woman of Passion: The Life of E. Nesbit, 1858-1924 by Julia Briggs (New York: New Amsterdam Books, 1987).

Preeminent Edwardian children's author, prolific novelist and poet, co-founder of the Fabian socialists, friend of George Bernard Shaw, H. G. Wells, Annie Besant, Lord Dunsany, and Noel Coward, Edith Nesbit was to the world at large a figure of conventional if progressive sensibilities. In the relative privacy of her home she was the Bohemian duchess, chain-smoking mother to five children, two of them secretly by her ever-philandering husband's live-in mistress, searcher for occult mysteries, lover of George Bernard Shaw – and afterward of an ever-younger string of adoring young men. A mesmerizing contrast of apparent acquiescence in the rigid conventionalities of late Victorian and Edwardian England, and quiet moral revolt against them.

I first encountered E. Nesbit, as she signed herself, when I was about twelve. I had been reprimanded by an officious librarian at the old Felipe De Neve branch library in Lafayette Park for trying to take out an adult book and was restricted to the children's section. I had worked my way through the Grimm Brothers, Hans Christian Anderson's often creepy tales, and Andrew Lang's Blue, Yellow, Green, Orange, and etc. Fairy Books. I much preferred the more contemporary, you-can-get-there-from-here, ones: the Doctor Doolittle series; Freddy the talking pig from Bean Farm in upstate New York; and the Oz books, which the library refused to carry and I had to buy one at a time from a used bookstore on Seventh Street across Alvarado from MacArthur Park.

And then there were the two odd books by E. Nesbit, *Five Children and It* (1902) and *The Phoenix and the Carpet* (1904). In the first, the five brothers and sisters, in the illustrations the boys in knee britches and the girls in loose old-fashioned dresses, move from London to the countryside in Kent. Exploring a gravel pit they unearth the It, a Psammead, an ugly sand fairy, with a small round furry body and eyes on stalks like a snail, so it can hide in the sand and poke its periscope eyes up for a look. The children call it Sammyadd and find it can grant one wish every day, though the wishes expire each nightfall. The story was quaint, the children speaking in the kind of formal way that one would suppose well brought up Edwardian children would do. And unlike most of the you-can-get-there-from-here books, like *Alice in Wonderland*, *Peter Pan*, or the Oz books, the children don't get to fly off to the magic country for long stays. Instead they are never far from their controlling parents for more than a few hours, forever having to hide what they are up to and living always under the adults' thumbs.

None of their wishes turn out very well. Riches prove to be a heap of gold coins that adults refuse to cash when presented at stores by children. Becoming beautiful only means being turned away at their home's door when they are not recognized. Yet this is not quite the old sausage-on-the-nose three wishes that go bad, where the last wish must be used to undo the second one. In that classic fable the fault lies with the stupidity of the wishers. In E. Nesbit the children are smart enough; they are just not free enough.

In *The Phoenix and the Carpet* a used rug bought for the children's nursery turns out to have a large egg wrapped within it. This hatches into an ancient phoenix, a narcissistic and imperious creature. The carpet itself is magic and takes the children on many brief adventures: to a remote island, to India, to Persia where they bring back 199 Persian cats, to France, where they give a treasure to a poor family. The phoenix demands to be taken to a temple in its honor, which it is certain from self-importance must exist. The children in a hilarious scene take the bird to the Phoenix Fire Insurance Company with results you may imagine.

Throughout the children are realistic. They quarrel among themselves, perceive the world as real children would. Their homes are middle class, but in straightened circumstances. I found something memorable about the intrusion of magic into this otherwise staid and old-fashioned England.

This was the sum of my encounter with E. Nesbit for the next fifty years. Then in the early naughts I "read" four more of her books: *The Enchanted Castle, The Magic City, The Magic World* short story collection, and one of

Nesbit's adult works, *Man and Maid*. I say "read" as much of E. Nesbit's work has been digitized and is available for free from the Project Gutenberg text archive and other such sources. I had my computer read these to an MP3 file and listened to them on my iPod. You are probably imagining Robbie the Robot, but in fact computerized voices have improved considerably in the last twenty years.

Becoming curious I next came on a 1965 piece on Nesbit by Gore Vidal. Unstinting in his praise, he declared her, next to Lewis Carroll, "the best of the English fabulists who wrote about children (neither wrote *for* children)." He comments, following a then-recent critical work on her writing by Noel Streatfeild, that "E. Nesbit did not particularly like children, which may explain why the ones that she created in her books are so entirely human. They are intelligent, vain, aggressive, humorous, witty, cruel, compassionate … in fact, they are like adults, except for one difference." The difference is that they are utterly powerless and controlled by their adult relatives.

Unhappily she was and is little read in the United States. Vidal attributes that to a tradition of narrow utilitarianism of American literary tastes in children's books then prevailing, which kept even the Oz books out of most public libraries for more than half a century. The vogue for realistic, "practical" literature was still riding high when Vidal penned his essay. By the time the tide shifted and the era of J.K. Rowling's Harry Potter and lesser series such as Philip Pulman's *His Dark Materials* and Susan Cooper's *The Dark Is Rising* came on the scene, too many years had slipped by for E. Nesbit's work to benefit.

There have been two full-length biographies, *E. Nesbit* by Doris Langley Moore (1933), and Julia Briggs' excellent and more extensive *A Woman of Passion: The Life of E. Nesbit, 1858-1924*. Langley Moore presented Nesbit as the long-suffering victim of her womanizing husband, Hubert Bland. Briggs, writing fifty years later, tells us that Edith got her own back, taking lovers as she pleased despite the hostile conventions of Victorian, Edwardian, and Georgian England.

Edith was born in South London on August 15, 1858. Her parents, Sarah and John Collis Nesbit, ran a small agricultural college on the property. She was the youngest of the couple's four children, two brothers and a sister, as well as an older half-sister from Sarah's first marriage. Her father died when she was four. In 1866 her older sister, Mary, was diagnosed with consumption and her mother entered on a lengthy period of abrupt relocations to try to save the child's life. Edith was often packed off to boarding schools or to stay with distant relatives. In September 1867 the family moved to France to escape England's damp climate. They stayed at spas in the Pyrenees, returned to England, moved to Dinan in French Brittany, sent Edith and her brothers to schools in Germany, and finally returned to London, where Mary died in November 1871 at the age of nineteen. Mrs. Nesbit then moved the family to the village of Halstead in her home county of Kent. This lasted until 1875, when whatever money they were living on ran out and they moved back to London in very reduced circumstances.

Hubert Bland Prevaricates

The story gets more interesting when, in 1877, at nineteen, Edith meets Hubert Bland, a twenty-two-year-old bank clerk. They were engaged the following year. Bland passed himself off as related to landed gentry, but Briggs describes him as "pure Cockney." He lived with his widowed mother on the outskirts of the south London suburb of Blackheath. Bland was already a political radical, having a nodding acquaintance with Eleanor Marx, Karl Marx's daughter, and Henry Hyndman, head of the Social Democratic Federation. He was also a cocksman of a high order. In later life Bland claimed to have first been engaged to be married at the age of twelve. At the least, at the time he became engaged to Edith Nesbit he had just gotten his mother's paid companion, Maggie Doran, pregnant. She bore him a son.

Edith's poems seem to indicate that she had sex with Bland in the summer of 1879. He was still postponing the promised marriage. In the meantime, Bland kept his engagement to Edith a secret both from his mother and from Maggie Doran. Edith nevertheless moved out of her mother's home and took rooms under the name Mrs. Bland. As for Hubert, he was spending four nights a week with Edith and the other three at his mother's, where he could be with Maggie, neither woman knowing about the other. Hubert continued the arrangement with Maggie long after Edith found out about it, at his mother's home until she died, in 1893, and for five years more elsewhere.

Edith, living alone and without aid from Hubert, struggled to make a living, selling her poetry to small magazines. Bland finally married her, seven months pregnant with their first child, Paul, in April 1880. Hubert did not move in with her but continued to live primarily with his mother.

Bland started a brush-making business, which quickly failed. Edith added short stories and home-made greeting cards to her output. Their second child, Iris, was born in December 1881. Around that time Edith finally found out about Maggie Doran and her child by Hubert, and Hubert told his mother about his marriage to Edith and of their two children. Hubert began to collaborate with Edith on her short stories.

The Fabian Society

Fabian socialism, named from the Fabian Society, became in Britain in later years the epitome of democratic, gradualist social reform, instrumental in winning the minimum wage and universal health care. The Fabian Society was founded on January 4, 1884, with a membership of fourteen. Hubert Bland chaired the founding meeting. He, along with Frank Podmore and Frederick Keddell, were chosen as the group's executive committee, with Bland as treasurer. Hubert held both posts until 1911. Podmore proposed the name, for the Roman general Fabius Maximus, nicknamed Cunctator, the delayer, for his strategy of avoiding head-on battles with the Carthaginian invader Hannibal, and by extension the strategy for bringing socialism to Britain in incremental stages. The Fabians played an important part in founding the Labour Party in 1900 and remain influential in the party. A number of Labour prime ministers have been members.

Edith was elected to the Fabian Pamphlets Committee, and soon she and Hubert were the co-editors of the society's journal, *To-Day*. The young George Bernard Shaw joined in September 1884. Other prominent early members included Edward Pease, Eleanor Marx, Annie Besant, suffragette leader Emmeline Pankhurst, H. G. Wells, Oliver Lodge, and the prolific Sydney and Beatrice Webb.

Edith had a third child, in January 1885. She named him Fabian.

Years later, in 1908, the Fabian Society published a book of Edith's socialist verse under the title *Ballads and Lyrics of Socialism*. Part of a poem titled "London's Voices" captures her feelings on the injustice and inequality of her society:

> Here, in the city, Gold has trampled Good.
> Come thou, do battle till this strife shall cease!'
> I left the mill, the meadows and the trees,
> And came to do the little best I could
> For these, God's poor; and, oh, my God, I would
> I had a thousand lives to give for these!
> What can one hand do 'gainst a world of wrong?
> Yet, when the voice said, 'Come!' how could I stay?
>
> The foe is mighty, and the battle long
> (And love is sweet, and there are flowers in May),
> And Good seems weak, and Gold is very strong;
> But, while these fight, I dare not turn away.

George Bernard Shaw, a bit more self-distancing, in an address to the Society in 1892 spoke of its state in 1885:

> [W]e denounced the capitalists as thieves . . . and, among ourselves, talked revolution, anarchism . . . and all the rest of it, on the tacit assumption that the object of our campaign, with its watchwords, 'Educate, Agitate, Organize,' was to bring about a tremendous smash-up of existing society, to be succeeded by complete Socialism. And this meant that we had no true practical understanding either of existing society or Socialism. (*The Fabian Society: Its Early History*, by G. Bernard Shaw, London: The Fabian Society, 1892)

By 1886 the group had grown to sixty-seven members.

Shaw and Edith

Though they had attended the same socialist meetings since early in 1884, George Bernard Shaw and Edith first seriously noticed each other at a gathering at the home of Karl Marx's daughter Eleanor in March 1885. Edith, in a letter to her friend Ada Breakell that summer described Shaw as "one of the most fascinating men I ever met."

Biographer Julia Briggs, who has dug through their diaries, letters, and manuscripts, writes that they had a passionate love affair between June and September 1886. Shaw turned thirty that summer, Edith twenty-eight. They went on long walks in the country, attended concerts and museum exhibits, he took her frequently back to his rooms — Shaw, like Bland a few years earlier, still lived with his mother.

Their affair was a major life event for Edith. But while it is very likely, it is not certain that it was physically consummated. This stemmed from Shaw's ambivalence about sex. Briggs comments that "At this stage of his life, Shaw was constantly playing with the idea of marriage, and proposing to any young women whom he felt confident would refuse him, while fleeing headlong from those who showed any interest in the idea."

Further, Shaw believed it was undignified for a man to pursue a woman, although he frequently did so. In later years he was anxious to portray the affair as largely Edith's obsession with him. Their many secret trysts, from his diary plainly at his initiative and expense, belie this.

Briggs writes:

"Edith had fallen in love for the second time in her life with a philanderer as compulsive, in his own curious way, as Bland, even though his anxieties and inhibitions made him sexually undemanding. The experience was to be a searing one."

And:

"Edith's passion for Shaw was intense. At one time she proposed leaving Hubert in order to run away with him, as he privately boasted to Doris Langley Moore." This exchange took place in 1931 when Moore interviewed Shaw for her biography of Edith.

It would seem that the affair in 1886 was not a fully conventional one. There was something in the acerbic future playwright that was more than shy about sex. When he did finally marry, to Charlotte Payne-Townshend, in 1898, their forty-five-year marriage was never consummated, ostensibly out of her refusal to have children. A 1996 book, *Bernard Shaw: The Ascent of the Superman* by Sally Peters, proposes that Shaw was a repressed homosexual.

Socialism and the Paranormal

The Blands, Edith more than Hubert, were interested in psychic phenomena and the esoteric as well as in socialism. This may seem incongruous in light of post-Lenin Marxism's narrow philosophic materialism and rejection of the occult as rank superstition. In late nineteenth century England, however, while there were some hard materialists, socialism and psychic phenomena were two mutually intertwined threads of the avant garde rejection of conventional politics and conventional religion.

Briggs is not much interested in this second thread and she refers to it only in passing. In mentioning Edith and Hubert's activities in 1885 other than the Fabian she notes their attendance at the Browning and Shelley Societies, but also "societies for psychic research." Briggs quotes a March 1884 letter from Edith to Ada Breakell listing several books she is reading. These include, Edith writes, "an intensely interesting book which Harry [her brother, married to Ada Breakell] would like called Esoteric Buddhism by Sinnett."

A. P. Sinnett was a recently converted disciple of the Russian mystic Madame Helena Petrovna Blavatsky, the founder of the occult Theosophical Society. Sinnett's book had little to do with any recognized school of Buddhism but was devoted to Blavatsky's schema of world evolution from the mythical continents of Lemuria and Atlantis, and the teachings of her claimed Mahatmas or Ascended Masters of Tibet, essentially all-wise spirit guides who live on the Astral Plane and from there influence the course of human history. Sinnett was the recipient of a series of alleged letters from the Mahatmas, the question of their authenticity raising a heated controversy even in circles sympathetic to the idea of spirit communication.

These could have been casual interests on Edith's part, but Alex Owen, in *The Place of Enchantment: British Occultism and the Culture of the Modern,* reports that Edith Bland was also an initiate of the Hermetic Order of the Golden Dawn, the preeminent occult organization of its day, and one requiring a demanding admission process. The Golden Dawn was famous for teaching the practice of magic. Its best-known members were the famed Irish poet William Butler Yeats, Irish socialist actress Florence Farr, Irish revolutionary Maud Gonne, and the infamous "black magician" Aleister Crowley.

Alex Owen offers an explanation of the affinity between political radicalism and the occult. The late nineteenth century was an age in which the rapid changes caused by industrialization and urbanism, the expansion and secularization of education, led to widespread questioning of the whole gamut of traditional values. Socialism was the defense of the oppressed poor against the indifference or worse of the dominant Conservative and Liberal parties. Spiritualist mediums, and the more academic and credentialed Society for Psychical Research, proposed and carried out empirical research into the claims of traditional scriptural religion that there was some kind of afterlife. Both currents were looked on in their day as the epitome of modernism.

Further, both the socialist organizations and the occult ones welcomed women into positions of leadership that were essentially closed to them in Victorian and Edwardian England. A good example was Anna Bonus Kingsford (1846-1888), only the second English woman to get a medical degree, a militant animal rights advocate and anti-vivisectionist who managed to get through medical school while refusing to dissect a living animal. She was both a prominent women's rights campaigner and at the same time rose to head Madame Blavatsky's Theosophical Society, where she claimed to get insights in trance states from nonmaterial beings.

Still more famous was Annie Besant (1847-1933), an early leader of the Fabian Society, a close friend of Edith Nesbit, and eventually also president of the Theosophical Society. Besant lost custody of her children in a famous court case because of her advocacy of birth control. In her socialist period she was a principal speaker at the November 13, 1887, rally in Trafalgar Square attacked by troops and remembered as Bloody Sunday. She was a leader of the London matchgirls strike of 1888. The girls worked a fourteen-hour day for pitiful wages. The phosphorus used in making matches was also used in rat poison and caused extensive liver and kidney damage. George Bernard Shaw and Hubert Bland raised money for the match strikers, which they distributed at the factory gates as strike pay.

During the 1880s Besant spent much time with Edith Bland and even took the two older children, Paul and Iris, home with her when Edith came down with the measles. Besant also, incidentally, fell in love with George Bernard Shaw. She proposed that he come live with her, but he refused.

She was won over to Theosophy in 1890, moved to India, where she claimed to have become a clairvoyant, and rose to head the organization which by then was international in scope. Her new associates were now people like Colonel Henry Steel Olcott and Charles Leadbeater, names to conjure with in the occult fraternity. Olcott had earned his military title in the American Civil War and had served on the official investigating commission into the assassination of Abraham Lincoln.

Nor was this mixing of socialist politics with the occult just a female proclivity. Two of the central founders of the Fabian Society were Edward Pease and Frank Podmore (1856-1910). Podmore's home was also for years the Fabian office. In his *The History of the Fabian Society* Pease describes how he and Podmore got the idea for the group:

> In the autumn of 1883 Thomas Davidson paid a short visit to London and held several little meetings of young people . . . I attended the last of these meetings held in a bare room somewhere in Chelsea, on the invitation of Frank Podmore, whose acquaintance I had made a short time previously. We had become friends through a common interest first in Spiritualism and subsequently in Psychical Research, and it was whilst vainly watching for a ghost in a haunted house at Notting Hill – the house was unoccupied: we had obtained the key from the agent, left the door unlatched, and returned late at night in the foolish hope that we might perceive something abnormal – that he first discussed with me the teachings of Henry George in 'Progress and Poverty,' and we found a common interest in social as well as psychical progress.

Frank Podmore is remembered as much for his books on psychic phenomena as for his role among the Fabian socialists. These include *Phantasms of the Living* (1886, coauthored by Frederick Myers and Edmund Gurney); *Studies in Psychical Research* (1897); *Modern Spiritualism* (1902); and *The Newer Spiritualism* (1910).

Oliver Lodge, mainly known as a physicist, was a long-time Fabian, author of two Fabian tracts and co-author of a third with Sidney Webb, George Bernard Shaw, and Sidney Ball. At the same time he conducted studies of telepathy in the 1880s and served as president of the Society for Psychical Research from 1901 to 1903.

Little Orphan Alice's Come to Our House

Edith made friends readily and always had an admiring circle of both men and women. Among her women friends the closest included Ada Breakell, who married Edith's brother Harry and moved with him to Australia, and Alice Hoatson. Edith first met Alice in January 1882 when Alice was working as reader for *Sylvia's Home Journal* and Edith visited their offices to try to submit a short story. Alice was six months younger, from Yorkshire. They were temperamentally opposites, Edith outgoing, strong-willed, prone to emotional extremes, overflowing with literary and other projects; Alice quiet, submissive, efficient, and home centered.

Alice was ineluctably drawn into the Blands' lives. She became Edith's most frequent companion. In 1884 she joined the Fabian Society where she became the organization's assistant secretary. Edith even urged Alice to distract Hubert's attention from his latest lover. Alice, who the Blands nicknamed the Mouse – they called each other Cat, which tells much – succeeded too well. The cat caught the mouse and she was soon pregnant with Hubert's child. Edith had for several years urged Alice to come and live with them. She finally did so in late 1886, where she discretely gave birth to Rosamund that November.

Victoria was still on the English throne. Had their domestic situation become public it could have destroyed the Blands still very marginal literary careers, on which their precarious livelihoods depended. Edith and Alice agreed that Edith would claim to be the mother. They maintained this fiction throughout their lives, repeating the ruse thirteen years later when Alice bore Hubert a second child.

Of course their close friends knew of the subterfuge. And there was always Maggie Duran, the mother of Hubert's other out-of-wedlock child. Even she joined the Fabian Society, in 1890, where that secret slipped out as well.

George Bernard Shaw's biographer described Hubert, as Shaw viewed him, as "a Tory Democrat from Blackheath, who sported fashionable clothes, wore a monocle, and maintained simultaneously three wives, all of whom bore him children. Two of the wives lived in the same house. The legitimate one was E. Nesbit." (cited by Briggs, p. 108)

The disparaging "Tory Democrat" reflected much that was conservative in Hubert Bland's outlook despite his socialist politics. Most notably he was firmly opposed to women's suffrage. He is said to have exclaimed, "Votes for women? Votes for children! Votes for dogs!" Edith under pressure from Hubert also opposed women's suffrage, arguing rather tendentiously that it would set back the movement for socialism by flooding elections with votes by Conservative women.

Julia Briggs describes the Bland menage of those years:

> Alice was socially unassertive, which allowed Edith to shine un-
> challenged; she was also capable and dependable, quite content to play
> 'the humble satellite to a comet', as she herself put it. She relieved Edith
> of organizing or undertaking the dull routine household tasks, and dealt
> more effectively and consistently with the servants, her steady tempera-
> ment acting as a foil to Edith's volatile nature.

Literature and Lovers

Edith Nesbit would be past forty before she wrote the children's classics
on which her reputation rests, as well as many adult novels and short story
collections. In the penurious eighties she survived by hand painting and writing poems on greeting cards, and publishing an occasional poem or short story
in various magazines and newspapers. Briggs writes: "She would allow the
butcher's and baker's bills to mount up to huge sums, and would then write
some verses or stories to pay them off. She liked this functional way of thinking about her work so that each piece of writing was destined to pay off some
particular household bill."

Hubert never made much of a living. For a few years he had a job with
the Hydraulic Power Company, and when he lost that, turned to journalism.
He and Edith in the early years collaborated using the pen name Fabian Bland,
under which they published a novel, *The Prophet's Mantle*, in 1885.

In her own name Edith concentrated on poetry, which she always believed was her true gift. She published three slim volumes of her poems in
1885. Then, in 1886, Longmans published her *Lays and Legends*. It had been
recommended by their reader, prominent author Andrew Lang, who coincidentally is also best remembered for his children's books, of traditional fairy
stories. The poems were praised by the widely popular poet Algernon Swin-
burne as well as by adventure novelist H. Rider Haggard. Oscar Wilde sent
her an encouraging letter.

As she neared thirty Edith also began to take lovers, generally younger
men from her circle of admirers among the Fabians. The first was Noel Grif-
fith, studying to be an accountant, twenty-three to her twenty-nine.

In the early nineties she began a long affair with Richard Le Gallienne
(1866-1947), a slim, elegant, and prolific poet, possibly best remembered for
his novel *Quest of the Golden Girl*. George Bernard Shaw wrote an extremely
hostile review of Le Gallienne's *English Poems* (1892), probably because
many of them were thinly disguised love poems to Edith Bland. At one point
Edith wanted to run away with Le Gallienne but was persuaded against it by

Alice Hoatson. The affair continued after Le Gallienne married Mildred Lee in 1891, and was the source of much guilt when Mildred died young in 1894. In 1903 Le Gallienne moved to the United States. There his esthete taste and archly traditional romanticism found little resonance and he never achieved the popularity he had in *fin de siecle* England. Still, I have long enjoyed Le Gallienne's *October Vagabonds*, a luminous account of his attempt, accompanied by a French artist, to walk four hundred and thirty miles from upstate New York to Manhattan.

Maturity and Success

As she aged, Edith drew around her an ever younger group of admiring young men. One of these, Oswald Barron (1868-1939) became her lover and her muse. A Fabian, a columnist for the London *Evening News* under the pen name The Londoner, Barron was more than anything else a scholar of medieval heraldry and noble genealogies. They wrote poems and short stories together, Barron proving to be an endless font of plot ideas. More than that, he imbued Edith with a sense of the importance of history and of the recollections of childhood. This transformed her writing and in the process won her a mass audience for the first time.

Her breakthrough book was *The Story of the Treasure Seekers* (1899), the first of a series of semi-comic novels about the Bastable children. Their names were taken from her coterie of young Fabian men, the hero being Oswald Bastable after Barron, though the children's personalities were modeled on Edith's brothers and sister. It was an immediate best seller. The self-important Oswald recounts in somewhat inflated style how he and his five brothers and sisters try many different ways to find some treasure after their mother has died and their father has been slipping into penury. There were two sequels, *The Wouldbegoods* in 1901, her most successful book, and *The New Treasure Seekers* in 1904. All remain in print a century later, the first of the Bastable books having been three times made into a television series and once into a TV movie.

Hubert's fortunes also improved. He was now doing book reviews for the *Daily Chronicle* and a popular column for the Manchester *Sunday Chronicle* that at its height claimed a million readers. The Blands had lived in numerous houses during their marriage. Now finally prosperous, they rented Well Hall in Eltham, on the border between Kent and London. This was a decayed eighteenth century mansion of thirty rooms. It stood on the grounds of a still earlier house built by Sir Thomas More, Henry VIII's martyred chancellor, for his daughter. She was said to have brought his severed head there for burial after the king had him executed for opposing Henry's marriage to

Anne Boleyn. The deep moat that had surrounded the original house was still intact in the back grounds when the Blands lived there. Edith did much of her writing in a rowboat on the water.

The old mansion was as dilapidated as the place Tom Hanks buys in the film *The Money Pit*. The main staircase suddenly collapsed, the gutters failed and the ground floor was flooded. Edith claimed the house was haunted by a ghost that played the piano when no one was in the room, and stood behind her when she was writing, quietly sighing. She began to gain weight, and chain smoked her hand-rolled cigarettes. The household was gregarious and saw many guests, parties, and lectures. Edith was especially fond of parlor games, skits, charades, and musical evenings.

Her initial literary successes were all in naturalistic settings, the fantasy works would come later. In both, however, she refuses to idealize her child characters or their powers. Her biographer writes:

> Over and over again Edith presents her child protagonists in un-manageable confrontation with irate adults whom they are quite unable to cope with. She is realistically aware of the child's lack of any real power other than the power of imagination. . . . It is her refusal to ideal-ize either the child's actual – as opposed to imaginative – power, or the nature of the world that children inhabit that constitutes E. Nesbit's great strength and perhaps her most important contribution to children's fiction.

Edith had three living children – Paul, Iris, and Fabian – but afterward she gave birth twice to babies that were still-born. She took these very hard, the blows magnified as Alice Hoatson gave birth in close proximity each time to a healthy child of Hubert's. The first dead baby was in April 1886 followed by the birth of Alice's Rosamund in November, when Alice joined the Bland household. This sequence was repeated in 1899, shortly after the move to Well Hall, when Edith bore a second dead child, and Alice gave birth to John Oliver Wentworth Bland. Edith, as she had done with Rosamund, adopted John and presented him to the world as hers while Alice continued to play the role of the spinster Auntie.

The following year Edith's youngest, Fabian, died, at fifteen, from a botched anesthesia during a routine operation conducted at Well Hall to re-move his adenoids. No one had thought to tell him not to eat the night before the surgery and he asphyxiated in his vomit while no one was watching him. The family was devastated.

Edith's turn to fantasy and magic was linked to the appearance of *The Strand* magazine in January 1891. Best known as the place where Sherlock Holmes pursued his trade, *The Strand* built a stable of well-known authors, besides Conan Doyle including Rudyard Kipling, H. G. Wells, E. W. Hornung (Doyle's brother-in-law, who wrote the Raffles the Gentleman Burglar series), and Max Beerbohm. The magazine strongly preferred fantasy. Edith published her first fantasy book, *Five Children and It*, serially in *The Strand* in 1901. The two sequels in the Psammead series, *The Phoenix and the Carpet* and *The Story of the Amulet,* followed in 1904 and 1906, then her two related time travel books, *The House of Arden* and *Harding's Luck* in 1908 and 1909. All the rest of her fantasy and magic books, such as *The Enchanted Castle, The Magic City,* and finally *Wet Magic*, about children who find a mermaid, also appeared first in *The Strand*. While the children in the Bastable books were modeled on her siblings, the fantasy book children were modeled on her own children. She also wrote eleven novels for adults between 1885 and 1922, none of which gained the audience her children's fiction did.

G. K. Chesterton's sister-in-law Ada, a frequent visitor at Well Hall, described Edith in her Bohemian prime:

> Mrs Bland . . . was always surrounded by adoring young men, dazzled by her vitality, amazing talent and the sheer magnificence of her appearance. She was a very tall woman, built on the grand scale, and on festive occasions wore a trailing gown of peacock blue satin with strings of beads and Indian bangles from wrist to elbow. Madame, as she was always called, smoked incessantly, and her long cigarette holder became an indissoluble part of the picture she suggested – a raffish Rossetti, with a long full throat, and dark luxuriant hair, smoothly parted. She was a wonderful woman, large hearted, amazingly unconventional, but with sudden strange reversions to ultra-respectable standards. (cited by Briggs, p. 233)

The Blands often took in strays in need of support. Edith even welcomed Maggie Doran, the mother of Hubert's first child, now in ill health, into her home, where she lived until her early death in 1903.

In 1907 Edith founded a short-lived literary journal, *The Neolith*, printed in hand-done calligraphy on oversized paper. Contributors included H. G. Wells, George Bernard Shaw, G. K. Chesterton, Andrew Lang, and Lord Dunsany. This last, in private life better known as Edward John Moreton Drax Plunkett, 18th Baron of Dunsany, became one of Edith's lifelong friends. She and Alice's son John visited Dunsany and his wife at their ancient Dunsany

Castle in Ireland in 1910. Lord Dunsany has long been one of my favorite authors, his ornate and archaic language and bizarre worlds with their own gods unlike the work of any other I can think of. Dunsany was also a playwright, and a financial supporter of Dublin's famed Abbey Theatre.

The H. G. Wells Fiasco

H. G. Wells and his wife Amy Catherine joined the Fabian Society in February 1903, beginning that fall to exchange regular visits with the Blands. For several years the two families were very close. Wells once showed up at Well Hall unannounced and stayed for a week, finishing his novel *In the Days of the Comet* in the back garden.

Distance set in during 1906 when Wells began a campaign to reorganize the Fabian Society. He demanded that it become more like a political party, adopt an official line in contrast to the wide spectrum of views currently tolerated, run candidates for parliament, and, stickiest of all, get rid of the existing Executive Committee, including Hubert Bland. There was also some suggestion in Wells' proposals that he wanted an endorsement of free love, which horrified the Edwardian sensibilities of many members.

Bernard Shaw supported the Old Guard against Wells and the thing came to a head in a couple of large meetings in December 1906 where Wells was roundly defeated.

The rift became a chasm when, in 1908, Wells, then forty-one, tried to run away to Paris with Hubert's beloved daughter Rosamund, twenty years his junior. The eloping couple were betrayed and Hubert caught them on a train at Paddington Station. Hubert Bland, monocle or not, was a large, powerful man and an excellent boxer. He thrashed Wells and carted his wayward daughter home. Wells in the appendix to his 1934 *Experiment in Autobiography* claimed that he was precipitated into adultery with Rosamund to save her from Hubert, saying that "her father's attentions to her were becoming unfatherly. I conceived a great disapproval of incest, and an urgent desire to put Rosamund beyond its reach in the most effective manner possible, by absorbing her myself." Such self-sacrifice!

Whatever the truth of Wells' accusation, he lost the sympathy of the Fabians when the following year he betrayed his wife again, getting Amber Reeves, a young member of the group, pregnant. She managed a hasty marriage with someone else, but Wells persisted in the affair after the marriage. Sidney and Beatrice Webb now broke off their friendship with Wells over his conduct. Wells got even in 1910 with a *roman a clef*, *The New Machiavelli*, in which the Webbs do not fare well and the Blands appear very negatively but unmistakably as the Booles.

Edith and Shaw Late in Life

Edith Nesbit and George Bernard Shaw remained close friends for life, though they never were again lovers. As they entered middle age their interests and outlooks began to diverge, without diminishing their mutual affection. Edith, while still retaining her interest in socialism, dropped away from active participation in the Fabian. Around the time she turned fifty she became passionately absorbed by the Baconian controversy. This in its simplest form was the claim that Francis Bacon (1561-1626) was the true author of Shakespeare's plays. That issue has sputtered on to our own day where a small group of irreconcilable conspiracy theorists still hold that Shakespeare was a village clod while Bacon wrote his plays, if not almost every other major work of Elizabethan England including the *Fairy Queen*.

For the more esoteric wing of the Baconian movement, the plays were only the appetizer. Just as the true alchemists of the Middle Ages regarded turning lead into gold as little more than a parlor trick on the road to discovering the Philosopher's Stone and achieving immortality, the occult Baconians hoped through secret ciphers hidden in the plays to unravel the Rosicrucian mysteries of which they believed Bacon to have been a master, and the hidden lore of the Freemasons, in Bacon's day a feared secret society and not yet the businessmen's club known for its funny hats and handshakes. Edith Nesbit was more drawn to the search for mystic enlightenment in her ciphering than the question of who really wrote Hamlet.

Edith invested large amounts of time and money, trying vainly to learn logarithms in hopes of finding secret ciphers hidden in Shakespeare's plays, buying rare books, and for years supporting an old neer-do-well known as Tanner who was said to be doing his own research on Baconian ciphers. By ciphers the devotees intended coded messages buried in the text to be extracted by discovering the pattern of the code.

Shaw at the same time was evolving in the opposite direction, toward a far harder version of socialism, and then beyond that to an admiration of all of the contemporary absolutist revolutions and their dictators of the far left and far right as superior to mere corrupt capitalist democracy. The worst of this would come in the quarter century in which he outlived her.

In the years of their friendship Shaw limited his advocacy of extremist propositions to selective human breeding according to the tenets of the Eugenics movement. He amalgamated his notion of socialism with calling for government and corporate directed breeding programs aimed at creating a race of Nietzschean supermen. This drew little adverse reaction, as he presented his view – notably in his 1901 play *Man and Superman* – in witty dialogue wrapped in the popular verbiage of onward and upward evolution, promotion of the Life Force, and as an egalitarian process blind to class differences.

Shaw had no patience for mysticism or the occult, though those beliefs were probably less harmful than the things he did advocate in the world of secular reality. He good naturedly lent Edith money to pursue her Baconian studies, and also his replica set of early editions of Shakespeare for her to test her cipher skills on. Still, he joked with her that he could show from textual comparisons that his own plays had all been written by Sidney Webb.

Last Years

Hubert in 1911 began to lose his eyesight. Soon he was blind. He continued to write his weekly column and do some book reviewing, Alice Hoatson reading the books to him and taking down his dictation. Edith's creativity began to flag, and in 1913, after the serial publication of *Wet Magic*, the last of her children's books, *The Strand* canceled her contract, leading to a drastic decline in her income. After more than a decade of prodigious literary output Edith fell silent for the next eight years, returning only a few years before her death with two adult novels. Hubert died suddenly, in April 1914.

There followed some years of financial hardship. Edith, Alice, and their children took in paying guests at Well Hall. They set up a roadside stand where they sold vegetables and flowers. For a while they raised chickens and sold the eggs, until an outbreak of disease killed the flock.

Three years after Hubert's death Edith remarried, not to an intellectual but to Thomas Tucker, known as "the Skipper," a marine engineer and ferry boat captain. She was defensive about his lower class bearing but they were very happy together. Alice finally left, after thirty-one years, moving to London where she worked as a nurse.

Edith's health began to fail, as her persistent smoking produced ever more serious attacks of asthma and bronchitis. She and the Skipper had in the end to abandon Well Hall as too expensive to maintain. From the grand house they moved to a pair of brick sheds recently built by the Air Force in the village of St. Mary's in the Marsh. The Skipper partitioned the open interiors into numerous rooms. In her last year Edith made friends with a new neighbor in the village, the young Noel Coward, who found her enchanting. He had read and collected her books as a child.

Edith died on May 4, 1924, of lung cancer. Alice Hoatson lived long enough to be interviewed by Doris Langley Moore for her 1933 biography of Edith, but to the end maintained the pretence that Rosamund and John were her niece and nephew. Paul, Edith's first born, always ill at ease with his Bohemian family, worked in finance, married unhappily, and committed suicide at sixty in 1940. Iris became a dressmaker. Rosamund cared for Skipper in his last years and published one novel, in 1934. Of Iris, Rosamund, and John and their later lives, Julia Briggs could discover only the probable decade of their deaths.

Julia Briggs closes her biography with an appreciation of Edith's work that Noel Coward wrote in 1956:

> I am reading again through all the dear E. Nesbits and they seem to me to be more charming and evocative than ever. It is strange that after half a century I still get so much pleasure from them. Her writing is so light and unforced, her humour is so sure and her narrative quality so strong that the stories, which I know backwards, rivet me as much now as they did when I was a little boy.

There was a copy of *The Enchanted Castle* next to his bed seventeen years later when he died.

November 8, 2011

George Bernard Shaw: Can His Reputation Survive His Dark Side?

It is with a certain sadness that I come to write this. George Bernard Shaw, through his plays, was one of my early heroes. I knew only the good of him then. More recently I have come to learn things, about his political views, that I could have known then but did not, and knowing, would have seen him differently. Learning them prompts me to want to know more about his contradictory character, to decide anew what we should think of him.

That kindly old gentleman pulling the strings attached to Henry Higgins and Eliza Doolittle on the cover of the vinyl album of *My Fair Lady* died in 1950 at the Methuselan age of ninety-four. Though remembered principally for his many plays, for which he won the Nobel Prize in 1925, Bernard Shaw (he hated George and didn't use it) was also an indefatigable essayist and public speaker. An early leader of the originally tiny Fabian Society, he was a lifelong socialist, but that narrow catechism could not contain his ebullient eclecticism. Shaw was not a Marxist but a Nietzschean, not an atheist but a believer in Bergsonian vitalism.

Always an iconoclast, Shaw's opinions, though generally on the left, ranged all over the map, were usually intended to shock, generally had a comic edge, and managed to infuriate almost everyone at some time. Unhappily, at an age when most of his contemporaries were dying off or in their dotage, beginning in his early seventies, and to the dismay of his friends on both the left and right, he lost faith in parliamentary democracy and lauded the famous dictators of the 1930s as leaders who could "get things done." Today the American right wing has discovered Shaw's more disreputable mouthings and found them to be a convenient club with which to beat today's liberals and the left. The reasoning is usually along the lines of those marvelous syllogisms so beloved by the Glenn Becks of the world: Shaw liked Mussolini, Shaw was a Fabian Socialist, Fabian Socialists are similar to liberals, therefore liberals like Mussolini, Mussolini was a fascist, Hilary Clinton and

Barack Obama are liberals, therefore Hilary Clinton and Barack Obama are fascists. If you think I exaggerate, take a look at *National Review* editor Jonah Goldberg's book *Liberal Fascism*, which was #1 on the *New York Times* best seller list.

Glenn Beck has an Internet post entitled "Who Are the Fabian Socialists?" that opens with an accurate if disturbing quote in which Shaw intones, "if you're not producing as much as you consume or perhaps a little more, then, clearly, we cannot use the organizations of our society for the purpose of keeping you alive, because your life does not benefit us and it can't be of very much use to yourself."

Beck, in his usual manner, judders in an ever widening spiral of accusation, from Shaw's distasteful declaration, to all Fabian socialists, and from there to all progressives, a category to which Shaw did not even belong, and then to Hilary Clinton, who was three years old when Shaw died, in the kind of broad-brush indictment that Jon Stewart loves to mock:

> The progressives and the Fabian socialists want to deny or distance themselves, all the while Hillary Clinton says I'm an early more than, early 20th century American progressive. That's who George Bernard Shaw was hanging out with and they had the same elitist kind of ideas. It is where it is where the idea of eugenics, breed the perfect race, breed a better voter. So, here's the Fabian socialists, their plan. These are just their these are just their goals and, again, there's no Star Chamber here. These are all stated.

This incoherent babble, whose meaning is just barely discernible, is from Beck's own personal website. It runs from guilt by association to guilt without any association.

One liberal website was so eager to dissociate from Shaw to escape Beck's rant they disparaged Shaw as a "eugenics-supporting lunatic," hastily adding that "He was also an avowed socialist, which, despite Beck's insistence to the contrary, is not the same as a progressive," seeming to imply that eugenics-supporting lunatics are more likely to turn up among socialists than among prim progressives.

Glenn Beck may not be the best example, as he is in somewhat bad odor even among conservatives as himself a lunatic. Shaw's excommunication, however, is fairly broad on the right. His entry on Conservapedia, the right-wing alternative to Wikipedia, provides two brief sentences listing without further elaboration the titles of five of his plays, followed by a long page devoted to Shaw's endorsement of eugenics and his late-life praise of dictators.

If you want the worst, up front, from an unbiased source, we have Stanley Weintraub's "GBS and the Despots" in the August 22, 2011, *Times Literary Supplement*. Weintraub is a distinguished Shaw scholar and editor of *Bernard Shaw: The Diaries 1885–1897*.

In 1927 Shaw published in the *London Daily News* a letter titled "Bernard Shaw on Mussolini: A Defence." He came under sharp attack for this by both socialists and liberals, but persisted in his admiration of Mussolini throughout the 1930s. While sharply condemning Hitler's anti-Semitism, he spoke positively about the Nazis for renouncing the Versailles Treaty, which Shaw had opposed, and for their supposed economic reforms, writing in 1935, "The Nazi movement is in many respects one which has my warmest sympathy." As late as 1944, deep into World War II, when he was strongly supporting the British war effort against Germany, he still in print had something positive to say about Hitler's *Mein Kampf*. He claimed that he was a National Socialist before Hitler was.

He was well-disposed toward Oswald Mosley, Britain's home-grown fascist demagogue, declaring Mosley "the only striking personality in British politics." He turned against the German Nazis and Italian fascists during World War II, but never wavered from his adulation for the Soviet Union, first under Lenin, and then, undiminished, under Stalin.

As it happens, George Orwell in his 1946 pamphlet *James Burnham and the Managerial Revolution* does shed light on the Glenn Beckish claim that Shaw's dual embrace of communism and fascism was broadly typical of Fabians or other sorts of socialists:

> English writers who consider Communism and Fascism to *be the same thing* invariably hold that both are monstrous evils which must be fought to the death; on the other hand, any Englishman who believes Communism and Fascism to be opposites will feel that he ought to side with one or the other. The only exception I am able to think of is Bernard Shaw, who, for some years at any rate, declared Communism and Fascism to be much the same thing, and was in favour of both of them.

Shaw also made extreme and indefensible statements about euthanasia. Glenn Beck doesn't even quote the worst, such as a 1933 suggestion that chemists develop a "humane" poison gas for the extermination of those he regarded as social parasites, those who refuse to work and insist that society support them (including the idle rich as well as the deliberately idle poor).

Eugenics

Reactionary columnist Jonah Goldberg in his risible book *Liberal Fascism*, a 467 page tome written apparently because some leftist called him a fascist, and amounting to a "Nyah, nyah, you're the fascist!", spills four or five pages of vitriol on "liberal heroes" who "shared Shaw's enthusiasm" for eugenics. What is dishonest about all this stuff is not the quotes from leftists but the claim that eugenics was widely supported by leftists and the omission of all those on the right who were eager, and very well-funded, champions of eugenics — for some, poison gas and all.

The problem with the right-wing use of Shaw to pillory moderate socialists and nonsocialist liberal progressives is not only that few of the latter held such views, but that this kind of cherry picking is ahistorical. It doesn't seek to understand how such now unacceptable opinions gained currency, or who held them and why. It is what Pascal Bruckner calls the sin of anachronism, which he contrasts to real history, which "forbids us to judge preceding centuries from the point of view of the present." Sympathy for Italian fascism, and even German Nazism, was widespread after the bloody debacle of World War I and the Great Depression, and far more so on the right than on the left, Shaw being an outlier here.

The very idea that there is such a thing as social change dates mainly from the Industrial Revolution, when it became obvious in daily life. Much of philosophy, social theorizing, and political organizing since has aimed to figure out to what degree we can have effective input into our own future, to guide the unfolding changes rather than simply submit to them. Many paths forward have been embraced only to prove disastrous later. Communism and fascism are the textbook examples. Darwin showed that there was biological change as well as political and economic change. Eugenics was an attempt to take charge of human evolution, which was ultimately found to be far more difficult and to involve a far greater potential for evil than its first advocates imagined.

Eugenics was generally thought of as a harmless way to take an active part in improving the "race." One of its main projects was simply to legalize and popularize birth control. That gave it a "progressive" tinge. But it was quickly harnessed to Social Darwinism and began to be invoked to bar immigration of Asians and other "undesirables," which was more popular on the right, along with some trade unions. It expanded in the United States to bar marriage or reproduction by those deemed mentally unfit, a category that began with the retarded and the mentally ill, and which expanded to swallow up many poor black women. These atrocious policies were widely enacted into

American law through the lobbying of major foundations, which were generally more conservative than liberal.

Eugenics was supported by some leftists and liberals, such as H. G.
Wells, John Maynard Keynes, Margaret Sanger, Sidney Webb, Virginia
Woolf, progressive Republican Theodore Roosevelt, and Stanford University
President David Starr Jordan. But similar advocacy was widespread on the
right and center, where eugenics champions included, in Great Britain and
Ireland, Conservative Prime Minister Arthur Balfour, Winston Churchill,
W. B. Yeats, T. S. Eliot, D. H. Lawrence, and Julian Huxley; in the United
States, Alexander Graham Bell, John D. Rockefeller, Andrew Carnegie,
Henry Ford, John Harvey Kellogg (founder of the breakfast cereal company),
and Clarence Gamble (heir to the Proctor and Gamble fortune). The main difference is that the Irish and Britons mainly talked about eugenics while the
American corporate foundations poured large amounts of money into its implementation. In the U.S., thirty states adopted involuntary sterilization laws
used to forcibly neuter 64,000 people between 1907 and 1963.

This was promoted by wealthy organizations such as the Rockefeller,
Ford, and Carnegie foundations. The Rockefeller Institute prominently employed the pro-Nazi French biologist Alexis Carrel, who wrote:

> Those who have murdered, robbed while armed with automatic pis-
> tol or machine gun, kidnapped children, despoiled the poor of their sav-
> ings, misled the public in important matters, should be humanely and
> economically disposed of in small euthanasic institutions supplied with
> proper gasses. A similar treatment could be advantageously applied to
> the insane, guilty of criminal acts.

Notice how the criteria becomes more and more sweeping as the list grows,
from murderers to armed robbers to mere swindlers and then to people who
spread false information, and finally the mentally ill who step over some legal
line.

The most prominent organizer of the eugenics movement in the United
States was the apolitical zoologist and geneticist Charles B. Davenport (1866-
1944), who headed the Cold Spring Harbor Laboratory in Cold Spring Harbor, New York, which was funded by the Carnegie Institute. Davenport's
eugenics creed included the proviso, "I believe in such a selection of immigrants as shall not tend to adulterate our national germ plasm with socially
unfit traits."

Notably the Conservapedia does not mention the association with eugenics of any of the conservatives. It does recount the state laws requiring sterili-

zation of the "unfit," but sanitizes its account by referring to the whole movement as "radical" and omitting all but the Carnegie foundation and Davenport from its summary.

Exterminationist ideas of the sort Shaw voiced in the 1930s were then, as they still are today, more common than we like to recognize, and not particularly linked to eugenics. In the early twentieth century colonialism and empire were more often the springboard. On the left it was H. G. Wells, not Shaw, who talked about exterminating "inferior" races. On the right, novelist D. H. Lawrence said such things. The British conservative author George Chatterton Hill in his 1907 *Heredity and Selection in Sociology* wrote that "Nothing can be more unscientific, nothing shows a deeper ignorance of the elementary laws of social evolution, than the absurd agitations, peculiar to the British race, against the elimination of inferior races." The British "race," he said, "by reason of its genius for expansion, must necessarily eliminate the inferior races which stand in its way. Every superior race in history has done the same, and was obliged to do it."

American diplomat and international lawyer Henry C. Morris in his *History of Colonization* (1900) insisted that if the native population of a colony could not be induced to produce a profit for the colonialists, "the natives must then be exterminated or reduced to such numbers as to be readily controlled." The Illinois Institute of Technology Chicago-Kent College of Law to this day sponsors the Henry C. Morris Lecture in International and Comparative Law.

It is not clear even that Shaw's few comments about euthanizing the congenitally antisocial and those who refuse to work were connected to his support for eugenics. He doesn't say that the antisocial are biologically inferior, which would be the eugenics argument. The quotations usually circulated or cited here are a fairly close paraphrase of Saint Paul's Second Epistle to the Thessalonians, 1:10: "For even when we were with you, this we commanded you, that if any would not work, neither should he eat." Shaw most likely picked the idea up from Lenin's *State and Revolution*, where it appears as "He who does not work shall not eat." The saint and the revolutionary don't spell out that the culprits will die, but generally not eating has that result. Yet, Shaw gives the premise a cruel activist twist that goes beyond his sources.

Of course, today loose exterminationist talk has, from overuse, lost much of its shock value. Its proponents only have to avoid the trigger word "poison gas." Right-wing radio talk host Michael Savage, with an audience of eight to ten million for his nationally syndicated show, The Savage Nation, in a July 21, 2006, broadcast on Iranian President Mahmoud Ahmadinejad's pending appearance at the United Nations urged, "I don't know why we don't use a bunker-buster bomb when he comes to the U.N. and just take him out with everyone in there."

Shaw's accuser, Glenn Beck, when asked about Iran, was superlative in his bloodlust: "I say we nuke the bastards. . . . In fact, it doesn't have to be Iran, it can be everywhere, anyplace that disagrees with me." (Premiere Radio Networks, The Glenn Beck Program, May 11, 2006).

Left, Right, and the Extremes

Shaw is useful to the right as one of the extremely few well-known socialists who also said some positive things about fascism. He fits into the current bizarre campaign to rewrite history and fob off fascism as a left-wing movement. This is in part merely a cynical attempt to unload on the opposition the crimes of one's own ancestors. But in part it is sheer ignorance of history. Many of today's Tea Party enthusiasts, when judging some snippet they read or hear about the past, decide who was left and who was right by consulting their own private convictions and seeing if they match. They seem blithely innocent of any notion of the history of ideas and take as a given that their own recently acquired small-government panacea has always been the hallmark of conservative thought.

Liberals from the eighteenth through the early twentieth century were champions of capitalism, political democracy, free elections, human rights, and religious tolerance. Conservatives were supporters of the absolute monarchies, established religions, aristocracy, and strict social hierarchy. Obviously there have been shifts since, and there were always individual thinkers who broke the pattern, but conservatives through the end of World War II were more likely to be in favor of strong central governments than liberals, except on the issue of social welfare measures such as the New Deal, which flowed from their disdain for the lower classes, not from their fear of big government. As recently as Reagan and Bush junior we have had conservative presidents who claimed they favored small government while greatly expanding federal power and costs.

It was the conservative parties and politicians that were the allies of Hitler, Mussolini, and Franco during their rise to power, and in Italy and Spain for the duration of fascist rule, not the liberal or left parties. The left has its own sins, in widespread illusions in Soviet Russia and the Lenin and Stalin dictatorships, but there is no grounds to foist on it responsibility for its adversaries' portion as well. In any case, many on the left and most liberals were opponents of Soviet communism.

The right-wing blogosphere, Glenn Beck, and the Conservapedia have a simple approach to someone like Bernard Shaw, apart from their attempt to use him to smear today's liberals: brand him as irremediably wicked and ex-communicate him from polite society. The difficulty is that many significant figures in our history have these kinds of dark sides to them, and the typology is far from following any clear left-right cleavage.

The problem with deciding what we should think of Bernard Shaw is the problem of historical context. Judged by the standards of our own day, many of the outspoken figures of our past have inexcusable blemishes. Yet to cast them all out would leave us without a history or a culture. Churchill admired Mussolini, approved of colonialism, opposed Indian independence till the end, and was a staunch eugenicist. Kipling was an anti-Semite. Yeats supported the Blueshirts, the Irish fascist organization. Brecht, Langston Hughes, Charlie Chaplin, Dashiell Hammet, and Frida Kahlo were Stalinists, and far from the only ones. Henry Ford promoted the anti-Semitic forgery *The Protocols of the Elders of Zion.* Mahatma Gandhi supported white apartheid in South Africa. Chaucer, Martin Luther, William Shakespeare, Immanuel Kant, George Washington, Benjamin Franklin, Karl Marx, Pierre-Joseph Proudhon (the founder of French socialism), H. L. Mencken, Mark Twain, Joseph Kennedy (father of JFK), G. K. Chesterton, and T. S. Eliot all said some pretty awful things about Jews. Abraham Lincoln, despite the Emancipation Proclamation, was a racist. Even Jesus, when approached by a Canaanite woman asking him to heal her daughter, first refuses, saying "I am not sent but unto the lost sheep of the house of Israel," and calls the non-Jews "dogs." (Matthew, 15:22-26)

Everyone must make their own judgment on whether a political or liter-ary figure of the past was so inexcusably far from an acceptable moral stan-dard as to write them out of the historical canon. I am not prepared to give up Yeats or Kipling, Churchill or Gandhi. I am not so forgiving of Henry Ford, the profascist poet Ezra Pound, or Brecht. I still listen to Wagner, but cannot silence the small voice recalling that Nietzsche broke with him over Wagner's anti-Semitism, or that his music was played over the loudspeakers at Ausch-witz.

My Encounters with Shaw's Plays

If all I knew about Bernard Shaw was what I read on Conservapedia there would be no reason to refrain from burning his books, or at least encour-aging libraries to discard them. But that is not how it was. In a certain sense I grew up with Shaw's plays. Somewhere I had seen the 1938 film of *Pygma-lion* with Wendy Hiller and Leslie Howard, for whom I was named. My fam-ily were Republicans, but my mother (who after I left home became a liberal Democrat) was an avid follower of television drama, and Shaw was frequently on the bill in the fifties. Particularly memorable was a production of *The*

Devil's Disciple in November 1955, when I was thirteen. Shaw's only play set in America, at the time of the American Revolution, it starred Ralph Bellamy, one of my favorite actors, as Pastor Anderson, and Maurice Evans as the clever and heretical Dick Dudgeon. Thought to be a useless wastrel, Dudgeon acts with matchless heroism when, while visiting the minister's home, he is mistaken for Pastor Anderson by General Burgoyne's soldiers, who have come to arrest Anderson to be executed as a hostage. Dudgeon lets himself be mistaken for the pastor to save the other's life.

The following spring there was *Caesar and Cleopatra*, with lots of clever dialogue between Cedric Hardwicke and Claire Bloom. Then came *My Fair Lady*. My mother took my sister and me to a rare outing, the 1957 West Coast touring company of the new musical, with Brian Aherne and Anne Rogers in the roles premiered by Rex Harrison and Julie Andrews. We bought the original cast LP, which my sister and I played until we knew every song by heart.

I was innocent yet of politics and caught only a whiff of the class divisions Shaw was satirizing. And it would be decades more before I could see something in Henry Higgins of Vandeleur Lee, the charismatic singing teacher and choral conductor who shared the Shaw home when Bernard Shaw was a child, phonetics substituted for voice instruction.

But my true fascination with Shaw came a year later yet, and this time it was focused directly on the playwright and his ideas.

Noel Swerdlow, a high school friend with advanced views, one day took me to Wallach's Music City in Hollywood, where he insisted that I buy the First Drama Quartet LPs of their reading of *Don Juan in Hell*, the lengthy dream sequence from Shaw's 1903 play *Man and Superman*. The cast was beyond superb: Charles Laughton as the Devil, Charles Boyer as Don Juan, Agnes Moorehead as Doña Ana, and Sir Cedric Hardwicke as the Statue. The LPs are long out of print but you can still download the MP3 version from Amazon at a minimal cost.

In Shaw's rendering of the Don Juan legend the story picks up after the living statue, Doña Ana's father, has dragged the lothario off to hell. Here Don Juan debates the Devil on the meaning of life. Hell is not a pit of fire and brimstone but a palace of hedonism. Heaven, which remains off stage during the play, is some kind of workshop where people toil selflessly to improve humanity.

The talk — and it is all talk, no action of any kind takes place, but the play in not less gripping for that — ranges over art, music, love, human cruelty and cowardice, marriage, evolution, the Life Force, and the quest for a superior mind, the superman.

The Devil champions his realm of love, art, music, and beauty against the brutality of human life on the physical earth in one vast speech that in print is a single paragraph three pages long. Here is just the beginning of it:

And is Man any the less destroying himself for all this boasted brain of his? Have you walked up and down upon the earth lately? I have; and I have examined Man's wonderful inventions. And I tell you that in the arts of life man invents nothing; but in the arts of death he outdoes Nature herself, and produces by chemistry and machinery all the slaughter of plague, pestilence, and famine. The peasant I tempt today eats and drinks what was eaten and drunk by the peasants of ten thousand years ago; and the house he lives in has not altered as much in a thousand centuries as the fashion of a lady's bonnet in a score of weeks. But when he goes out to slay, he carries a marvel of mechanism that lets loose at the touch of his finger all the hidden molecular energies, and leaves the javelin, the arrow, the blowpipe of his fathers far behind. In the arts of peace Man is a bungler. I have seen his cotton factories and the like, with machinery that a greedy dog could have invented if it had wanted money instead of food. I know his clumsy typewriters and bungling locomotives and tedious bicycles: they are toys compared to the Maxim gun, the submarine torpedo boat. There is nothing in Man's industrial machinery but his greed and sloth: his heart is in his weapons.

Don Juan concedes that human society is often brutal but he rejects the Devil and his proteges' escape into a ghostly world of beauty, art, and love, the aristocratic retreat into cultivated living. The Devil tries to tempt him, saying, "Here, I repeat, you have all that you sought without anything that you shrank from."

Don Juan rejects this:

On the contrary, here I have everything that disappointed me without anything that I have not already tried and found wanting. I tell you that as long as I can conceive of something better than myself I cannot be easy unless I am striving to bring it into existence or clearing the way for it. That is the law of my life. This is the working within me of Life's incessant aspiration to higher organization, wider, deeper, intenser self-consciousness, and clearer self-understanding. It was the supremacy of this purpose that reduced love for me to the mere pleasure of a moment, art for me to the mere schooling of my faculties, religion for me to a mere excuse for laziness, since it had set up a God who looked at the world and saw that it was good, against the instinct in me that looked through my eyes at the world and saw that it could be improved.

Read that in your head in Charles Boyer's imperious French accent and see if you are not moved!

Naturally at sixteen I was attracted to what sounded like a life dedicated to such a higher purpose. I didn't fail to notice Shaw's particular take on this, that the job to be done was to aid the evolution of humanity toward the creation of the superman. I had read *Thus Spake Zarathustra* and grasped that this was a Nietzschean idea. But Nietzsche himself presents the search for the superman as a lonely personal spiritual and intellectual quest, not a government program in selective breeding. In any case I didn't feel I had to take seriously the goal of a biological superman to be inspired by the idea of a life of service to humanity in some form.

We now know some very negative things and a few positive ones about the old playwright. What else would I need to know about GBS, as he styled himself, to decide if his works are worth keeping and his life worth recalling? I turned to the fat one-volume edition of Michael Holroyd's magisterial biography.

Shaw's Early Life

Shaw was born on July 26, 1856, in Dublin. His father, George Carr Shaw, was an alcoholic. He married Lucinda Elizabeth "Bessie" Gurley for her money, but her father outsmarted him and put it in a trust that wouldn't come due for many years. It was a loveless marriage. Whatever small ability the pair had to display affection was exhausted on their two daughters. None was left for their third-born, George Bernard. When young George was around six, to make ends meet they shared a house with music impresario and voice teacher George Lee, who later called himself Vandeleur Lee. Lee was captivating and the household became a platonic *menage a trois*, with Lucinda Shaw far closer to the music teacher than to her useless husband. This was a pattern that GBS imitated many times in his life, in passionate but usually unconsummated love affairs with other men's wives.

Called Sonny as a boy, he did not get on in school but was a voracious reader, steeped in Shakespeare, Homer, Sir Walter Scott, Alexandre Dumas, Shelley, and Byron. By the time he was ten he lost his belief in religion. Through Vandeleur Lee he developed a love of music.

At fifteen he took a job as an office boy in a land firm. In June 1873, when Shaw was sixteen, Vandeleur Lee left their home in Dublin and moved to London; Shaw's mother, now called Bessie, followed. Her two daughters went with her, leaving Sonny behind with his father. The three women in London lived separately from Lee, Bessie and her younger daughter Lucy pursuing musical training with him. Missing her, as well as the music that had been so central to the household, GBS taught himself the piano, becoming a fairly accomplished classical pianist. Early in 1876 his older sister Agnes died of a wasting disease. Shaw took the occasion of her funeral to move to London, where he lived with his mother and Lucy, though as ever on remote terms.

Vandeleur Lee had not prospered in England. He hired Shaw to ghost write music criticism for a paper called *The Hornet*, which was the beginning of Shaw's first career, as a music critic. Lee unexpectedly proposed marriage, to Lucy rather than to Bessie, which led both Lucy and her mother to break all ties with him. Shaw continued the association, as writer and as piano accompanist in Lee's voice lessons.

Shaw had a striking appearance. When grown he stood six feet two, but weighed only 140 pounds, almost a stick figure. He grew a distinctive red beard to cover scars from a bout of smallpox. When he was twenty-nine he bought his first new suit, the then distinctive if faddish Jaeger woolen set, widely promoted for its purported health benefits. It included wool underwear, a tweed coat and waistcoat, and short breeches with long stockings. This became his trademark garb, more and more unfashionable as the decades passed.

The London GBS discovered was the one described by Charles Dickens, who had died at fifty-eight in 1870, only six years before Shaw's arrival. The city's slums were a cesspit of squalor and wretchedness whose like can be seen today only in third world countries, though they are making a comeback in the wake of the current world recession. Horror at this human misery led Shaw to hopes of reform and, after some years, to the budding socialist movement.

In the meantime he tried to break into the literary world. Between 1879 and 1883 he wrote five novels, all of them rejected by every publisher he approached. The first, *Immaturity*, did not see print for fifty years. The other four were eventually serialized in two socialist periodicals, between 1884 and 1888.

Following a brief stint at the telephone company, he spent the next eight years studying at the British Museum, supported by his mother, a favor he would return when he became a successful playwright. In this period he adopted vegetarianism, in part from his reading of Darwin, which led him to see animals as fellow creatures. He also abstained from alcohol, having seen his parents' marriage ruined by his father's drinking.

He trained as a boxer, had his first girl friend, and, in 1882, attended a lecture by the American reformer Henry George that set him on the road to political radicalism. He soon discovered Karl Marx and ploughed through *Das Capital*, not yet available in English, in a French translation. In September 1884 Shaw joined the Fabian Society, which had been founded earlier that year. For the next eight years, until his first performed play, *Widowers' Houses*, in 1892, he devoted most of his energies to the new organization.

The Fabians were opposed to forming a socialist political party. Instead they pursued a strategy of permeation, by which they meant patiently persuading influential figures and leaders of the existing Liberal and Tory parties. They advocated a range of moderate reforms that would come to be widely accepted in Europe and North America in the century that followed: a welfare state on the model of Bismarck's Germany, women's suffrage, slum clearance, for a national health service, a minimum wage. Of the various English socialist groups the Fabians were the least proletarian. Their views were the soul of moderation, their members thoroughly respectable, their outlook mostly local and provincial. It would be years before they would even discuss their position on foreign policy and British colonialism.

Shaw quickly became one of the small group's most effective platform speakers and pamphleteers. The leadership team that would cohere for the next half century was complete with the adherence of Sidney and Beatrice Webb. Shaw was the inspired propagandist, the Webbs the statisticians and careful researchers. In the thirty years before the bloody slaughter of the Great War, the Fabians were essentially the liberal wing of the great mass of Victorian believers in the inevitability of onward and upward progress. Portions of their list of reforms were often endorsed by Tory as well as Liberal politicians.

In 1900 Shaw drafted the Fabians' first declaration on foreign policy, "Fabianism and the Empire." It was anything but radical, viewing empires as a progressive step beyond narrow nationalism, rating the British empire as the most worthy, and endorsing the British side in the Boer War. By the late 1880s Shaw, and the Fabians with him, had rejected Marxist class struggle. Shaw envisioned the split in society as between those who worked at something for a living and those who did not. This differed from the Marxian class theory in that it condemned only that part of the rich who lived off rents and interest, and with them those of the lower classes who chose not to work or who chose to be criminals.

The Fabians were instrumental in founding the Labour Party, also in 1900, and became the party's brain trust for decades afterward, several British prime ministers ranked among their growing membership.

Meanwhile Shaw was establishing himself as a book reviewer and music critic, and even as an art critic. In February 1889 he became music critic for *The Star* under the pseudonym Corno di Bassetto, and then switched to *The World*, now signing himself GBS. During these years he gave a thousand unpaid lectures for the Fabians and was much sought after as a platform speaker and teacher.

As the nineteenth century closed, GBS continued his work with the Fabians on a reduced level. He spent six years as a local elected London official. In the British system he served in the St. Pancras Vestry as vestryman, a member of the elected parish council, changed to a borough in 1900. Here he worked effectively and amiably with moderate and conservative members of the local government.

During the 1880s he had several mainly platonic affairs: with Karl Marx's youngest daughter, Eleanor, who was living with Edward Aveling and would commit suicide when Aveling married someone else; with later-famous children's author Edith Nesbit, married to the Tory socialist Hubert Bland; and with May Morris, William Morris's daughter. Morris, best remembered as a central figure in the Arts and Crafts movement and the Pre-Rafaelite artists, was an early socialist leader and headed the Socialist League, a more proletarian rival to the middle-class Fabians. Shaw admired Morris but counted him "a privileged eccentric and in no way an authority as to socialist policy." Shaw's biographer adds that this was "almost exactly in the same manner as the Labour Party was later to regard G.B.S. himself." May, impatient with Shaw's reticence, married, prompting Shaw to renew the attachment, on the pattern of Vandeleur Lee with his own parents. The marriage failed, but Shaw by that time typically withdrew again.

Shaw's one seriously consummated affair was with Jane Patterson, an older woman and close friend of his mother's. This lasted, with some interruptions, from April 1885 until the beginning of 1893. During one of the interstices he was offered a contract of terms for living together by Annie Besant, then a Fabian firebrand but later the head of Madame Blavatsky's occult Theosophical Society. He turned her down.

GBS Becomes a Playwright

A more serious affair led to a final break with Jane Patterson and helped redirect Shaw toward his ultimate vocation. In 1890 at May Morris's home he met and fell in love with Florence Farr. She was then at the very beginning of a career that would make her a leading figure of the English and Irish stage. Shaw saw and reviewed for the press her performance in *A Sicilian Idyll* by John Todhunter. This event drew together several of the major strands of Victorian Irish culture. Todhunter was a close friend of Irish poet and playwright William Butler Yeats, and a member of the Hermetic Order of the Golden Dawn, the occult organization in which both Yeats and Farr would become prominent. Farr would be a frequent lead in plays by both Shaw and Yeats, and through her Shaw established his own links with Yeats' Abbey Theatre in Dublin and a long personal friendship with Yeats and his patron, Lady Gregory.

Another influence on Shaw in the period was seeing Janet Achurch in 1889 in the first English production of Ibsen's *The Doll's House*, shocking in Victorian England when Nora dares to break free from her stifling marriage. Shaw saw the play five times. He was inspired by Ibsen to see the theatre as a venue for serious ideas, at odds with the drawing-room comedies and bedroom farces that were the staple of the Victorian stage. He was inspired enough to write one of his few nonfiction books, *Quintessence of Ibsenism* (1891).

Then, in 1892, his first play, *Widowers' Houses*, opened. It ran for only two performances. Creaky though it was, it previewed much that became typical of Shavian drama. It took stock figures of Victorian theatre but inverted their characters. The young hero, Trench, falls in love with the daughter of a wealthy man. Discovering that his prospective father-in-law is a slumlord, Trench demands that his fiancee reject any money from him. The reversal is that she refuses and breaks off the engagement. It is discovered that Trench's trust fund is equally tainted and the lovers reunite, accepting their unscrupulous financial foundation. Add witty dialogue and many humorous turns of phrase to coat the social problem under examination and you have a Shaw production.

His biographer, Michael Holroyd, makes a pithy summary of what distinguished his subject's work:

"Shaw's plays were not plays. Archer [an early collaborator] had no trouble in spotting this. His friend had dispensed with plot, with character, with drama and the red corpuscles of life, to demonstrate that argument squeezed into a well-built dramatic machine was as good as any play."

His first three plays were not financial successes. *Widowers' Houses* was followed by *The Philanderer,* the title suggesting the content and based loosely on some of Shaw's own adventures in other people's marriages, and then in 1893, *Mrs. Warren's Profession*, in which Vivie Warren discovers that her genteel upbringing was financed by her mother's brothel, with undertones of possible incest, as there is doubt about which of her mother's several lovers is her father, and her own fiance is the son of one of the possibles.

These plays were disturbing in their day and had a hard political message not far from the surface. Shaw resolved in future to write plays more about people and their situations, with more humor and less message. He published the three early efforts together as *Plays Unpleasant*. Afterward he arranged book-length collections of his further plays, setting a new pattern for play publication on both sides of the Atlantic, prefacing each play or volume with a lengthy essay on the social ill motivating the sparkling dialogue.

He followed with *Arms and the Man*, a romantic comedy with a feminist theme set in Bulgaria during the 1885 Serbo-Bulgarian war. This was his first well-received effort. He had written it for Florence Farr, who played Raina Petkoff, the female lead. Raina rejects her Bulgarian war hero fiance Sergius Saranoff to marry a Swiss mercenary, Captain Bluntschli, who had fought on the Serbian side. Bluntschli may have been an enemy but he at least respected her while her lout of a war hero was out with other women. In later years the play ran seven times on Broadway, and between British and American productions has had casts that included Ralph Richardson, Margaret Leighton, Laurence Olivier, Marlon Brando, Len Cariou, Kevin Kline, Raul Julia, John Malkovich, and Helena Bonham Carter.

Having lived in poverty his first forty years, financial success came only with his eighth play, *The Devil's Disciple*, which in 1897, mainly in America, earned him £2,000 (about $272,000 in today's dollars). In his long life he published no less than fifty-nine plays and was the most performed and honored playwright in the English language for several generations, second only to Shakespeare. Most of these works have not survived, but a core canon have remained staples of theatre companies in many countries: *Arms and the Man, Candida, The Devil's Disciple, The Doctor's Dilemma, Captain Brassbound's Conversion, Caesar and Cleopatra, Man and Superman* and its dream sequence *Don Juan in Hell, Major Barbara, Androcles and the Lion, Pygmalion, Heartbreak House*, and *The Apple Cart* are all still performed on stage and for television. His most popular play was his vision of Joan of Arc, *Saint Joan* (1923).

GBS wrote only one thoroughly Irish play, *John Bull's Other Island*, 1904, focused on the conflict between a British land developer in Ireland and a priest who opposes him. Though the premiere was ultimately moved to London from the planned Abbey Theatre opening, over disputes on length and Shaw's negatively realistic portrayal of his native Ireland, the episode cemented a lifelong friendship with Yeats and still more so with Lady Gregory, central figures of the Irish Literary Revival.

The Internet Movie Database lists no fewer than 175 film and television productions of Shaw plays, in multiple languages, from a 1921 silent Czech film of his early novel *Cashel Byron's Profession* to a 2009 Canadian film of *Caesar and Cleopatra* starring Christopher Plummer. The entries cluster between 1938 and 1985, a bit heavier in the 1950s and 1960s. On television he is well represented in the Hallmark Hall of Fame and the BBC Play of the Month.

Saint Joan was filmed by Otto Preminger in 1957 with Jean Seberg in the title role, screenplay by Graham Greene. On stage Shaw's Joan has been played by Sybil Thorndike, Katharine Cornell, Wendy Hiller, Uta Hagen, Siobhan McKenna, Joan Plowright, Genevieve Bujold, Lynn Redgrave, Amy Irving, and Judi Dench. Unexpectedly for a man of the left, Shaw did not take the predictable path of glorifying the rebel Joan and casting her interrogators and executioners as consummate imperialist and ruling class villains. In his only tragedy he insisted there were to be no villains, each side acting as their beliefs told them they must.

By 1894 GBS and Florence Farr ended their affair, her occultism grating too harshly against his Fabianism. He more and more in his writings and in his life began to elevate work above love. He formed repeated intense romantic attachments to women, usually prominent actresses, but withdrew from physical sex. His compulsorily chaste lovers included Janet Achurch, Ellen Terry, and Stella Campbell, stage stars of their day. His pattern included long walks, visits to museums, and always an extensive exchange of letters, many of them at least verbally passionate.

Then in 1898 at the age of forty-two he married for the first time. His bride was Charlotte Payne-Townshend. She was Irish, rich, six months younger than he, intelligent, and with a certain inclination toward radical politics, but plain of face and figure. And, perhaps essential to their marriage, deathly afraid of childbirth. They were happily married for forty-five years. It is said that the marriage was never physically consummated. He had lived with his mother, though not on very good terms, until their wedding. He and Charlotte in 1906 bought a house in the village of Ayot St Lawrence in Hertfordshire, just north of Greater London. They lived there for the rest of their lives. They traveled widely together until quite late in life. After a time Shaw resumed his flirtations and heavy correspondence with other women, which Charlotte tried to ignore. He seems to have abstained from sex with them as well as with his wife, with the possible exception of a young American beauty, Molly Tompkins, who pursued him, then already seventy, during several of his prolonged visits to Italy beginning in 1926.

The Life Force versus Darwin

Shaw updated and published his nonfiction *The Perfect Wagnernite* in 1898. A major change was taking place in his thinking. He was inspired by the Ring cycle, but unhappy that in Wagner the heroes are liberated only after death, by ascending to heaven. He needed an earthly salvation and wanted something more than ordinary politics as the sole vehicle to achieve the egalitarian future he hoped for. He began looking for an additional ally on that road. He believed he found it in his own interpretation of evolution.

It was typical of the Victorians to embrace Darwin but miss the point of what he was saying. Darwin's natural selection made no promise as to outcomes, only stating that successive generations of organisms favor genetic variants and mutations that advantageously adapt them to their environment. Many Victorians chose instead to read "Evolution," as a straight road to ever greater physical and mental perfection alongside the social and political perfectability they also believed in. Most of those who championed this ideological version of evolution thought of themselves as Darwinians. Some, looking for a more definite and rapid promise of improvement, professed versions of evolution that explicitly differed from Darwin.

Marx and Engels rejected natural selection, with Marx instead endorsing a little-known crank geologist who claimed to be able to predict stages of steady improvement in animal species from changes in the earth's soils. Shaw abandoned atheism and created a creed he called Creative Evolution in which the Life Force was an immanent power driving the human race toward rapid (by geological standards) improvement in mind and self-consciousness. This Life Force was a mystical biological field of some kind, whose strength was being added to the mere human efforts of social reformers such as the Fabians. Humans and other living things were said to be endowed with a self-determining essence separate from the physics and chemistry that ordinary science recognizes.

Looking back some years later, in his preface to the five *Back to Methuselah* plays, published in 1921, he acknowledged that he had intended the *Don Juan in Hell* dream sequence in *Man and Superman* to be the founding document of a new religion:

> Accordingly, in 1901, I took the legend of Don Juan in its Mozartian form and made it a dramatic parable of Creative Evolution. But being then at the height of my invention and comedic talent, I decorated it too brilliantly and lavishly. I surrounded it with a comedy of which it formed only one act. . . . Also I supplied the published work with an imposing framework consisting of a preface, an appendix called *The Revo-*

lutionist's Handbook, and a final display of aphoristic fireworks. The effect was so vertiginous, apparently, that nobody noticed the new religion in the centre of the intellectual whirlpool.

GBS was never modest, but he is right that *Don Juan in Hell* was perhaps his most brilliant piece of writing, new religion of selective breeding of the superman at its core notwithstanding. The critic Max Beerbohm wrote of it, "In swiftness, tenseness and lucidity of dialogue no living writer can touch the hem of Mr Shaw's garment. In *Man and Superman* every phrase rings and flashes." Beerbohm became a close friend. In a letter decades later on Shaw's ninetieth birthday he articulated what many thought:

"My admiration for his genius has during fifty years and more been marred for me by dissent from almost any view that he holds about anything." For Beerbohm the secret of disentangling Shaw's extremist preaching from his plays was his odd combination of seriousness and irrepressible frivolity, the comic side that invaded all his productions.

Shaw was no scientist. He appropriated the idea of Creative Evolution from the literature of his day that could offer support to his faith in a radical improvement in humanity and eliminate the evils of his own time. In part he seems to have found what he was looking for in the French philosopher Henri Bergson, whose 1907 book *Creative Evolution* advocated a form of vitalism in living organisms and coined the term that Shaw officially adopted in the preface to *Back to Methuselah*.

A more immediate influence was the novelist Samuel Butler, best remembered as the author of *The Way of All Flesh* and *Erewhon*. Butler was also a tireless adversary of Darwin, promoting his own version of evolution. Butler's two key differences with Darwin were that Butler wanted to claim a role for some kind of innate intelligence in directing evolutionary change from within organisms, and he wanted to resurrect Lamarck's idea of the inheritance of acquired characteristics.

Shaw at one point wrote: "What damns Darwinian Natural Selection as a creed is that it takes hope out of evolution, and substitutes a paralysing fatalism which is utterly discouraging. As Butler put it, it banishes Mind from the universe." In a 1911 debate over religion with G. K. Chesterton, who would convert to Catholicism in 1922, Shaw staked out his own ground:

As for my own position, I am, and always have been a mystic. I believe that the universe is being driven by a force that we might call the life-force. We are all experiments in the direction of making God. What God is doing is making himself, getting from being a mere powerless will or force. This force has implanted into our minds the ideal of God.

> We are not very successful attempts at God so far, but . . . there never will be a God unless we make one . . . we are the instruments through which that ideal is trying to make itself a reality. (Cited by Holyroyd.)

Inheritance of acquired characteristics was a second arrow in the quiver for hastening evolutionary change. It proposed that building up muscles through exercise or energetic use of the brain through study, or other environmental influences on an organism could be passed on to offspring. Plainly if this were so, evolutionary change would be perceptible in a generation or two instead of the eons-long process of random genetic adaptation to particular environments. Accepting Butler's revival of discredited Lamarckism led Shaw in the 1930s to give credence to Soviet claims about the agricultural miracles of the quack plant geneticist Trofim Lysenko, later shown to be fraudulent.

The point is not so much to show that Bernard Shaw believed things that were at variance with scientific knowledge — a great many Republicans do that — but that he was a man in a hurry to see the change he had aspired to from his early youth, and was trying to enlist both supposed natural and mystical forces to bring it closer. Michael Holroyd describes Shaw's new religion as "a moral commitment to progress thorough the Will, answering the need for optimism in someone whose observation of the world was growing more pessimistic." This turn toward a form of forced-hope mysticism took place in Shaw before the cataclysm of World War I, in his recoil from the more ordinary evils of poverty, injustice, inequality, and inertia of the political leaders of Victorian England. (The long-lived Victoria died only in January 1901, as GBS was formulating his response to the age to which she gave her name.) Pessimism would slowly gain the upper hand after the debacle of the war. His eventual turn toward what he thought of as strong leaders was part of the same process.

World War I

The world war marked the end of the long nineteenth century and with it much of the Victorians' hopes for social improvement. Shaw was particularly shaken, as he took more seriously than most of his comrades the long-standing socialist credo of internationalism, which in the climate of feverish patriotism after August 1914 left him open to charges of being pro-German. The parties of the Socialist International had pledged before the outbreak of hostilities to refuse support to their own governments in the event of war. They overwhelmingly turned patriotic when the artillery began to fire. A few in Britain, such as Bertrand Russell, declared themselves pacifists and went to prison. Shaw on November 14 published a long supplement to the *New*

Statesman entitled "Common Sense About the War." It earned him immediate obloquy.

He accused Britain's rulers of being little better than their Prussian opponents, hypocrites who had planned war with Germany since the latter's victory over France in 1870 and now played the innocent victim of Junker militarism. The Americans would have to come in, he said. "They will have to consider how these two incorrigibly pugnacious and inveterately snobbish peoples, who have snarled at one another for forty years with bristling hair and grinning fangs, and are now rolling over with their teeth in one another's throats, are to be tamed into trusty watch-dogs of the peace of the world."

He was immediately shunned as a traitor. Prime Minister Asquith's son said he should be shot. Dramatist Henry Arthur Jones declaimed that Shaw's mother was "the hag sedition." In America, Theodore Roosevelt called him a "blue rumped ape."

But he was not actually against Britain's participation in the war. Instead he proposed, quixotically, that war aims be reconfigured along democratic and socialist lines. He demanded democratic rights for the troops, trade union representation in the army, an end to secret diplomacy, and a pledge not to take drastic reprisals against Germany at the war's end. Finally, he agreed with the government that the German invasion of France, though not Belgium, merited Britain's entry into the war:

"It left us quite clearly in the position of the responsible policeman of the West. There was nobody else in Europe strong enough to chain the mad dog." And: "We must have the best army in Europe." He quietly donated £20,000 to the British War Loan, about $2.8 million in today's dollars. The acrimony over his pamphlet was a measure of the wave of heady war fever that swept Britain in the early days of the fighting. It would take several years for him to be forgiven. Churchill in his 1937 *Great Contemporaries* showed that he still bore a grudge. There were a few who took Shaw's side. Bloomsbury author Lytton Strachey, who would later win fame for his *Eminent Victorians*, described Shaw as "our leading patriot." In 1917 at the invitation of Douglas Haig, commander-in-chief of the British army, Shaw spent a week at the front in France.

He wrote only a few skits during the war, but followed afterward with several of his most successful plays: *Heartbreak House* in 1920, the five *Back to Methuselah* fantasy plays on Old Testament themes in 1922, and his triumphant *Saint Joan* in 1923. He was awarded the Nobel Prize for literature in 1925. One newspaper dubbed him "the most famous author in the world."

In this period he and Charlotte deepened their friendship with many prominent figures who crossed the whole political spectrum: John Galsworthy, G. K. Chesterton, Lady Gregory, Arnold Bennett, James Barrie, author of Peter Pan, and composer Edward Elgar. Of course Fabians Sidney and Beatrice Webb remained among their dearest friends. They were especially close to T. E. Lawrence, Lawrence of Arabia, a frequent house guest. Shaw had provided editorial help and Charlotte served as proofreader for his *The Seven Pillars of Wisdom*. She and Lawrence over the thirteen years before his death exchanged six hundred letters. Shaw added regular radio talks over the BBC to his other activities.

Disillusionment and the Dictators

Shaw began his drift toward the dictators in the usual left-wing way, by imagining that the Russian Revolution of October 1917 was ushering in the egalitarian utopia he had dreamed of. A decade later he thought he saw almost comparable signs of progress in Mussolini's corporatist state. The Fabian strategy of permeation seemed to be having meagre results. Labour was in power briefly in 1924, with Ramsay MacDonald at its head. Then MacDonald headed a second Labour government from 1929 to 1931, but, disastrously for the left, continuing as Prime Minister in August 1931 in a coalition with a Conservative and Liberal majority. MacDonald, the first Labour Prime Minister, was expelled from the party. Labour would not return to power until the end of World War II.

Where, Shaw asked, was the socialism? In part his disappointment rested in the ultamatistic concept of socialism he had been carrying around in his head since the end of 1910, when he wrote that he advocated "a state of society in which the entire income of the country is divided between all the people in exactly equal shares, without regard to their industry, their character, or any other consideration except the consideration that they are living human beings . . . that is Socialism and nothing else is Socialism."

It would be hard to find any living socialist or even communist who would endorse this proposition. But as that is what he was looking for it would help explain his attraction to forceful extremists. He joined a large swath of the population throughout Europe that had lost faith in official parliamentary parties and their governments after the bloodbath of World War I and the prolonged economic collapse of the Great Depression.

It was the age of totalitarian fantasies. The dictatorships that came to power in Russia in 1917, in Italy in 1922, and in Germany in 1933 and their many followers shared a disdain for parliamentary democracy and personal liberty. They promised a new prosperity and security through a semi-militarized mobilization of the population and giving free rein to police agencies to suppress dissent. Millions who in the past had hankered after liberty found themselves equally willing to give up their liberty to be welcomed into the powerful national fold.

These movements transcended the customary governmental limits of both left and right. The Soviet revolution of 1917 won a wide following among workers and intellectuals in the West, while radical rightists in Italy and Germany were indisputably popular on their home ground and had large numbers of sympathizers abroad. Partisans who looked only at "left" and "right" saw these two rival currents as mortal enemies. There was an argument to be made, and it would get more of a hearing after the second world war, that they were similars. Shaw took the latter view, and as he already approved the Russian version he saw no reason to withhold at least qualified endorsement of the other two.

In 1931, as he turned seventy-five, GBS visited the Soviet Union, accompanied by Conservative MP Lady Nancy Astor, a long-time friend and militant anti-Communist whose own views leaned more toward Hitler. He was met at the train station by Karl Radek and Anatoly Lunacharsky. Radek had been Vice-Commissar for Foreign Affairs in the early days of the Russian Revolution. A former Trotskyist, he was purged, then capitulated to Stalin in 1929, and was enjoying a brief rehabilitation when he met Shaw, before Stalin had him shot in 1939. Lunacharsky had been Commissar of Enlightenment, in charge of education and the arts, in the first Soviet government. He was already in semi disgrace and would escape the purges only by dying in 1933. His works would soon be banned in the USSR.

Shaw was given a staged tour of happy workers and peasants. He believed it all, imagining it to be Fabianism triumphant. Lady Astor was unimpressed, declaring, "I think you are all terrible." She was applauded when her translator, no doubt deliberately, misstated her remarks. Stalin gave the pair a lengthy interview in which he succeeded in charming Shaw, who managed to miss all the brutality of the Soviet system. This trip converted him to communism.

Churchill, who always had a keen eye for such things, in his *Great Contemporaries* mocked GBS's Soviet excursion:

> The Russians have always been fond of circuses and travelling shows. Since they had imprisoned, shot or starved most of their best comedians, their visitors might fill for a space a noticeable void. And here was the World's most famous intellectual Clown and Pantaloon in one, and the charming Columbine of the capitalist pantomime. . . . Arch Commissar Stalin, 'the man of steel', flung open the closely guarded sanctuaries of the Kremlin, and pushing aside his morning's budget of

death warrants, and *lettres de cachet*, received his guests with smiles of overflowing comradeship.

For Shaw, all of this was a matter of abstract ideas, chimeras whose content bore almost no relation to the realities of life in Stalin's Gulag or one of the fascist states. One right-wing website today calls him a murderer. That's absurd. Probably the worst thing he did in life was to convert the Webbs to Stalinism when he returned to England, spoiling forever their reputation, which rested on their political convictions far more than his did.

Another figure who attracted Shaw for the next few years was Oswald Mosley. In November 1932 he described Mosley as "one of the few people who is writing and thinking about real things and not about figments and phrases."

Mosley the previous month had founded the British Union of Fascists. That he still had credit anywhere on the left might seem surprising, but not if you know his trajectory over the previous fourteen years. Scion of an aristocratic family, Mosley was a decorated veteran in World War I. He was a Conservative Member of Parliament from 1918 to 1922, when he became an Independent, then joined the Labour Party, and still later the Independent Labour Party, an older group to the left of the official Labour Party. He served as a minister in Ramsay MacDonald's 1929 Labour government. In early 1931 he formed the New Party, with a generally Keynesian program to help the unemployed in the Depression. After a visit to Mussolini, Mosley lurched to the right and was converted to fascism. This was still before Hitler became chancellor of Germany, whose National Socialists never called themselves fascists, and there were still widespread illusions in Italian fascism on both the right and the left.

Not seeing much motion toward communism in England, Shaw now looked to fascism as the next best thing, calling it "the only visible practical alternative to Communism." In retrospect one would have to say that Shaw was unusual, but not alone, in his day in seeing the striking similarity in methods and governmental forms of the two dictatorial systems, the hyperstatist extremes of left and right. Both professed an extreme populist rhetoric while busily eliminating all sources of opposition, especially from the very people they claimed to champion.

Usually their partisans could see only the differences. If anything, Italian fascism, the only one then extant, was a noticeably less repressive form of government than Leninist or Stalinist Russia, which had very large partisan support among the European working class and intelligentsia. Hitler would permanently brand fascism as consummate evil, but that would become apparent outside of Germany only as World War II approached, inflated a hundred-fold with the revelations of the Holocaust later. The fever of the totalitarian virus was coursing through the blood of Western society and had not yet run its course.

Shaw did denounce Mosley's anti-Semitism, and within a few years lost interest in him. What had briefly attracted him was the image of a charismatic leader. That seems to be mostly what he saw in Lenin, Stalin, Mussolini, and, for a while, Hitler. When challenged by Beatrice Webb as to why he should see something positive in the rightist figures, who had "no philosophy, no notion of any kind of social organization," he replied that it was their powerful personalities. These were men who broke through the paralyzing inertia of the parliamentary systems of their day.

Even in his late years, as misanthropy crept into his view of the human race, Shaw rejected racism and misogyny. He and Charlotte made a world tour by ship in 1933, stopping in South Africa, India, China, and the United States. The next year he published *The Adventures of the Black Girl in Her Search for God (and Some Lesser Tales),* where he proposed that "the next great civilization will be a black civilization," and, as Holroyd summarizes, "that future gods may be female rather than male; and that the biological solution to the race war between black and white is intermarriage." This, as can be imagined, created a great furor, in England almost as much as in apartheid South Africa.

In a certain way Shaw in his prolonged old age used his fancifully re-imagined dictators to threaten England: if you don't carry out serious reforms these are the kinds of leaders who will do it for you.

Two Decades of Peace and a New War

His plays were less widely performed in the 1930s. They were more modern sounding than Oscar Wilde but nevertheless had a certain Victorian mustiness about them. Intellectuals in particular were now looking on him as a figure out of the past. Holroyd says that *The Apple Cart,* finished in 1929, "was to be the last of Shaw's plays to win a regular place in the standard repertory." He wrote fourteen plays after that. He had begun in 1921 to prepare a collected edition of his works. The first volumes appeared in 1930. When it was finally complete the ultimate edition ran to thirty-seven volumes.

Shaw's circle of friends in his late years expanded beyond theatre people and Fabians. He was close to world heavyweight champion boxer Gene Tunney and the Catholic Prioress of Stanbrook Abbey, Dame Laurentia McLachlan. He wrote admiringly of Einstein and Churchill, the latter returning the compliment.

In his last decades much of his thought and writing delved into fantasy and surrealism. This brought him closer to W. B. Yeats, whose work had always mined that vein. At the first meeting of the Irish Academy of Letters, in September 1932, Shaw was elected president, Yeats vice president.

He and Charlotte lived quietly at Ayot. A non-Christian, he made large contributions to the local church to repair the roof and the organ. He underwrote replacing the windows in the village school. Each year he sent the headmistress a check to pay for sweets for the children at the village shop. He received endless requests for donations, for aid, for letters of support or endorsement. He responded to many of them. One poet wrote to say his clothes had been destroyed in a fire. Shaw sent him a check for £400 with a note saying how much he disliked the fellow's poetry. One street person asked for a pair of boots. Shaw had them sent, then found that the man returned them several times to be repaired.

A German actress wrote saying she had the perfect body and wanted to have his child so it would inherit his great brain. He responded, "What if the child inherits my body and your brains?" In a bookstore he noticed a copy of one of his books with a handwritten inscription. He bought it, packed it up, and sent it to the original dedicatee with a note, "With the author's renewed compliments." Invited to a party by a note saying the hostess would be "At Home" on a certain date he fired back, "So will G. Bernard Shaw."

Years before, he had inherited a building in Ireland, which he donated to the Catholic Bishop of Kildare and Leighlin to serve as a school; it became the Technical College. Leonard Woolf described him as "personally the kindest, most friendly, most charming of men."

After Hitler became chancellor in 1933 Shaw declared the Nazis "a mentally bankrupt party" and called for an anti-German pact between Britain, France, the United States, and the Soviet Union. He described Hitler as a new Torquemada and compared his anti-Semitism as akin to a case of rabies. These are significant qualifications on the few positive things he said about the Nazis. He still counted the Nazis as in the right in abrogating the Versailles Treaty and claimed that he was the only one in England who was still polite in writing about Hitler.

Shaw was far more sensible about the second global war than the first. He refrained from denouncing British "Junkers," and for the first months limited himself to hopes for an early negotiated settlement. At the beginning of 1940 the BBC asked him to make a broadcast on the war. The Ministry of Information vetoed his script. Harold Nicolson, then Churchill's official Censor, rejected the speech, saying, "Shaw's main theme is that the only thing Hitler has done wrong is to persecute the Jews. As the Minister [Duff Cooper] remarks, millions of Americans and some other people [believe] that this is the only thing he has done right."

Shaw came out for uncompromising war against Hitler and Mussolini. Early in 1941 he told an American reporter, "[T]here is a very dangerous madman loose in Europe who must, we think, be captured and disabled. If we are right, he is as dangerous to you as to us; so we ask you to join the hunt."

Where he had been persona non grata during World War I, his plays experienced a major revival during the second war. There were many productions in the early years and by 1944 there were nine Shaw plays running simultaneously in London. Casts in the wartime period included Robert Donat, Vivien Leigh, John Gielgud, Edith Evans, Deborah Kerr, Laurence Olivier, Ralph Richardson, Sybil Thorndike, and Margaret Leighton. Traveling companies took his plays to rural towns, munition factories, and mining outposts.

His generation was dying off, even the long-lived ones. He had served as one of the pall bearers when Thomas Hardy, fifteen years his senior, died in January 1928. The others ranked around the coffin were James Barrie, John Galsworthy, the poet Edmund Gosse, A. E. Houseman, and Rudyard Kipling. T. E. Lawrence, thirty-two years Shaw's junior, was killed in a motorcycle accident in 1935. Beatrice Webb, one of his closest friends since the 1880s, died in April 1943. Charlotte developed osteitis deformans, a debilitating bone disease that left her hunchbacked and unable to walk unaided. She began to hallucinate. She died that September. H. G. Wells followed in August 1946, and finally Sidney Webb in October 1947.

For his ninetieth birthday, in 1946, the newly founded Penguin paperback publisher issued the "Shaw Million," simultaneous publication in Britain of ten of his titles in editions of 100,000 each. The lot sold out in six weeks.

In his last years he suffered from anorexia; his weight, never much, fell to 126 pounds. On September 10, 1950, GBS fell in his garden, fracturing his thigh. He died on November 2. In his will he left art works to public galleries and theatres in Britain, Ireland, and the United States.

Orwell and Churchill on Shaw

Before submitting the question we began with for your decision I want to call two of Shaw's contemporaries for their views, one from the left, one from the right. First, George Orwell, who lived just half as long as GBS but whose years matched precisely the second half of Shaw's life. Orwell was also a socialist, but unlike Shaw, one who understood better than almost anyone the horrors of totalitarianism.

Orwell seems never to have written a piece devoted solely to Shaw. His comments are scattered in essays with broader themes. He admired Shaw's plays but not his politics. On the positive side he wrote:

> It would be an absurdity to regard Shaw as a pamphleteer and nothing more. The sense of purpose with which he always writes would get him nowhere if he were not also an artist. In illustration of this I point once again to *Arms and the Man*. . . . Nowhere is there a false emphasis or a clumsily contrived incident; the play gives the impression of having grown as naturally as a plant. There are not even any verbal fireworks; brilliant as the dialogue is, every word of it helps the action along. (Cited by Loraine Saunders, *The Unsung Artistry of George Orwell*.)

Orwell made a three-fold criticism of Shaw's politics, grouping him with other writers who shared one or another of Shaw's attitudes. First, that as rebels such authors failed to anticipate that if they were successful in shattering the status quo the results might be much worse rather than much better. Second, that most British authors of Shaw's vintage were extremely provincial, which led them to magnify the evils of British society while not grasping the true scope of foreign repressive regimes toward which they were too tolerant. And finally, that those writers who embraced Soviet communism — or fascism — constituted a dangerous totalitarian current that other socialists should be wary of.

The first criticism appears in his essay "Notes on the Way" in the British weekly *Time and Tide* of April 6, 1940, in the dark early days of World War II:

> [T]here was a long period during which nearly every thinking man was in some sense a rebel, and usually a quite irresponsible rebel. Literature was largely the literature of revolt or of disintegration. Gibbon, Voltaire, Rousseau, Shelley, Byron, Dickens, Stendhal, Samuel Butler, Ibsen, Zola, Flaubert, Shaw, Joyce — in one way or another they are all of them destroyers, wreckers, saboteurs. For two hundred years we had sawed and sawed and sawed at the branch we were sitting on. And in the end, much more suddenly than anyone had foreseen, our efforts were rewarded, and down we came. But unfortunately there had been a little mistake. The thing at the bottom was not a bed of roses after all, it was a cesspool full of barbed wire.

He developed his second theme in a BBC broadcast on March 10, 1942, titled "The Rediscovery of Europe." He posed 1914 as the dividing line between two ages. Before 1914, "The giants of that time were Thomas Hardy — who, however, had stopped writing novels some time earlier — Shaw, Wells, Kipling, Bennett, Galsworthy and, somewhat different from the others — not an Englishman, remember, but a Pole who chose to write in English — Joseph Conrad." What strikes him about the prewar figures is their provincialism on international issues and a naive trust in the future of middle-class reform:

> I think the basic fact about nearly all English writers of that time is their complete unawareness of anything outside the contemporary English scene. Some are better writers than others, some are politically conscious and some aren't, but they are all alike in being untouched by any European influence." The provincialism was not only geographical but historical as well. "To Bernard Shaw most of the past is simply a mess which ought to be swept away in the name of progress, hygiene, efficiency and what-not.

His point is that the writers of the prewar period took for granted the middle-class life of isolated England. Their rebellion against it was a narrow one, over issues that would look small after the trenches of France. He contrasts the whole lot of them to Joyce, Eliot, Pound, Huxley, Lawrence, and Wyndham Lewis:

> To begin with the notion of progress has gone by the board. They don't any longer believe that men are getting better and better by having lower mortality rates, more effective birth control, better plumbing, more aeroplanes and faster motor cars. . . . All of them are politically reactionary, or at best are uninterested in politics. None of them cares twopence about the various hole-and-corner reforms which had seemed important to their predecessors, such as female suffrage, temperance reform, birth control or prevention of cruelty to animals.

He contrasts this new cynicism to "the shallow Fabian progressivism of writers like Bernard Shaw." What did it signify?

> Partly that was the effect of the war of 1914-18, which succeeded in debunking both Science, Progress and civilized man. Progress had finally ended in the biggest massacre in history. Science was something that

created bombing planes and poison gas, civilized man, as it turned out, was ready to behave worse than any savage when the pinch came.

He adds:

> One effect of the ghastly history of the last twenty years has been to make a great deal of ancient literature seem much more modern. A lot that has happened in Germany since the rise of Hitler might have come straight out of the later volumes of Gibbon's *Decline and Fall of the Roman Empire*. Recently I saw Shakespeare's *King John* acted — the first time I had seen it, because it is a play which isn't acted very often. When I had read it as a boy it seemed to me archaic, something dug out of a history book and not having anything to do with our own time. Well, when I saw it acted, what with its intrigues and doublecrossings, non-aggression pacts, quislings, people changing sides in the middle of a battle, and what-not, it seemed to me extraordinarily up to date. And it was rather the same thing that happened in the literary development between 1910 and 1920. The prevailing temper of the time gave a new reality to all sorts of themes which had seemed out of date and puerile when Bernard Shaw and his Fabians were — so they thought — turning the world into a sort of super garden city. Themes like revenge, patriotism, exile, persecution, race hatred, religious faith, loyalty, leader worship, suddenly seemed real again.

Orwell addressed his third charge, the totalitarian strain on the British left, in a passage worth recalling in his 1944 essay "Raffles and Miss Blandish":

> The interconnexion between sadism, masochism, success-worship, power-worship, nationalism, and totalitarianism is a huge subject whose edges have barely been scratched, and even to mention it is considered somewhat indelicate. To take merely the first example that comes to mind, I believe no one has ever pointed out the sadistic and masochistic element in Bernard Shaw's work, still less suggested that this probably has some connexion with Shaw's admiration for dictators. Fascism is often loosely equated with sadism, but nearly always by people who see nothing wrong in the most slavish worship of Stalin. The truth is, of course, that the countless English intellectuals who kiss the arse of Stalin are not different from the minority who give their allegiance to Hitler or Mussolini, . . . nor from that older generation of intellectuals, Carlyle, Creasey and the rest of them, who bowed down before German

militarism. All of them are worshipping power and successful cruelty. It is important to notice that the cult of power tends to be mixed up with a love of cruelty and wickedness *for their own sakes*. A tyrant is all the more admired if he happens to be a bloodstained crook as well, and 'the end justifies the means' often becomes, in effect, 'the means justify themselves provided they are dirty enough'. This idea colours the outlook of all sympathizers with totalitarianism, and accounts, for instance, for the positive delight with which many English intellectuals greeted the Nazi-Soviet pact.

This concern appears to be why the dictatorship in *1984* is said to have arisen from a British socialist revolution, not a fascist one, or the Russian socialist one, as a warning to his fellow socialists of this fatal train of thought. And then there is Mr. Whymper in Orwell's *Animal Farm*. Whymper is a man the pig ruler Napoleon hires as his agent to lobby for Animal Farm to the humans. Whymper is widely said to be based on Bernard Shaw.

Orwell and Shaw both died in 1950. Despite all that is worthy and memorable in Shaw's writings, it is not surprising that in the sixty-two years since, Orwell's reputation has grown larger while Shaw's has greatly diminished.

I will call one last witness, staunch British bulldog Conservative Winston Churchill, who lived seventy-six of his ninety years in the same England as Bernard Shaw.

Churchill did write a piece exclusively about Shaw, in his 1937 *Great Contemporaries*. He notes Shaw's early poverty, his recoil while still in Ireland from forced conventionality, his embrace of all the "New" movements of the 1890s. He had dined with Shaw, saying of the occasion, "I possess a lively image of this bright, nimble, fierce, and comprehending being, Jack Frost, dancing bespangled in the sunshine, which I should be very sorry to lose."

He held the plays in unreserved esteem:

> *Candida*, *Major Barbara*, and *Man and Superman* riveted the attention of the intellectual world. Into the void left by the annihilation of Wilde he stepped armed with a keener wit, a tenser dialogue, a more challenging theme, a stronger construction, a deeper and more natural comprehension. The characteristics and the idiosyncrasies of the Shavian drama are world-renowned. His plays are today more frequently presented, not only within the wide frontiers of the English language, but throughout the world, than those of any man but Shakespeare. All parties

and every class, in every country, have pricked up their ears at the coming and welcomed their return.

Shaw, he argued, in his life was radically divorced from his own political views, not by a crude hypocrisy but by an odd ability to in all sincerity believe many contradictory things at the same time:

> Few people practice what they preach, and no one less so than Mr. Bernard Shaw. Few are more capable of having the best of everything both ways. His spiritual home is no doubt in Russia; his native land is the Irish Free State; but he lives in comfortable England. His dissolvent theories of life and society have been sturdily banished from his personal conduct and his home. No one has ever led a more respectable life or been a stronger seceder from his own subversive imagination. He derides the marriage vow and even at times the sentiment of love itself; yet no one is more happily or wisely married. He indulges in all the liberties of an irresponsible Chatterbox, babbling gloriously from dawn to dusk, and at the same time advocates the abolition of Parliamentary institutions and the setting up of an Iron Dictatorship, of which he would probably be the first victim. . . . He is at once an acquisitive capitalist and a sincere Communist. He makes his characters talk blithely about killing men for the sake of an idea; but would take great trouble not to hurt a fly.
>
> He seems to derive equal pleasure from all these contrary habits, poses and attitudes. He has laughed his sparkling way through life, exploding by his own acts or words every argument he has ever used on either side of any question, teasing and bewildering every public he has addressed, and involving in his own mockery every cause he has ever championed. The world has long watched with tolerance and amusement the nimble antics and gyrations of this unique and double-headed chameleon, while all the time the creature was eager to be taken seriously.

Churchill adds some more bitter comments on Stalinist Russia beyond the passage quoted earlier on Shaw's 1931 visit:

"In Russia we have a vast dumb people dwelling under the discipline of a conscripted army in war-time. . . . a people ruled by terror, fanaticisms, and the Secret Police. . . . where liberty is unknown; where grace and culture are dying; and where armaments and preparations for war are rife." He continues: "Decent, good-hearted British men and women ought not to be so airily detached from realities, that they have no word of honest indignation for such wantonly, callously-inflicted pain."

He upbraids Shaw for his role in World War I, describing him as the country's chief jester:

> If the truth must be told, our British island has not had much help in its troubles from Mr. Bernard Shaw. When nations are fighting for life, when the Palace in which the Jester dwells not uncomfortably, is itself assailed, and everyone from Prince to groom is fighting on the battlements, the Jester's jokes echo only through deserted halls, and his witticisms and commendations, distributed evenly between friend and foe, jar the ears of hurrying messengers, of mourning women and wounded men.

Nevertheless, once peace is restored "we can be proud of our famous Jester." He concludes with fulsome praise:

"Saint, sage, and clown; venerable, profound, and irrepressible, Bernard Shaw receives, if not the salutes, at least the hand-clappings of a generation which honors him as another link in the humanities of peoples, and as the greatest living master of letters in the English-speaking world."

I think it best to leave this review here, a picture of a greatly flawed man with great gifts, who dreamed of a totalitarian future while making the present better in many ways. His principal contribution, apart from the obvious in lifting the spirits of several generations of theatre goers, was to have helped move the British public and government to give women the vote, to tend to the health of their people, to clear the odorous slums. He had fantasized about achieving more, but luckily, for him and for us, that more — the messianic utopia of a society remade by dictatorial fiat through a murderous and super-centralized state — was denied him.

February 1, 2012

The Magic of Lord Dunsany

When the world is too much with you, the inanities of politics have you down, and the fount of insoluble crises discourages, it is a good time to read something by Lord Dunsany. An Edwardian Irish aristocrat, much of his voluminous work is long out of print, but what is available is mostly his early wonder tales, probably his best. Dunsany is usually described as a fantasy or science fiction writer, but such terms mislead. He is often compared to the more widely read H. P. Lovecraft, who readily acknowledged Dunsany's influence, yet their work shows more differences than similarities.

I had a taste for Lovecraft in my teens, but reading him now I am put off by his sodden load of manipulative adjectives. The first page of "The Dunwich Horror" gives us "squalor," "dilapidation," "gnarled solitary figures," "crumbling doorsteps," "creepily insistent rhythms," "rotting gambrel roofs," "tenebrous tunnel," "malign odour," "stigmata of degeneracy and inbreeding," "unhallowed rites."

Dunsany's style changed several times over his lifetime, but it was always clear, simple, and relatively adjective-free. His early work owed much to the King James Bible, then came a poetic period in modern prose, and in the final laps, straight story telling. Accompanying this change of style there is a migration also from imaginary cities and countries to actual places and from magical or mystical forces to the merely extremely improbable.

Where Lovecraft sought to create an atmosphere of repellent horror, Dunsany's writing more often exudes a melancholy poetic beauty, though he delved into horror, more often when he used settings somewhere in the real world, rather than his dream lands. Their oeuvres run in parallel in their interest in strange forgotten gods, Lovecraft's Cthulhu Mythos and Dunsany's gods of Pegana, but Lovecraft's gods are always sinister, threatening to return to earth to the detriment of humanity, while the gods of Pegana are mostly far away and indifferent to humans, rather on the Gnostic model. Oddly, the Irish lord's outlook, something of a country squire lamenting the expanding evils of the machine age and its threat of destroying both Nature and humanity, his pervading sense of the fragility of civilization, and of Time as a wrecker rather than an engine of progress, a century later can seem to merge with to-day's fears of impending ecological cataclysm, though at an eerie remove. A leitmotif of his work is that humans are becoming ever more disconnected from and damaging to the natural world and in so doing both risk and deserve extinction.

There are not any individualized humans in *The Gods of Pegana*, Dunsany's first book. The personifications Fate and Chance cast lots to begin the Game. We never know which won, but he chooses Mana-Yood-Sushai as his player. Mana-Yood-Sushai in turn creates the gods, among them Skarl the Drummer. As Skarl begins to drum, Mana-Yood-Sushai falls asleep, the lesser gods create the worlds, and the play begins. When Mana wakes, "the gods and the worlds shall depart, and there shall be only Mana-Yood-Sushai."

There is creation but it doesn't start with origins as Genesis does. The Game in which we are tiny pawns begins "Before there stood gods upon Olympus, or ever Allah was Allah" but still long after when time and space came into being:

"When Mana-Yood-Sushai had made the gods there were only the gods, and They sat in the middle of Time, for there was as much Time before them as behind them, which having no end had neither a beginning." The gods in turn make the worlds, not for some grand purpose as the God of Genesis does but to amuse themselves. After a million years, through which Mana-Yood-Sushai slumbers, the god Kib creates the beasts of Earth to play with. After another million years "Kib grew weary of the second game, and raised his hand in The Middle of All, making the sign of Kib, and made Men: out of beasts he made them, and Earth was covered with Men." All this time Skarl beats on his drum so that Mana-Yood-Sushai will not wake, which would destroy the gods and their plaything worlds, including us, to begin a new Game.

The Gods of Pegana was published in 1905, an intriguing vision for an Edwardian Irish lord. It contained many more tales, of the doings of Kib, the Sender of Life in All the Worlds, of Sish, the Destroyer of Hours, Slid, Whose Soul Is by the Sea, and Mung, Lord of All Deaths between Pegana and the Rim. Many lesser gods are added. And then come human prophets, powerful figures in their human communities for their supposed influence with the gods, but generally ignored by the lords of Pegana.

In preparing publication Dunsany enlisted Victorian-Edwardian artist Sydney Sime as his illustrator. Sime was a prominent magazine illustrator, and did drawings for other authors of fantastic and macabre literature, such as William Hope Hodgson and Arthur Machen. The collaboration lasted until

Sime's death in 1941, in most cases Sime producing drawings for Dunsany's stories, but sometimes the reverse, with Sime submitting a set of drawings and Dunsany inventing stories to explain them.

Dunsany (pronounced Dun-SAY-nee) followed with more tales of the Pegana universe in *Time and the Gods* (1906), its amused tone captured in the story "The Relenting of Sarnidac." Sarnidac is a lame dwarf shepherd boy, the butt of jokes in his home city. One day Sarnidac sees a line of tall strange figures walking southward on the dusty road. Out of curiosity he falls in behind them, marching on until they come to the neighboring city of Khamazan. There the people recognize the marchers as the gods of the Earth, but as they approach the city gates the figures begin to rise into the air, higher with each step until they are gone into the sky. The people call on the gods not to desert them, and then they are all gone except the lame dwarf who is seen to remain on the road. The lame boy is taken in triumph to occupy the king's palace. "And the Book of the Knowledge of the Gods in Khamazan tells how the small god that pitied the world told his prophets that his name was Sarnidac and that he herded sheep, and that therefore he is called the shepherd god."

Dunsany rarely returned to the Pegana gods. Indian-American literary critic Sunand Tryambak Joshi in his *Lord Dunsany: Master of the Anglo-Irish Imagination,* comments, "But the themes that were broached in these two books — fantasy as Nature, the glories of the unmechanized past, antihumanism, the awesomeness of Time and the power of art and dreams to combat it — would receive many distinctive variations and elaboration in his subsequent story collections, plays, novels, and poems."

Between 1908 and 1916 Dunsany produced five slim volumes of wonder tales, his most lasting work, beginning with *The Sword of Welleran.* There followed stories of the world war, plays (forty-seven of them), nine novels, and in his later years, the tall tales of Jorkens the London clubman, and several books of poems. For purists, including H. P. Lovecraft, Dunsany never surpassed his early naive, childlike tales, in *The Sword of Welleran* (1908) and *A Dreamer's Tales* (1910). His language does become flatter in the later work and an element of tongue-in-cheek creeps in already in the later of the stories in *The Book of Wonder* (1912). An example from this last is the opening of "The Hoard of the Gibbelins," which Wikipedia cites as most typical of Dunsany's prose. It does capture one side of him, when he is after a kind of ironic horror:

> The Gibbelins eat, as is well known, nothing less good than man. Their evil tower is joined to Terra Cognita, to the lands we know, by a bridge. Their hoard is beyond reason; avarice has no use for it; they have

a separate cellar for emeralds and a separate cellar for sapphires; they have filled a hole with gold and dig it up when they need it. And the only use that is known for their ridiculous wealth is to attract to their larder a continual supply of food. In times of famine they have even been known to scatter rubies abroad, a little trail of them to some city of Man, and sure enough their larders would soon be full again.

Dunsany doesn't abandon his lovely or evil fantasy cities until his Jorkens books, and his second Irish novel, *The Story of Mona Sheehy* (1939).

Lord Dunsany, the scion of an ancient Irish peerage, was born in London on July 24, 1878, his proper name being Edward John Moreton Drax Plunkett. Through most of his life he alternated living in England, at a small family estate called Dunstall Priory near Shoreham, Kent, and at Dunsany Castle, twenty miles northwest of Dublin. The family is said to have come from Denmark and to have settled in Ireland in the tenth century, before the Norman Conquest. They intermarried with the Cusacks, a Norman family, who built Dunsany Castle between 1180 and 1200, making it probably the oldest continually inhabited structure in Ireland. Edward inherited the title on his father's death in 1899 and signed all of his many published works Lord Dunsany. His life is chronicled in a 1972 biography by Mark Amory. S. T. Joshi's *Lord Dunsany: Master of the Anglo-Irish Imagination* (1995) offers a critical appreciation of his writings.

Edward attended Eton, then Sandhurst, Britain's preeminent military academy. In 1899, at twenty, he joined the Coldstream Guards and served under fire in South Africa in the Boer War, where he was friends with Rudyard Kipling. He left the army in 1901. By this time he had acquired two of his lifelong interests: hunting and chess. He grew a deep love of nature, somehow reconciling that with all the killing he was doing, paired with a deepening abhorrence of industrial civilization. His hunting took him outdoors, where he spent endless hours in the woods, claiming he shot his own dinner from October to March. In later years he went on shooting expeditions to Africa, India, and the Middle East.

Dunsany, as he came to be known, was among the pro-British Irish. More typically these lived in Northern Ireland and were Protestant by religion. Lord Dunsany's Irish connections were in the south and whatever his religious views he was not a Christian. S. T. Joshi calls him an atheist based on the universe depicted in *The Gods of Pegana*. While strange and multiple gods predominate in his fiction, and there is also a pronounced sympathy for paganism in his few Irish-themed books, there are a few stories, such as "The Kith of the Elf-Folk" and "Where the Tides Ebb and Flow," that refer to a single god and

Paradise, while "The Sailors' Gambit" concerns a traditional pact with the Devil for a crystal that allows its users to win at chess. Even in these few stories, gods singular or multiple have no real interest in humans except occasionally to punish them for their impudence, as in his play *The Gods of the Mountain* (1910), where a band of beggars impersonate the seven jade gods of a mountain to get the credulous villagers to bring them food and gifts. The gods retaliate by turning the imposters into jade statues, which the villagers continue to worship, quite ignorant of the real import of the transformation.

Dunsany married Lady Beatrice Villiers in September 1904, he twenty-six, she just short of twenty-four. Beatrice proved to be level headed and literate, Mark Amory relying heavily on her diaries for his biography. In August 1906 their only child, Randal, was born.

Hunting and the military were conventional activities for a landed aristocrat. Writing strange fiction was not, and it took several years before Dunsany's reputation shifted from that of a lord who wrote on the side to a writer who also happened to be a lord. Some critics were never convinced that he was not a dilettante. Archaic as always, he did much of his writing with a quill pen on large sheets of paper in an oversized looping calligraphy, or he dictated to Beatrice, who took it down in shorthand.

As an increasingly prominent Irish writer, based at least part of the year near Dublin, he developed a prickly friendship with William Butler Yeats, though Beatrice came to dislike Yeats's patron, Lady Gregory, accusing her of stealing Dunsany's plots. Nevertheless, Yeats edited a collection of Dunsany's writings that appeared in 1912.

At Yeats's suggestion, Dunsany wrote his first play, *The Glittering Gate*, in 1909. Bill, a burglar, dies and finds himself facing a great golden gate, presumably the gate to heaven. His old friend Jim is there, unhappily locked out and continually opening beer cans lying on the ground, each one proving to be empty. Bill eventually goes to work on the gate with his burglar tools, forces it open only to discover empty space filled with stars.

The Irish Renaissance, or Celtic Revival, was in full swing, with authors such as W. B. Yeats, Lady Gregory, George Russell, J. M. Synge, Oliver Gogarty, and Sean O'Casey. They approached Dunsany, but he never really fit in, both because of his pro-British politics and because there was nothing Irish about his work. This distance continued for decades. In 1932 Yeats was instrumental in founding the Irish Academy of Letters, with George Bernard Shaw as its first president and Yeats as vice president. It had two classes of membership, the higher called "Academicians," the lower, "Associates." Academicians had to have done work "Irish in character or subject," Associates needed only to be of Irish descent. Dunsany was furious at being offered only an Associate membership and refused. Amory records that

> Dunsany . . . writing over ten years later says only that he retaliated in private with a society to honour writers of the 14th century in Italy. 'Who, I asked, would they suggest? Dante of course was suggested; but I was shocked. "Most certainly not," I said, stroking my hair as Yeats used to stroke his. "Dante did not write about Italy, but of a very different place. Most unsuitable."' He went, however, to Yeats' memorial service to show no animosity remained.

The slight prompted him to write his first sustained Irish-themed piece, his novel *The Curse of the Wise Woman* (1933), considered one of his best works. The wise woman, Mrs. Marlin, curses a British development company that has brought earth moving equipment to drain the historic bog where she lives. A great storm of possibly supernatural origin buries their building site and saves the natural enclave. It won the Irish Academy of Letters' Harmsworth Literary Award as best Irish novel of the year and Dunsany was elected to full membership in the Academy.

Though Dunsany knew all the major figures of the Celtic Revival, most of his close friends were Unionists. The only one of the republican writers he became really close to was Oliver Gogarty, a romantic if overly plump figure, poet, medical doctor, gossip, and militant Nationalist. Among the Dunsanys' friends was Edith Nesbit, the English Fabian activist and children's' author, who was one of his earliest readers. He contributed to her short-lived magazine *Neolith*, and on a visit to Dunsany Castle she played with him at building houses in the drawing room out of furniture and bric-a-brac, a central plot device in her 1910 *The Magic City*.

In early 1913 Dunsany and Beatrice went to Algeria, where he did his first big game hunting. He returned to Africa alone that fall, this time to Kenya, where he conducted a killing spree that would freeze the blood of any animal lover: fifty-five beasts including 4 warthogs, 6 zebras, 3 jackals, 8 impalas, a lion and a rhinoceros.

The heyday of his career as a dramatist ran from his 1909 *Glittering Gate* through the end of the Great War, with productions of such plays as *King Argimenes and the Unknown Warrior* (1910), *Alexander* (1912), *The Queen's Enemies* (1913), and *If* (1919). *The Queen's Enemies* is based on an account in Herodotus in which Egyptian Queen Nitokris invites her enemies to a banquet in an underground temple, then kills them by opening floodgates to the Nile. *If* is an early time travel story in which a mysterious man from the

East offers the hero a crystal that allows him to go into the past to make changes in his life. It ran for two hundred performances in London in 1921-22, Dunsany's swansong when he briefly stood in the first rank of British playwrights. His exotic locales and royal protagonists lost their savor after the war and his plays were rarely performed.

When World War I broke out in 1914 Dunsany joined the Royal Inniskilling Fusiliers, where he was made a captain. He was slated to be sent to Gallipoli, but against his will, probably because of his age, was transferred to a reserve unit in Derry in the north of Ireland. He was on leave at Dunsany Castle when the week-long Easter Rising broke out in April 1916, during which the Nationalists captured Dublin and held it for a week, hoping to win Irish independence while England was tied down in France. Dunsany reported to British GHQ in Dublin and was sent with a group in a car to relieve an outpost in a Dublin neighborhood. They were ambushed by a Nationalist squad and a ricochet bullet hit him in the face. The Nationalist fighters who took him prisoner apologized and drove him to a hospital. At the end of the week pro-British forces recaptured the hospital. One side of his lip was paralyzed. His recovery was prolonged and he was not ruled fit for service until October, and then only for light duty.

A year later he was posted to France. Shortly after his arrival he wrote to Beatrice from Amiens:

> Imagine Waterloo, Sebastopol, Ladysmith, Pompeii, Troy, Timgad, Tel el Kebir, Sodom and Gomorrah endlessly stretching one into the other; and twisted, bare, ghoulish trees leering downward at graves; and scenes very like Dore's crucifixion and realities like the blackest dreams of Sime [Sydney Sime, Dunsany's illustrator]; tanks lying with their noses pointing upwards still sniffing towards an enemy long since stiff or blown away in fragments like wounded rhinoceros' dying. Imagine the wasted ruin of a famous hill that once dominated all this, now no more than a white mound with a few crosses on it, standing against the sky to show that Golgotha was once more with us.

In January 1918 he was transferred to the War Office in London, where he wrote propaganda for the home front and the world press, simple stories of soldiers' lives, incidents from the front. He wrote sharply against the Kaiser but his materials were singularly free of the animosity toward ordinary Germans that was so prevalent at the time. He also wrote two books about the war, *Tales of War* (1918) and *Unhappy Far-Off Things* (1919).

The war ended in November 1918. From October 1919 through January 1920 he made a triumphal tour of the United States. Many of his plays were being performed and he lectured in many cities. Two of his plays were running in New York when he was there, and while in New Hampshire he saw a performance of his *Fame and the Poet* by inmates at the Portsmouth Naval Prison. Yet he had been changed by the war. Mark Amory says of him and Beatrice, "before the war they had been young, now they were not. Dunsany's greatest friends were dead and he did not replace them." He lost touch with the Irish Renaissance group. Amory adds, "He believed as a matter of course that the task of an artist was to produce Beauty, but in the 1920s there was little demand for what was small and exquisite." Though short stories were his metier he turned in the interwar years to novels, publishing nine between 1922 and 1939.

Dunsany and Beatrice, as firm Unionists, were at risk after Sinn Fein declared Ireland independent in 1919 and waged its guerrilla war through 1921. Their gamekeeper at Dunsany Castle, Toomey, was a staunch Republican and helped to divert threatened attacks by his political cothinkers. The Anglo-Irish Treaty established the Irish Free State in the predominately Catholic twenty-six southern counties, breaking off Northern Ireland's six counties with their Protestant majority to remain part of Britain. The Nationalists split over acceptance of the treaty and a civil war followed with Eamon de Valera leading the anti-Treaty forces in a bitter struggle that lasted until 1923. An anti-Treaty band burned the Kilmessan station near Dunsany Castle and burned a train. Several of their neighbors and the local township were burned out. A car was commandeered from the Dunsany stables to be used as a car bomb, but was found abandoned. The raiders said they "heard his Lordship was a good man and they didn't wish to disturb him or his family."

Beatrice wrote in her diary on April 12, 1923, "it is little bits of personal cruelty that throw such a nasty light on the Irish character. When for instance they burnt the stationmaster's house at Kilmessan (Mrs. Preston and we had to refit them entirely with clothes and furniture last March) they would not let him run upstairs to save his dead wife's pictures and his money." In May they returned to England, where Dunsany wrote his second novel, *The King of Elfland's Daughter*, which still had eight editions printed between 1969 and 2001.

Chess had always been one of Dunsany's passions. In the spring of 1928 he played José Raul Capablanca, world chess champion, 1921-1927. The showy match pitted the Cuban grandmaster against twenty-one opponents in simultaneous play, three from each of seven countries. Dunsany fought the champion to a draw.

A shooting expedition took Dunsany to India at the end of 1929, lasting into the next year, where he killed more animals, this time from elephant back, accompanied by the Nawab Hamid Ali, ruler of the princely state of Rampur. On his return he plunged into his Jorkens period. Dunsany had invented Jorkens in 1925 with "The Tale of the Abu Laheeb." Jorkens is the star attraction of the somewhat seedy Billiards Club, a dimly lit male retreat in London. Plied with a few whiskeys, Jorkens entertains the members with accounts of his fabulous adventures. The Abu Laheeb, to begin with, was a legendary sort of Yeti, an intelligent giant sloth living in the reed marshes of the upper Nile in Sudan. Jorkens tells his audience that he had set out to hunt the Abu Laheeb, but after tracking it into the deep reeds saw that it had mastered the art of fire and that made it too close to humans to shoot it. The first of five collections of these stories, *The Travel Tales of Mr. Joseph Jorkens,* was published in 1931.

Dunsany changed his style several times, from the biblical prose of the Pegana books to the elegiac adventures in mythical cities or on remote English moors, and finally to the realistic locations of Jorkens' accounts in which improbable events take place. He prided himself on simplicity, and did not consider his work "literary" in any high-flown sense. He prized pure imagination, and so never did research for any of his locales. He loved to make up the names of people and places, an eclectic mixture of sounds pilfered from Latin, Arabic, and Greek. He had a great animosity for modern factories and smoky urban slums. Most of the imaginary cities he created had a vaguely Middle Eastern setting and were made of marble and onyx, with merchant bazaars where emeralds and diamonds were on plentiful display. The Jorkens tales differed in using as settings places he had been on his expeditions.

The Jorkens stories were clever but lacked the esoteric magical feel of his early short story collections or several of his novels. Those remain readily available while the Jorkens books are out of print except for a three-volume hard cover edition edited by S. T. Joshi issued by Night Shade Press in 2005, and even there the first volume can be found only used at exorbitant prices.

Still, Kipling thought highly of the bibulous raconteur. In a 1931 letter to Dunsany he wrote:

> At first I resented the introduction, as camouflage, of your *Mister Jorkens*. Now I begin to see why your imagination *in vacuo* (and you've got more of it than anyone I know) had to have that peg and the background of the Billiard Club's atmosphere. . . . For sheer 'cheek' the Mermaid yarn ["Mrs. Jorkens," in which Jorkens marries a mermaid, but

she swims out to sea at the end.] is the best. I am not thinking for the minute of anything except the audacity of it.

World War II found the Dunsanys at Dunstall, just south of London on the flight path of German bombers. They took to sleeping in the cellar and invited the gardener's family to join them. Dunsany was sixty-one, Beatrice fifty-nine. He joined the Local Defence Volunteers.

The couple had one last great adventure. In September 1940 the British Council asked him to accept a professorship of English Literature in Athens. They were sent to Glasgow, where they took ship, which under wartime conditions kept its route and destination secret from the passengers. It landed them in Sierra Leone on the West African coast, the more direct Mediterranean route considered too unsafe. Then on to Cape Town, where they transferred to a plane that skipped up the east side of the continent, stopping in Mozambique, Kenya, and Sudan, ending in Cairo. While enroute, Greece, which had been neutral, had been attacked by Italy and was now in the war. They crossed the Suez Canal in a rowboat, then went by car and train up the Mediterranean coast to Turkey. They reached Greece at the beginning of January, arriving in Athens eighty-three days after leaving home.

Dunsany lectured two or three times a week, to a standing-room-only crowd when he spoke on Byron. On April 6 Germany declared war on Greece and began bombing the capital. On April 16 the Greek army line broke and refugees began to stream out of Athens. The Dunsanys were offered a no-food place in the hold of a Polish cargo ship leaving for Haifa. They took it. Dunsany slept on the deck while Beatrice and three other women slept on straw mattresses in a small cabin. Water was too scarce for bathing and bread was about the only food available. Dunsany was enjoying himself immensely, writing in a letter, "The lives of refugees are full of interest. One learns what a lot of places there are to sit down, and how to be comfortable. with the help of one's life-belt. And one learns what good food bread is; water is grand stuff too when you can get it."

Their ship joined a convoy with a cruiser, two destroyers, and two Greek submarines. Machine guns were mounted on their deck, which fired on a German Stuke. The Stuke bombed a nearby ship but didn't sink it. They reached Port Said on April 24. Their luggage came on another ship, which was sunk. They went on by ship to South Africa, where they remained the rest of the year, arriving back in Ireland only in March 1942 after a year and a half away.

They spent the next six years at Dunsany Castle. Gasoline was unobtainable so they traveled locally by dog cart. Lacking tea they brewed a drink from garden flowers. The castle did not have electricity until 1946. The lamp oil ration was just enough for cooking, so their cook made tallow candles for light and they used battery lamps for reading. Their son Randal had married a woman named Vera in Brazil just before the war, then served in the British army in India. In 1946 he returned to Brazil, where he first saw his six-year-old son Edward. Randal and his wife brought Edward to Ireland, then broke up the marriage, Randal returning to duty in India, Vera sailing for Brazil, while six-year-old Edward was left permanently with his elderly grandparents. Dunsany was sixty-eight, Beatrice sixty-six. "Little Eddie" did not speak English.

In 1947 Randal remarried, prompting the Dunsanys to deed the castle to him and return to their home at Dunstall in Kent. Little Eddie went with them. In England Dunsany was president of the Author's Society, he continued writing, and lectured widely. In August 1952 California poet and author Hazel Littlefield Smith visited them, inviting them to come to California. Beatrice had injured her leg, but Dunsany went. Smith wrote an account of their friendship, *Lord Dunsany: King of Dreams*. He returned to the United States twice more, in 1954 and 1955, including successful lectures during his visits.

Dunsany published a book almost every year: Collections of short stories, *The Man Who Ate the Phoenix* (1949), and *The Little Tales of Smethers and Other Stories* (1952); three more novels, one each between 1950 and 1952, and the last of the Jorkens, *Jorkens Borrows Another Whiskey,* in 1954. Two of his later novels involved men who lived in the bodies of animals. *My Talks with Dean Spanley* (1936) has the Dean, whose name suggests Spaniel and also Dean Arthur Penrhyn Stanley of Westminster, reminiscence about his previous life as a dog, a far superior animal to a human. This was one of the very few of Dunsany's books that made it to the screen, in a 2008 production with Sam Neill as Spanley and Peter O'Toole as his attentive audience. Dunsany returned to this idea in 1950 in *The Strange Journeys of Colonel Polders,* in which the colonel is forced to sequentially inhabit the bodies of many different animals, generally illustrating the evil treatment of animals by humans.

Edward Plunkett died on October 25, 1957, during a visit to Dunsany Castle. Beatrice lived on until 1970.

Many of his stories, including a good number written when he was only in his thirties, are of the devastation, by Time or the gods, of lost causes and doomed cities. "In the Land of Time" has Karnith Zo, the young king of Alatta, literally lead an army against Time's castle.

> From one of his towers Time eyed them all the while, and in battle order they closed in on the steep hill as Time sat still in his great tower

and watched. But as the feet of the foremost touched the edge of the hill Time hurled five years against them, and the years passed over their heads and the army still came on, an army of older men. But the slope seemed steeper to the King and to every man in his army, and they breathed more heavily. And Time summoned up more years, and one by one he hurled them at Karnith Zo and at all his men. And the knees of the army stiffened, and the beards grew and turned grey, and the hours and days and the months went singing over their heads, and their hair turned whiter and whiter, and the conquering hours bore down, and the years rushed on and swept the youth of that army clear away till they came face to face under the walls of the castle of Time with a mass of howling years, and found the top of the slope too steep for aged men.

A similar story is "Carcassonne." Actually a city in the south of France, Dunsany chose the name only because one of his correspondents had quoted a phrase, "But he, he never came to Carcassonne." In Dunsany's rendition, Camorak the lord of Arn musters his knights to dare to challenge the prophecy of a diviner that he would never come to Carcassonne. Camorak sets out with his troops, fighting their way from fiefdom to fiefdom. Years go by and the knights become fewer and older until only Camorak and one other are left. "Then they drew their swords, and side by side went down into the forest, still seeking for Carcassonne. I think they got not far; for there were deadly marshes in that forest, and gloom that outlasted the nights, and fearful beasts accustomed to its ways."

Then there are Dunsany's misanthropic pieces. In his 1933 radio play *The Use of Man* a group of fox hunters debate which animals are the most useless and could be done without. Lord Gorse swears he will kill all the badgers in the county. Pelby raises the ante, declaring "if a thing's no good, it doesn't seem to me that it has any right to exist." (A thought Bernard Shaw incautiously voiced in his less judicious moments.) Stags are to be allowed because their heads look good on walls. But the hunters can see no use in crows, mice, rabbits, and so on, the most useless of all being the mosquito.

A spirit wakes Pelby, leads him out among the asteroids, and in a gathering of the spirits of the animals asks him, "What is the use of man?" Pelby speaks of building cities, roads, and harbors. The spirits reply, "That is only for man." He is told that if the animal spirits can find no witnesses in man's behalf, humans will be eradicated. The dog speaks up, worshipfully, but his testimony is discounted. The crow, bear, and elephant tell how they have been treated by humans (Pelby's effort to ingratiate the bear by saying he has seen many of them in zoos doesn't help his cause). And so on through horses, cows, mice, cats, and many more. When the last three minutes is up and sentence is about to be passed one more creature asks for the floor. It is the mosquito.

> THE SPIRIT: What use is Man? Tell this assembly.
> MOSQUITO: I speak for Man. I, the mosquito. Man is my food."

And the sentence is stayed.

In a more pensive vein we have the brief prose poem "Charon," here condensed to its essentials:

> Charon leaned forward and rowed. All things were one with his weariness. It was not with him a matter of years or of centuries, but of wide floods of time, and an old heaviness and a pain in the arms that had become for him part of the scheme that the gods had made and was of a piece with Eternity. . . . It was strange that the dead nowadays were coming in such numbers. They were coming in thousands where they used to come in fifties. . . . Then one man came alone. And the little shade sat shivering on a lonely bench and the great boat pushed off. . . . Then the boat from the slow, grey river loomed up to the coast of Dis and the little, silent shade still shivering stepped ashore, and Charon turned the boat to go wearily back to the world. Then the little shadow spoke, that had been a man. 'I am the last,' he said. No one had ever made Charon smile before, no one before had ever made him weep.

Lord Dunsany's legacy is undeservedly obscured. S. T. Joshi, in his preface to *Lord Dunsany: Master of the Anglo-Irish Imagination,* suggests the reasons:

> Dunsany lives, if at all, as a respected but ill-understood figure in the modern fantasy movement, an acknowledged influence on such later figures as H. P. Lovecraft, J.R.R. Tolkien, Ursula K. Le Guin, and others." Joshi attributes this neglect to the ghettoization of fantasy and other genre fiction in reaction to "the dominance of cheap pulp magazines," especially in America. "As a result, there developed a rather ignorant and small-minded unwillingness on the part of mainstream critics to consider any material of this type as falling within the realm of genuine literature. . . . Dunsany naturally suffered from this prejudice, even though he had never appeared in the pulp magazines.

Dunsany is most of all an antidote to the addiction to politics, to over-absorption in questions of rulership and policy. A reminder that advocacy of protecting nature is not the same as experiencing the natural world. There is a beautiful little vignette, "The Day of the Poll," in his *A Dreamer's Tales* in which a poet persuades a dedicated voter to accompany him on election day to the top of a hill outside of town overlooking the sea.

> And for long the voter talked of those imperial traditions that our forefathers had made for us and which he should uphold with his vote, or else it was of a people oppressed by a feudal system that was out of date and effete, and that should be ended or mended. But the poet pointed out to him small, distant, wandering ships on the sunlit strip of sea, and the birds far down below them, and the houses below the birds, with the little columns of smoke that could not find the downs.

Happily for us some possibilities remain. Skarl continues his drumming and Mana-Yood-Sushai sleeps on, at least for a while.

March 1, 2012

Part 6:
West Adams Sketches

Wyatt Earp

Wyatt Berry Stapp Earp (1848-1929) was one of the Wild West's most color-ful and famous lawmen, best remembered as a survivor of the storied and much filmed encounter known, somewhat incorrectly, as the gunfight at the OK Corral, which took place in Tombstone, Arizona, in October 1881. Wyatt Earp spent his last years in West Adams, Los Angeles, living with his com-mon-law wife Josephine Sarah Marcus Earp, in a bungalow at 4004 West 17th Street, between Arlington and Crenshaw and Venice and Washington Blvd.

Wyatt was one of eight children of Nicholas Porter Earp and Virginia Ann Cooksey. He was born in Monmouth, Illinois, on March 19, 1848. The parents moved often and far, and their children when grown followed their example, crisscrossing the mid and far West many times. The family lived for a while in Pella, Iowa, then left by wagon train for California in 1864. Broth-ers Virgil and Wyatt worked as stage drivers for a San Bernardino freight company, driving a run that went to Salt Lake City.

Later the family moved to Lamar, Missouri, in 1869, where the father, Nicholas, became constable. When Nicholas was elected Justice of the Peace, Wyatt took his job as town constable. Wyatt Earp's only documentable legal marriage was to Urilla Sutherland in Lamar in January 1870; she died in childbirth.

Wyatt was indicted but never tried for horse theft in Indian territory in Arkansas in November 1871. He left the area and moved on to Wichita, Kan-sas, where he joined the police force in 1875. From there he went to Dodge City where he worked as a policeman during the years 1877-79, and spent some of his time in Fort Worth, Texas. He was made assistant marshal of Dodge in 1878.

On a trip to Griffin, Texas, on the trail of train robber Dave Rudabaugh, Wyatt became friends with John "Doc" Holliday (1851-87). Holliday had completed his training as a dentist in Atlanta, Georgia, in 1872. He almost immediately developed tuberculosis. He went west to Texas for his health but quickly found he was unable to practice because of his illness. Holliday turned to card playing to make a living and, knowing the risks of such a profession, trained himself in the use of guns and knives. Expecting, wrongly, that he would die in a few months, he was unafraid to take reckless chances. Leaving a string of bodies behind him, he fled to Colorado and Wyoming, but was back in Texas at Griffin when Wyatt Earp arrived. After he killed another man with a knife in a poker game, Holliday was rescued from a lynch mob by his lover, "Big Nose" Kate, and hastily headed for Dodge City.

Tombstone

Meanwhile, Wyatt's older brother Virgil moved to Prescott, Arizona, with his wife Allie. He first worked as a stage driver. After he joined a local sheriff in gunning down a group of outlaws he was elected constable in November 1878. The next year Virgil was named Deputy U.S. Marshall for Pima county, Arizona Territory. He was sent to the new silver mining town of Tombstone, where he was the senior law enforcement figure, sharing authority with the city marshal (chief of police) and local sheriff. This was a great opportunity and his brothers packed up to join him. Morgan left his job as a policeman in Butte, Montana, and arrived in Tombstone in 1880; Wyatt came in from Dodge City with his common-law wife Mattie (Ceelia Ann Blaylock). He became a deputy sheriff in Tombstone in July 1880. He also invested in the Comstock Mine. Morgan worked for Wells Fargo as a shotgun messenger. Wyatt also bought an interest in the Oriental Saloon, where he gambled frequently.

While in Tombstone, Wyatt broke with Mattie Blaylock and began an affair with Josephine Sarah Marcus (1861-1944), a San Francisco actress, who had been living with the local sheriff, Johnny Behan. The two men became instant enemies.

Josephine Marcus was born in Brooklyn to German Jewish immigrants Hyman and Sophia Marcus. Her family moved to San Francisco when she was seven. At fifteen she ran away from her staid Jewish family to join Pauline Markham's touring company, performing Gilbert and Sullivan's *H. M. S. Pinafore*. On tour in Arizona she met the dashing Johnny Behan, who followed her back to San Francisco to court her. She gave in and went with Behan to Tombstone, where he became the sheriff of Cochise County, which included Tombstone. She lived with Behan for a year. She had only recently broken up with him when she fell in love with Wyatt Earp. She and Wyatt remained together for the rest of Wyatt's life, almost fifty years. Though there may not have been a formal marriage, Josephine was always presented as Wyatt's wife, and after his death she left behind two manuscripts incorporated in a book entitled *I Married Wyatt Earp*.

The city marshal, effectively the local chief of police, Fred White, was killed in October 1880 and Virgil was given his job, at first temporarily and then permanently in June 1881. The town was divided between law-abiding citizens and a semi outlaw faction called the Cowboys led by "Curly Bill" Brocious, the Clantons, and the McLaurys. Sheriff Behan sided with the Cowboys, the Earps with the more respectable side.

The town adopted an ordinance prohibiting carrying firearms within the town limits. The October 26, 1881, OK Corral fight, which actually took place in an empty lot down the street next to Fly's boarding house, was over the Earp's insistence that there was not going to be any "open carry" in Tombstone, which no doubt would have displeased today's NRA. In the much-told story, Virgil, backed by his brothers Wyatt and Morgan, and with Doc Holliday walked down to the empty lot where they confronted Ike and Billy Clanton, Tom and Frank McLaury, and Billy Claiborne.

Virgil and Morgan were wounded; Billy Clanton and the two McLaurys were killed. According to witnesses, Doc Holliday and Morgan Earp drew first. Billy Clanton and Frank McLaury were armed and had threatened to kill the Earps; Ike Clanton was unarmed and tried to run away. Supporters of the Cowboys later claimed that Tom McLaury was unarmed, while supporters of the Earps claimed that he was the one who shot Morgan Earp and that his friends removed his gun from the scene after he was killed. Sheriff Behan charged the Earps with murder, but they were acquitted after a 30-day trial.

The Cowboys sought revenge and a wave of bloodletting followed. On December 28, Virgil was fired on from ambush by three men with shotguns in the dark on a Tombstone street. His left elbow was destroyed, crippling him for life. On the night of March 18, 1882, Morgan was assassinated by a shot in the back from outside through the glass door of a saloon where he was playing billiards. At an inquest the next day a witness identified the murderer as Frank Stillwell, one of Sheriff Behan's former deputies and an associate of the Clantons.

On March 20 in Tucson, Wyatt and Doc Holliday put Vigil and his wife, with Morgan's body, on a train to their parents in Colton, California. As the train left, Wyatt spotted Frank Stillwell. He followed him and shot him dead.

The Earp party returned to Tombstone where they organized a posse of dubious legality and went on what has been called the Earp Vendetta Ride, tracking down and killing at least four of the Cowboys who had shot Virgil and killed Morgan. Presented by the Earps as a lawful effort to arrest criminals, the posse took no prisoners. The dead included Curly Bill Brocious, the best known of the outlaw faction. Meanwhile Sheriff Behan recruited his own much larger posse, made up mostly of accused cattle rustlers and the Earps' Cowboy enemies. The two groups never met.

A court in Tucson issued murder indictments against Wyatt Earp and several of his group for the killing of Frank Stillwell despite support for the Earp side by acting territorial governor John Gosper and U.S. Marshall Crawley P. Drake. The Earps and Doc Holiday left the state and went to Colorado, where the governor refused to extradite them, ending the legal matter. John Ringo, the surviving leader of the Cowboys, was murdered under mysterious circumstances while the Earps were in Colorado. Josephine, after Wyatt's death, said she believed that Wyatt and Doc Holliday returned to Tombstone briefly to kill Ringo.

Idaho, San Diego, the Harquahala Mountains, San Francisco, and Alaska

In 1884 Wyatt and Josephine, as well as his brothers James and Warren, who were not involved in the famous shootouts, went to the Idaho silver fields of Coeur d'Alene where they bought mining claims and opened a saloon. Virgil set up a detective agency in Colton, California, where his parents were then living. Wyatt and Josephine went from Idaho to Texas, then on to California, where they settled for some years in San Diego. There they bought real estate and Wyatt became well known as a referee in boxing matches in San Diego, Tijuana, and San Bernardino. He also owned harness racing horses and drove them himself in races.

By this time his gunfighting days were in the past, but in an interview with an agent of California historian H. H. Bancroft in 1888 Wyatt claimed to have killed "over a dozen stage robbers, murderers, and cattle thieves" in his time as a lawman (quoted in *The Earp Papers*, p. 141). Wyatt and Josephine were back in Arizona in 1889 where he became a part owner of a gold mine in the Harquahala Mountains northeast of Yuma. (Coincidentally, in 1950 my father joined two other men in buying a gold mine in the Harquahala Mountains, possibly the same one. My sister and I spent a few days there in the summer of 1951.)

By the mid-1890s Wyatt and Josephine were living in San Francisco, where they owned a small stable of race horses.

In December 1896 Wyatt was induced to referee a San Francisco boxing match between Bob Fitzsimmons and Jack Sharkey. Wyatt declared a foul against Fitzsimmons and gave the bout to underdog Sharkey, provoking an unjustified outcry that the fight had been fixed. In the scandal that followed the Earps sold out their holdings and returned to Arizona.

Ever on the move looking for the big score, they next moved to Alaska to join the Klondike gold rush in 1897. After numerous adventures they settled in Rampart, Alaska, 100 miles northwest of Fairbanks, toward the end of 1898, living in a dirt-floored log cabin. By the next year they were in Nome, where Wyatt and a partner built the Dexter Saloon, the first two-story building in town. They furnished it lavishly for the period. The business boomed. When the Earps sold out and returned to the U.S. in the fall of 1901 they had $85,000 from the sale of their holdings, equivalent to $2.2 million in 2010 dollars.

Los Angeles, and Mojave Desert Mining Camps

Wyatt Earp, 1929, at 4004 W. 17th Street

They returned to California. Josephine described the next part of their lives, from 1901 to Wyatt's death in 1929, as "our happiest years together" (*I Married Wyatt Earp*, p. 206). She said of those days, "We would wander over the deserts of Nevada, Arizona and California with a camping outfit during the pleasant fall, winter and spring months. The hot summer months would be spent in Los Angeles" (p. 207).

Although automobiles did exist, their first expedition, from Los Angeles to Tonopah, Nevada, early in 1902, was made with a horse team and wagon. It took several weeks to get there. Shortly after they arrived they opened the Northern Saloon, "Wyatt Earp, Prop." They divided the next few years between gold mining in Nevada and living in Los Angeles.

In 1906 Wyatt and Josephine opened mining claims in the Whipple Mountains in the California Mojave desert near the Colorado River. They owned a small cottage at Vidal, halfway between Needles and Blythe, near the Arizona border. They spent their winters there and worked their claims until 1928, the year before Wyatt's death. They generally spent the hot summer months in Los Angeles, where they rented various small houses, the last of which was the house at 4004 W. 17th Street in West Adams.

In the early 1920s Wyatt tried to get the silent film industry to take up his story. He became friends with early Western stars William S. Hart and Tom Mix, and in several letters suggested that Hart use Wyatt's biography as the basis of a film (see excerpts from their correspondence in *The Earp Papers,* pp. 217-23).

Wyatt Earp died at the house on 17th Street on January 13, 1929. William S. Hart served as a pallbearer and Western actor Tom Mix attended, as did many of the old timers from Tombstone, the Klondike, and the Nevada and Whipple Mountain mining camps. A lengthy obituary in the *Los Angeles Times* said in part, "it was like a reunion of the sturdy men and women who knew Wyatt as a wiry, six-foot, two-gun officer of the law in mining town, cow camp and almost anywhere along the frontier where trouble was apt to pop loose."

Josephine arranged to have Wyatt buried in the Hills of Eternity Jewish cemetery in Colma, California, in the San Francisco Bay Area. At the time of her death in 1944 she was living at 1812 W. 48th Street in South Los Angeles. The house at 4004 W. 17th Street was demolished to build the Mount Vernon Junior High School, since renamed Johnnie Cochran Middle School.

An enormous literature has grown up around Wyatt Earp and his brothers. Some is highly fictionalized. Most of it is either adulatory or part of a subgenre of hostile debunking. Some of this material includes:

W. A. (Bat) Masterson, *Famous Gunfighters of the Western Frontier* (1907).

Stuart Lake, *Wyatt Earp: Frontier Marshal* (1931). The first major biography and a keystone in the heroic Earp legend. Lake interviewed Wyatt Earp extensively, but later admitted that he had no direct quotes in his book but had embroidered on somewhat terse things Wyatt had told him.

Ed Bartholomew, *Wyatt Earp, The Untold Story* (1963). A debunking biography.

Josephine Sarah Marcus Earp, *I Married Wyatt Earp.* Collected and edited by Glenn G. Boyer (1976). Based largely on two manuscripts that Josephine wrote after Wyatt Earp's death, though Boyer has been criticized for some fictionalization..

Richard E. Erwin, *The Truth About Wyatt Earp* (1993). Regarded as a solid factual work by an attorney.

Don Chaput, *The Earp Papers* (1994). Excerpts from documents and newspaper accounts of all of the Earps' lives.

Wyatt Earp has been a central character in at least 10 films and a secondary one in dozens more. He has been portrayed on screen by Randolph Scott, Guy Madison, Henry Fonda, Joel McCrea, Burt Lancaster, James Garner, Jimmy Stewart, Hugh O'Brian, Kevin Costner, and Kurt Russell, to name only the best known. Josephine's book was filmed for television in 1983 (*I Married Wyatt Earp* starring Marie Osmond, with Bruce Boxleitner as Wyatt).

July 22, 2007

Dirty Dan Harris

**Only known photo of Dirty Dan Harris, on his dory
in Bellingham Bay, Washington**

I have a particular affection for Dirty Dan Harris, pioneer trader and smuggler
in Bellingham Bay, Washington, and founder of the town of Fairhaven, having played him in one of the annual West Adams Heritage Association's Living History Tours at the Angelus Rosedale Cemetery, where his remains lie.
In these events the volunteer actors learn what they can about the lives of their
characters, are costumed for the period, and set up at the character's grave-
stone to assume their parts.

For weeks I studied the history and maps of Bellingham Bay and the
Skagit River, as well as the few articles in local Bellingham magazines about
Harris' extraordinary life: whaler, Indian trader, smuggler, fighter in the
Yakima Indian War, packer on the Cariboo Trail, and then hotel owner and
founder of the town of Fairhaven, which grew into Bellingham, a better
known place. A man of incredible physical strength and indifferent personal
hygiene, who late in life married a much younger woman on whom he doted

286

who died young. Briefly rich, Harris was ultimately poisoned by his wife's Los Angeles doctor, which is how I came to be standing next to his grave chanelling his unhappy spirit.

Daniel Jefferson Harris, 1826-1890, was born in Patchogue, Long Island. After a family quarrel, he left home for Sag Harbor, New York, where he boarded an Alaskan whaler for a life at sea. In 1852 he deserted his ship in Honolulu, eventually reaching Victoria, British Columbia, and later Bellingham Bay in 1853, the same year that Washington Territory was created. Harris befriended John Thomas, who in 1853 had taken up a donation claim covering what was later the location of much of site of the town of Fairhaven at the south end of the bay.

Thomas hired Harris to help build a cabin on the beach at Padden Creek near the present location of 7th and Harris Streets in the city of Bellingham. Thomas died before the cabin was complete, but Harris finished the structure and made it his home while Thomas' estate languished in probate. In 1861, Harris officially took over the Thomas donation claim.

Harris was a big man, just under six feet and weighing 200 pounds. He typically wore a red undershirt, frock coat, unlaced boots or no shoes at all, and a top hat. His unkempt appearance earned him the nickname of "Dirty Dan." He had an independent spirit and declined to work in the Roeder Mill or the Sehome Mine where many of the early settlers earned their wages. Instead, between 1854 and 1858 Harris became a trader and smuggler. He would row 50 miles from the mainland to Victoria on Vancouver Island, sometimes once a week, stopping at several of the smaller islands on the way. He carried local produce and other agricultural goods to Victoria, returning with rice, fancy women's hats (which he sold to the Indians), and whiskey.

He served in the local militia during the Yakima Indian War of 1855-58 and again in the brief Pig War of 1859, and earned the rank of colonel when he brought the *USS Massachusetts* back to Bellingham Bay from San Juan Island and saved the town from the Nooksak Indians.

In 1858 Dan Harris bought a sloop and began trading at the mouth of the Fraser River in Canada and with Vancouver. Once a group of Samiahmoo Indians boarded Harris's sloop off Point Roberts. They tossed him overboard, and sailed off with his cargo, especially the whiskey. He later found the beached craft. He prepared a special barrel of whiskey spiked with an emetic, sailed back to the place his boat had been seized, and let the Indians capture him again. They left him alone after that.

In the early days, smuggling was not considered a serious offense and Harris was only reprimanded once by Whatcom County pioneer Edward Eldridge, then serving as Deputy Collector of Customs, who sold Harris's cargo at public auction in Port Townsend.

In 1861, Harris purchased a tract of 43 acres from Americus Poe covering the present site of southwestern Fairhaven and northern Post Point for the sum of $53.75. He meant to raise sheep there. He took ship to San Francisco, then went on to Utah where he bought 700 sheep. He drove them back to California alone with the help of some sheep dogs and bought passage on a ship to Bellingham Bay. The ship's captain, however, refused to provide water for the sheep, and by the time they arrived in Washington the sheep were so thirsty they ran off the ship to the beach, drank salt water, and all but 22 died.

Harris traded his remaining sheep for a string of horses and became a packer on the Cariboo Trail, taking trade goods overland up to the gold fields around Ruby Creek on the Skagit River .

In 1877, working alone, Harris cleared and graded a road from Sehome to Lake Whatcom to move supplies and machinery to the newly established Blue Canyon Mine. In 1881, the Kansas Colony re-established the mill at Whatcom Creek and the community anticipated an economic revival following the decline precipitated by the closure of the Sehome Mine in 1878. Harris plotted the town site of Fairhaven and became a real estate magnate and promoter. He demanded a fixed payment in cash only and soon had more money than anyone else in town. It is estimated that Dan realized $32,000 from the sale of lots created from his property holdings, about $714,000 in 2010 dollars.

With the money he built the Northern Hotel at the foot of Harris Avenue and constructed a deep water dock adjacent to the hotel. The hotel had marble topped tables and one of the only pianos in the area. In the election of 1884 Harris backed Democrat Grover Cleveland, who won as the first Democratic president since the Civil War. In celebration on inauguration day in 1885 Harris threw a huge party at the hotel and purchased a 50 foot flag and a 125 foot flagpole. He and his friends were too drunk to raise the pole and relied on a group of sailors who were passing by to do it.

In October 1885, Harris married Bertha Wasmer, at 28 some 31 years younger than he was. Bertha had tuberculosis and the couple relocated to Los Angeles in hopes that the drier climate would help her. In 1889 Harris sold his Fairhaven property to I.M. Wilson, E.L. Cowgill and Nelson Bennett for $70,000, about $1.7 million in 2010 dollars. Bertha continued to decline, and died in 1888. Harris was devastated. He became a recluse in a Los Angeles hotel, drinking heavily. He was attended by Bertha's doctor, A. S. Shorb, and his pretty wife Mattie.

The Shorbs took over Dan's finances, including purchasing property in Los Angeles and San Diego. Doctor Shorb prescribed medications for Harris and encouraged him to drink whiskey. In a short time Harris' health began to fail and he became bed-ridden. In May 1890 Harris gave Mattie Shorb a certificate of deposit in the amount of $25,000. She was told to put it in a bank of her choice in Dan's name. She didn't do so. He died five weeks later. Doctor Shorb signed the death certificate. The Shorbs were accused of poisoning Harris for his money. Dan's nephew sued the Shorbs to recover the money, but it had been hidden in many banks under false names and all that even a court order could recover was $45 and a pocket watch.

A statue of Dan Harris was erected in the Fairhaven Historical District of Bellingham in 2003.

October 6, 2007

Leslie Evans as Dirty Dan Harris, September 2004

Katharine Putnam Hooker

An early leader of West Adams society, survivor of two shipwrecks and the San Francisco earthquake, noted travel writer about Italy, and close friend of astronomer George Ellery Hale, naturalist John Muir, and psychologist William James, Katharine Putnam (1849-1935) was born in Milwaukee, Wisconsin. Her mother, was Elizabeth Noble Whitney. Elizabeth's brothers, Katharine's uncles, were Josiah Dwight Whitney and William Dwight Whitney. Josiah (1819-1896) was a Harvard professor of geology who became chief of the California Geological Survey (1860-1874) and for whom Mt. Whitney, the highest peak in the United States, is named. William (1827-1894) was a professor at Yale and the leading Sanskrit scholar of his day.

Katharine's father, Samuel Osgood Putnam (1820-1906), in 1849, almost immediately after Katharine was born, left for California to hunt for gold. He sent her and her mother to Elizabeth's parents' home in Northampton, Massachusetts. Putnam crossed the plains in a covered wagon, then rode a horse through the Rocky Mountain passes. In Nevada, Indians stole his horse and he went on to California on foot.

Three and a half years later Samuel Putnam sent for his wife and daughter. Elizabeth and the toddler Katharine took ship for Panama, where they trekked through the jungles on mule back to the Pacific. From Panama they sailed on the *SS Tennessee* for San Francisco, arriving in March 1853. On the approach to San Francisco Bay the ship struck the rocks in a fog and went to the bottom, at a spot still called Tennessee Cove in memory of the event. The passengers, including four-year-old Katharine, took to lifeboats and were rescued by the crew of a nearby whaling ship.

After the family was reunited they lived in San Francisco for a short time, then bought a farm forty miles to the south where Katharine grew up. Elizabeth, Katharine's mother, died in 1862 when Katharine was fourteen. Later that same year Katharine suffered her second shipwreck. Invited on a bay cruise on the steamer *Paul Pry*, the ship ran aground on Alcatraz Island and burst into flames. Curiously, in a piece of synchronicity, she found herself in a lifeboat with the same Mrs. Chenery who had shared a cabin with her and her mother on the *SS Tennessee* nine years earlier and abandoned ship with her once before.

Always athletic and adventurous, as a teenager Katharine climbed Half Dome in Yosemite National Park by rope. She once walked to the bottom of the Grand Canyon and back, disdaining to take the easy way down on mule back.

In 1869 at age twenty Katharine Putnam married the much older John Daggett Hooker (1838-1911). They moved to Los Angeles, although I have been unable to determine the dates. John Hooker becames vice-president of the Baker Iron Works, the company that built the first locomotive constructed in Los Angeles, and president of the Western Union Oil Company. He was also an avid amateur astronomer and inventor and a founder of the California Academy of Sciences.

Around 1886 they built a house at 325 West Adams Street at the north-west corner of Grand Avenue and Adams, in the very early development of the West Adams section of the city. This later became the site of the Orthopedic Hospital. (In the nineteenth century it was West Adams Street; sometime later it was renamed Adams Boulevard.) The house was an enormous colonial revival mansion with decorative porch columns.

John and Katharine had a son, Lawrence (1878-1894), who died of anthrax while attending Yale Law School. Their daughter, Marian Osgood Hooker (1875-1968), became a physician and published numerous medical and scientific books. She was also a prominent amateur photographer whose photographs illustrated Katharine's travel books. Marian was the first woman to scale Mt. Whitney, in 1903 in a group with the famed naturalist John Muir, who was a close family friend.

Katharine had a lifelong interest in books. She learned French and German in her youth, read voraciously, and maintained a large library. She became a skilled bookbinder as a hobby. She was a talented writer and regularly published short stories. Once as a gift Katharine financed the republication of a novel by her friend and early feminist author Elizabeth Stoddard (1823-1902).

Marian lived with her mother through most of Katharine's life and was her best traveling companion. The two made an extended trip to Europe in 1896 with a family friend, Samuel Marshall Ilsley. Always incensed by needless cruelty, Katharine attended a bullfight in Madrid and was so horrified at the torture of the bull that she made the party leave the city the same day.

The trio then went on to Italy, which captivated Katharine and became a central interest for the rest of her life. She began the serious study of Italian, and by 1899 on a return visit had become fluent. She wrote three influential books about her adopted country, *Wayfarers in Italy*, which was first printed privately then brought out in an edition by Scribners (1902); *Byways in Southern Tuscany* (1918); and *Through the Heel of Italy* (1927). *Wayfarers* went through four printings by 1905 and is still occasionally quoted today. All three books were illustrated with photographs by Katharine's daughter Marian.

Katharine and John hired an architect to build formal gardens as part of their home, and John maintained a stable and horses before automobiles were common. Samuel Marshall Ilsley in a brief biography of Katharine wrote of their home, "It became one of the beauty spots in Los Angeles, and many notable gatherings were held there, brilliant teas, philanthropic meetings, and later for a number of years . . . lovely children's festivals" (*Katharine Hooker: A Memoir*, 1935, p. 30). The house was later donated to a family friend, Maude Thomas, who turned it into her St. Catherine's School.

Katharine was the center of the social life of the home on Adams Street. She was a close friend for decades of philosopher and psychologist William James, who enjoyed lengthy stays at the Hooker home, and the conservationist John Muir, despite the fact that Muir carried on a famous and prolonged dispute with Katharine's uncle Josiah Dwight Whitney over the geological origins of Yosemite Valley. Muir lived at the West Adams home for months at a time and wrote some of his enduring works there. Another friend was scholar and peace activist David Starr Jordan, president of Stanford University. Beginning in 1904 Katharine introduced George Ellery Hale, the country's foremost astronomer, to her circle and he became a frequent guest at the Adams Street house, as well as a source of friction between Katharine and her husband John.

Hale had turned down an offer to head the Smithsonian Institute in order to build observatories in the far west. In February 1904 he first visited the Hooker home, intending to cultivate John Hooker as a donor for the newly created Mt. Wilson Solar Observatory.

Helen Wright in her biography of Hale writes of his first visit to the Hooker home,

> On his arrival he found a large yellow house, surrounded by elaborate grounds. He was ushered into a large living room, its floors adorned with magnificent Persian rugs. Here he was greeted by Hooker, who then led him on a tour of the house and grounds, of which he was inordinately proud. In the stable behind the house he kept two fabulous trotters; in the garden, which was surrounded by a high spite fence [i.e., a fence erected to annoy neighbors] that he had built to keep out the eyes of inquisitive

neighbors, he had a fantastic collection of roses that ran to thousands of varieties. He also kept his telescope in this garden. (*Explorer of the Universe: A Biography of George Ellery Hale*, p. 181.)

Hale had founded the Mount Wilson Solar Observatory in the San Gabriel Mountains above Pasadena in December 1903. He soon turned the conversation to astronomy and Hooker agreed to pay to bring a 10-inch telescope to California. Over the next decade and a half the Mt. Wilson Observatory would grow into the greatest observatory in the world.

A long-lasting friendship blossomed between the Hale and Hooker families. At the core was George Ellery Hale's fascination with Katharine Hooker and her close friend Alicia "Ellie" Mosgrove. This does not appear to have been romantic, as Katharine was almost twenty years older than the astronomer, but of a deep platonic and intellectual character.

Helen Wright in her biography of Hale recounts,

> Soon after his first visit to the house on West Adams Street in Los Angeles, Hale had met the beautiful, highly cultured Katharine Hooker. From the first he was charmed. . . . Behind the yellow house on West Adams Street she had a charming Italian garden, and here, as time passed, George Hale was to spend some of his happiest hours. (*Explorer of the Universe*, pp. 197-98)

Katharine would recite long poems in Italian, and Hale, whose Italian was very limited, would memorize them and repeat them in turn. Although Katharine was almost twenty years older than Hale, she and Ellie Mosgrove brought out a hitherto unseen playful side of the country's most famous scientist. Helen Wright comments:

> Soon after their first meeting [Hale] invented a saloon on the Embarcadero in San Francisco in which the fascinating Ellie became the "gal" with diamond heels and a red dress who sold drinks at the bar. To strangers he would often say quite seriously, "By the way, did you know that Ellie once kept a saloon in the Seraglio in Constantinople, and there shanghaied sailors into the bar?"

When in a more serious mood, Wright continued, "the house took on an added glamour. In those stimulating surroundings he became, as a younger woman who met him there recalls, 'the charming center of a great deal of admiration.'

When he talked of his work on the sun, of his great telescopes and the universe they revealed, his listeners sat entranced." (p. 199)

Alicia Mosgrove, like Katharine, was highly accomplished. She had climbed Mt. Whitney, sailed on a yacht to Tahiti, and traveled a thousand miles down the Nile in a native boat. She founded a school in the Westlake district of Los Angeles sometime around 1906. In her later years she founded a children's museum and hospital in San Francisco and served as director of the California Institution for Women, the women's prison in Tehachapi.

Katharine adopted Ellie Mosgrove into the family and Mosgrove lived with the Hookers, continuing on living with Katharine and her daughter Marian after John's death in 1911 when Katharine left Los Angeles and moved to northern California.

Katharine was visiting her father Samuel in San Francisco in April 1906 when on the 18th the famous earthquake took place. The house survived the shaking, but the fire that swept the city reached it during the night, burning it to the ground. The family evacuated at 3:00 am, enlisting aid to carry Samuel, who was eighty-five and an invalid. They took him to a tent hospital at Fort Mason, then to a Red Cross hospital. The rest of the family lived in an evacuee camp run by the military for five days. John Hooker, who had remained behind in Los Angeles, sent an agent with a belt full of gold pieces who finally found them. Samuel was taken to his ranch, where he died a few months later.

George Hale, Katharine, and Alicia mostly excluded John Hooker and Hale's wife Evelina from their sessions in the back garden. In 1906 Evelina was institutionalized with a nervous breakdown, and George Hale turned even more to the companionship of Katharine and Ellie.

In 1906 Hale asked John Hooker for his support for the 100 inch telescope he wanted for his observatory. In California historian Kevin Starr's account, John was "just barely" tolerated in the little circle of Hale, Katharine, and Alicia Mosgrove (*The Dream Endures: California Enters the 1940s*). Hale's wife Evelina was also kept away. She was institutionalized that year with a nervous breakdown, and George Hale turned even more to the companionship of Katharine and Ellie. John Hooker, hurt by his exclusion, sought entry into the circle by offering $45,000 — a little over $1 million in 2010 dollars — to fund the Mt. Wilson telescope that was eventually named for him. This donation paid only for the casting and grinding of the giant mirror. The housing and observatory dome were to cost hundreds of thousands more, in part paid by the Carnegie Institute.

The reflector was to be 100 inches in diameter, the largest mirror telescope attempted up to that time. The disk for the telescope's mirror was cast in France and weighed four-and-a-half tons. Polishing it after it arrived took nine years. Apart from its giant mirror the Hooker telescope required a precision mount and clock drive, and a motorized dome. The fragile components were hauled up a primitive mountain road by mule and by trucks with mule teams harnessed on as auxiliary power. The site, so close to Los Angeles, might seem a bad choice, but the perennial inversion layer over the Los Angeles basin actually improved visibility from the overlooking mountaintop.

Early in 1909 an estrangement began between John Hooker and George Hale. This started with doubts about the quality of the glass lens cast in France, which had been delivered in Pasadena in December 1908. Hale's technical assistant, George Ritchey, a woodworker and self-taught astronomer, believed the glass was fatally flawed. This later proved to be untrue, but Hooker flew into a rage. He made common cause with Ritchey in castigating Hale for accepting the delivery.

But soon a hotter issue arose, in John Hooker's jealousy of Hale's friendship with Katharine, despite the fact that Hooker was seventy-one and Katharine already sixty. John's jealousy was general — he came to prohibit any man to visit their Adams Street home when he was not present — but he was particularly resentful of George Hale. This estrangement and Hale's continued deep regard for Katharine and her friend Ellie Mosgrove, were a major element in Hale's 1910 nervous breakdown. The breakdown caused Hale to flee to Europe for a prolonged recovery. His symptoms included seeing a little man who would appear in his rooms at night to offer sage advice.

John Hooker died in May 1911 with the rift still active. He never paid the last $10,000 installment of his $45,000 pledge for the telescope. The difference was made up by the Carnegie Institute; the telescope was given Hooker's name despite his default.

The telescope was completed and operational only in 1917, years after John Hooker's death. With this telescope in the 1920s, astronomer Edwin Hubble measured the distances and velocities of galaxies, work which led to today's concept of an expanding Universe. The Hooker remained the largest telescope in the world until 1948 when the 200 inch Mount Palomar Telescope was put into operation. In 1981 the Hooker Telescope was dedicated as an International Historical Mechanical Engineering Landmark.

Another figure important to the Hooker household was John Muir (1838-1914), America's most influential naturalist and conservationist, founder of the Sierra Club, and often called the "Father of our national parks." In the foreword to the collection of Muir's letters from his later years, *John Muir's Last Journey,* Robert Michael Pyle writes of the period around 1910,

Muir returned four times to Los Angeles to lodge and write at the home of his wealthy friend John D. Hooker, the amateur astronomer and retired ironmaster. Muir's friendship with the Hooker family was vitally important to him during these years. Most of his best writing from this period was accomplished not in the "scribble den" of the old Martinez ranch house, but in the garret of the Hooker's home on West Adams Street in Los Angeles.

Samuel Ilsley in his brief biography of Katharine Hooker recalled of Muir, "He had made long stays with the family in Los Angeles, while writing some of his books. His personality was as picturesque and distinguished as his books, a wonderful talker and story-teller about the many adventures of his life."

Muir, at the time of John Hooker's death in 1911, was preparing for his last major journey, up the Amazon River in South America and then on to Africa to explore the Nile and Lake Victoria. Muir was close to both John and Katharine. He lived in their house for long periods, and when away corresponded with Katharine for more than twenty years. This correspondence intensified from the lonely way stations of his final long journey, which lasted from August 1911 to March 1912. By the time Muir had sailed from Philadelphia in August, Katharine had abandoned Los Angeles and moved to San Francisco.

John Muir wrote many letters to Katharine in San Francisco from the stopping points on his journey. In a letter of September 19, 1911, from Para, Brazil, a thousand miles up the Amazon, he wrote:

Away up in that wild Manaos region, in the very heart of the vast Amazon basin I found a little case of books in a lonely house. Glancing over the titles none attracted me except a soiled volume at the end of one of the shelves, the blurred title of which I was unable to read, so I opened the glass door, opened the book, and out of it like magic jumped Katharine and Marian Hooker, apparently in the very flesh The book needless to say was *Wayfarers in Italy*. This joy-shock I must not try to tell in detail for medical Marian might call the whole story an equatorial fever dream. (*John Muir's Last Journey*, pp. 67-68)

Katharine built a house on Pacific Avenue in San Francisco that she shared with Alicia Mosgrove. Later they moved to Berkeley, where they were joined by Katharine's daughter Marian. Katharine and Alicia are recorded as among those who attended John Muir's funeral in San Francisco in December 1914.

In 1915, Katharine, now 66, made a car trip to Death Valley. This was "before the days of good roads and comfortable inns," Samuel Ilsley wrote, "when it was a real adventure fraught with some danger."

At George Hale's invitation, Katharine and Alicia went to New York in May 1917, a month after the United States entered World War I, to hear the great physicist Ernest Rutherford, who was part of a French-British delegation appealing for American aid in the war. In his 1918-19 report, the president of the University of California acknowledged donations of specimens by Katharine for the natural history museum in San Francisco.

Katharine returned to Italy on a trip with Marian in 1922. In 1924 she, Marian, and Alicia Mosgrove moved to Santa Barbara, where they were joined by their old friend Maude Thomas. George Hale and his wife Evelina would take their summers in Santa Barbara, where George would spend much time with Katharine, Marian, and Maude Thomas.

At the age of 85 Katharine took a trip to Vancouver by car. She died in July 1935 at eighty-six.

July 2007

William G. Kerckhoff

William G. Kerckhoff, 1856-1929, was German-American lumber and electric power millionaire and land developer who bequeathed buildings in his name to USC, UCLA, and Cal Tech, and endowed a cutting-edge heart research institute in Germany. Kerckhoff came to Los Angeles from Indiana with his young wife Louise Eshman Kerckhoff in 1878 or 1879. He began his California career with the Jackson Lumber Company, serving the whole of the Los Angeles basin. To transport lumber, Kerckhoff in 1887 built the first ocean-going vessel in the United States to use oil for fuel.

In the 1890s he formed the San Gabriel Power Company, initiating the use of hydroelectric power in Los Angeles. By the turn of the century, with his partner A.C. Balch, Kerckhoff owned almost half the stock of Henry Huntington's Pacific Light & Power company, which had been formed to generate electricity for the Pacific Electric Railway and Huntington's Los Angeles Red Car line. Kerckhoff served as president of PL&P. In 1902, Kerckhoff and Balch were approached by the bankrupt San Joaquin Electric Company and agreed to purchase its assets. This put them in contact with its principal engineer, John Eastwood, who had a visionary plan to tap potential hydroelectric power in the San Joaquin River in the western Sierras. Eastwood for years had surveyed the Big Creek area of the Sierra Nevadas between Yosemite and Sequoia Parks, looking for the ideal places for a hydroelectric system. Eastwood took his drawings involving a vast system of reservoirs and tunnels to Kerckhoff, who agreed to back the effort. On Kerckhoff's recommendation Huntington agreed to the project and it was financed in the amount of $12 million by Pacific Light & Power.

In 1910, work was begun on the Big Creek project, encompassing the entire watershed of the upper San Joaquin River. At the time it was the largest construction project in the world, rivaled only by the construction of the Panama Canal. The system was cut into steep mountain terrain through solid granite, with picks and shovels, horses, oxen, and a small railroad. The dam and reservoir system created a series of artificial lakes including Shaver Lake,

Huntington Lake, and Florence Lake. This last was so high in the mountains that there was snow on the ground six months of the year and Alaskan sled dogs were used to deliver supplies during the two years of its construction. Pacific Light & Power also built a number of railroads, including the San Joaquin & Eastern Railway. The Southern California Edison Company absorbed Pacific Light & Power in 1917.

William G. Kerckhoff also invested in natural gas, buying his own gas company and building a 120 mile pipeline from the San Joaquin Valley to Los Angeles. He and his partners formed the Southern California Gas Corporation in 1910.

If this was not enough, Kerckhoff was also a big-time land developer. He was a founder of Beverly Hills in partnership with Burton Green, Max Whittier, and Charles A. Canfield. In San Diego County and the San Joaquin Valley, three land companies collectively owned 50,000 acres. He was president of the South Coast Land Company and masterminded the initial phases of the city of Del Mar just north of San Diego. Eryka Dennis. in the April 2-8, 2004, *Del Mar Times*, writes,

> As the South Coast Land Company acquired the land of Del Mar, the company's president, William Kerckhoff, imagined a village of cottages, 'ultimate bungalows,' and homes with an English influence to resemble Stratford-on-Avon. His vision resulted in the commission of Greene and Greene Brother's architect, John C. Austin, who along with the Greenes of Pasadena, had become nationally celebrated for New England style California Craftsman bungalows.

The Kerckhoffs lived in a grand mansion at 734 West Adams Blvd. After his death the home was donated to USC, where it was named Kerckhoff Hall. Today it serves as the offices of the Annenberg Center for Communication. The 1908 two-and-a-half story English Tudor Revival house is described on the Annenberg Center website:

> The exterior of the 18,000 square foot home features a sandstone block lower level and half-timbered upper stories. Multi-light windows with diamond shaped leaded glass, several balconies and patios, along with three tall cut stone chimneys further accentuate the structure's exterior richness. Inside, the building contains elaborate plasterwork on the ceilings and walls in the central rooms of the first floor, in addition to inlaid oak paneling and an ornate, sweeping stairway leading to the second floor.

This gift typifies the philanthropy for which, of all his various activities, William G. Kerckhoff is best remembered. Shortly before his death Kerckhoff was asked to fund a new building at UCLA. On his deathbed, he told his wife Louise to "build the building Dr. Moore wants." Louise Kerckhoff spent $815,000 to build and furnish the original student union, completed in 1931 and named Kerckhoff Hall. A formal portrait of William Kerckhoff hangs on a wall on the fourth floor. On the window side of the room, stained glass images of a redwood tree and a dam are a reference to Kerckhoff's life.

William Kerckhoff was equally generous in his bequests to the California Institute of Technology. He funded two different laboratory buildings for Cal Tech, both still in operation today under his name: The William G. Kerckhoff Laboratories of Biological Sciences at the Cal Tech main Pasadena campus, and the William G. Kerckhoff Marine Laboratory operated by Cal Tech in Corona del Mar.

Kerckhoff's most generous gift was not to an American institution but in the construction of the William G. Kerckhoff Herzforschungsinstitut, a clinical and experimental cardiology center in Bad Neuheim, Germany, a health resort known for its hot mineral water springs. William Kerckhoff had a bad heart, and for years had been a patient of Germany's foremost cardiologist, Franz Groedel, a pioneer of cardiac radiology, electrocardiography, and scientific hydrotherapy, whose practice was in Bad Neuheim. Kerckhoff died in Bad Neuheim, bequeathing $4 million to Groedel to found a heart research institute and affiliated clinic in Kerckhoff's name.

Groedel founded the William G. Kerckhoff Herzforschungsinstitut (Kerckhoff Heart Research Institute). The institute included clinical and research units as well as departments of experimental pathology, statistics, and education. The result was a cardiovascular research institute unmatched by anything in Europe or the United States. Groedel never enjoyed the fruits of this work. His mother was Jewish and the Nazis labeled him a "non-Aryan" despite his conversion to Christianity. He fled to the United States in 1933, where he became the founder of the American College of Cardiology. The Kerckhoff Institute became part of the Max-Planck-Society in 1951, retaining its distinct name and identity at Bad Neuheim. Today both the Max-Planck-Institute for Heart and Lung Research and the Max-Planck-Institute for Physiological and Clinical Research in Bad Neuheim trace their origins to the William Kerckhoff Heart Research Institute.

July 2007

John Randolph Haynes

John Randolph Haynes: California Progressive by Tom Sitton. Stanford University Press, 1992. 348 pp.

This is the first of Tom Sitton's notable series of biographies of shapers of Los Angeles and Southern California in the late nineteenth and early twentieth centuries. Sitton is a curator and head of the history department at the Natural History Museum of Los Angeles County. John Randolph Haynes, 1853-1937, was a physician, millionaire socialist, and probably the central figure in adding the rights of initiative and referendum to the California state constitution, in their day progressive reforms that have since become, by the law of unexpected consequences, the tool of special interests to bust the state budget and cater to the phobias of religious conservatives. Later from the same author there are biographies of Southern California transportation and port magnate Phineas Banning, and Fletcher Bowron, Los Angeles's long-serving reforming mayor, 1938-1953.

Born in Fairmont Springs, Pennsylvania, to parents of British descent, John R. Haynes grew up in the state's anthracite coal region where his father, James Sydney Haynes, was a coal operator. His mother, Elvira Mann Koons, was of British and Dutch ancestry. On the British side her forebears arrived in America in 1635 and fought in the American Revolution and the War of 1812.

At the age of ten, John and his family moved to Philadelphia. They fell on hard times and John went to work at fourteen. He became a carpenter's apprentice and worked his way through medical school, where he earned an M.D. and Ph.D. from the University of Pennsylvania. He opened his own practice in a poor Irish and Jewish part of the city, where he developed a life-long sympathy for the plight of the poor. In 1882 he married Dora Fellows, a cousin from central Pennsylvania, who worked with John in the medical office and in his later reform endeavors. They had a son named Sydney who died of scarlet fever at the age of three. For health reasons, most of the Haynes family moved to Los Angeles in 1887, including his parents, his brothers

Francis and Robert, and sisters Florence and Mary. All three brothers held MDs and at first lived together with their parents in a house at 8th and Main where they established an active medical practice. During the decade from 1880 to 1889 the city grew from 11,000 to 50,000 inhabitants.

In his first decade in Los Angeles John became personal physician to some of the most powerful families in the area: the Otis family who owned the *Los Angeles Times*, as well the Newmark, Rindge, and Rosecrans families. John became a director of the new California Hospital and practiced there after it opened in 1898.

In the same years John and Dora invested heavily in real estate and became extremely wealthy. They bought house lots, a commercial building in Monrovia, and a 2,700 acre ranch in Riverside County. John also had investments in two downtown theaters, in banks, the Union Oil Company, and the Pacific Railroad Company. He served on the board of directors of several local corporations and as director of the Los Angeles Chamber of Commerce, 1895-97.

At the age of forty-four in 1897, John Haynes became a follower of the Christian socialist movement promoted by Reverend William Dwight Porter Bliss. This led to involvement in a long series of reform organizations. Bliss had founded the Union Reform League in San Francisco. John Haynes became a leader of its Los Angeles chapter, which soon also became the national office of the organization. The League's long-range goal was Christian socialism, but in the meantime it settled for immediate reforms: woman suffrage, direct legislation (the initiative process), public ownership of utilities, merit-based civil service hiring and promotion, graduated taxes, and other objectives of Progressive-era crusaders.

Though nominally a Democrat, John R. Haynes retained good friends among leading Republicans. With an unusual ability to bridge almost the whole political spectrum while remaining firmly at the left end, Haynes gave public support to the cause of socialism in Los Angeles. He became friends with millionaire socialist Gaylord Wilshire, the developer of Wilshire Blvd., and contributed to his journal *Wilshire's Monthly*. He lent and then gave money to Job Harriman, an attorney from Indiana who ran for governor of California in 1898 on the Socialist Labor Party ticket and was Eugene V. Debs' vice presidential running mate in Deb's bid for the U.S. presidency on the Socialist Party ticket in 1900. And he donated to the Socialist Party directly and later to the Intercollegiate Socialist Society.

Haynes' most sustained effort was to win adoption for "direct legislation," which were the now familiar rights of ballot initiatives, referendums, and the right to recall public officials. Haynes viewed these reforms as a form of direct democracy that would weaken the power of special interests. His biographer writes that in the years after 1900 John Randolph Haynes became "the most significant reform figure in Los Angeles."

Adding Direct Legislation to the Los Angeles City Charter

In 1900 Haynes was one of 15 members elected to an official city Board of Freeholders with the mandate of revising the Los Angeles City Charter. Through heavy lobbying of the other members he persuaded the board to endorse adding initiative, referendum, and recall, of which recall was then the most controversial. It did not exist in any U.S. city or state charter or constitution. The new city charter was approved locally but the State Supreme Court invalidated it. Two years later Haynes was able to revive the issue when a new Los Angeles charter revision committee was created. Though not a member this time, he sponsored an elaborate banquet for the members where prominent defenders of the reforms spoke. The committee agreed to support the direct legislation issues as amendments to the existing city charter. These were adopted in December 1902 by strong majorities in a citywide election. He next successfully lobbied the state legislature, which in that period had to approve changes in the Los Angeles charter.

Haynes and Gaylord Wilshire went to London in 1903 to meet with leaders of the Fabian Socialists. They had discussions with H. G. Wells and George Bernard Shaw. Back in Los Angeles, Haynes was appointed to the city's Civil Service Commission, where he served for twelve years, having special responsibility for the health and medical issues affecting city workers.

The first recall under the new Los Angeles ordinance took place in 1904 when labor groups and several of the city's smaller newspapers successfully removed an allegedly corrupt member of the city council, who had the backing of the *Los Angeles Times* — the *Times* in those years was extremely right wing, antilabor, and hostile to the Progressive movement. This led to a personal break between Haynes and *Times* publisher H. G. Otis. Previously the *Times* had supported Dr. Haynes' reform campaigns, but from this point on it denounced him repeatedly and ran hostile political cartoons portraying him as inciting violence.

Haynes responded by making an alliance with William Randolph Hearst's *Los Angeles Examiner*. The Hearst press was famous for its sensationalist coverage, but in those years Hearst was also pro-union and backed numerous reforms.

The *Examiner* also supported John Haynes' new interest in promoting city ownership of gas and electric utilities. In 1905 Haynes threw his support to City Engineer William Mulholland, best remembered from his unflattering depiction in the 1974 film *Chinatown*, during the construction of the aqueduct system to bring water to Los Angeles from the Owens Valley. Mulholland had overseen the building of several electric generating plants along the aqueduct route where waterfalls could provide energy for power generation. Mulholland proposed that these continue to be city owned when the project was finished, while the *Los Angeles Times* advocated that they be sold to private companies.

On April 18, 1906, the famous San Francisco earthquake shattered the Bay Area. The same night, Los Angeles city officials assembled a team of 25 doctors and 50 nurses to be sent by train to the beleaguered city. Dr Haynes was elected medical director of the team. They arrived in San Francisco by 1:00 pm the next afternoon. Sitton writes:

> In the midst of this chaos Haynes and his cohort established five makeshift hospitals to provide medical and surgical attention to the injured and to distribute food supplied by the Hearst organization. Haynes took charge of a hospital set up near Golden Gate Park that became the headquarters of the Los Angeles expedition. There he cared for whoever came in, and occasionally ventured out into the streets and rubble in search of those trapped and needing attention. (p. 62)

That same year Los Angeles meatpacking interests mounted a lawsuit challenging standards imposed on them in a city initiative, arguing that laws made by ballot initiatives were unconstitutional. Haynes supported the City Attorney's defense of the law before the State Supreme Court, even hiring his own group of lawyers. The court upheld the Los Angeles ordinance.

Still later that year Haynes and a friend made a fact-finding trip to Europe that included spending time in Russia during the still-continuing revolution that had broken out in 1905.

On his return he served for three years as a clinical professor at the USC College of Medicine. At the end of 1907 he became Clarence Darrow's doctor. The famous lawyer had just returned from defending Big Bill Haywood and George Pettibone of the Western Federation of Miners in a bombing trial in Boise, Idaho. Darrow had an infection of the mastoid bone of his inner ear. Haynes assisted in an operation to remove the bone. Darrow took more than a year to pay his bill.

The *Los Angeles Times'* War with the Millionaire Socialist

The battle between Haynes and the *Los Angeles Times* became more bitter in 1908, as the *Times* printed scores of hostile cartoons of Haynes, denounced him as a dangerous crank, and in March attempted to tie Haynes to an alleged plot by Chicago "Reds" to murder the Los Angeles chief of police. The *Times* also threw its backing to a proposed bill that would allow the U.S. postmaster-general to permanently ban from the mails any publications deemed "improper," but particularly socialist and anarchist publications. Haynes wrote to every member of the California congressional delegation urging them to reject the repressive measure. "In this episode Haynes again had the last word, further infuriating the *Times* editors" (Sitton, p. 78).

The tenor of the *Times'* campaign against Haynes can be gauged by its headline when his term as chair of the Los Angeles Civil Service Commission expired in February 1908: "Scandals During the Freakish Reformer's Regime Furnish Material for Grand Jury Investigation." Four other city newspapers refuted the *Times'* charges, and a new mayor reappointed Haynes to the commission chairmanship the following year.

For years John R. Haynes had systematically lobbied the state legislature personally and through paid lobbyists to adopt the three pieces of direct legislation that were his hallmark issue. These were blocked in Sacramento repeatedly by the extensive control over the legislators by the Southern Pacific Railroad. Ironically it was a revolt within the Republican Party that broke this logjam. In preparation for the 1910 gubernatorial elections, a breakaway section of the state GOP calling themselves the Lincoln-Roosevelt Republicans promoted a slate of anti-SP reform candidates lead by gubernatorial nominee Hiram Johnson. Haynes attended some of their meetings and cemented agreements that they would support his direct legislation proposals, although he did not join the Republican Party or participate further in their organization. He accepted an appointment to the Republican State Committee on Direct Legislation and helped to draft the amendments on those issues.

Hiram Johnson and the Lincoln-Roosevelt Republicans were elected in a landslide. In the 1911 session of the California legislature their draft constitutional amendments passed by the legislature and were put on the ballot for an October 1911 vote. They would establish initiative, referendum, and recall, as well as women's suffrage, workmen's compensation, and regulation of the railroads and public utilities. If Ronald Reagan would be too liberal for today's Republican Party, these long-gone brethren would be denounced as Communists.

The "Father of Initiative, Referendum and Recall"

John Haynes, through the Direct Legislation League which he headed, heavily financed the campaign to win support for the pending constitutional amendments. He made a personal thirty-day speaking tour of the state. The amendments were approved by the voters in October. Thereafter John Randolph Haynes became known as "the Father of Initiative, Referendum, and Recall."

Unhappily, a century later these originally liberal provisions have been coopted by nativists, oil companies, anti-taxers, right-wing billionaires, religious extremists, and just-plain well-meaning interest groups intent on earmarking large parts of the state budget for their own worthy cause. Some of the most notable have been:

- Proposition 13, 1978, the most financially disastrous, locked in extremely low property taxes and imposed a two-thirds legislative requirement for budget votes or tax increases, resulting in gridlock in the legislature, while stripping local schools of a large part of their financial base.
- Proposition 98 in 1988 required that a large minimum part of the state budget — 39% in the initial years after adoption — go to K-14 school funding with fixed annual increases, depriving the legislature of leeway for other pressing needs in recessionary times.
- Proposition 187, 1994, denied illegal immigrants eligibility to receive public services (later declared unconstitutional).
- Proposition 22, 2000, banned same-sex marriage (later declared unconstitutional).
- Proposition 8, 2008, resubmitted the wording of Prop 22, eliminating the right to same sex marriage, that had in the interim been approved by the courts, trying to skirt the ban on a statute by this time making it an amendment to the state constitution. This one is still under appeal.

If his centerpiece reform today needs itself to be reformed, John Randolph Haynes had many other contributions to make to our political system. From 1911 on, Haynes, already fifty-eight, withdrew further and further from the practice of medicine to devote his time to public service. He campaigned for improved working conditions in mines on the national level, and was one of the very few of the upper-class reformers who championed unions and workers' rights. Governor Hiram Johnson appointed Haynes a special commissioner to investigate mine safety in the U.S. He also worked to establish the minimum wage in California and shorten the work day. He served for years on a state commission to reform prisons and mental institutions, and in Los Angeles worked to increase affordable housing.

In 1912 he and Dora built a large house on the east side of Figueroa just north of Adams Blvd. in West Adams, just across the street from the Doheny compound at Chester Place. The architect was Robert D. Farquhar, who designed a two-and-a-half story French-Norman chateau. Haynes' biographer describes the house as "one of the city's most stately residences of the time," with "a richly appointed interior of fine woods, silk damask panels, and exquisite furnishings." Visitors included novelist Upton Sinclair, a long-time friend. Back in 1905 Haynes had helped subsidize Sinclair's novel *The Jungle,* the famous expose of the Chicago meatpacking industry.

During World War I Dr. Haynes served prominently in state relief and war support efforts. In this period he broke with the Hearst press because of its antiwar and somewhat pro-German editorial policies. He several times during the war served as a local, state, or federal mediator in strikes or threatened strikes, where he generally took the side of labor rather than management. By the end of the war Haynes had shifted his priorities from direct legislation to public ownership of utilities.

The 1919 Red Scare and Post-World War I Politics

In the Red Scare of 1919 Haynes was subpoenaed by a local grand jury to testify about his support of socialist causes. He feigned illness and refused to appear. The *Los Angeles Times* denounced him repeatedly as a "parlor Bolsheviki." Haynes got a comeback when *Times* publisher Harry Chandler invested in a joint effort with the Soviets to develop oil fields in Siberia. Haynes in an open letter challenged Chandler to explain how he could "enter into a business deal with Lenin, a man you had been daily denouncing as a blood thirsty fiend."

Despite the *Times'* hostility, Haynes returned to prominence in the postwar period. He headed the gubernatorial campaign committee of William D. Stephens in 1918, a Republican Party progressive on some issues. After Stephens was elected, Haynes was appointed to the State Committee on Efficiency and Economy, where he spearheaded a major simplification of California government, finally consolidating some 70 agencies into 5 departments. Stephens also appointed Haynes as a Regent of the University of California, an appointment unsuccessfully challenged by Stephens successor as governor, right-wing Republican Friend Richardson.

Haynes, probably the city's leading advocate of public ownership of water, gas, and electric utilities, was appointed to the Los Angeles Public Service Commission in 1921 and served for sixteen years. In the early 1920s, working both as a commissioner and through private lobbying organizations, he was instrumental in getting the Edison Company and the Los Angeles Gas and Electric Company to sell their distribution facilities to the city.

In 1924 Haynes was a leader of the independent Progressive Party presidential effort of Robert La Follette, which in California had to run on the Socialist Party ticket to gain ballot status. Haynes denounced the Democratic nominee, John W. Davis, as a corporate mouthpiece and the Republican, Calvin Coolidge, as a "moron."

Another of his causes was the construction of Boulder Dam. Haynes promoted the dam itself and the proviso that the electricity it generated would be sold to the city rather than to private companies. The dam was not actually built until the early 1930s, but Haynes was instrumental in winning public support for the project, which was opposed by the *Los Angeles Times*, reportedly because publisher Harry Chandler owned thousands of acres of farmland in Mexico that would be less profitable if the dam helped to irrigate California's Imperial Valley.

The John Randolph Haynes and Dora Haynes Foundation

Reaching their early seventies, John and Dora began to consider how to preserve their considerable fortune — some $2 million, $24.4 million in 2010 dollars — to continue after their deaths to promote causes they supported. In September 1926 they cofounded the John Randolph Haynes and Dora Haynes Foundation. The foundation was committed to enhancing democracy and promoting public ownership of utilities. Another goal was improving the living conditions of workers. On this score Haynes was particularly concerned with mine safety.

Haynes committed the foundation to several other causes, although the directors he chose generally avoided funding them. These included his support to the then-fashionable eugenics movement, which called for selective breeding of humans and preventing the "feeble minded" from reproducing; endorsement of Prohibition; and support to Margaret Sanger's birth control organization. Haynes was also a major supporter of the American Indian Defense Association.

In the mid-1920s Haynes, as one of the four University of California Regents based in Southern California, was intimately involved in the construction of the Westwood campus of UCLA, which began in 1927, and the transfer of the university there from its Vermont Avenue campus in 1929. Haynes put up some $25,000 of his own money to help purchase the Westwood land, and was a major donor to the original UCLA library.

In preparation for the construction of Boulder Dam, Los Angeles in 1928 created the Metropolitan Water District, entrusted to build the Colorado River aqueduct to bring water to Southern California. Haynes, already a city Department of Water and Power commissioner, was appointed to the MWD board, where he worked to safeguard DWP interests in this broader Southern California forum.

Haynes and city ownership of water and power utilities came under sharp attack during the administration of Mayor John C. Porter (July 1929-July 1933). Porter, a protege of the fundamentalist minister, Ku Klux Klan supporter, and anti-Semite publicist Robert Shuler, packed the DWP board with supporters of private electric companies who sabotaged its work. A major political battle erupted in the city, in which supporters of municipal ownership succeeded in winning a majority on the city council. The new city council refused to confirm three consecutive appointments to the DWP board by Mayor Porter. Porter dismissed Haynes as president of the DWP board, but the city council refused to approve the action and it failed. Haynes, at 79, continued in office.

Haynes played a large part in selecting Frank Shaw to run, successfully, against Porter in the 1933 elections. Shaw was later recalled, in 1938, in a series of corruption scandals and revelations of criminal activity by members of the LAPD, the first such recall in a major U.S. city. But in 1933 he had a reputation as a progressive and was active in providing jobs for the unemployed. He supported municipal construction projects to aid both the city and the large number of workers suffering from the Depression.

Haynes acted as an advisor to Shaw and helped to secure the appointment of many public officials committed to city ownership of utilities and other reforms. During the two-term Shaw administration the city completed its independence from private water and electric companies, most importantly through the completion of Boulder Dam, now renamed Hoover Dam, which began to furnish electricity to the city in October 1936. The conversion to all-city-owned electric power was completed at the end of 1937. The *Los Angeles Times,* a bitter opponent of public ownership, built its own generators in its building's basement and refused to buy electricity from the city-owned utility.

The Haynes Foundation after the Deaths of John and Dora Haynes

John Randolph Haynes died on October 30, 1937, at the age of 84, still in office as president of the Board of Water and Power Commissioners. Flags on all city buildings were flown at half mast. Dr. Haynes was buried at Rosedale Cemetery in West Adams, next to Dora, who had died in November 1934.

The Haynes Foundation, which had become moribund in the first years of the Depression, revived after Dora's death. The foundation received $140,000 at the settlement of her estate in mid-1935. On John's death the majority of his wealth passed to the foundation as well. Under the administration of his nephew, Francis Haynes Lindley, the foundation drew back from activist progressive political causes and turned instead to support of research and community forum programs. It used the Figueroa and Adams Haynes home as its headquarters until 1952 when the building was demolished to construct the Harbor Freeway.

The John Randolph and Dora Haynes Foundation today is located at 888 W. Sixth Street, Suite 1150, in Los Angeles. It continues to fund social science research about Los Angeles, awarding grants of some $3 million each year. Its special concern is social problems in the city of Los Angeles.

July 2007, revised in March 2012

The Amazing Doctor
Margaret Chung

Doctor Mom Chung of the Fair-Haired Bastards: The Life of a Wartime Celebrity by Judy Tzu-Chun Wu. University of California Press, 2005. 282 pp.

I first encountered the above photo while working on a set of links to the Photo Database of the Los Angeles Public Library for a neighborhood website in the West Adams district of Los Angeles. The caption was "Chinese American woman in automobile." It was dated 1909. I thought, how unusual to have a Chinese American woman driver. I was struck by her American version of high Edwardian fashion. I had a wistful thought that there was too great a gap in time for me to ever know anything more about this young woman. The description in the library's database added that the photo had a caption, "Want a ride?" The subject was named Margaret Chung, and she was plainly no shrinking violet. She was further described as the first Chinese American physician in Southern California, a graduate of the University of Southern California.

I wanted to see if there was anything more I could find out and did an internet search. Among the many personal current websites of Margaret Chungs, one a minor actress, I turned up several references to a Doctor Margaret Chung, and even a full-length biography by Ohio State University historian Judy Tzu-Chun Wu. This, it proved, was my subject, and a good deal was known about her.

Margaret Chung (1889-1959) proved to be an amazing, and once-famous, person. Chameleon-like she had invented and reinvented herself, living in many worlds. Daughter of a Chinese prostitute and a vegetable peddler, she had become a Hollywood surgeon. Later, in San Francisco, she moved in early lesbian circles and dressed in men's clothes. She became the mentor of a group of Navy pilots and created an organization of pilots and submariners called the Fair-Haired Bastards, from the ethnicity of most of its members and the fact that Chung was unmarried. It grew to some 1500 members during World War II. Senators and Congressmen became her friends, and she invented the Waves, and Navy auxiliary for women. Even the Los Angeles Library's scant description as the first Chinese American physician in Southern California proves to have been an understatement, as Chung was the first-known American-born Chinese woman physician in the whole country.

Judy Tzu-Chun Wu's biography tells the story of Doctor Margaret "Mom" Chung, an irrepressible and incredible life. Wu's book descends at times into long sociological digressions on the status of Chinese American women and such, obstructing the flow of her narrative, but Margaret Chung's life has such vibrancy that it emerges from these pages unscathed.

Margaret Chung was born in Santa Barbara, California, the eldest of eleven children. Her parents emigrated separately from China in the 1870s. Her father worked as a merchant, then went bankrupt and became a fruit peddler, dairyman, and ranch foreman. Her mother was rescued from a brothel. Both became invalids when Margaret was very young, and Margaret took over supporting the family by the time she was ten, as well as caring for her

younger siblings and nursing her mother who was slowly dying of tuberculosis. She drove a horse-drawn freight wagon alone when she was ten and later
worked 12-hour days in a Chinese restaurant when she was in the seventh
grade. The family moved first to Ventura, then to the East Adams section of
Los Angeles near San Pedro Street.

Margaret managed to put herself through college and medical school by
winning scholarships, selling medical supplies, and lecturing on China. In
1916 she graduated from the University of Southern California's College of
Physicians and Surgeons, becoming the first American-born Chinese woman
physician in the United States. After a brief stint at Kankakee State Hospital
in Illinois, she returned to California and worked as a surgeon at the Santa Fe
Railroad Hospital. She also developed a clientele in the Hollywood crowd,
and removed Mary Pickford's tonsils. Chung moved to San Francisco in
1922, where she worked as staff physician at the Wiltshire Hotel and opened a
medical office in Chinatown.

In 1931, Dr. Chung became friends with a young aviator from Berkeley.
Soon she was entertaining a group of his Navy Air Reserve friends for dinners. This grew into an American aviators' club called the "Fair-Haired Bastards," which became famous in World War II. She was known to the flyers as
Mom, and "adopted" them, numbering her "sons" and giving each a silver
ring with a jade Buddha.

When Japan invaded China in 1937, Margaret Chung began making
speeches to organizations and at local colleges in support of China. After the
Japanese attack in December 1941, she helped send emergency medical supplies to Pearl Harbor, for which she received a citation from President Truman. During the war, Doctor "Mom" Chung added a section for nonflyers,
called Kiwis (for a flightless bird), and the Golden Dolphins, a submarine
auxiliary. High ranking officers attended her Sunday dinners where from 75 to
100 military personnel came to her house each week. By her rules the men did
the dishes and mopped the floors, including Admiral Chester Nimitz, commander of the U.S. Pacific Fleet. Concerned above all with promoting U.S.
support to China in its struggle with the Japanese invaders, Chung recruited
the first 200 American aviators for the renowned Flying Tigers.

By the end of the war the Bastards, Kiwis, and Dolphins included 1500
"sons," some of whom were U.S. senators and congressmen. Using these connections, Doctor "Mom" Chung virtually invented the WAVES, the women's
auxiliary of the U.S. Navy, holding lobbying meetings in Washington with her
"sons" and committing them to backing the idea. The organization was officially inaugurated on July 30, 1942, as a women-only division of the U.S.
Navy. The name stood for "Women Accepted for Volunteer Emergency Ser-

vice." Margaret Chung was never given public credit for this achievement, or even permitted to join the WAVES, which she ardently wanted to do. The government secretly blacklisted her because they suspected that she was gay. Her sexual orientation has never been established, but she had friends who were lesbians and she had a long and very close friendship with the Jewish singer Sophie Tucker. The two exchanged very affectionate notes and letters, but even Chung's biographer is uncertain of the character of their relationship.

When Margaret Chung died in 1959 her pallbearers included Admiral Nimitz, San Francisco Mayor George Christopher, and famed conductor Andre Kostelanetz.

March 7, 2009

About the Author

LESLIE EVANS was born in New York City in 1942. He grew up in Los Angeles, and has lived since in San Francisco, Manhattan, and Virginia, Minnesota. He has worked as a carpenter, a Marxist militant, an iron miner on the Mesabi Iron Range, an editor for UCLA's Asian studies centers, the World Health Organization, and the World Bank, and as reporter for UCLA's International Institute. He is the author of the memoir *Outsider's Reverie*. He lives with his wife, Jennifer Charnofsky, their dog and five cats in a 1910 Craftsman house in the West Adams section of Los Angeles.

Index